Operation Abonar

Inside story of Britain's biggest gunrunning scandal government officials didn't want told

by Michael Hallowes

Former Scotland Yard Senior Investigating Officer

Published by Clink Street Publishing 2023

Copyright © 2023

First edition.

Diagrams are the original work of the author.

The photographs are either the property of the author or used with kind permission from the Metropolitan Police Service and the Royal Armouries National Firearms Centre, with very special thanks to Mark Murray-Flutter, Senior Curator, Firearms, Royal Armouries.

Also, an enormous thank you to Rebecca Hallowes and William Price for the additional editing.

ISBN:
978-1-914498-88-6 - paperback
978-1-914498-89-3 - ebook

For the victims

Foreword

The compelling story of Britain's biggest gunrunning investigation, known as 'Operation Abonar', is based largely on real events that have remained mostly unreported for twenty-five years. It is told from a personal perspective by the former Detective Inspector who led the enquiry as his first major Scotland Yard investigation. Only weeks before he had joined the shadowy 'Directorate of Intelligence, SO11 Branch'. The context is 1997, a time of escalating gangland violence in Glasgow, Manchester, Dublin and London. Rivals are fighting over drugs and turf, seeking to settle feuds with fully automatic machine guns needing thousands of rounds of ammunition. Some are also wanting silencers to surprise their enemies in drive-by shootings. Others have got hold of even heavier weaponry not previously seen in the UK.

Author's caveat

Certain events, names and identifying details have been changed to protect the privacy of individuals, and some characters are an amalgam of many and created to help the story flow. Any similarities between these and a real person are purely coincidental. The reader should also understand that conversations are an indication rather than a verbatim account of what was said. This book is dedicated nonetheless to my former colleagues who worked with me on 'Operation Abonar' and in Specialist Operations at New Scotland Yard.

PROLOGUE

Conservative Party Conference, 6th October 1993

"Prison works. It ensures that we are protected from murderers, muggers, and rapists, and it makes many who are tempted to commit crime think twice...This may mean that more people will go to prison. I do not flinch from that. We shall no longer judge the success of our system of justice by a fall in our prison population."

– Michael Howard, MP, Home Secretary, 1993 to 1997.

1997
Monday, 20th January

It was just before midnight in Moss Side, Manchester. For a brief moment, the moon shone through before surrendering the night sky again to heavy clouds. The street lighting coloured the drizzly air in a hazy amber hue. A group of four young men had gathered outside a house in Westerling Way talking loudly and aggressively. Given the upsurge in violence between rival gangs on the estate, an anxious neighbour had dialled 999. As PC Kennedy turned the marked police car slowly into the road, he gave his younger less experienced colleague, PC Thompson, a reassuring smile. They scanned the street looking for the suspects. Between the intermittent sweeps of the windscreen wipers the Constables soon spotted them outside number 29. Each was wearing an anorak with its hood pulled up partially hiding their faces.

Not sure what they would encounter, PC Kennedy parked a few yards short and, leaving the headlights on full beam, he and PC Thompson stepped out to investigate. The young men each extended a hand to protect their eyes so as not to be dazzled. PC Kennedy spoke into his radio to update the station of their arrival. That immediately warned the group that the two silhouetted men now approaching were police officers. They chose not to retreat and instead purposefully crossed the road to take advantage of the shadows there. As they did so, the shortest of them swiftly pulled a black object he had been hiding inside his anorak and pointed it at the Constables. Then the terror began.

A deafening burst of automatic gunfire tore through the air like the amplified sound of ripping cardboard. From the machinegun's barrel, furious white flame lit up she shooter's face exposing his wide-eyed stare as his hand jerked uncontrollably upwards. Ducking instinctively, the Constables both felt and heard the first bullets whistle past only inches from their heads. The gunfire went on punctuated by the stream of spent cartridges ringing emptily on the tarmac.

"Fuck. Get down! Get down!" PC Kennedy screamed as he scrambled almost on all fours to find cover behind the nearest parked car. PC Thompson dropped to the ground too and did his best to roll towards what he hoped would be safe refuge under a van. Both heard the repeated thuds and whistles as the bullets intended for them smacked into a house wall and ricocheted off just feet away.

Neither Constable had been shot at before and both now feared they would die ignominiously on this dismal wet road in Moss Side. Feeling his heart racing with fear, from his crouched position behind the car, PC Kennedy frantically rubbed his hands across his body checking for wounds and, finding none, raised his head skywards and mouthed "*Thank you God*". At that same moment, PC Thompson had gone into shock. With the gunfire still making his ears ring, he was agitatedly mouthing words into the radio but found his voice had shut down.

The shooting seemed to last forever but had ended in just two seconds. Once PC Kennedy was convinced it had stopped, he nervously raised his head just above the bonnet of the car he had used for cover. Wiping away sweat and drizzle from his face, he watched with huge relief as the four men jumped a garden wall and fled the street cheering with delight. Choosing not to pursue them, he radioed for assistance before going to help his colleague. PC Thompson too had not been shot but was unable to stand unaided due to his state of shock. So instead, PC Kennedy helped him over to a low garden wall where he sat shaking, speechless and staring fixedly ahead.

Forensic officers later recovered twenty-one 9mm cartridge cases along with fragments of six bullets. Each of these had copper jackets with an unusual blue tip.

More than a month later, in the early hours of Wednesday, February 26th, acting on intelligence about this shooting, detectives from Greater Manchester

Police (GMP) executed a search warrant at 67 Anthony Close, West Gorton. The three occupants woke to the double crash of the battering ram breaking down the front door followed by the repeated shouts of "Armed police! Armed police!" The six-man team of Specialist Firearms Officers (SFOs) swarmed through every room to contain those inside. Once they had secured the property and handcuffed the two men and a woman found upstairs, their team leader handed over the scene to the detectives waiting outside.

Climbing into the loft, DC Balfour's torch picked out a holdall-sized embroidered tapestry bag beside the water tank. He crawled across the dusty rafters to reach it. The fact it showed no signs of dirt suggested someone had only recently hidden it there. Lifting the bag awkwardly in his crouched position, he was surprised by its weight.

"*This better be what we came for*" he thought, now noticing the dust on his clothes. He unzipped the bag and the matt nickel plating of the objects inside reflected his torchlight. DC Balfour had found three Smith & Wesson 'Model 36', snub-nosed .38 calibre revolvers. With them were two clear plastic food bags full of '.38 Special' ammunition with lead bullets.

He called out to his supervisor, DS O'Neill. Poking hid head through the open loft hatch, the DS responded, "what you got mate?"

"A holdall with three revolvers and a couple of sandwich bags of bullets," DC Balfour told him in a hushed voice, not wanting to alert the people detained downstairs.

"No machine guns then?" asked the DS.

"No, not yet."

As he spoke, DC Balfour swung his torch back around the loft until its beam landed on a red carrier bag branded 'Kwik Save'.

"*Oh hell*," he thought as he scrambled precariously back along the rafters to get it. As he lifted the plastic bag, the five-kilo weight alerted him to something big inside. He nudged open the edges with his torch.

"Bingo, sarge!" he whispered. Taking his trophy back to show the DS, he told him excitedly, "two MAC-10s with two 30-round magazines". Then checking the latter he added, "and they're fully loaded with those same blue-tipped 9mm bullets we keep finding at shootings".

Subsequent forensic examination and comparisons with the spent ammunition recovered on January 20th identified one of these two MAC-10s had been used in the Westerling Way shooting. In addition, both guns were stamped on the right side of the receiver with the manufacturer's name, 'SF FIREARMS P.O. BOX 218 TUNBRIDGE WELLS KENT'. However, someone had obliterated the serial number using an electric TIG welder thereby creating a line of dots of melted metal. This method prevented any chance of recovering the digits forensically. The examining scientist also found a combination of gunsmithing features that made these MAC-10s unique when compared to all the others he had seen. These included:

- a smooth bore barrel with an external screw thread to allow a silencer to be fitted
- the breech bolt (that works on springs, sliding back and forth when the trigger is pulled to both fire the bullets and eject the spent cases) was of a never-seen-before design with the extractor set at forty-five degrees
- the feed ramp (over which the bullet slides from the magazine into the barrel) was a new design too with a seam weld setting it in place, and
- the loading port and pistol grips had been modified to accept magazines from an 'Uzi' machine pistol.

Sunday, 23rd March

Gangland shootings continued almost daily in Manchester due to the ongoing feuds over turf and drugs. The night shift had become the most dangerous time for GMP officers, as most incidents happened after dark.

It had just gone 10pm as the two uniformed Constables on foot patrol turned the corner into Lydbrook Walk in Ardwick. The noises of the council estate settling down for the night gently reverberated around them in the chill dampness of early spring. The bright street lighting allowed the Constables to easily spot two men ahead of them dressed in dark clothing acting suspiciously. Their behaviour suggested one was buying drugs from the other. The Constables looked for somewhere in the shadows from which they could observe and move closer without being seen. Disappointingly, the streetscape offered no such cover, so the two men had spotted the officers too. At first, they hesitated, not sure whether to bluff it out or run. But, as the officers picked up pace, the two decided to sprint up an alley heading off the estate to the west. The officers gave chase.

"16-53 to Charlie Kilo, urgent assistance!" PC Newberry shouted into his radio as they pursued their quarry. "Chasing suspects, Lydbrook Walk, across the recreation ground towards Langport Avenue."

As they left the alleyway, one of the men dropped a small plastic bag, which the second Constable, PC Woodage, deftly scooped up as he continued the pursuit. Subsequent forensic analysis found it contained a gramme of brown heroin.

The two fugitives separated in Langport Avenue. Their pursuers decided to go after the slower one, who was now weaving through the tangle of back alleys leading to Dartford Close.

As more officers joined the chase and closed in, the fleeing man realised he was cornered. Stopping next to a parked BMW, momentarily he crouched down behind it. As he stood up again, the two pursuing officers caught up with him. PC Newberry put the suspect in a wrist lock and then slammed him face-down firmly on the BMW's bonnet.

"Why did you run, mate?" he asked while his colleague bent down, shining his torch under the car. The light illuminated the matt black finish of a small-framed submachine gun.

"I think I know why," PC Woodage announced as he extended his baton to drag the gun out from under the car. "So what have you to say about this then? Is that why you ran?"

The gun found was another MAC-10, with all the same distinctive features of the two recovered in West Gorton. Its Uzi magazine contained another twenty-one blue-tipped 9mm bullets.

Wednesday, 23rd April

Devon Dawson was known to the Metropolitan Police in Brixton, south London. Originally from Jamaica and aged 29, he was an active drug dealer who regularly used violence to secure and enforce his share of the lucrative local market. He had spent the evening standing outside the 'Green Man' pub at the busy junction where Coldharbour Lane crosses Loughborough and Hinton Roads. This was his turf for selling one-gramme bags of cocaine. He hid these down his underpants along with the cash, so kept one hand almost permanently in the elasticated waist band of his shell suit ready to trade. It was around 10pm when a young man approached and stopped short of

Dawson. He nodded to him, signalling he wanted to buy. Dawson shouted out, "yo, so you want some blow? Better show me the money. Not doing credit for no one."

Given the constant vehicle traffic around him, Dawson hadn't noticed the car drawing up alongside with its windows down. It's doubtful he even had time to comprehend what was about to happen. The ten-round burst of fully automatic gun fire tore through his body. Each bullet jerked him around as if he was doing some frenetic dance move. His life ended in that single second it took for the gunman to squeeze the trigger. Whilst everyone else on that stretch of narrow pavement ran and ducked for cover, Dawson fell dead. His blood had spattered across the now bullet-chipped drab brown tiles of the pub wall. It marked out where some had ripped clean through his body due to the close range of the shooter.

Detectives recovered at the scene ten 9mm cartridge cases. The pathologist who conducted the subsequent autopsy removed four bullets from Dawson's body; each had a distinctive blue tip.

Five days after the shooting, police were searching for Michael Senior, another Jamaican-born drug dealer. As Dawson's fiercest business rival, he was the principal suspect for his murder.

Two detectives in an unmarked car radioed for armed backup when they spotted Senior in Branksome Road, Clapham, south London. He was a rear-seat passenger in a red Nissan saloon being driven by a close associate.

The Armed Response Vehicle (A-R-V) crew in the marked Rover 800 were quickly up behind the Nissan with blue lights and headlights flashing indicating to the driver to stop. As soon as he did so, two armed officers ran forward; each with a hand on their Glock 9mm pistols ready to draw if threatened. Seconds later, the detectives pulled up in their car behind.

"Keep your hands where I can see them," the armed officer told Senior firmly as he opened the car door next to him.

"Why you stopping me? All this police harassment," he protested, sucking his teeth. Begrudgingly, Senior then got out of the car shouting, "I've not done nothing!"

Stepping forward, DS Harvey immediately handcuffed the man, telling him, "I doubt that cos' you're nicked for the murder of Devon Dawson."

Later that same day, the detectives searched Senior's home at Dumbarton Court, Brixton Hill. They recovered a MAC-10 that Senior had hidden in a kitchen cupboard. The gun was still loaded with twenty-five 9mm bullets in its Uzi magazine; each one with a blue tip.

Subsequent forensic examination confirmed it was the gun used to kill Dawson. Senior only admitted to storing it for someone he wouldn't name. To this day, Devon Dawson's murder remains unsolved.

Senior's MAC-10 shared all the features of the three recovered by GMP in January and March. It was now evident someone was arming gangs with these easily concealable submachine guns along with the blue-tipped 9mm ammunition. They were doing so in numbers that foreshadowed a murderous escalation in violence that the police in London and Manchester had to stop.

CHAPTER 1

Scotland Yard

April 1997

The whole wing of the eight-storey 'Victoria Block' at New Scotland Yard (NSY), where my office was on the fourth floor, had recently been refurbished to allow new cabling to connect us to the digital age. Contractors had raised the floors and lowered the ceilings to accommodate the improvements. Sadly, they had done nothing to upgrade the original toilets. Purpose-built in 1967, ours and the interconnecting eighteen-storey 'Tower Block' were approaching the end of their utility as the headquarters of the Metropolitan Police Service (MPS). Extraordinarily, the structure held out another 16 years until its closure in 2013.

My narrow, seven-foot-by-fifteen-foot office had two desks on either side of the window at the far end away from the door. One provided a home to a desktop computer, the other was where I did most of my work, with two chairs alongside for visitors. Next to the first desk was a heavy duty, four-drawer steel cabinet for storing classified files. Above that, screwed to the wall, was a large whiteboard. A tall two-door steel locker behind the door acted as a wardrobe. The office was on the gloomy north side of the building, overlooking the junction of Caxton Street and Broadway. I had been promised one on the south-facing sunny side, overlooking Victoria Street, but my boss had taken it instead. He was Detective Superintendent Anton Baxter. I had readily accepted the compromise because I largely owed my new position to him.

In mid-1995 I had been a uniform Inspector on the Territorial Support Group (TSG[1]) based at the high security Paddington Police Station. A year later, I was asked to do a three-month attachment to the Support Services

---

1   TSG: Territorial Support Group – teams of specialist uniform officers highly trained in public order policing.

Review as an operational adviser. The job entailed identifying cost-savings that would not hinder policing capability by outsourcing many of the support services the organisation had built up over its 150+ years. The review resulted in savings totalling £400 million. I was then at a loose end.

It was by happy coincidence I bumped into Anton in the corridor. We knew each other from when he was an Inspector and I a probationary Constable at the same police station in 1981. We had a friendly catch-up, during which I mentioned my need for a new challenge. He was on his way to a meeting with the Director of Intelligence, Deputy Assistant Commissioner (DAC) Alan Fry. His boss, the Assistant Commissioner (AC) for Specialist Operations, David Veness, had just tasked him with delivering an 'Aglow Level[2]' counter-terrorism exercise. DAC Fry needed a team to get it done and had summoned Anton to find them. Fortuitously, DAC Fry also knew me from the early 90s when I had been a uniform Inspector at Hammersmith and Shepherds Bush. He had been the DAC in charge of '6-Area' that covered the west of London. We had got to know each other very well due to my successful handling of several high-profile major incidents. Within minutes, my desk phone rang, and later that day I was in a meeting with him and Anton. The following morning, I started a six-month secondment to the Anti-Terrorist Branch, known as 'SO13'. The role reached its natural conclusion with the running of the exercise over the first weekend in January 1997.

Anton had encouraged me to apply for a permanent role at Scotland Yard. After a competitive selection process, I was delighted to be the successful candidate. And so it was, once the secondment to SO13 ended, I was appointed as a Detective Inspector to the Directorate of Intelligence, known as 'SO11'. Anton was my new boss. Without that chance corridor-encounter, I would never have had the incredible opportunity to make a level transfer from uniform to become a 'Scotland Yard Detective'. Hence, I was very happy to let Anton have the better office.

SO11 was known as the '*covert policing branch*'. Our primary responsibilities were technical and conventional surveillance. We worked alongside other specialist units in the police, intelligence, military and law enforcement agencies, both nationally and internationally. We gathered information on London's most dangerous gangland criminals. To protect our often-sensitive

2   Aglow Level: highest level of counter-terrorism exercise involving senior officers, government officials, and Ministers playing out their roles in person in a three-day scenario that usually ends with UK Special Forces effecting a hostage-rescue.

methodologies, we rarely gave evidence in court. Instead, we provided actionable intelligence 'products' to other branches in Specialist Operations (SO), who then acted as our executive arm to make the arrests and bring prosecutions. Hence, the media liked to call us the 'Shadowy Intelligence Branch'. Our Latin motto was 'Skelatus Non Skelus' [The criminal not the crime] to reflect our focus on covertly gathering intelligence about the people committing the most serious crimes and so catch them in the act.

I was head of what was euphemistically titled 'Corporate Services', managing a mix of 50 experienced detectives and civil staff in a cooperative of nine business units. We were the strategic hub for all criminal intelligence gathered and processed by the MPS. Our principal purpose was to identify linked series crimes. The nine included **InfoS** (Information Systems), the central unit that processed all intelligence held by the MPS about criminals and their addresses. The **Firearms Intelligence Unit** (FIU) that monitored the criminal use of firearms and all recoveries of guns and ammunition around the UK. The team liaised directly with the Forensic Science Service, MI5 Weapons Intelligence Branch and other law enforcement and intelligence agencies. A group of Sergeants worked in the **Prison Intelligence Unit** (PIU) embedded within the Security Sections at each of London's nine prisons. They gathered information on every inmate while incarcerated. The **Telephone Intelligence Unit** (TIU) provided the focal point between detectives and the UK Communications Service Providers (CSPs), processing telephone data to support major crime investigations. The **Computer Crime Unit** was in its infancy then and focused largely on researching Suspicious Activity Reports (SARs) submitted to us from London's financial institutions. My only operational role was managing the Covert Operations Room, known as '**Central 500**'. This was at the western end of the fourth-floor corridor and where we ran all life-at-immediate-risk operations, such as kidnap and extortion investigations. It was within the secure 'Fordham Suite' of rooms, so named in memory of DC John Fordham. He was killed in 1985, and many would argue strongly it was murder, whilst on surveillance duties for 'C11', as the Branch was then known.

Mine was meant to be very much a Monday to Friday, nine-to-five job based for the most-part on the fourth floor. Having been operational since joining the MPS in November 1980, this was not what I was used to. Thus, to compensate, I put myself permanently on call, turning out at all hours to open and manage Central 500. That had already helped me gain valuable experience, working alongside senior detectives from the Organised Crime Group (OCG), known as SO7. They were based on the fifth floor. When necessary, we brought in tactical advisors from other units, such as those from SO19, the Specialist Firearms Command. In addition to kidnap investigations, during my two tours in SO11, we also took charge of the arrests of Edgar Pearce, the 'Mardi Gra[3] Bomber', and David Copeland, the 'London Nail Bomber'.

---

3   Mardi Gra: although he misspelt it, this was the pseudonym Edgar Pearce gave himself.

CHAPTER 2

Week 1

Tuesday, 29th April

I sat at my desk reading the FIU reports into the murder of Devon Dawson and the firearms' recoveries in Brixton and Manchester. I was fortunate to have DC John Bryan running the unit. He was an exceptionally diligent detective who made sure I was well-briefed. In his mid-fifties, he was a career detective and still full of energy despite his approaching retirement. He was generous in spirit; especially towards me, and I was grateful for his active support. He became a good friend and mentor in my early months in the Directorate.

John's frequent exits from the building to smoke his pipe would often follow with a knock on my door. He would then pass on some piece of thoughtful analysis about the intelligence he was working on. This morning was no exception. I felt his presence darken my office doorway and the aroma of recent pipe smoke told me who it was without looking up.

"Guvnor, may I?"

"Of course, John," I said, pointing to the nearest 'visitor chair'. Instinctively, he glanced at the papers on my desk. A common trait of detectives is to check what the boss is reading. It's part of the survival instinct, as it provides early warning of a file that is either about you or some 'grief' heading your way.

"Ah good, I see you've got my reports. I think I've spotted a pattern," he said with a hint of excitement in his voice.

"Yes, thank you. Good analysis by you and Mark. I read your note saying while no one's yet naming the supplier of these guns, it's the same gunsmith who manufactured the four MAC-10s."

"Not just that, Guv," the excitement in his voice rose, "may I get the files and show you?"

"Sure, meet me in the Fordham Suite briefing room. There aren't any ops on right now, so we can make use of the extra space and its free coffee machine."

Ten minutes later we reconvened in the briefing room. This was a large, light-grey painted room, dominated by a twelve-seat, rectangular boardroom table filling the centre. Along the right side was a bank of three desks with computers for use by analysts. A locked door in that wall gave access to the secure corridor that led to the actual Operations Room. Two large whiteboards covered the opposite wall. A large projector screen dominated the back wall alongside the offset doorway. At the far end of the room, the windows provided a view of Victoria Street and the offices opposite. However, we kept the blinds drawn permanently to avoid giving away when the suite was in use.

John had brought along his civil staff analyst, Mark. He was a shy, quiet man in his late twenties. His modest persona belied a sharp mind that, like John's, could quickly assess contrasting pieces of information, sometimes in minute detail, to identify a pattern others might easily miss. John and Mark were ideally suited to their jobs. With eight other units to manage, I relied on shrewd, analytical and meticulous people like them.

"Okay Guv. Look at these," John began, visibly excited by what he was about to reveal. "A linked series of three arms caches. The first on November 12th last year. Customs called the SO13 Reserve to say they'd got anonymous information about a load of guns hidden in an A-reg Ford Fiesta abandoned in Whitechapel. SO13 passed it on to the local uniform, who found the car unlocked. In the boot was a green holdall containing twenty handguns of various types."

"Wow," I uttered almost involuntarily in surprise, to acknowledge I knew such a large find was extremely rare.

"And that's not all, Guv. There were several plastic sandwich bags containing all the different calibres of ammunition needed for each gun. Oh, and seven half-kilo blocks of cannabis."

Mark passed the photographs for me to thumb through as John continued, "the important commodity here are thirteen Russian Tokarev pistols. That's because they also appear in the other two caches. Nasty handgun. Its 7.62 bullet can defeat our body armour."

"I don't recall you showing me Tokarevs before," I commented.

"No, they're a first for the FIU. But here's another interesting common denominator. Mark, show the Guvnor the next set of photographs, please."

Mark handed me another album.

"Someone's used an electric TIG welder to remove all the identifiable marks we need to trace their origins. That's unusual too. We've not seen that before either."

I nodded to concur the obliteration marks all looked to have been made with the same tool.

"Right, the second cache," John carried on with more energy, now reassured by my interest. "February 26th this year, Customs called SO13 again. This time it's with anonymous information about a B-reg Vauxhall Cavalier abandoned in the Wickes car park in Plaistow. As before, the caller said we'd find guns hidden in the boot. SO13 passed it on to the locals and, again, uniform found the car unlocked."

He paused while Mark handed me the corresponding album.

"So, as you'll see, the same type of green holdall as the Whitechapel job, but this time it's twenty-seven handguns."

"Wow," I said again, confirming he had got my attention. "So that's now forty-seven from just these two."

"Yes, and remember, there's another to come. So this second cache included six more Tokarevs. Again, we've got sandwich bags filled with ammunition for them and the others. Oh, but no cannabis this time."

I looked at the pictures before commenting, "okay, I get the Tokarevs linking these two, but in this second one are some nickel finish Smith & Wesson revolvers. I just read in the GMP reports they also found three like these. What do we know about them?"

"Nothing yet, but I'll check and get back to you. Mark, can you pass the Guvnor the photographs of the third cache, please? You'll see more Tokarevs amongst them."

Mark spread out another set of photographs for me to view.

"This third cache was found on March 1st," John continued, "someone left them in the boot of a D-reg white Maestro, unlocked and abandoned in the car park of the Tollgate Hotel near Gravesend, Kent."

"Don't tell me, another call from Customs."

"Absolutely right, Guv. This time, though, they called Kent Police HQ. The caller claimed he was acting on anonymous information. When the locals searched the car, they found eighteen guns and, as before, sandwich bags with the right ammunition for each one."

"I see some interesting variations this time," I commented looking at the variety of guns in the photographs.

"Yes, Guv, it's a much more eclectic mix than the previous two. This time someone had wrapped each one in an oil-soaked hessian-type cloth and marked them in pen with a three-letter Cyrillic code. We haven't seen that before either." His tone suggested some annoyance at this being another factor beyond his knowledge. He paused while Mark showed me the relevant photographs.

"As you'll see," John explained, "there's also a World War Two era 30-calibre 'Browning Automatic Rifle', a BAR. It was wrapped in blue towelling strapped up with brown packing tape. Its serial number was removed in the same way as the others using a TIG welder. Odd that because the gun's so old it's unlikely to be traceable."

"It's a particularly unusual addition compared to the previous two," I commented.

"Yes, Guv, and there's another more exciting one," he said with great relish. "This time two cardboard boxes branded 'Emerald Margarine' containing four new MAC-10 submachine guns, four silencers, and eight Uzi magazines. They were also wrapped in the same blue cloth as the BAR."

Wanting to show I had been paying attention, I commented, "and I see they're stamped with the same 'SF Firearms' markings as the MAC-10s recovered by GMP. They're also of the same type used to murder Devon Dawson".

John looked impressed as he said, "yes, and there's another connection I want to show you." The excitement in his voice was building as he said, "one of the sandwich bags contained over 100 rounds of the blue-tipped 9mm bullets. We'll need to check with the Lab, but these appear to be identical to what GMP recovered and the MAC-10 ammo used in the Brixton murder."

He paused, politely waiting for me to catch up as I went through all the photos.

"What's with these blue-tipped bullets? I've not seen these before," I asked.

"No idea, Guv. We can ask Marco and Hamish. They're bound to know."

"I'm surprised you haven't done that already, John," I said jokingly.

"I'm on to it, Guvnor, just haven't done so yet," his voice feigned annoyance. "Marco will know where else they're turning up from his Lab[4] reports. I'm hoping Hamish over at MI5 will know who makes them."

"Okay, so what do you both think is going on with these three caches?" I asked, wanting their knowledge to help steer my thoughts on our next steps.

"We've got a series of common denominators," John replied, sounding authoritative, "not least that Customs are in the middle of this. Same types of

---

4   Lab: short for Metropolitan Police Forensic Science Laboratory.

handguns, including the nasty Tokarevs in all three, and each comes with the matching calibre ammunition."

"And," Mark added, "they've all had their serial numbers removed in the same distinctive way. Plus, as you've just pointed out, Guv, we've got the nickel finish Smith & Wessons that may be the same as those found by GMP."

"Right. So what do you propose guys?" I asked.

John hesitated as he summoned the courage to ask for something outside his usual remit. "Well, Guv, I think we're dealing with one source of supply, and I'd like to start an investigation to identify who it is."

I delayed replying while I considered how to run such a major investigation, as this would be a first in my new role, but something we should lead.

"Okay, agreed," I announced. "Yes, we should ramp up an investigation to identify the source, and quickly. We need to get ahead of whoever's involved. John, I want you to take some initial actions, please."

Eagerly, he opened his daybook. This A4-size, half inch thick red notebook is standard equipment amongst Scotland Yard detectives. Known by its stores' inventory as '*Book 40*', we used them as both a diary and notebook. John clicked his biro in readiness.

"First, I want you to contact the three SIOs[5] at Greenwich, Plaistow, and Gravesend. Find out where they've got to with their enquiries. I'm hoping they've done house-to-house, reviewed CCTV, and all the usual background enquiries into the three cars."

"Yes Guv."

"Second, run transaction enquiries on the PNC[6] in case they haven't. Hopefully the cars have been stopped or sighted by police and we'll get some helpful leads."

"Yup, we can get those done very quickly." The fervour in his voice confirmed he agreed with my thoughts so far.

"Third, talk to your equivalent in GMP. Ask them whether they know who's supplying these guns to their gangs. Ask the three SIOs for our caches who they think supplied theirs and who they were meant for."

I waited while John furiously finished writing, his pen moving so fast it was scratching the paper.

"And fourth, call the wonderful Marco at the Lab and ask him whether he's seen the guns yet and, if so, what he knows."

I let John catch up before continuing.

---

5   SIO: Senior Investigating Officer - the most senior detective assigned to lead a major criminal investigation.
6   PNC: Police National Computer - database of all registered vehicles and their owners and all persons with a criminal record.

"For my part, I'll have a word with Hamish at MI5. I'll also visit SO13 Reserve to check their records for the two calls from Customs. John, would you phone Kent about theirs?" I noted his nod and so carried on, "and get the name of the Customs officer and their phone number too. Unless you can think of anything else, that should be enough to kick us off."

"Yup, that's all good. We should have some if not all the answers for you in the morning."

"Great. Meet me in my office tomorrow at 9:30 for a catch-up. Oh, and one more thing."

"Yes Guv?" John said, sounding apprehensive.

"Let 'Information Room'[7] know of our interest in shootings involving submachine guns. If they get reports of one anywhere in London, I want them to call me immediately. Give them my pager and mobile numbers."

I left the briefing room knowing we were on to something major but, at that point, I had no idea of the enormity of what was to come. Going back to my office, I dialled the number for SO13 Reserve.

---

7   Information Room: short for the Central Command Complex - Information Room (CCC-IR) based on the second floor of New Scotland Yard, which was the communications hub for 999 call-handling and despatch for police in London.

CHAPTER 3

SO13 Reserve.

I buzzed the intercom on the fifteenth floor to gain access from the lift lobby. I could see DS Tim Broughton observing me through the glass screen of the SO13 Reserve Room opposite. I waved and he pressed the door-release.

Tim had a reputation as a formidable detective during his time on the Flying Squad. He had been in the thick of high-risk operations arresting armed robbers in the 90s. He and his team had often taken them out 'across the pavement' as they fled from a bank after robbing it at gunpoint. He had a friendly but assertive manner that came with the confidence of knowing his job. He was the perfect choice as the guardian and gatekeeper in charge of SO13's Reserve. Like our own facility downstairs, it acted as both a call centre and visitor reception point. Anyone coming to our floors had to convince the staff they had a genuine reason to enter the restricted areas beyond.

Tim ushered me into his office. I could see he had tried to bring order to the clutter on his MPS regulation black linoleum-topped teakwood desk. His attempts at filing papers in various trays had spilled out to cover the surface. The bookshelves behind had exceeded their capacity too, with the excess files lying horizontally, perched precariously above the ones stacked below.

"Well Guvnor, we haven't seen you in a while. What can I do for you?" he asked, welcomingly as he cleared papers from a chair to let me sit.

"I've just picked up a gunrunning investigation, and I need your help with one of my enquiries."

"Okay, what did you have in mind?" his tone suggesting some hesitation in case it was onerous.

"I'd like to see your logs for two calls to the Reserve from Customs." His face relaxed as I continued, "they were on November 12th last year, and February 26th just gone. They called to let you know where to find firearms hidden in two cars."

"I remember them. As it happens, Guv, I took both calls," he said, now delighted at the ease with which he could help. "The Customs guy didn't want to give me anything to identify a suspect. He was keen we just go and get the guns. He told me there's no point plotting up to see who might collect them. It was as if we were doing him a favour," he sighed in obvious frustration. "Typical Customs. You know what they say, Guv, it's all about product not prisoners with them. Doesn't matter whether anyone gets arrested. They're measured on seizures not prosecutions; you know."

I nodded to acknowledge his greater experience, although I suspected it was a myth perpetuated by detectives after years of jealous rivalry between our two organisations.

"I'm hoping you recorded the caller's name and phone number?" I then asked.

Tim eased the ring binders with the handwritten call logs out from the shelf behind him. He thumbed through the one for November first and then February's. He left them open at the relevant pages before sliding both towards me.

"Harrison, Ben Harrison is the name he gave. Same guy both times," he announced, clearly pleased at proving his diligent record-keeping.

"And these are his phone numbers?" I asked reading the content.

"Yes, but that's the odd thing, Guv. I could see from my phone screen he was calling from a mobile, so I wrote the number down immediately. But when I asked him for his number, he gave me a landline instead. I wrote that down too, as you can see."

"I'm going to need photocopies of these, please. That won't be a problem, I hope?"

"No, not at all, Guvnor," he said, immediately getting up to run the two logs through the photocopier in the corner.

I started making notes in my daybook while he carried on recalling the conversations with the Customs officer. "On both occasions, Harrison told me he'd received a call only a few minutes before from an informant about where to find the guns. As you can see, that informant knew the street names and precise location where the cars were parked. He even knew the car registration numbers." His voice changed to reflect the wisdom of his experience as he continued, "now, that's too much detail for an informant, unless they've got a hand in the job themselves. I imagine you get something similar through your Crimestoppers unit too, Guv."

"Yes, we do, but you've got me thinking why Customs called you and not Crimestoppers."

"Well, I imagine it's because he or she is getting some form of reward way beyond just the cash you offer. How many guns have you recovered so far?"

"Well, forty-seven from Whitechapel and Plaistow and another eighteen from a third find in Gravesend, so that's sixty-five in total. Plus, there's more than a thousand rounds of assorted ammunition." I noticed Tim was losing interest, so I added, "we need to find who supplied these, because the same types are being used in shootings; one with a MAC-10 where GMP officers were targeted. Another MAC-10 was recovered only yesterday used in a Brixton murder."

"Well, I wish you luck, but don't expect much help from Customs, Guv," he told me as I left.

CHAPTER 4

SO11 TIU

My priority on returning to the fourth floor was to catch up with the Telephone Intelligence Unit (TIU) supervisor, Pete Dobson. I needed him to fast-track some discreet enquiries. Pete was in his early thirties, with boyish good looks and a pale complexion that he kept overly moisturised. It gave his face a semi-permanent sheen. He used a rather camp mannerism to display disapproval that I was very much alive to. Lowering his head enough to stare at me over the rim of his glasses, he would then cup his cheek in one hand and cover his mouth with the little finger. The accompanying frown warned that he wanted to dissuade me, for example, from tasking his staff with what he perceived would be something tedious.

I had to tread carefully with Pete. Until my arrival, he had taken great pride in his role as Secretary of the national 'ACPO(S)[8] Telecommunications Industry Strategy Focus Group', known for short as 'ACPO Telecoms'. Chaired by DAC Fry, membership was limited to senior law enforcement officers, government officials, and some talented people from the confidential side of the industry: the CSPs. However, DAC Fry had replaced Pete with me to reward my drive to put the TIU at the forefront of pioneering the formidable techniques we were developing with the CSPs. Together, we had made major advances in the use of telecoms data to investigate organised crime gangs and arrest people for some very serious offences, including murder.

Pete had resisted my wanting to create a 24-7 response involving an on-call rota for his staff. He wanted instead to maintain more regular hours and weekends off. I needed his team to step up and share the burden of supporting live operations. Reluctantly, he had allowed them to participate, but chose not to do so himself. DAC Fry liked what we were achieving; especially through our support to Central

---

8   ACPO: Association of Chief Police Officers, the collective term used for the overarching business leads for the 43 police forces of England, Wales, and Northern Ireland. The eight Scottish forces used the term ACPOS – 'S' for Scotland.

500 operations. In a fast-moving, high-risk kidnap investigation, the TIU was critical to identifying the telephone used by the hostage to give '*proof of life*', as this would also locate the stronghold where they were being held. Until my arrival, Pete restricted the TIU's services to mostly fulfilling requests for subscriber checks and itemised billing. This had limited the tactics available to the OCG. It meant their principal option had been to put the ransom on the road in the hope it would draw the hostage-takers into bringing their captive to the pay-off. I was able to change that by demonstrating how we could now use data to get ahead of them to locate and rescue the hostage with much greater certainty. All this innovation had earned me the nickname of '*Whizzy*'.

I punched in the six-digit code to unlock the door to the TIU. Pete had arranged the office into three banks of four desks for his twelve-strong team made up entirely of civil staff. Each had a computer and a three-tier document tray. Pete had positioned his own desk separately at the far end of the room, with two large whiteboards behind him and a bank of fax machines alongside. It gave the appearance of a classroom with the teacher at the front. Almost full height windows overlooked Victoria Street on the left. That glimpse of the outside world somewhat compensated for the intensity of the administrative work undertaken in the room.

Respectfully, Pete stood up acknowledging my arrival, "yes Sir. Is this a social or do you need something?"

"Bit of both, please, Pete. How are you? How's the team?"

"Under pressure, as usual, Sir. Thankfully no kidnaps this week so I've still got all my staff," he commented, with his right hand now cupping his cheek.

I noted the warning signal and quickly added, "I do appreciate what you all do here, Pete. Having two of yours on call has radically changed things for the better. And I'd say that's good for Corporate Services too, wouldn't you?"

He sat back down in his chair; his expression remained disapproving as he glared at me over his glasses. Sensing he was about to list all the negatives; I changed the subject. "I need your help with the subscriber for this mobile," I said, writing the number for Ben Harrison into his daybook. "I also need the itemised billing for the period from October 1st last year through to today."

Pete now took over writing his own notes to keep up.

"I'll need all the incoming calls for the same period. Cellsite[9] locations too. Going forward, I want the mobile on live trace, so we get all its incoming

---

9   Cellsite (locations): the capability of the CSPs to locate a mobile handset by either triangulating its position live on the network through its connections with the closest masts or historically by the mast(s) used during a call.

and outgoing calls immediately. Keep it running until May 31st. By then we should know enough to tell whether it's worth continuing."

Pete looked as if he was going to protest, so I kept talking to prevent the interruption.

"Can you also get the subscriber for this landline?" and I copied Harrison's other number into his book. "I'll type up the Data Protection authorisations and have them back to you in a few minutes. I'd be grateful if you'd start working on them right away, though. It's for a confidential investigation I've kicked off into gunrunning."

"Interesting," he commented, "not had one of those before."

"Yes, and I want single line reporting, Pete. That means, for now, only you know what's going on and only you report back to me directly. I've no problem with you tasking my enquiries out to your staff, but I don't need them knowing the context. Is that clear?"

"Yes, Sir. I'll get on to it now."

"Thank you. When can I expect the results back?"

Looking over his glasses at me impatiently, he replied, "subscriber checks could take an hour. As you know, itemised billing takes a day or more. Incoming, and cellsite locations take longer."

"Okay, but press the CSPs to fast-track these, please," I added as I walked away.

Sitting back at my desk, I typed up the data protection authorisations on my computer. As a Detective Inspector, I could only authorise a subscriber check. Everything else needed a Superintendent to approve. Having printed off mine and the Superintendent's authorisations, I tucked them into a folder and then went to find Anton, hoping he would be in his office.

I had quickly learned the language used by Scotland Yard detectives when addressing each other. 'Guvnor' for Inspectors and Chief Inspectors, and 'Boss' for Superintendents and Chief Superintendents. 'Sir' tended to be reserved for more senior ranks. Of course, we mixed them up to suit the circumstances; particularly if a well-timed 'Sir' conciliated a quicker path out of trouble.

I knocked on Anton's open door, "Boss, may I? I need a couple of telecoms data requests authorising." I noted the difference between our two offices, as unlike mine his was filled with mid-morning sunshine.

He looked up and, thankfully, broke into a welcoming smile. He had a reputation for disliking interruptions and not suffering fools gladly. Having worked for him before, we knew each other socially. He lived not far from me and often when he had a duty car, would give me a lift home. Anton was in his forties, so ten years older than me. He preferred navy blue suits, which complemented his height and solid build. He had thick dark brown hair, with no obvious signs yet of greying or thinning. He would often brush his fringe back vigorously with one hand, as if conscious he'd let it grow a little too long to remain smart.

I explained my rationale for the call data requests.

"Interesting approach. Okay, I'll authorise these, but be careful. I don't want you making an enemy of Customs."

"No Boss," I replied quickly by way of reassurance.

"And you better create an official docket for the investigation. Get an operation codename from Special Branch too. Document everything."

"Will do."

"Oh, and remember," he added, running a hand through his hair, "your role is here on the fourth floor, not galivanting out in the field. Let me know immediately if you get something significant. I'll then decide who's going to develop the job operationally." He paused to let me acknowledge his instruction with a nod before continuing, "and let me have whatever you've got so far on Friday. We can then catch up on Monday after 'prayers'[10]. Okay?"

"Yes, Sir."

---

10 Prayers – colloquial term for the weekly catch-up meeting between senior officers.

CHAPTER 5

First Lines of Enquiry

Wednesday, 30ᵗʰ April

The following morning, as planned, John and Mark came to my office for our first review of the investigation. On the way in, I had collected from my pigeonhole in the '*Branch Office*[11]' two envelopes that Pete had left for me. These contained the subscriber checks confirming the mobile and landline recorded by Tim were registered to HM Customs' National Investigation Service (NIS) in London.

"We've been in touch with the CID[12] at Whitechapel and Plaistow," John began, and then waited for me to open my daybook while I also mentally noted the aroma of pipe smoke. "Well, it's pretty much the same story for both," he continued. "The cars were bought for cash a couple of days before they were found with the guns. Advertised in the '*Thames Valley Trader*', both sellers met the buyer in Eltham, somewhere just off the High Street. No address. They did the deal on the roadside and didn't get the details of the new owners. Nothing helpful on the PNC either."

"Damn," I said, despite expecting that would be the outcome. "Still worth checking, though."

"Yes, Guv. Sadly, there is no CCTV where we need it in Eltham High Street." Then with a more positive voice, he added, "if you're in agreement, I'd like to offer the SIOs our E-fit[13] people to work with the car-sellers. Hopefully, they can create a face from the descriptions. Are you okay with that?"

"It's worth a try. Yes, make the offer. Let me have the numbers for the sellers' phones too. I'll get reverse billing authorised in the hope it identifies the ones used by whoever arranged to buy them."

---

11 Branch Office: administrative secretariat.
12 CID: Criminal Investigation Department.
13 E-Fit: police forensic artist.

"Will do, Guv," Mark replied enthusiastically.

"What more have you got?" I then asked them.

"Both cars have been forensically examined," John added in a manner that forewarned of the outcome. "No useful marks. Wiped clean, and still with all the rubbish the previous owners had left."

"Damn. And the guns and ammunition?" I asked, hoping for something we could exploit.

"No fingerprints on the guns and nothing useful on the sandwich bags either. Whoever's involved made sure they left nothing to help us identify them."

"What about CCTV? There must be some of the Wickes' car park, surely?"

"Nothing for Whitechapel, and the system in Plaistow wasn't working."

"Hmm, so, have the SIOs sent the guns to the Lab?"

"No, Guv," Mark said, clearly wanting to contribute too. "Neither are willing to go to the expense of forensic examinations unless there's an arrest. All they've done is take photographs. I've been in touch with NCIS[14], but they can't help unless we can provide serial numbers. I've asked them anyway to check whether they've seen these makes and models before. Hopefully, they have, and we can connect ours with whatever intelligence they've got about a supplier."

"Thanks Mark, good idea," I said, wanting to encourage his proactivity.

"Guv," John cut in, sounding a little more positive now, "GMP confirmed a TIG welder was used to remove the marks on their MAC-10s and Smith & Wesson revolvers. Marco said the same had been done to the MAC-10 used to murder Devon Dawson."

"Okay, so the TIG welder is certainly a common denominator in London and Manchester. Any intelligence on who was hiding the guns found in Whitechapel, Plaistow and Gravesend?"

"None at all," John said in a tone that reflected his growing annoyance that none of his enquiries had born fruit. "All three SIOs drew a blank. They've got no possible lines of enquiry."

"What about GMP? Any information about who's supplying theirs?"

"No, they're as mystified as we are. They assume it's someone down here because the MAC-10s were manufactured by a Kent-based company, SF Firearms in Tunbridge Wells."

---

14   NCIS: National Criminal Intelligence Service, which ran the National Firearms Tracing Service within its INTERPOL National Central Bureau. They took responsibility on behalf of UK investigators to trace through the global firearms market the ownership of a firearm used in crime to identify the point where it was either stolen or passed into the illicit gun trade.

"Okay, so what do we know about them?"

"No longer in business," Mark said, again keen to show his enthusiasm. "I'm waiting for confirmation from the Sussex Force Intelligence Unit, as the business was actually on their turf, not Kent's. The guys at NCIS said the company went bust a year or so ago. They've had multiple police enquiries since about its MAC-10s, but always drew a blank with the former owner, Christopher Perkins. He told them that in '95 he surrendered all his surplus stock to Sussex Police for disposal as scrap. He can't explain how they keep turning up."

"We'll be making our own enquiries, Guv," John added.

"Not yet with Perkins," I told him firmly. "We don't want to alert him right now to our enquiries, as he could well become a suspect."

John nodded saying, "sure Guv, we'll work around him for now."

"Good. Let me know what you turn up. I read that GMP thought theirs had been reactivated. The similarities with the ones found at the Tollgate Hotel suggest they were too." Looking at John to reinforce this as an action, I added, "we need to look into that possibility too."

"Yes Guv, we'll add that to our enquiries."

"What news from the Kent SIO about their job at the Tollgate Hotel?"

"Well, she's done a far more thorough job examining their guns," Mark said, handing over an album of detailed photographs. "She sent me these this morning via one of their traffic officers, who came up on a solo motorcycle. As you can see, the same TIG welder marks as Whitechapel and Plaistow. There's no doubt all three are linked to the one supplier."

I flicked through the images. "Very impressive. Any chance we can get our SIOs to do the same."

"No. We'll have to do it ourselves," John answered. "If we want to see the guns, they're now in the property stores at Greenwich and Plaistow."

"We do, and all together. Get the three SIOs to send everything to Marco at the Lab," I told John. "I want to make our own comparisons to confirm they all come from the same source."

"I'll get that done," John replied, still with his head down writing.

"Thanks. So, Mark, what more from Kent? Forensics? CCTV? Anything helpful?"

"Same as the others, I'm afraid. The car was bought for cash a day or so before. Interior wiped clean. No forensics. No CCTV, and no one saw the car being left in the hotel car park. Interestingly, though," and he paused momentarily for effect, "the deal to buy it was done in the same side road off Eltham High Street."

"Wow. Okay, do we have anything about suspects associated with that area?"

"Nothing immediate," John cut in, "but I've asked InfoS to see what they can dig up."

"Right, what about the original call to Kent Police?"

"They faxed me a copy of their CAD[15] record," Mark said eagerly, passing over the paper for me to read. Once again, it was Ben Harrison from Customs using the same numbers as for his calls to SO13.

"Okay, so have the three SIOs now spoken to Harrison?"

The sigh that preceded John's reply signalled more bad news, "they've all tried the mobile and landline numbers, Guv, but both go to voicemail. They've left messages, and a guy from NIS did call back. Wouldn't give a name. Said Harrison wasn't available, and the investigation was confidential, so he couldn't say any more."

"How very odd. What else? There must be something positive from all your enquiries," I asked.

John and Mark just shrugged to confirm they had not got very far.

I paused to gather my thoughts before asking them, "okay, I'd love to get your first impressions of what we've learned so far?"

John looked at Mark and then spoke for them both, "first, it's clear we're on the receiving end of an informant-led Customs' job. Clearly, they've got their own agenda, which means they're not fussed about who supplied the guns and their end-users. They're just happy we got them off the street, for which they'll take all the credit." Then, just like Tim had commented, he added, "since their objectives won't include identifying the supplier, they won't be interested in helping us do so instead. I sense the three SIOs know this too, which is why they're not doing more."

"I keep hearing this about Customs, but let's not make any assumptions until we've asked them ourselves," I said firmly.

"Yes Guv, but us taking on an investigation that might compromise their informant means they won't be happy with us poking around."

"I understand that John, so we need to find a way to secure their cooperation," I replied, not wanting to allow his negativity to prevent us from persevering. "With sixty-five firearms and a thousand rounds of ammunition

---

15   CAD: Computer Aided Despatch – record of the initial call to police, action taken and result.

now recovered, it appears at least one crime gang wanted to stockpile weapons. That foreshadows an escalation in violence, which means we must find their armourer quickly."

"It's early days for us, Guv, but we're focused on doing just that," John responded more positively.

Good, so we need Customs and the SIOs to work with us too, as we should anticipate more guns to come."

"Why's that," John asked, clearly trying to catch up with where my thoughts had got to.

"Well, after the Whitechapel seizure, the gang sought to replace what they lost with the ones recovered at Plaistow and more. Having lost them too, they tried again at Gravesend, only this time with the MAC-10s and the BAR thrown in. Whilst Customs have disrupted whatever was going on, I think we should expect whoever lost it all will want to replace everything and quickly."

"So, you think there are more in the pipeline, Guv?" Mark said, obviously energised by the prospect.

"Right now, we can't be sure, Mark, but, yes, we should anticipate there are. So we can't just leave it that Customs won't talk to us. Every day increases the risk of another murder or shooting as more guns leak on to the criminal market. There may even be more unrecovered arms caches out there waiting to be distributed." I paused to note both were nodding as they recognised the potential.

"Therefore," I continued, "we must find out who's behind the supply chain."

"We're right with you, Guv," John said, now sounding much more enthusiastic. "Are we going after the Customs' informant too?"

"Yes, but let's keep that to ourselves. Mr Baxter has given permission for us to make discreet enquiries about Ben Harrison's mobile. Let's see what that turns up. Hopefully, it'll provide the leverage we need to convince him to help us."

"Sounds good. We'll hold off making enquiries with our Customs' contacts until you say so, Guv."

"Thank you, John. That would be wise. Once we've got enough, I want you to set up a meeting with Harrison. I want the SIOs for Whitechapel, Plaistow and Kent there too. Invite GMP's to come along as well. We also want someone from the Brixton homicide squad." To emphasise my objective, I told them forcefully, "We must get all the SIOs to put pressure on Customs. Hopefully, they will help convince Harrison to task his informant with giving us the source, his network, and who he's supplying."

"Absolutely, Guv. We'll start getting that meeting organised."

"Thank you. Oh, and please let me have your file on these three recoveries. I want to send a copy over to Hamish."

"Sure, I'll have it topped and tailed and back to you shortly."

"Good. I'll use it to convince him to host our meeting with the SIOs at Thames House. Hopefully, MI5's involvement alongside our own will stimulate greater collaboration."

John and Mark nodded.

"Okay. Thank you both for the briefing. Early days, but we're making progress. This is the biggest gunrunning job we've had. Reconvene tomorrow, please, same time, and for the rest of the week."

As they stood up to leave, I added, "oh, and John, would you do me another kindness please?"

I saw him flinch momentarily as he responded with, "Sir?"

"Phone Special Branch and ask them for an operation codename." His face revealed his relief at this simple task. "Mr Baxter wants to get our investigation registered formally. That way he can give us the necessary top-cover should Customs start questioning why we're investigating them."

"Sure, I'll get that done too."

I had adopted the expression 'Would you do me a kindness?' from my time working for AC Veness. He used it to great effect whenever he wanted you to do something that was likely to be onerous. You felt obliged to get it done because it would be a 'kindness' to him and he was our big boss. My own staff quickly recognised the significance of this term when I used it too. Hence, I noticed, like John, they often flinched in anticipation of what might be coming.

Picking up my desk phone, I called Mark Daly, my opposite number at HM Customs. He advised that Ben Harrison was a Senior Investigator in the NIS and one of their foremost informant handlers. He was rarely at Customs House, so Mark kindly gave me the contact details for his boss, Mick Burridge.

CHAPTER 6

Get it Done

Sitting at my desk later that morning, I noticed my open doorway darken. Instinctively, I looked up. It was Detective Chief Superintendent (DCS) Brian Mills, the SO11 Branch Commander. An absolute gentleman in every way. Courteous to a fault, with steely blue eyes and an air of supreme confidence gained from years of hands-on operational experience as a career detective. Much of it involved running the types of high-risk intelligence-led investigations SO11 was renowned for. His office was next to mine, on the right. He was a smoker, and so his was tainted by the smell of stale tobacco. Sometimes, it permeated through to mine to warn when he was alongside. Brian was in his 50s and so old-school he refused to have a computer. Instead, he hand-wrote everything. Occasionally, he would pop in and ask me to type up his notes, leaving behind the relevant file. I did so willingly, as the documents were always an interesting read.

Brian had called me into his office soon after I joined SO11. The previous week he had brought his daughter into work and introduced us. She said my face seemed familiar but could not recall where from. Two years earlier, I had agreed to have some family pictures taken by a photographer friend. He promised me he'd use them just for his stock library. "My daughter's remembered where she'd seen you," Brian announced as he handed me the magazine '*More*', aimed at a readership of mainly teenage girls. His mischievous look told me he was rather pleased with himself as he said, "you'll find your photograph in a double-page article. It's under the banner headline, '*My baby's father is the married man next door*'."

Brian laughed at my obvious embarrassment as I recognised myself from the photograph. Thankfully, he accepted my innocent explanation. However, for weeks afterwards he would produce the magazine to his visitors and bring them to my door. Almost proudly, he would point at me saying, "and that's the married scoundrel right there."

Wondering why Brian was standing in my doorway this time, I asked, "Boss, do you need my secretarial skills?"

"No, not on this occasion, Michael. My office, please."
I grabbed my jacket from the back of the chair and followed him.
"Push the door to, would you, and have a seat." His flat tone signalled bad news. He reclined in his executive-level chair and revolved it slightly side-to-side, revealing his discomfort at what he was about to say. I too had one of these chairs, despite them being the preserve of more senior ranks. I had "borrowed" mine on leaving SO13 and moved it into my new office. I was conscious, though, that Brian had earned his by privilege of rank.

I followed the protocol and looked at the papers on his desk hoping to glimpse what might be coming my way. My mind began to race: '*had Customs already called him wanting to know why I was making enquiries about Ben Harrison?*'

Lifting a brown folder from his desk, Brian let me know what was troubling him. "Michael, I'll get straight to the point, I'm not able to support your application for promotion this year."

I sat back and took a deep breath. Then, with a voice of resignation quietly exclaimed, "sugar, bloody, damn." My wonderful godmother, Mrs Elizabeth Ive, had taught me this reaction to adversity. Her Methodist upbringing meant she found it almost impossible to swear. This was as bad as her language got. I too rarely swore, so found her three words a useful way to express my emotion without causing offence. Brian sensed the disappointment I was suppressing.

"Look Michael, the facts are these," his voice was now matter-of-fact. "I know you've had six years in the Inspector rank but until now in uniform. You're a '*Branch Detective*' here in SO11; not a real one who's been through the Detective Training School like the rest of us. To be a DCI, you still need to earn your colours as a true detective. I've been allocated three slots to recommend DIs for selection and, I'm sorry, I've got three far more qualified than you."

I considered the ramifications as he spoke. I had been the youngest Sergeant ever at twenty-two, with just four years' service. I had made Inspector within ten years at twenty-nine. I was ambitious but, in 1995, the MPS placed a moratorium on promotions. I then looked for broader experience to give me a better chance when the system re-opened. Since I had chosen to become a detective, I could not now revert and try for a uniform promotion instead.

"Shame we couldn't have done this over a pint, Boss," I said, trying to appear positive.

Brian smiled, "we can still have a chat over a pint," he said, warming to the idea of staying on after work. Reassuringly, he then added, "look, I'll get you on the next Detective Inspectors' Course. That'll get you qualified for the CID. You can then move around without being returned to uniform."

I nodded to indicate my appreciation.

"And you'll be in a far better position for promotion to DCI too. How does that sound?"

"Thank you, that's most kind," I replied, still suppressing my disappointment.

"Good. That's it for now. Let's go for a pint this evening."

Returning to my office, I closed the door and slumped into my borrowed executive chair wondering if I'd ever rightfully be entitled to one. I stared at the framed photograph on the desk of my wife, Olivia, and our four-year-old daughter, Rebecca. This career setback would only add to the tensions at home. It meant I would have to put in even more hours at work to get the recognition needed for a decent chance at promotion. The phone rang as I pondered on this. Answering it cheerily, I hoped not to give away my underlying frustration.

"Michael, how are you? It's Stuart Jackson."

Stuart and I first met in 1996 when he was the Staff Officer to the Commissioner, Sir Paul Condon. He was then a Chief Superintendent awaiting promotion to Commander. As part of the Support Services Review, I had helped assess the value-for-money of maintaining the 'MPS Band'. Based on its high costs and unproven benefits, our recommendation was to close it down. Returning its forty or so members to full-time operational duties would immediately achieve a benefit from the £3 million in opportunity costs alone. The Management Board listened to us and, whilst its chair, The Receiver[16], Philip Fletcher, agreed, the Deputy Commissioner, Sir Brian Hayes did not. He was incandescent with rage. Anticipating Sir Brian's reaction, I had briefed Stuart in advance. He in turn told the Commissioner. According to Stuart, when Sir Brian then stormed into the Commissioner's office declaring, "have you heard what they want to do with the Band?" Sir Paul replied, "yes, just think what else we could do with the three million. Time it was disbanded," and chuckled at his pun.

Returning my thoughts to Stuart's phone call, I said, "are we re-forming the Band, Sir?"

Laughing, he said, "no, no, I think you're forgiven for that." Then with a hint of uncertainty in his voice, he asked, "I'm hoping my research is correct and you now look after prisons, guns and telephones?"

---

16 The Receiver: formal title for the equivalent of a Chief Financial Officer.

"Yes, Sir, that's correct."

"Good," and with more confidence he continued, "can you be in the Commissioner's Private Office in thirty minutes? I have something you might be able to help me with."

Half an hour later, Stuart welcomed me to the eighth floor. I could not help noticing his bright new Commander's epaulettes. "Congratulations on the promotion, Sir, is that very recent?"

"Thank you, yes, last month."

"Dare I ask which ACPO job you got?"

"Police Adviser to the Prison Service based at the Home Office, which is why I need to see you." Then in a more hushed voice he asked, "first, may I check you are security cleared?"

"Yes, I am."

"Good, good. What I'm about to tell you is highly confidential," he said still in a semi-whispered voice. "It'll soon become clear why I want your knowledge of prisons, guns and telephones."

Placing my daybook on my lap, I asked, "do you mind if I take notes?"

"Not yet," he replied sternly, before lowering his voice again to say, "let me explain things first. If you convince me you can help, then certainly, take notes. Otherwise, I'll ask you to forget the whole conversation."

I looked past him momentarily at the sign on the closed door. It read '*Commissioner*'. Stuart followed my gaze. "Oh, he isn't in. Out on a visit with his new Staff Officer. It's given me the opportunity to meet you here. I'd rather not do so at the Home Office, as will become clear. Sir Paul may return soon and also want a word."

Stuart was softly spoken and surprisingly mild mannered for a man who held considerable authority. I felt sure that if provoked, he could also bang the table. This was the first time I had been into the Commissioner's private suite. Everything was so different compared to the more stark, functional surroundings and drab grey colours of the other floors. Thick carpet replaced the standard linoleum, and armchairs and sofas offered much more comfort than the regulation upholstered hardwood seats the rest of us were used to. As I drank the coffee Stuart offered, I noted even the crockery and spoons were more upmarket than those available in the fourth-floor canteen.

"Michael, I'm going to run past you a scenario I've had dropped on me very recently," his voice suggested some annoyance. "I'm keen to know what you can do to help me. You see, we need to get ahead of a situation that's both operationally and politically challenging. It's also potentially career-damaging for some very senior government officials involved."

"Sir, I'd be delighted to help in whatever way I can," I answered, my mind now racing.

"Thank you. Oh, and the Commissioner has taken a keen interest, so you'd better be confident about what you can deliver."

"Of course, Sir," I said with confidence to reassure him.

"Right, to summarise, in March, someone senior in the Home Office began negotiating on behalf of the Home Secretary with a solicitor acting for a serving High-Risk Category A[17] prisoner. The latter wants to trade his early release by telling us where some very heavy weaponry is hidden in London."

Silently, I mouthed my usual "wow."

"So now the background," he began to explain, "the inmate is in a prison outside London, so not one of yours. His solicitor contacted the Home Office direct to say his client had picked up information on his wing that a London crime gang is holding rocket propelled grenades, RPGs. He's offering to help the Home Secretary seize them in exchange for immediate parole. He's not offering anything to help us make arrests, so he won't name his source."

"Goodness," I said, not knowing what more I could add.

"Yes, and I'm sorry to tell you the Home Secretary has already agreed, but only in principle, not yet in writing. Now, all that is very likely to change in twenty-four hours. With everyone predicting the Conservatives will lose tomorrow's election, and Labour will get in, we'll shortly have a new Home Secretary. He or she will want to know about this immediately, as finishing the deal will be on their watch. Still with me?

"Yes Sir. I'm just surprised the Home Secretary agreed, even if it was only in principle. The political fallout will be massive when the media gets hold of this."

"Precisely, and not only will Michael Howard be made to look an absolute fool, so will every one of the officials who've been advising him. Their jobs aren't at risk with a change of Minister, but their reputations are. We can expect them to do everything to protect their careers and pensions." With a sense of foreboding he added, "thus, you can see how very messy this could get."

"Yes, which means we'll have to be very careful with our enquiries."

"Quite so. I only got to know of this last Friday when the Home Office official acting as the go-between asked for my advice. He said the Home Secretary had

---

17   Category A: highest security risk, with the potential for extreme violence, or likelihood of escape.

finally realised that dumping the job of recovering the RPGs on us without warning would not look good; especially after nearly two months of negotiations. When I briefed the Commissioner, well, as you can imagine, Sir Paul was none too impressed to learn the Home Secretary hadn't come to him immediately."

"This begs the question as to what precedent the Home Secretary thought he was setting," I commented. "I mean, once word gets out, solicitors by the dozen will be queuing up offering to trade every type of contraband imaginable to negotiate their clients' release too."

"Quite so, Michael, quite so." Stuart then paused before continuing, "now, despite all the obvious distractions Michael Howard has due to the election, the Commissioner has got him to agree on how to proceed. The Home Office official I mentioned will, for now, continue to be the point of contact with the solicitor. He will act only on my instructions. It must be that way, as the Commissioner doesn't want to alert the solicitor to wider police involvement."

I nodded, following the logic of this approach.

"He wants to give the appearance that we're nothing more than the recovery agency once we've been told where to find the RPGs. That gives us the opportunity to run a discreet investigation in tandem so we can get ahead of what's going on."

"That makes sense," I said, getting excited by what was potentially coming my way.

"Yes, the Commissioner is very keen we develop a negotiating strategy that does just that. I'll be meeting your boss, DAC Fry, at 5pm to get it sorted. I'll then be briefing the Home Office official about what to say in his next call to the solicitor."

Stuart paused to look at me and seemed reassured by my nods.

"The matters I want your advice on are these. First, what can we do about the Category A prisoner and his solicitor? Second, what can you do to put us on the front foot in these negotiations so we can seize the RPGs before any trade? And third, what intelligence is available to confirm they even exist?"

I paused before replying; both to give me time to think and also sound convincing when I did that I knew what to do. "Okay Sir, in response to your first question, I'll use my Prison Intelligence staff to talk to their opposite numbers at the prison and quickly develop a full profile on the inmate. We'll be asking for his associates on the wing, especially those with London connections; visitors; telephone conversations, dates and times, etc. I'd also want to know every time the solicitor visited."

"Sounds good. What else?"

"Second, I'll get my TIU to build a profile on the solicitor from his mobile phone calls, including the locations where he made them. We'll check his office and home phones too. We'll start with the very first call he made to the Home Office. I'd also want to go back in time to identify who he called and vice versa to initiate it."

I paused to check that Stuart's expression had confirmed I was on the right track.

"That should give us a solid picture of who the solicitor is talking to about the trade, both inside and outside the prison," I then added. "I'll also put all the numbers on live monitoring going forward. Do you have the phone numbers being used by the solicitor and the Home Office official, Sir?"

"Yes, I do," his voice now sounding less guarded.

"And the dates and times for that very first call right up to and including their most recent one?"

"Yes, I can let you have those, and the accompanying notes of what they discussed," he added. I was relieved his voice now revealed an enthusiasm to proceed.

"Excellent. Well, that's how we would help you get ahead of what they're planning. As to your third question," again, I paused to inject some gravitas to my thinking, "I'll do my own research with MI5's Weapons Intelligence Branch. I'd want their take on whether such weaponry could be in London and, if so, where it came from. Those would be my first three actions. Do they help?" I finished, hoping to have displayed sufficient rigour in my approach.

"Yes, yes, bloody perfect, Michael," he replied, his voice now evidently excited. "It's much more than anyone has done in the Home Office and what I can do from where I sit. I'm very grateful for our chat. Thank you."

I waited in anticipation of him now giving me the full facts. After a period of extended silence that made me feel uncomfortable, I asked, "would you like me to make a start now, Sir?"

"Sorry, Michael, yes, yes, of course. I was just thinking about the consequences of failure. Hmm, let me worry about that." Then, picking up a brown folder from the chair next to him, he said, "right, here's the file I've put together for my own purposes. I've drawn it mostly from what the Home Office official gave me." As I reached to take it, Stuart hesitated, saying, "but I can't let you take it away or photocopy it. You're very welcome to read it here, make notes, and then give it back to me." In a hushed tone, he continued, "you'll understand there are sensitivities about there being any official record. That way, if it all goes wrong, it's easier for the Home Office to deny everything."

"If you say so, Sir," I replied, unhappy with the implications of his statement. I chose to move on, though, by asking, "would you help me with a 'who's who in the zoo'?"

"Yes, of course," he replied encouragingly, "the senior Home Office official is Colin Murray, deputy head of the Prison Service. You'll find his phone numbers in the file, with a chronological list of dates and times along with his own notes of each conversation with the solicitor."

Stuart paused helpfully while I copied the information.

"The inmate's name is Fred Donovan. He's a major Manchester criminal. Sentenced in late '95 for conspiracy to supply amphetamines, he's fifteen months into a ten-year stretch at HMP Full Sutton on the Category A Wing."

Stuart waited for me to catch up with my notes while I scribbled hurriedly, hoping I would be able to decipher them later.

"His solicitor is Patrick Gudgeon, also from Manchester. You'll find his mobile and office numbers in the file. Colin Murray indicated there's some history between them, so you might want to look back further than March 13th when this all started. Colin said he couldn't discuss whatever had gone before, so I didn't enquire further."

"If you don't mind Sir, I need to spend a few minutes writing down the dates and times for all these calls and copying the notes about what they discussed?"

"Carry on, but remember, when the time comes, we'll need to review whether any of it can or should be turned into evidence." Once again, he lowered his voice before adding, "I sense the Home Office won't want the full story coming out in court should your enquiries lead to an arrest."

I nodded to let him know I had heard him but kept my head down while continuing to make detailed notes. When I finished, I told him, "I need to manage expectations, Sir. It may take the CSPs a week to get all the data we want."

"Okay, we'll just have to be patient then," he said with some resignation. "Whilst the Home Office is doing what it does best, prevaricate, speed is still of the essence. Gudgeon is putting Colin under considerable pressure to give him a letter from the Home Secretary to confirm the agreement. He's claiming any delay risks the RPGs moving and Donovan not then hearing where to. He's upping the ante all the time, warning they could be used any day in some horrendous crime."

I picked up on his anxiety and replied reassuringly, "I'll press on everyone that speed is of the essence, Sir."

"Thank you. For now, the election has bought us a couple of weeks, maybe a month at most. Gudgeon does accept the Home Secretary's attention is elsewhere right now. Colin's assured him he'll brief the next incumbent, if there is to be one, very soon after he or she takes up office."

"Sir, in addition to you talking to DAC Fry, would you also call my immediate boss, Detective Superintendent Anton Baxter? It will help me enormously if he hears it from you direct that you want me working on this."

"Yes, of course," he replied immediately in a reassuring tone, before saying enthusiastically, "I'm going to recommend you be my first point of contact. I will let you know immediately about any calls between Murray and Gudgeon. That way you can react to what's happening on the telephones."

"That makes sense, Sir. In the meantime, I'd like to put Colin Murray's phones on live monitoring, so we know immediately either the number he called or just called him. We wouldn't have to wait days for the billing. Live monitoring will also reveal the caller's number even if they think they've blocked it by prefixing their call with 1-4-1."

"That seems very sensible." Then in a more hushed voice he asked, "I assume you'll only go digging further when I tell you a particular call is relevant."

"Yes, and that's how I'll write it up."

"Good, well I'm happy with that. Now, here's my card, with my new phone numbers so you and I can keep in touch." I took it, handing him mine in return.

"As regards the negotiating strategy," he added, "I'll be briefing DAC Fry that our primary objective is to recover the RPGs by any lawful means. The Commissioner made it abundantly clear to the Home Secretary he has great difficulty doing deals with prison inmates. He doesn't want Donovan getting any benefit; especially if he won't name his source."

"I agree."

"So part of your job, Michael, is to find the evidence, even if it's only on balance of probability that Donovan hasn't been straight with us."

"All received and understood, Sir." I thought for a moment before asking, "when should I tell Mr Baxter to expect your call?"

"Within the hour, oh, and recommend he join me at 5pm in my meeting with DAC Fry."

I was about to get up when I stopped to impart some of my own knowledge on the subject, "You know, Sir, an RPG is a very unlikely weapon for London criminals to use." Looking him in the eye to reinforce my point, I told him, "I get to see a lot of intelligence files on weapons. There's never been any mention of RPGs in a UK context. That may be because they've got no practical use, not even for cash-in-transit robberies. As Michael Caine once said in the 'Italian Job', they're likely to do more than just "*blow the bloody doors off*"."

Stuart laughed, "yes, quite so."

"My knowledge comes from monitoring the biker-war going on in Sweden. It's between the 'Hells Angels' and 'Bandidos' outlaw motorcycle gangs. They've been firing RPGs and bombing each other's club houses for a couple of years now. Thankfully, we just don't have that type of weaponised gangland violence on our streets." I then added, "well, not yet anyway."

Stuart nodded as he took in the information.

"I should tell you I'm also running an investigation that could be related," I decided to tell him. I then explained what we knew about the three recent recoveries of firearms and ammunition in Whitechapel, Plaistow and Gravesend.

"My goodness, Michael," he said when I finished, "if all these are connected, it could be that what we're witnessing is, as you suggest, the build-up to a massive surge in gang violence across the UK."

"Yes, Sir, quite possibly it is."

Just then, Sir Paul Condon entered the room. Instinctively, I stood up. His expression suggested he recognised my face but could not recall the name.

"Sir, you'll remember this is Detective Inspector Michael Hallowes," Stuart said helpfully. "He's now in SO11. Head of guns, phones and prison intelligence,"

"I do recall Michael, I do. Good to see you, again. I think we're all forgiven for the Band. Are you fully briefed?"

"Yes Sir, I am."

"Good. Remember the objectives: protect the integrity of Scotland Yard, and recover the weapons, if they exist. Oh, and make sure Donovan stays in prison. If I have my way, he'll serve out his sentence in full. Understood?"

"Perfectly, Sir."

"Good, well, get it done, Michael, get it done."

CHAPTER 7

Tasking and Coordination

As before, my first port of call on return to the fourth floor was to see Pete in the TIU.

"Good afternoon," I said on finding him at his desk. "Thanks for the results on the subscriber checks for the Customs' numbers. How are you getting on with the other data?"

"I've had the billing through. Vodafone are cursing you, though, for the other stuff. If you're lucky they'll get it to us later today."

"Okay, let me have whatever they send through as soon as it comes in."

"Sure."

Taking the pages of billing he had just given me, I asked, "would you do me another kindness?" and saw him flinch, which was deserved. "While we're waiting for the rest, would you ask one of your team to start transferring all this on to an Excel spreadsheet?" I knew how much work was involved, and, justifiably, Pete gave me one of his disapproving stares.

I persevered, "I know, I know," I responded, hoping to sound sympathetic, "but the analysts will find it so much easier to process in electronic format. Please, let's get into the habit of doing it from the start. Better still, ask the CSPs to send it in soft copy, not paper, and let me have it all on disc. Thanks."

Pete nodded, but not enthusiastically.

"I've got another similar enquiry, please," I announced as I gave him the numbers for Patrick Gudgeon. He sat down and began writing.

"First, subscriber-checks on these mobile and landline numbers for confirmation. As before, I need incoming and outgoing on the mobile going back six months from today, so October 1st onwards. Get what you can from BT on the landline for the same period. Until further notice, I need live monitoring for all incoming and outgoing calls to both the landline and mobile, plus cellsites on the mobile's location."

Pete now wrote furiously in his daybook without looking up.

"And I'll need the same for this mobile and landline," I said, giving him the numbers for Colin Murray. "Don't be concerned if the subscriber comes back to the Prison Service or Home Office."

This time he did look up and I got all his warning signs as he responded, challenging my request, "first, you start investigating Customs and now you're looking into the Home Office."

"Yes, Pete, it's all authorised and, this time, from the very top."

He looked at me suspiciously saying, "I'll need the paperwork".

"Of course. Have I ever let you down?"

He thought for a moment before replying, "no Sir, but the phone companies will moan. I'll make sure they get it done, though. Will there be many more such extended-period requests for data?"

"Very likely, Pete, yes. Same rules apply. Speak only to me about this job. Okay?"

"Yes Sir."

I noted in my daybook the instructions I'd given him, and then headed out along the corridor to the 'Main Office'.

I scanned the sea of heads of the forty or so people who worked there at the rows of desks. In the middle of the room, I spotted DS Dermott Logan at his. As the most senior Sergeant, he supervised the Prison Intelligence Unit. Every police force around the country had a similar setup for monitoring prisons within their jurisdiction.

"Dermott, good afternoon. How are you? How's the team?"

"Hello Guv. Good to see you. All good apart from my ongoing grief at home. The others are all fine. As you can see, I'm the only one in the office today. Got some HR matters to sort out."

"I'm sorry about the domestic situation. How are the children?" I asked sympathetically. A week before he had a tearful private chat in my office about his wife leaving him to set up a new life with a woman she knew from work. He was devastated.

"Well, now my wife's moved out leaving me the kids, I've got all the childcare responsibilities. Another reason why I'm in the office rather than at Belmarsh; it's closer for collecting them from school."

"Not a problem. I can cut you as much slack as you need. Now, not wishing to add too much to your burdens, would you mind popping into my office, please? I'd appreciate your help."

"Give me five minutes, and I'll be in, Guv."

I went back to mine and found that John had slipped his report on the three firearms recoveries under the locked door. Picking up the file to read later, I left the door open, and Dermott soon joined me.

"Would you push the door to, please? Thanks."

He did so and, before sitting down, glanced quickly over at the files on my desk. To his disappointment, I had left them closed and face down.

"I need you to call your opposite number at Full Sutton Prison, please, and find out everything you can about an inmate on the Category A wing there. His name is Fred Donovan."

"Okay," he said, clearly relieved I was not asking him to do one of my '*kindnesses*'.

"Upstairs wants us to have a thorough look at every aspect of his prison life. Who he's talking to on the wing could well have a major impact on gangland crime in London. If I asked you to do the same for one of your inmates at Belmarsh, what would you give me?"

"Oh, I can do better than that. I know my oppo at Full Sutton. It's DC Des Overton. If you like, we can call him now."

I let Dermott use my desk phone to dial the number.

"Des, hello, it's DS Dermott Logan in the Met, SO11 … Yes, I'm fine thanks. How are you? … Good, good. Look, I've got my boss here who'd like your help. He's got an interest in one of yours on the Cat A wing, Fred Donovan. Do you have time now for a confidential chat, or do you want to call back from somewhere more secure? … Okay, good, I'll hand you over. It's DI Michael Hallowes."

He passed me the handset and I switched the call across to the handsfree speaker.

"Des, thanks for taking my call. Do you know Fred Donovan yourself?"

"Yes, as a Cat A he's a big player in the prison. Let me grab his file from the cabinet. One minute Guv." I was delighted he sounded energetic and immediately helpful.

A minute later, after the sounds of a metal filing cabinet drawer sliding open and then closing, Des was back on the line. "Okay, Fred Donovan. Yes, he's serving ten years for supplying amphetamines. Went up before the judge at Manchester Crown Court in November '95 and was sentenced to ten years. He was on remand here from July that year. The file says he was arrested in a joint operation between GMP, North-West Regional Crime Squad and Customs."

"Okay, who does he associate with?" I asked, wanting quickly to get to the relevant points.

"Donovan mixes with all the main players here on the Cat A wing, most of whom have also been convicted of supplying drugs. He's well behaved and doesn't give us any aggro. He was also good mates with Haase and Bennett for a few months until they got released by the Home Secretary last year. What more do you need on him?"

"Whoa, can I just rewind a moment, Des? Who are Haase and Bennett and why did the Home Secretary release them?"

"Oh, they're John Haase and Paul Bennett. Major league Liverpool heroin dealers. Last year, it was a big story up here. The Home Secretary pardoned and released them less than a year into an eighteen-year stretch for smuggling £18 million worth of heroin."

"What?" I said, unable to contain my shock.

"Yes, it was in return for information leading to the recovery of a load of firearms hidden away by gangs up here. I'll find you the confidential Merseyside Police report on the job. I know we've got a copy filed here somewhere. When I do, I'll fax it down. It'll make interesting reading." Des's voice faded slightly as he turned his head away to look around the room for where the file could be.

"Yes, please fax it to me. As regards Donovan, I want everything about his associates on the wing; especially any with connections to London and firearms."

"Sure, Guv, leave it with me. It'll be easier if I fax you his complete file. Sorry, I won't have time today, but I'll make sure you get it by close of play tomorrow. Is that okay?"

"Thanks, Des, yes, that's perfect."

Ending the call, I turned to Dermott and thanked him. He then quickly left to get home.

I sat back in my chair excited by the interesting developments about Donovan. In particular, his association with two other inmates who had already done a deal with the Home Secretary and that Customs were also involved.

Having typed up the authorisations for the telephone data arising from my meeting with Commander Jackson, I realised an obvious oversight. I had forgotten to brief Anton. Grabbing my daybook and the authorisations from the printer, I headed to his office hoping he was still there. Thankfully, he was, with his head down working on papers at his desk. I knocked.

"Boss, may I?"

"Michael, I've only got a couple of minutes. What do you want?"

"First, the easy part. A few more authorisations, please."

"Briefly, what are the circumstances?" his tone suggested impatience.

Speaking quickly due to his time constraint, I told him, "the context is there's a Manchester solicitor acting for an inmate at Full Sutton Prison who's trying to trade his client's early release with the Home Secretary. He's offering RPGs, which he's told the deputy head of the Prison Service are in the possession of a so far undisclosed crime gang somewhere in London."

"Stop, stop, where did you get this from?" his voice sounded annoyed as he brushed his fringe back rather more vigorously than usual and swivelled in his chair to face me.

As I explained the background, Anton's expression changed from anger to surprise. Trying to head off any repercussions, I added the positive news about Commander Jackson wanting him in the 5pm meeting with DAC Fry. I finished saying, "I had hoped he'd called you already, but the look on your face suggests not."

"No, he hasn't. And as I think you can tell, I'm a little annoyed. However, it sounds like it's not entirely your fault." He sat back and paused before adding, "Look, we have an unwritten protocol here about handling requests from senior officers outside the Directorate."

"It would have been helpful to know that in advance, Sir," I commented, hoping it didn't sound rude.

"Yes, well, when Commander Jackson called you, you should have let either me or Brian know before you went upstairs. I appreciate you've known him a while and, given his rank, you're keen to help. But really, one of us should have been there. That's how we operate. Next time, build in a delay before agreeing to a meeting. Okay?"

"Understood."

He then took a few minutes to read the authorisations.

"Okay, Michael, I'll authorise these. However, I want you to see DCS John Bunn in SO13. I want you to make sure we're not treading on one of his live CT[18] investigations."

"I'll do that next."

"Look, I admire your energy. You're making the right enquiries about this inmate Donovan and his solicitor Gudgeon. As with the firearms' job, remember, I want to know the moment you find anything significant."

"Yes Boss, of course. Oh, and I'm happy to join you at 5pm in the meeting with DAC Fry, if that would help."

---

18   CT: Counter Terrorism.

"No, that won't be necessary," he said quite dismissively, reminding me where I sat in the chain of command. "At some point," he added, "I'll catch up and update you." Finishing our conversation he added, "so much for my only having two minutes!"

Returning to my office, I typed up and printed off my notes of the conversation with Stuart Jackson. Having inserted the pages into the folder with John's report, I headed along the corridor to the Director's outer office. This was the only room in SO11 with a 'Brent Phone'. This large black desktop telephone enabled secure and encrypted landline and fax communications between UK law enforcement and intelligence agencies. Turning the key to switch it on, I waited a minute as the device completed its authentication process. Once the screen said, 'Dial number', I selected "Fax" on the keypad and loaded the loose pages from the file and sent them over to the MI5 Weapons Intelligence Branch. I addressed the cover sheet to Hamish, my principal contact there, and added a note saying, "Please call me".

Hamish was a quietly spoken Scotsman in his mid-50s. He was tall, with the obvious bearing of a former army officer. He wore small-framed glasses that gave him a slightly academic look that perfectly suited his role now as an intelligence officer. I had learned very quickly from our first conversations that he was meticulously thorough, with an encyclopaedic knowledge of weapons and ammunition. He was, therefore, the perfect choice for his role. He had earned a reputation as one of the foremost experts in weapons identification and the habits of those involved in the global illicit arms trade. Quite regularly, he proved himself instrumental at solving investigations into the criminal use of firearms. A recent one involved a murder in Scotland. The offender left behind the AK47 assault rifle used in the attack. Hamish recognised marks in Arabic painted on the buttstock as matching those on others recovered during the Gulf War. Realising this weapon was almost certainly a battlefield trophy brought home by a British soldier, he set about identifying the suspect. Service records revealed one living in the neighbourhood where the murder took place. Hamish let Strathclyde Police know, and they made the arrest. The soldier was later convicted of the murder.

I stood waiting by the Brent Phone. As I had anticipated, it rang and the number on screen told me it was Hamish.

"Thank you, Hamish, I thought the reports would get your attention."

"Yes, they did. First, these RPGs, what do you want to know?" His quiet Scottish voice did not soften the curtness of his questioning.

"Likelihood of them being here in London?"

"We haven't heard that, but there's always the potential for someone to smuggle them in from the former Soviet-bloc. It would be a first if that's what's happened."

"Do I also need to ask Fort Halstead[19]?"

"No, no, they update us with everything they see too. I'll need you to pop over and meet a couple of people here who'll find your reports very interesting. Next Thursday at 10am. Will that suit you?"

"Yes, but time is pressing, Hamish. We need to get on top of what's going on."

"Hmm, yes, I read that in your report, but I can't get these people to meet you any sooner."

"Anything you can help me with right now?"

"No, other than you need to read the Merseyside Police report on Haase and Bennett."

"Now that is a coincidence, Hamish. I hadn't heard of them until a few minutes ago. What's the relevance?"

"You need to talk to Merseyside Police. Best you get the story from them first. We have our own very fixed views on the case."

"Well, I should get their report tomorrow. Can you be a little more helpful with what I should be looking for?"

"No, not right now. You need an open mind when you read it. I can then give our perspective."

"Hmm, okay. So, about the RPGs, when asked by my bosses, can I say that neither you nor Fort Halstead have any knowledge of them being in the UK?"

"Yes, you can say that on good authority. Sorry I can't be more helpful. I'll be able to say more when we meet."

Returning to my office, I telephoned Tim in the SO13 Reserve. A few minutes later, my mobile rang. The screen showed 'No Caller ID'.

"Michael, John Bunn. DS Broughton passed on your message. Would you be in my office tomorrow at 7am?"

"Of course, Sir."

"Good, Anton Baxter already let me know why you need to see me. I suggest you reschedule whatever you had planned and spend the day up here. Alright?"

"Sir."

I then sent a text to John Bryan apologising for having to miss our 9:30 in the morning and re- scheduled it for the next day back in the Fordham Suite.

---

19   Fort Halstead: part of the Defence Science and Technology Laboratory (DSTL) that examined weapons and explosives recovered by the police and military here in the UK and overseas.

CHAPTER 8

My First Major Scotland
Yard Investigation

Friday, 2ⁿᵈ May

The previous day with SO13 had been useful to catch up with colleagues but proved worthless in terms of moving forward both our firearms and RPG lines of enquiry. None of our intelligence cut across theirs. Thankfully, that meant DCS Bunn was happy for us to continue as an SO11-led operation. I cursed, though, the loss of a day I could ill afford given the urgent nature of our enquiries.

I was grateful this morning to get a seat for my Tube journey into St. James's Park. It allowed me to read the newspaper more comfortably, albeit I had to keep my elbows in so as not to annoy the people either side. The front page declared Labour's predicted victory over the Conservatives. Tony Blair was now Prime Minister and Jack Straw his Home Secretary. I wondered what he would make of the briefing his officials would be giving him about the unfinished business with Fred Donovan.

I popped into the SO11 Branch Office to check my pigeonhole and collected a brown A4-size envelope that was sticking out. I recognised Pete's handwriting. Tucking it into the side pocket of my briefcase, I headed through the double-doors to my office.

As I unlocked it, I found John had slid another file under my door. He seemed to prefer this method of postage to the more conventional use of my pigeonhole. As instructed, he had created a Registry File. Across the top, written in thick black marker pen, was the name, '*Operation Abonar*'.

To avoid different squads choosing their own and, potentially, the same title for their investigations, Special Branch issued all operation codenames. They based these on a monthly theme that they then allocated in strict alphabetical order. Some SIOs could get annoyed by this process. I recall one who, on taking over a job named 'Heath', from a theme for open spaces, had exclaimed, "Heath?! Heath! I'm investigating bloody terrorism, not a walk in the countryside. What's next month's theme?"

"Greek gods, Sir," the frazzled registrar offered.

"What are my choices?" the SIO raged as he thumbed down the list to the end. "Perfect. I'm having 'Zeus', book that one out to me. Far more appropriate!" And that's how the 1998 OCG-SO11 investigation to arrest the '*Mardi Gra Bomber*' got its name.

Opening the Abonar file, I saw John had inserted a handwritten note saying, "*Abonar. Portuguese verbs this month. Means 'to pay'!!! Clearly, it's a warning to those we're coming for*". I smiled in agreement.

I put his note on my desk before checking the file. Helpfully, he had also typed a one-page outline of the investigation so far. I added the pages he had given me previously on the three firearms' recoveries along with my own typed notes on the lines of enquiry. Operation Abonar was now formally underway. It was my first major Scotland Yard investigation.

Next, I opened the envelope from Pete. It contained the Vodafone records for Ben Harrison's mobile giving all the incoming and outgoing calls from 1st October 1996. Disappointingly, in the same timeframe, BT had only been able to provide the outgoing ones from his office phone. Helpfully, Pete had included a floppy disc with all the data in a series of Excel spreadsheets. I loaded it into my computer and entered the password provided. Looking at my watch, I saw I had only a few minutes before my 9:30 with John and Mark. I decided to focus on the mobile data. I entered the search parameter of November 12th, 1996, to find the call from Harrison to SO13 about the first recovery in Whitechapel. I then searched for incoming calls immediately before. There was only one. It was from a mobile some ten minutes earlier. I made a note of it in my daybook. I then ran the same searches for the other two calls about the second and third recoveries on February 26th and March 1st. Again, Harrison had received just one beforehand. It was the same mobile number each time. It registered in my mind. I flicked through my daybook to check. Thankfully, I only had to go back as far as Wednesday. There it was and I already knew the subscriber. My thoughts were racing as I processed what I had just discovered whilst rushing to the Fordham Suite.

"Good morning gentlemen. You are now my modestly sized, two-person Major Investigation Team," I declared to John and Mark as I took my seat.

"And I'd like to thank you for making Operation Abonar my very first Scotland Yard investigation."

They both smiled encouragingly.

"Sorry I missed our catch-up yesterday. I haven't had time to tell you, but I picked up a new job following an unexpected meeting with Commander Jackson."

They both looked at me quizzically.

"It meant Mr Baxter had me spend yesterday with SO13 cross-checking the new intel with theirs to make sure we're not treading on one of their jobs." I paused to let them grasp the significance and noted their looks of alarm. I quickly allayed them saying, "and, thankfully, we're not. So Abonar and the new job remain with us."

"Well, that's a relief, Guv," John said with obvious cheer. "So, are you going to enlighten us about the new one?"

"Yes, of course, but let's first catch up on Abonar. For my part I've just received the call records for the Customs' man, Harrison, going back to October 1st last year. Before I tell you what I've found, I'd like to hear about your progress. John?"

"Well, we've got the incoming call data requests you asked for, which Mr Baxter now needs to authorise. They're for the phones for the three people who sold the cars in which the guns and ammo were found in Whitechapel, Plaistow and Gravesend. As you requested, we've included the time and date parameters for the CSPs to search for the incoming caller IDs for the buyers. Other than that, there isn't very much more to add."

"Okay, thanks. Mark?"

"No, Sir."

"Oh, and Guv," John interrupted, clearly wanting to add something helpful, "I've also arranged for all the SIOs to send their exhibits to Marco at the Lab. We're meeting him there next Tuesday morning at 10:30, and I've organised a photographer. Hope that's okay with you?"

"Of course, great. Right, let me fill you in on my surprise meeting with Mr Jackson."

John and Mark looked at me intently as I read my notes of the meeting, before handing the typed copy to John along with the Abonar file.

"Goodness. Well that trumps Abonar for sure," he announced.

"Actually it doesn't, and I'll explain why." I could feel my own excitement rise as I spoke. "I've only had time to quickly scan the calls for Harrison's mobile. But, from what I've found, I'm confident Abonar and the RPG jobs are directly connected."

"How so?" John asked, obviously excited too.

With that I got up and loaded the floppy disc into the computer next to me and projected the overlaid spreadsheets on to the big screen for them to see.

"Right, here we go," I said, moving the cursor around the points of interest. "Call number one to Harrison's mobile immediately before he phoned SO13 Reserve about the Whitechapel recovery. Make a note of that incoming mobile number guys, as it appears again."

I then repeated the process for the calls about Plaistow and then the Tollgate Hotel.

"See, it's the same mobile. Chaps, this is our first major clue towards identifying Harrison's informant."

"Do you now know who it is already, Guv, and you're just teasing us?" John asked.

"I do and I am, yes." Pausing for a couple of seconds to heighten their excitement, I then announced, "it's the solicitor, Patrick Gudgeon. As I just briefed you, he's the one representing Fred Donovan in the negotiations with the Home Secretary about the RPGs."

John reacted instantly, "Oh my God. Yes, yes so it is."

I then briefed them on my conversation with DC Des Overton about Donovan's association on the prison wing with John Haase and Paul Bennett; their successful negotiations with the Home Secretary for early release, and the case also being linked to a Customs' operation.

"Guv, that's shocking!" Mark almost shouted, his voice filled with obvious scorn.

"Yes, and I'm waiting for the confidential Merseyside Police report to explain how many firearms they recovered and what types."

John interrupted, "I'm thinking it has to be significant for the former Home Secretary to release them so early into an 18-year sentence. Must be hundreds."

"Yes, and interestingly, when I asked Hamish about this, he just told me to read the Merseyside report."

"Be interesting to see if the Merseyside guns have TIG weld marks too," Mark queried.

"Yes, it would," I replied.

"So when can we expect to see the report?" John asked, also now keen to get his hands on it.

"Well, DC Overton said he'd fax it to me as soon as he found it. I'll check my pigeonhole straight after this."

"I'll check our files too, Guv, but it doesn't ring any bells," John commented.

"So, with Gudgeon the common denominator in both Abonar and our new RPG job, we now need to know who he's representing in his dealings with Customs over the firearms."

"You know Sir," Mark interjected, "as Manchester is where the firearms from our Abonar source are also turning up, it could be the Customs' informant is someone up there. Maybe they used Gudgeon to warn Harrison to stop the three consignments before they could reach the Manchester gangs."

"Interesting idea, Mark," I said, recognising his valid thought process, but then cautioned him and John, "possibly, but we must keep an open mind. A detective's worst enemy is confirmation bias. Remember our ABC: 'Assume nothing, Believe nobody, and Check everything'. Understood?"

"I thought it stood for 'Arrest everyone, Bail nobody, and Charge the lot'," John countered, laughing at his own joke.

"Thank you, but no," I said firmly. "Right, moving on, our priority is identifying who Gudgeon is acting for."

"Absolutely Guv," John responded excitedly. "You know, I can't believe how much this job has grown since we first briefed you on Tuesday."

"Yes, I know, which is why we need to approach this scientifically. Would you find us an analyst, please, to now help? Hopefully, we can borrow one from Angela Dawes' team in the Main Office. I need them to create an 'i2'[20] chart. I want to map the phone data and firearm recoveries along a timeline plus every conversation between Murray in the Prison Service and the solicitor Gudgeon about the RPGs." I was pleased to see them both nodding in agreement. "Combining both jobs on the one chart will help identify more easily any other common denominators, and faster than I just did manually."

"Sure, Guv. The Strategic Analysis Unit is over in the corner near my desk. I'll ask one of them after this," John advised.

"Goodness," I said, pausing to reflect, "I've just remembered something else Commander Jackson told me. He said Murray had a history with Gudgeon but wouldn't tell him more, so didn't ask. Hopefully, given the data I've requested goes back to October, it will reveal what that was about too."

---

20 i2: the software package used by many police forces to process and overlay data from multiple sources to help identify connections and patterns between otherwise disparate pieces of information.

"Maybe it's that Gudgeon was also the solicitor acting for Haase and Bennett in their negotiations with Michael Howard," Mark suggested.

"Well that would be a coincidence," I said, "which, of course, only the Merseyside report will tell us. Hopefully, DC Overton has now sent it. Oh, and John, he's also faxing Donovan's prison intelligence file. Once we've got it, I'll need everything relevant mapped on to the i2 chart too."

"This is going to be a lot of work, Guv," he cautioned.

"Yes, I know, so the sooner we start the chart and populate it with what we know so far, the better prepared we'll be for all the new data when it comes in." I noted John was now nodding in resignation that I was right.

"And, given the negotiations on the RPGs have been running since March 13th," I reminded them, "we need to accelerate everything. We must catch up and get ahead of whatever Gudgeon and Donovan have planned."

"Yes Guv," John responded, trying to sound positive despite knowing the work involved.

"Okay," I continued, "Mr Baxter is going to meet me on Monday to explain the negotiating strategy with Gudgeon and Donovan to secure the RPGs."

"Knowing that would certainly help us get ready."

"Quite so, John. If necessary, guys, we may have to work the weekend and ask the analyst to do the same. Sorry, but that's the good old exigencies of duty."

"Understood, Guv, if that's what you need,"

"Thank you, it is. I'm going to need your help too with proving my hypothesis about Gudgeon is right. There's too much at stake politically for me to go in half-cocked; no firearms'-related pun intended, when I brief Mr Baxter on Monday. Help me avoid having to tuck copies of the Sunday papers down the back of my trousers in case he beats me for getting it wrong."

John and Mark both laughed.

"That's all good, Guv. We'll protect your backside. I'll find us an analyst too."

"Thank you, John. Now, I better ask Mr Baxter if he'll allow me to pay you overtime for the weekend. If not, it will fall to me to come in, and my wife is already fed up with the hours I'm keeping."

"But, hopefully, Guv, not with your company," John said, looking at me sympathetically.

CHAPTER 9

Haase and Bennett.

I left the meeting and went to the Branch Office to check my pigeonhole. I was delighted to find two envelopes sticking out. The first contained the faxed copy of Fred Donovan's prison intelligence file. The second was the Merseyside Police report on Haase and Bennett. I walked into the Main Office with them both to find John.

"Here you go. Donovan's file from Full Sutton. Please make a start on it. I'm going to read the report on Haase and Bennett. I'll be in my office if you need me."

John examined the multiple pages inside the envelope, and his expression warned that processing it would take time.

Pushing my office door closed, I sat back in my chair to start reading. My staff knew that when the door was shut, disturbing me was not an option unless there was a crisis; hopefully, theirs not mine. I wanted no interruptions so I could read the report properly. I then immersed myself in its contents.

John Haase and his younger nephew Paul Bennett were career criminals. They each had multiple convictions for armed robbery and, more recently, drug smuggling. They first came to the attention of Merseyside Police as serious criminals in the 1980s. This was when they were members of an armed gang robbing cash-in-transit vans.

The report stated that in 1990 Haase and Bennett had progressed to the murkier underworld of international drug smuggling. They travelled frequently to London to collect high-grade heroin from a Croydon-based Turkish crime family. They then took the drugs back to Liverpool to distribute in the north-west. The Turks were bringing in the drugs from their home country. That brought them to the attention of Customs, who began a lengthy investigation involving surveillance on all the main players. The principal Turkish target was referred to as 'The Vulcan'.

In July 1992, police and Customs began making arrests across Liverpool following the seizure of a major shipment of heroin, worth approximately £18 million. It had been intended for the city's drugs market. Haase and Bennett evaded the initial arrests and laid low in a caravan on a site in Wales. From there they arranged to meet their Turkish counterparts and travelled by car to London, staying overnight in a cheap hotel. Both men had a reputation for carrying guns for protection and enforcement. At around 11am the next day, as they drove to the meeting place along Croydon High Street, two white vans overtook their car. The first of these rammed them off the road and the second blocked their escape from behind. Fearing some rival gang wanted them dead, and realising they were totally outnumbered, Haase and Bennett were terrified as they had no choice but to surrender. They seemed almost happy to discover it was a team of plain-clothes Metropolitan Police SFOs who had rushed from the two vans.

Merseyside Police transferred Haase and Bennett to Liverpool under armed escort. They later charged them and all the others involved, including the Turkish crime family, with a conspiracy to smuggle and supply heroin. They were all remanded in custody at HMP Liverpool, also known as 'Walton Gaol', where the Prison Service classified them as Category A prisoners.

The report then described Haase's first meeting with the Liverpool-based solicitor representing him and Bennett. With some disappointment, I read the solicitor's name was Tony Nelson, and the senior Customs officer was Paul Cook. That news destroyed our earlier optimism that it would be Gudgeon and Harrison.

Haase wanted Nelson to arrange a meeting with Cook to discuss getting a reduced sentence. Cook agreed to meet him at the prison. Nelson was also present. Haase asked whether he could do a deal based on information about where criminal gangs in the north-west of England had stored their drugs and guns. He indicated he also had information about weapons held by the IRA. The latter was to prove hugely influential in Cook's negotiations with the Home Secretary, because the IRA had only recently agreed to a truce brokered under the watch of President Bill Clinton. However, in 1995, the IRA breached it with the infamous Canary Wharf lorry bomb, which killed two and devastated multiple buildings.

Cook reported Haase's request to his superiors and they in turn to the Home Office. The Conservative government had pledged to fight serious crime and Michael Howard, as Home Secretary, had publicly declared his determination "to make prison work". The government was also committed to reinstating the delicate 'Northern Ireland Peace Process'.

Cook returned for a second meeting with the news that the Home Secretary was prepared to reduce Haase's sentence in return for the promised information. Haase then insisted his nephew, Paul Bennett, be included in the deal. The Home Secretary subsequently agreed to extend the benefit to both men. He made two conditions: one, that they provided the information whilst on remand and, two, they pleaded guilty at their trial.

Within weeks, Nelson contacted Cook providing him with precise details of where to find the first cache of guns and ammunition. From then on until a few days before their trial, Haase and Bennett gave information resulting in the recovery of thirty-five individual caches of firearms, ammunition and drugs. Each time, Customs directed police to the hiding place. Some were in abandoned cars; all recently purchased for cash and untraceable, and others in an empty council flat in Toxteth. Bizarrely, Haase and Bennett also gave Cook a 'treasure map' for a Squirrel Sanctuary in Formby. They had marked out in exact detail the locations of different stashes of guns buried there, such as '10 paces west, 5 east'. Haase told Cook, as with all the information, he had acquired it from an unnamed prisoner on the Category A Wing.

Extensive forensic work at the time failed to identify anyone involved in either hiding the guns or their supply. Helpfully, the report listed one hundred and fifty assorted firearms had been recovered in total along with fifteen hundred rounds of assorted ammunition.

The most interesting recovery was from a car bought for cash in Liverpool a couple of weeks before. Someone had abandoned it close to the Holyhead-to-Dublin ferry port in Anglesey, North Wales. Through his solicitor, Haase let Cook know it was intended for the IRA. Consequently, an MI5 surveillance team spent three days watching the car waiting for someone to collect it. When no one did, MI5 directed police to move in and search it. They recovered from the boot multiple rifles with ammunition and 'Semtex'. The latter, though, turned out to be fake. But MI5 and Customs were convinced they had successfully intercepted a major cache of IRA weapons intended for use by a terrorist cell operating both on the mainland and in Ireland.

Closer to the trial, Haase informed Cook that the Turks involved in the conspiracy planned to kill him and his family. Consequently, police moved Cook temporarily into 'Witness Protection'.

The report also mentioned that Prison Security staff at Walton Gaol had warned Cook of their strong suspicions that Haase and Bennett were using mobile phones smuggled into the prison with which to coordinate these finds. However, frequent searches of their cells failed to recover the devices.

Despite seizing their assets, police and Customs believed that Haase and Bennett still had hidden away, perhaps, as much as £1.5 million in cash and drugs. Detectives suspected they had used some of these funds to purchase all the weapons. However, they could not find any evidence to substantiate it. Hence, reluctantly, Merseyside Police agreed to Cook's demand that they advise the Home Secretary to reduce Haase and Bennett's sentences after trial.

The report included well-reasoned suspicions by Merseyside detectives that others had used a similar ruse previously. They too had bought illegal guns prior to trial; hidden them, and then provided information about where "other criminals" had stored them in return for a reduced sentence.

Haase and Bennett appeared before Liverpool Crown Court where they pleaded guilty to the conspiracy to smuggle and supply heroin. In advance, Cook provided a confidential report to the judge, His Honour David Lynch. In it, he detailed the help both defendants had given whilst on remand. He claimed it had led directly to the removal of firearms and ammunition from British streets held by criminals and the IRA. To protect Haase and Bennett from potential reprisals, in open court the judge sentenced them each to eighteen years' imprisonment. Behind the scenes, though, he wrote to the Home Secretary recommending, as requested by Cook, that he subsequently shorten the period as a 'reward' for the value the two men had brought to reducing harm. Haase and Bennett began to serve their sentences at Full Sutton Prison.

Having read about the police and prison officers' suspicions that the firearms' recoveries had all been a scam, I was shocked by what I read next. It was a separate note on their release from prison. *In 1996, and less than twelve months into their eighteen-year sentences, the Home Secretary granted both men a 'Royal Prerogative of Mercy'. In effect, he pardoned them for their leading roles in a massive drug smuggling conspiracy. Consequently, Full Sutton Prison released them. The report finished by advising that, currently, both Haase and Bennett were living at addresses in the north of Liverpool. Haase was now running a security company in Crosby, named 'Big Brother', which looked after commercial properties across Liverpool.*

I checked again the list of what Merseyside Police had recovered. Amongst the heavier weaponry were Soviet era AK47 assault rifles; Second World War American 'Thompson' submachine guns and British 'Bren' light machine guns, and eighty assorted new shotguns and rifles, plus assorted ammunition in all the appropriate calibres.

Of relevance to Abonar I noticed a Smith & Wesson nickel-finish revolver, and a '*Cash Converters*' plastic bag containing three silencers. I made a note to ask John to find out whether Merseyside Police still had these in storage and could send us photographs.

Whoever was involved in supplying the firearms had removed the serial number on each gun. This identifier, along with the make, model and type are the standard features used to trace the origins of illicit firearms. I had learned very quickly the principle that '*almost every illicit firearm was once on the legal market*'. That meant tracing the provenance through to the point of diversion was critical to successfully identifying the source of illicit supply. Ordinarily, criminals don't worry about the serial number. At most, police might link the gun to the record of its theft, most commonly a burglary. The fact every one had its traceable marks removed was a clear indication the source of supply was someone involved in the legal market. Obviously, he or she feared those marks would lead to us identifying them, and so they had everything useful obliterated.

Once I finished reading the Merseyside report, I sat back in shock as I considered what the lessons it had revealed would mean for Abonar.

CHAPTER 10

The Analysis Begins

Heading back into the Main Office, I spotted John over in the far corner with the Strategic Analysis Unit. Having watched me navigate between the desks, John stood up as I reached him.

"Well, here's the Merseyside report on Haase and Bennett," I told him as I handed it over. "Loads of similarities with Abonar in terms of Customs' involvement and negotiating with the Home Secretary. Let me know what you think."

"Did they use the same Customs officer and solicitor?"

"No, sadly not."

"Shame."

"Yes, but I'm certain we'll find that Harrison knows the other man. His name is Paul Cook. They're both in the National Investigation Service. I just hope they're not in cahoots."

"Well, if they are, that will give us more leverage."

"Yes, indeed it would. Oh, and you'll see I've highlighted where it mentions a nickel-plated Smith & Wesson revolver, and three silencers. Would you ask your contacts in Merseyside whether they have photographs of these and, if so, send us them?"

"Sure, I'll get Mark on to it."

"Would you also ask them Mark's question as to whether a TIG welder was used to remove their serial numbers."

"Yup, I'll pass that on too."

"Good, thanks. You'll find the report makes shocking reading," I commented as John now thumbed through its pages. "It warns of a carefully orchestrated scam that officials ignored. What concerns me is that Whitechapel, Plaistow and the Tollgate Hotel look to be a repeat performance."

"How so?" John asked, with a worried look.

"Well, so far in Abonar we've got sixty-five firearms and a thousand rounds of ammunition, yes?"

"Yes."

"Haase and Bennett helped recover one hundred and fifty and fifteen hundred respectively. That reduced their sentences by seventeen years."

"Yeah, just incredible."

"Which means if the person involved in Abonar is another inmate serving a long sentence, then by now he or she could be expecting almost immediate release."

"Yes, I suppose they would. We might even be in for another couple of recoveries, Guv, to finish off the deal."

"Yes, that's my worry too. And as for Donovan, he'll expect his offer of RPGs alone will secure his release."

"Good grief, yes, I suppose he would."

"So, John, we've got to accelerate Abonar. I want to get on top of this ridiculous trade Customs and the Home Secretary have foolishly allowed. We need Harrison's informant to identify the source of supply so we can prevent him from arming more gangs across the UK."

"As I said before, I'm right with you on that, Guv."

"Good. I'll be adding a note to the file saying much the same. When Mr Baxter reads it, that should convince him to grant the overtime and give me a few more resources."

John had been nodding as I spoke, and then looked sideways at the young woman next to us. Turning back to me, he said, "on that point, Guv, your arrival is well-timed. Let me introduce you to Alice from the Strategic Analysis Unit. She's kindly agreed to help us create the i2 chart."

Alice stood up to shake my hand. She was in her early-twenties, tall, with shoulder length blonde hair, and remarkably pretty. The fact she did not wear any make-up beyond lipstick and eyeliner told me she was confident in her looks. Her glasses gave her face a nerdy, student look, and the lenses magnified her striking blue eyes. She wore a white blouse under a short black bolero-style jacket and black leggings. This smart business-like outfit combined to show off her slender figure and long legs. I sensed she would turn the heads of many men in the building.

"Excellent, well good afternoon, Alice. Very good to meet you," I said, shaking her hand. "Thank you for agreeing to help."

She gently pulled hers away from my more robust grip and ran it through her hair. Then, slightly nervously, said, "good to meet you too 'Mr H'."

"Thought you'd prefer Mr H to Whizzy, Guv," John said playfully.

"Thank you, John. Yes, I'd be very happy to lose Whizzy for good."

"This job looks hugely interesting," Alice said, interrupting the banter. "I'm delighted to be invited to help."

"Have you cleared borrowing Alice with Angela Dawes?" I asked John.

"No, no, I haven't, Guv."

"Not a problem, I'll do it. Alice, when I'm speaking to your boss, how long should I tell her we'll need you for?"

She did not speak but stared at me intently for a moment longer than I felt comfortable with. Then, having thought about her answer, forthrightly replied, "well, from what John's shown me, let's say a couple of hours a day, sometimes maybe four."

"Can you be spared for that amount of time?" I asked.

"I think so. If not, I'll find a workaround. I'm new here, Mr H. I only graduated a couple of months ago and this is my first job. Your investigation will be great experience, because it's both operationally active and reactive." The excitement in her voice reinforced a genuine interest. "It'll be very different to the rapes and homicides I'm usually asked to analyse looking for a linked series. If you tell Angela that Abonar will broaden my knowledge, I think she'll be happy for me to help you."

"Okay, thank you. I'll confirm with her and come back to you. In the meantime, please crack on."

As John ushered me towards his desk, I commented, "Great choice in finding Alice".

"Yes Guv, she is rather easy on the eye."

"No, I didn't mean that. I meant she's got energy and enthusiasm. Just what we need."

"Of course, Guv. Of course, that too."

"And, if you haven't noticed, she's wearing an engagement ring on her left hand."

"Oh, really. Sugar, bloody, damn," he added, deliberately poking fun at me.

"Really John, is that what it's come to? Mocking me."

"Just a bit of fun Guvnor," he responded defensively.

"Yes, but only when no one else is around. So, what have you given Alice as a priority?" I asked, wanting to get back to the task in hand.

"Umm, just as you said. To reconstruct the events leading up to each firearms' recovery and then working backwards to identify how Harrison knew to call SO13 and Kent. Similarly, how Gudgeon knew to call Colin Murray about the RPGs."

"Very good, that's exactly what we need. When she finds a gap in our data, fill out a request and I'll get it authorised. "

"Yes, sure."

"Right, so how have you got on with Donovan's prison intelligence file? Do you want to go through it with me now?"

"Actually Guv, can we do it later. Right now I'd like to get Alice focused on building the chart."

"Okay, that's fine."

"Oh, there is one thing you could do for us. Can you get the data on a phone number I found in the file? It's the one Donovan's allowed to call from the phone on the prison wing."

"Sure, put it on a data request form and I'll get it done."

"Did you get the chance to ask Mr Baxter about the overtime this weekend, Guv?"

"Damn, no I haven't. I'll call him and get back to you."

"Please do, otherwise, Mrs Bryan and I have plans, and I need to let her know soonest."

I headed out into the corridor to speak with Angela. Her office was to the left of mine and the door was shut. I decided to write her a note, which I then popped into her pigeonhole in the Branch Office.

As I reached the corridor heading back to my office, Anton called out my name from behind me.

"Boss, good afternoon," I said, turning round.

"Have you got that file for me to read?"

"I have. It's now Operation Abonar. A lot has happened since we last spoke. In fact, I'm hoping you'll authorise overtime for an analyst along with John and Mark to work the weekend."

"Doing what exactly?" he asked curtly.

"Mapping everything on to an i2 chart. There's a lot to do."

"Well, I can tell you right now, that's a 'no'. I don't have an overtime budget for Corporate Services unless it's for Central 500 operations."

"I had hoped, Sir, given the eighth floor's interest, we could offer overtime to catch up on mapping the data; especially given the speed of negotiations on the RPGs."

"Well, to summarise what came out of my meeting with the Director and Commander Jackson, we've agreed to slow everything down. That's to give us time to brief the new Home Secretary and get his views. I also want to be sure we've got proper control over what the Home Office are up to. That means I won't need your team working any overtime just now. Okay?"

"Sir, may I suggest you take a look at the Abonar file."

Anton looked at me in a way that acknowledged he had heard the exasperation in my voice. He took the file and then moved swiftly past me along the corridor to his office.

Just then Angela appeared from the Branch Office. She and I got on well. She was in her 50s and dressed in a cardigan over a long skirt in the style I associated with my former schoolteachers. Her glasses added to a serious, academic look that some might find fearsome.

"Ah, Michael, how fortuitous. Just found your note. Yes, that should be fine. In fact, I'm happy to let you borrow Alice full-time. You made a good point about 'broadening her experience'. I'll review the arrangement with you at the end of the month. Until then, she's yours."

"Thank you very much."

I walked back to my office and flopped down in the chair wondering how we could catch up without overtime. As I did so, Angela reappeared in my doorway.

"Michael, this might sound odd, in fact I know it does, but a favour, please. I'm stuck on the right word for a report. You had a private education. Your Latin will be better than mine. When a woman does it to a man, it's called 'fellatio'. What's the word when a man does it to a woman?"

"Ah, Angela, um, I only took Latin to O' level, and what you're asking definitely wasn't in the syllabus. I believe the word you're looking for is 'cunnilingus'."

"Yes, yes, that's it. Somehow, I thought you'd know. Thank you."

I was so taken aback I didn't think to ask the context, and then decided it was best I hadn't anyway. It took me a moment to recover my thoughts before heading back to the Main Office to break both the good and not so good news to the team.

Alice was delighted she was now officially part of Abonar. Understandably, John and Mark were not impressed with Anton's denial of overtime to get on top of the data.

Almost begrudgingly, John handed me the data authorisations for the number he had taken from Donovan's prison file. I signed mine for the subscriber check and took it to Pete. I held off asking Anton to sign his for the billing to give him time to read the Abonar file and find my warning.

When I did go and see him, he graciously signed the authorisation. However, he dismissed my negotiations on the overtime saying, "let me finish reading the file. So far, I'm not convinced."

CHAPTER 11

Week 2

Monday, 5th May

Unlocking my office door at the start of a new week, I looked along the corridor and saw Anton's was open. I could expect him to pass by at any moment on his way to prayers. Whilst I waited, I scanned through each of the unit updates from across Corporate Services that I had just collected from my pigeonhole. They consisted mostly of performance metrics, such as how many taskings received, alongside a rolling annual total and any notable intelligence identified as a result. Finding nothing of sufficient importance to raise with Anton, I placed them all in a folder ready for his collection. A few minutes before the 8:30am start, he was at my door. His heavy footfall forewarned me of his approach. In anticipation, I was already on my feet, file in hand.

"All correct Sir, no reports of any note. Just the usual performance stats. Are you still available for our catch-up later about Abonar?"

"Yes, I am. I read the file and I get your concerns."

Anton also had responsibility for SO11's live operations involving our technical and conventional surveillance assets and the Special Intelligence Section's multi-agency investigation teams. These worked from our four covert satellite offices and a commercial airfield in the south-east. Consequently, he had enough to deal with reporting on all their activities. The look on his face as he took my file revealed he was grateful I wasn't adding to that burden.

My use of, "all correct Sir, no reports" has a long history in the MPS. It's commonly used when confronted unexpectedly by someone more senior. PC Trevor Lock famously did so following his heroic role in the 1980 Iranian Embassy Siege. Invited afterwards by a staff officer to use the private bathroom in the Commissioner's suite to freshen up, Sir David McNee surprised Trevor when he walked into his bathroom and found the Constable naked in the shower. Trevor's fabled response was, *"All correct Sir, no reports"*.

As Anton's heavy footfall faded, Pete appeared at my door. He handed me two envelopes. One contained the result of the subscriber check to the number in Donovan's prison intelligence file; the other, all the call data for the mobiles and landlines used by Gudgeon and Murray. Thankfully, this time, the CSPs had sent everything electronically and the TIU staff had copied it on to a set of floppy discs. I was pleased with the speed at which they were now processing our requests. Pete sensed my surprise and delight.

"I told the CSPs how important these are to you, Sir. They all seem happy to help. I think it may have something to do with you being the new Secretary." He couldn't help but then give me one of his disapproving looks.

"Good, because there's going to be a whole lot more," I told him. "Getting the CSPs on board now will help me accelerate this investigation, and time is not our friend."

"Yes, but it may well affect all our other work if they give you precedence," and he carried on staring to reinforce his displeasure.

I felt the sting in his words, but commented, "well Pete, that's why I've got you in charge of the TIU; to help keep everything in perspective and running smoothly."

"Yes Sir."

I heard the exasperation in his voice but chose to ignore it. I was saved by John loitering at my door, which encouraged Pete to leave.

"We stayed as late as we could on Friday, Guv, so I think you'll be happy with our progress. In fact, if I may be so bold, can we forego our 9:30. My time will be better spent helping Alice continue building the i2 chart."

"Yes, of course. I'm sorry I couldn't get you the overtime. I'll pop by your desk once Mr Baxter's finished with me."

"Okay, Guv, we should have most of it done by then. Oh, and you'll find us in the Fordham Suite. More discreet in there."

"Oh, sorry, before you go, Pete's just given me all this," and I handed him the envelopes. "Thankfully, it's all on disc. It's what you need to map the calls between Gudgeon and Murray. Pete's also confirmed the subscriber to the number Donovan phones from the prison wing. It's for his family home in Manchester."

John took it gratefully as I added, "I'm still waiting for the itemised calls, though. As usual, BT are pushing back on the incoming ones, but they're working on it. Fortunately, going forward, live monitoring will capture everything."

John looked troubled, as the delay would put back his hopes of getting on top of the data. Trying to be helpful, I said, "start by looking at Gudgeon's calls seven days either side of each Abonar recovery. They might throw out some leads we can quickly follow."

"Yup, I'll let Alice know."

At just before 10am, I heard the thump as Anton entered the corridor, shoulder-barging the swing doors accompanied by his distinctive heavy footfall. Passing my open door, he paused momentarily to say, "my office, please, Michael," before carrying on.

After his rather forthright instruction, Anton was reassuringly welcoming as I entered his office.

"Right, I've read the file and your warning about the risks if we don't accelerate getting on top of the investigation."

I nodded in appreciation.

"Identifying Gudgeon as the common denominator was good work by the way. What's his call data showing?"

"John has only just started working on it. Angela has lent us Alice to help map everything on an i2 chart."

"Ah, Alice, yes, the new analyst. Good looking lass."

"Yes Sir, and I don't want anyone distracting her. She needs to stay focused firmly on Abonar, please," I warned him with a smile.

"What?" he countered defensively.

"You know very well, Sir. We had enough trouble previously with that other Superintendent having a messy affair with a pretty young analyst. The Branch can do without a repeat performance."

"Yes, yes of course," he replied, looking wistful. "So, when can I see Alice's chart?"

"Forgive me, but without that overtime, it won't be before Wednesday."

"Ouch. Okay, I hear you. I may be able to divert something to Abonar from another budget."

"Thank you."

"Are you now combining both jobs under the one operation name?"

"Yes, and the i2 chart. That way we can constantly check for common denominators."

"Perfect. Oh, and I read the piece about Haase and Bennett," his voice now sounding annoyed. "I had no idea. That was an SO11 job too, you know. We did the surveillance bringing them down from the caravan site in Wales to their overnight stopover in Croydon. We then handed them over to SO19, who did a spectacular job the next day with making the arrests."

"Yes, I'm shocked Michael Howard released them even though Merseyside detectives and prison staff had warned him it was a scam."

"Yes, and whilst I blame Customs for their naivety, the Home Office behaved appallingly too. That leads me neatly on to the outcomes from my meeting with Commander Jackson and DAC Fry. We've agreed you're the first point of contact for Mr Jackson to call whenever Gudgeon gets in touch."

"Thank you, that will help enormously with monitoring the call data. What's the negotiating strategy?"

"Undoubtedly, Donovan is getting the information from outside the prison and not on the wing as he wants us to believe. We'll need your analysis to tell us how he gets it and who's involved. I read your comment, however, that it might take your team a couple of weeks."

"Yes, at least two."

"Right, so as a result, Mr Jackson and Colin Murray won't be saying anything to the new Home Secretary until you tell me you've worked it all out. At that point, Murray will tell Gudgeon to advise Donovan he'll have to prove his information is genuine."

"Okay, interesting. How do you plan to make that happen?"

"The idea is to convince him to arrange a sample. Without it, there can be no deal. A bit like a kidnap when we won't negotiate until the hostage-takers give us 'proof of life' their captive is alive."

"But won't that cause Donovan some difficulties? I mean, if he does provide a sample, then it's obvious to everyone he's controlling the RPGs, albeit remotely from inside."

"Exactly, which is why we need you and your team to identify who's holding them beforehand. Murray won't be making any more calls to Gudgeon until; one, you tell me you've got to grips with the solicitor's communications and, two, you're all over what's going on both inside and outside the prison. Are you okay with that?"

"Yes, that's all very clear, Boss. May I float something by you for your advice, please?"

"Go on."

"I think it's time we called Ben Harrison to push him into naming his informant and identifying the source of supply. We now know it's the same person who's arming the gangs in Manchester and London. Who do you think should make that call, you, or me?"

He thought for a moment and then said, "you make it. If he blanks you like he's done with the SIOs, then escalate it to me. I'll then take it to the DAC. He'll go over his head direct to the boss of the National Investigation Service. I don't want to go in at the top first, as that could leave us no room to manoeuvre if we fail."

"Okay, all understood."

"See if you can build a relationship with Harrison, and let me know what happens?" I nodded as Anton turned away to make notes in his daybook. Having finished, he swivelled in his chair to face me and asked, "right, so what are your priorities for the week ahead?"

"Well, first, it's to build that i2 chart and see where the analysis leads us." I watched as he wrote down what I said. "Second, we're going to see all the Abonar exhibits at the Lab tomorrow to make our own comparisons between the recoveries. Third, I've got DC Bryan organising a 'show and tell' meeting with the London, Kent and Manchester SIOs over at Thames House. I want Customs there too in the hope we can collectively put pressure on Harrison."

"Perfect," he said looking up from finishing his notes. "As before, call me as soon as you discover something significant. I don't want to hear it from someone else. Alright?"

"Yes Boss."

"Good. I'm off now to meet with the Home Office to see what we can do about that corrupt solicitor, Gudgeon."

CHAPTER 12

A Breakthrough

I walked back to my office feeling very positive that Anton was satisfied with Abonar's progress. The desk phone rang as I sat down.

"Have you got time to meet us in the Briefing Room?" John Bryan asked excitedly, "we've made some interesting discoveries."

"Sure, I'll come now."

Moments later I was standing next to him looking over Alice's shoulder. She was sat at a computer screen ready to guide me through her newly created chart.

"I've set the timeline out across the top," she began enthusiastically. "Under that, I've mapped all the events for each person of interest, Gudgeon, Donovan, Harrison, Murray and so on. I've included each of the firearm recoveries too and the purchases of the cars they were found in. For example, along this line, I've mapped Harrison's calls to SO13 and Kent Police. Below that, along this one, I've added Gudgeon's incoming and outgoing mobile calls going back to October 1st."

"Wow, very good," I said with genuine encouragement, "you've obviously been busy."

"Yes, and it's so much quicker when the data comes on disc," Alice said, as she looked up at me smiling before turning back to the computer. "Once I loaded the data for Gudgeon's mobile, I thought I'd reconstruct some events working backwards, as John suggested."

"Ah, I think it was the Guvnor who asked for that, Alice. I just passed on what he wanted," John corrected her.

"Sure, sure," Alice continued, somewhat bemused. "So building on *your discovery, Mr H*, that Gudgeon called Harrison each time before he in turn phoned the police, I thought I'd see who if anyone Gudgeon had spoken to beforehand."

"And?" I asked.

"Well, that's why John wanted you to see this. It's the same pattern for all three. Look." She pointed to the screen and the lines now linking a series of calls. "Do you see it Mr H?"

"Yes, yes I do," I said, my voice now matching the excitement in hers. "So, let me just confirm how I'm reading this. Each time Gudgeon phoned Harrison, minutes before that he received a call from a Manchester number."

"Yes, that's exactly it," Alice said jubilantly.

"Okay, so I better get you the subscriber."

"Done it already, Guv," John interrupted gleefully. "I ambushed DCI Woodfield in the corridor while you were in with Mr Baxter and got him to authorise it."

"Okay, good initiative, John. So, what do we know about them?"

"It's a 'TK'," he announced forthrightly, but noted my quizzical look. "Telephone Kiosk in old SO11 Surveillance parlance, Guv; a payphone or phone box to anyone else."

"So, are you saying that whoever is using this phone box-come-TK is the Customs' informant, and Gudgeon is acting as their go-between?" I asked.

"Something like that, Guv, yes," John responded cheerily, "and we've got a very good idea who it is."

"Who?"

"First!" Alice interrupted bluntly, somewhat annoyed we were getting ahead of the logical process she wanted us to follow, "let me take you through my reasoning, Mr H, to see if you reach the same conclusion, rather than John make you jump to one."

"Sure," I said, feeling rebuked as I realised Alice had just told me off for the first time.

"So, I checked the Manchester street atlas in Central 500 for the location of that phone box, oops, sorry, TK. I think it's more than a coincidence it's 100 yards from Donovan's home address."

"That is interesting," I said, enthused by this development. "Can you actually make the connection between the Donovan family and that TK?"

"No, not yet, Mr H, but I'm hoping the data will as we expand our enquiries."

"Okay, so let's keep an open mind for now," I cautioned.

"There's more we need to show you," John cut in. "Having also loaded all of Donovan's prison visits, we found another piece of the jigsaw. Look." He now leaned forward and ran his finger across the computer screen.

"On both November 12th, the day of the Whitechapel recovery, and February

26th, the day of the Plaistow one, there's a gap of about two hours between Gudgeon receiving the calls from the TK and then phoning Harrison."

I noted the sequence on the chart as he continued. "In those hours, Gudgeon visited Donovan at Full Sutton Prison. His calls to Harrison came only after Security logged him leaving. Harrison phoned SO13 Reserve immediately after each one."

"Good grief!" I said almost shouting. "So are you saying Fred Donovan, our man for the RPGs, is also the informant for the firearms' recoveries?" I asked, eagerly wanting confirmation.

"Yes, Mr H, it certainly looks that way," Alice stated confidently.

"But as you've just seen," John added, "the chart is telling us it's more likely to be Gudgeon who took the information into prison to tell Donovan, and not the other way round."

"Excellent work team!" I said, recognising the huge significance of their discovery.

"But there's still more Guv," John said, eager to show me. "The sequence for March 1st for the Tollgate Hotel has one significant difference. Look, this time Gudgeon didn't visit Donovan until after he'd spoken to Harrison," and John banged his fingertip against the screen to show me where to look.

"Holy shit… Oh, I'm so sorry, Alice. As John will tell you, I don't normally swear, but I think you'll forgive me this time."

"That's okay, Mr H," she said, smiling at me and lowering her glasses in mock disapproval. "In fact, John said something far worse when he made the connection."

"Which confirms, Guvnor," John interrupted swiftly, "that Gudgeon can't claim he got the information from Donovan."

"Wow, I'd say it does, but what have we got to prove it?" I asked.

"Only what you see here on the chart, Guv," John said as both he and Alice looked at me intently.

"Okay, I need to brief Mr Baxter on these developments. May we go through them again in a logical order to make sure I've got them right?" I asked.

Noting that Alice had given me an approving nod, I began. "First, you've confirmed my theory that Gudgeon is the go-between with Harrison for both the firearms job and the RPGs?"

"Yes, Guv," John said confidently.

"Second, you suspect Gudgeon got the information in phone calls from the Manchester TK that told him where all three consignments of firearms were hidden?"

"Yes," Alice and John said in unison.

"The TK is only yards from Donovan's home, so you suspect one of his family members made those calls?"

"Yes," again said in perfect harmony.

"And that was ahead of Gudgeon visiting Donovan?"

"Absolutely Guv, it's the same call pattern for all three," John confirmed.

Alice interrupted, "so you can tell Mr Baxter that Donovan can't claim he got the information from overheard conversations on his prison wing. Gudgeon brought it in to him from outside."

"Yes, I got that, which is my third point: we can confirm it unequivocally due to their mess-up with the timings for the Tollgate Hotel recovery."

"Yes Guv," John agreed confidently.

"Good grief, that's one hell of a result for us," I told them. "What I don't understand is why they would risk exposing their deception by doing that."

"Yes, it is odd," John mused. "I mean, they could have got away with it for the first two. But Gudgeon blew it completely the third time when he chose to call Harrison before he'd seen Donovan. I wonder why."

"Maybe they just got complacent," I offered.

"No, Guv, I think we'll find there was something else going on."

"Like what?" I asked, hoping he had an easy answer.

"I don't know yet, Guv, sorry."

"Okay, so Alice, your next step will be to make the connection between the Donovan family and that Manchester TK."

"Yes, Mr H, and to do that I need you to ask Mr Baxter to please authorise all the historic incoming and outgoing calls for it and the same for Donovan's home phone?"

"Yes, of course. I'll do my best to convince the CSPs it's worth doing such a massive reverse search."

"Let's hope you can, as this phone box, er, TK, appears pivotal to Abonar," Alice added with an almost pleading stare.

"Back to the chart, Guv," John said, wanting to redirect our attention. "We also need to check the data for the RPG negotiations to test whether it's the same pattern for how Gudgeon is getting the information about them."

"Absolutely right John. If that also shows it's not coming from Donovan, but from outside the prison via that same TK, then we've got him and Gudgeon for running another scam."

"We're working on that, Guv. Right now, I'd say you've got the leverage you wanted to demand Harrison speaks to you about Gudgeon and Donovan."

"And Colin Murray," Alice chipped in.

"Why's that Alice?"

"Because the call data shows he's been talking to Gudgeon since last October. I think we'll find the two of them have been negotiating a deal for Donovan that started back then, possibly with the firearms as the commodity."

"Holy…" I stopped myself before continuing, "show me?"

"I haven't finished adding all the calls," Alice said, rapidly moving the cursor around the chart, "but I can show you the first in the series."

"And these align with both Gudgeon and Mrs Donovan visiting Donovan at Full Sutton," John added.

"Fantastic work guys. Fantastic. What we're missing, though, is why Donovan is now offering to trade RPGs. As I discussed with you earlier, John, given he's doing 10 years, by comparison to Haase and Bennett, Donovan could claim from what we've recovered so far, he's provided enough to secure his immediate release. He must be very frustrated at still being inside. Maybe that's why he now needs the RPGs to finally get him out. What do you think?" I asked, looking at them both for a reaction.

"Maybe it's because something went wrong with getting hold of any more firearms," Alice suggested with faltering confidence, "so he's had to go bigger to accelerate his release."

"Maybe, Alice, maybe. Okay, I've got enough to brief Mr Baxter. Thank you both. Please remember the ABC. Make sure you back everything up with facts. I'd hate to look foolish by jumping to the wrong conclusions; especially with this being my first major investigation."

"Understood Mr H. John and I will go through it to check. In the meantime, can you please hurry along the call data for the Donovan's home number and the TK," her tone warned she now felt quite comfortable with tasking me.

"Of course," I said, smiling at her confidence. "I'll also press on the CSPs to make Abonar a priority; especially given the extreme threat of the RPGs."

As I stood up to leave, I paused for a moment before saying, "just a reminder; I don't want you discussing this investigation with anyone outside our team. Is that clear?"

Both looked at me while nodding.

"Whenever you can, work in here away from the Main Office. Let's keep knowledge of Abonar really tight. Only confide in others when we need their expertise. Alright?"

"Yes, of course," they replied in unison.

"I want a clear desk policy on everything too, please. At the end of the day, John, I want you to lock all the papers in the cabinet in my office. Don't just post them under my door!"

He looked at me sheepishly for a moment while I continued, "if I'm not in, borrow my spare keys from the Branch Office. I'll let them know you have my permission."

"Okay, Guv, I'll do that from now on."

"Alice, I need you to give any documents and discs you're using back to John when you've finished for the day. And, if you haven't done so already, password-protect your i2 chart, and let John and I have the details."

"Yes, I'll do that now."

"Anything else?"

"Oh, Guvnor, there is one thing," John replied, "Hamish has agreed to host our meeting with the SIOs. It'll be on Thursday-week, May 15th, at 10am. Hopefully, you can get Customs along too."

"Excellent. I'll add that to the conversation."

I checked Anton's office as I passed while heading to my own, but he was out, so I called his mobile.

"Michael, is this urgent?"

"Yes, Boss."

"Is it about Abonar?"

"Yes. Do you have two minutes?"

"Hold on. I need to step out of a meeting. I know what your 'two minutes' can be like."

I could hear him apologising and then a door opening and closing.

"Right, what is it?"

"Are you over at the Home Office?"

"Yes."

"Then you need to know that John and Alice have done fantastic work with their analysis. It shows four significant points about Gudgeon you need for your meeting."

"Okay, go on."

"First, Gudgeon's client, the Customs' informant for the firearms recoveries, is the same as for the RPGs; it's Fred Donovan."

"Bloody hell!"

"Second, Gudgeon knows the firearms job is all one big scam."

"How?"

"Because the analysis shows Donovan did not get the information from inside prison. Instead, Gudgeon brought it into him when he visited. Gudgeon got it from calls to his mobile from a Manchester phone box. Gudgeon disguised this by waiting until after he visited Donovan before he then called Harrison. The pattern is the same for Whitechapel and Plaistow."

"Excellent! Great work. Third?"

"Gudgeon slipped up on the Tollgate Hotel job, though. He didn't wait to visit Donovan before he called Harrison. He didn't see Donovan until two hours later. So, Gudgeon knows Donovan isn't the real source and it's actually someone on the outside."

"This is sounding good. Fourth?"

"The 'history' between Colin Murray and Gudgeon is also explained by their call data. The two of them started negotiating the firearms' recoveries last October."

"Holy shit! Okay, that is great work. Are you sure you're right about all this?"

"I'm convinced. The analysis proves Donovan is manipulating all this from inside and Gudgeon is knowingly facilitating it."

"Those bloody idiots in the Prison Service and Customs," Anton said, trying not to let his obvious anger be overheard. "That Gudgeon is a fucking shit too. Customs are bloody fools for not seeing they've been hoodwinked from the start. Have you called Ben Harrison yet?"

"No. He's next on my list."

"Don't. Phone his boss, Mick Burridge, instead. Get a meeting between the three of us this afternoon. I want it on our turf at NSY. Don't agree to doing it at Customs House. Make it really clear to Mick it's in his best interests to see us today. I'm available after 4pm."

"Sure. I'll call him now. Where'd you like to meet?"

"The Director's office would be good if it's available."

"Okay, I'll check. Sorry, again, for the interruption."

"Not a problem, Michael. It's what I asked you to do. It's also perfect timing. I hope your update is enough now to convince Legal Advisory to let us to do more with Gudgeon's phones. Because he's a solicitor, NCIS[21] won't play unless the Home Office lawyers approve it."

"Okay, well good luck with that."

---

21 In this context, NCIS provided the capabilities to monitor telephone communications for serious crime investigations that were beyond our systems in the SO11 TIU.

CHAPTER 13

HM Customs

Returning to my desk, I picked up the phone and called the National Investigation Service at Customs House.

"Mick Burridge," the voice answered, sounding quite casual.

Having introduced myself, I got straight to the point of my call, "I'm leading an investigation that's identified a compromise with one of your informants. We'd like you to meet us urgently today at the Yard to discuss the implications."

From the other end I could hear breathing but no other sound. Changing to a more challenging tone, which was made harsher by the roughness of his heavy east-end of London accent, Mick asked, "Sorry, who did you say you are?"

I repeated my name and spelled it out.

"I'll call you back on the 'GTN[22]', once I've confirmed who you are with the NSY switchboard?"

"Of course. I'll be waiting. I'm in my office."

A couple of minutes later my desk phone rang.

"Michael, Mick Burridge. I hope you understand my caution."

"Of course. I'd do the same."

"Now, what were you saying about a compromised informant and a meeting?"

"I'm investigating three firearms recoveries that your chap, Ben Harrison, kindly alerted SO13 and Kent Police to. My investigation is focused on identifying the source of supply."

"Okay, yes, I know something about this," he said dismissively, which annoyed me. So, I decided to up the ante by being more robust, hoping not to sound disrespectful.

---

22   GTN: The secure Government Telephone Network that users access from their standard desk phone by dialling a specific prefix code for the agency and then the extension for the individual number.

"Mr Burridge, we've linked the types of MAC-10 submachine gun recovered in the latest seizure to ones used in a murder in Brixton and a shooting at police in Manchester. So, we urgently need your help with using your informant to identify the supplier."

"Really?" he said in an unnecessarily challenging way that further irritated me.

"Yes, we can unequivocally connect them to one source of supply. You'll understand we must find that person, seize their arsenal of guns and ammunition, and put a stop to a worrying escalation in gangland violence."

"Um, I have to ask, why do you think any informant of ours can help with that?"

"Because your informant is running a scam using guns from the same supplier to hoodwink NIS into giving false information to the Home Secretary."

"What?!" he shouted indignantly. "You better be able to prove that."

"I can. We've been monitoring him and his Manchester-based solicitor. It's evident from our analysis your informant is controlling the delivery of those guns. That means he knows the source and their supply network. So, we need your help now to identify them."

"That's not operationally possible. Our informant is working on a major drugs job. I can't compromise that." I sensed something in his voice betrayed he was not being entirely truthful.

"Well, here's the situation," I decided to go in hard, "we will shortly be briefing the new Home Secretary on how his predecessor got sucked into a scam by Customs NIS. We'll be explaining how your team allowed this to happen while ignoring our calls to help identify the supplier. He's the same person who's been simultaneously providing the guns used in gangland shootings."

Sounding angry, he demanded, "How do you *know* it's a scam?"

"Oh, we do, Mr Burridge, we do. You'll appreciate it's not something I can discuss like this. Which is why my boss wants to meet you face-to-face this afternoon at 4pm here at the Yard."

Rather abrasively he asked, "Who's your boss?"

"Detective Superintendent Anton Baxter."

"Hmm, why can't he do this over the phone or meet me at Customs House?" he asked impatiently.

"Because of the sensitivities, he wants to meet you in-person, and since we have all the information here, it's better you come to us. We're on the fourth floor."

"4pm? Hmm, that gives me an hour to get over there," I noted his tone had changed to one of resignation. "Okay. Do I ask for you at reception?"

"Yes, and I'll come straight down to collect you."

"Fine, tell your boss I'll be expecting some hard facts to justify my making the journey."

"Of course. I look forward to meeting you."

Putting down the phone I heard Anton's distinctive footfall heading up the corridor. I got up to give him the news, but he had already walked into my office.

"Sorry Michael, the Home Office won't play. Their advisor, Rupert Smedley, said we don't yet have enough on Gudgeon for them to let us monitor his mobile. That means NCIS won't play either. You've got to provide much stronger evidence than just call data to prove he's knowingly involved in the conspiracy!"

"Damn!"

"Yup, and I warned Smedley any delay only risks Donovan dumping the RPGs on us before we know where they are and how he's going to do it. But that didn't seem to bother him one jot."

"Whose bloody side are the Home Office on? You know, Boss, this only confirms what Commander Jackson predicted. He said they'd behave like this to protect their reputations."

"Oh yes, that's very evident."

"Well, there is some good news. I've convinced Mick Burridge to meet us. He'll be here at four. And I've got the DAC's office arranged."

"Excellent, that is good news."

Just before 4pm, my phone rang. It was Debbie in Back Hall[23] to tell me our visitor had arrived. I walked to Anton's office and let him know.

"Good but, first, some house rules. Let me do the talking unless I ask you to chip in. Otherwise, I just want you to observe without commenting, alright? Take detailed notes too. Understood?"

"Yes, perfectly."

A few minutes later I showed Mick Burridge through to the outer office. The Director's staff officer, Sam, welcomed us and asked, "Tea or coffee anyone?"

"Nothing for me thanks," Mick replied.

"No thanks, Sam. I'm good," I added.

"Well there's water and glasses on the table. I'll show you through."

Anton got up from his chair as I introduced the two of them. They shook hands uncomfortably. We then each settled into the three armchairs evenly

---

23   Back Hall: the traditional name for the reception desk at New Scotland Yard.

spaced around the circular mahogany coffee table. The latter had a decanter of water on it, with a glass for each of us. I had my daybook open ready to take notes. Mick Burridge had a closely shaved head, and his remaining grey hair made him look older than the mid-40s I guessed he was. His heavy build and slightly unshaven face complemented the rough and abrasive character I had encountered over the phone.

Somewhat amused, I watched while these two alpha males began to assess each other's strengths.

"So, Anton, you needed an urgent meeting. Can I ask what you do here in SO11?" Mick began with his opening parry.

Brushing his hair back, Anton expanded his chest slightly before replying, "I'm the head of Covert Operations and Investigations. You probably know of my other office at Putney. I've got a couple of your people on loan to me there." Then, in a similar move to Mick, he checked out the worthiness of his adversary by asking, "and so what do you do at Customs House?"

"I lead on international drugs smuggling investigations in the NIS. These three firearms recoveries are a by-product of a much larger investigation."

"Oh, and what is that?" Anton asked in what I knew was his deliberately combative manner.

"Drugs."

"And that's an active investigation?"

Guardedly, Mick replied, "no, not yet. Our informant is testing us to make sure we can protect him before giving us more."

"So it's just a promise to the future?"

"Yes."

"So, no hard facts?"

"No."

"Nothing yet to justify putting the protection of your informant over and above helping us identify who's supplying all these guns?"

"Look…" Mick started to protest, but Anton carried on regardless.

"You see, your man Ben Harrison was happy to recover three consignments whilst ignoring the possibility the same supplier is simultaneously arming gangs in Manchester and London?"

"Well," again, Mick tried to speak, but Anton carried on talking, not wanting to give any ground until he'd got all his points across.

"So, which is it Mick; protect your informant or work with us to stop the flow of guns now fuelling an escalation in gangland violence?"

"Look, you know how it works, Anton," Mick answered, now determined to continue speaking. "You must give your own informants a degree of latitude while they develop a job and build trust."

"Not if it means lives being lost. You see, Mick, the reality of what we're dealing with here is that while you've been protecting your informant, guns from the same supplier killed a man in Brixton and very nearly two constables in Moss Side. It's time you told us exactly what's going on and who's involved. My job is to stop the killing and I need your cooperation!"

Dropping his defiance momentarily, Mick's mood changed to be more collaborative, "Okay, okay, I get that. I came here to be told the facts, not be attacked. Michael said you've identified our informant, and you've got evidence to say they're part of a scam. Why don't you tell me about that?"

Anton replied in a deliberately provocative manner, "Okay, so first your informant. It won't surprise you to know we've employed some advanced covert techniques to identify him. And, if I may say so, all rather too easily."

"Look Anton, instead of you carrying on trying to make me feel as uncomfortable as you obviously are, why don't you just get to the point? Given the urgency I was led to believe is the reason for this meeting, I'd appreciate you telling me *now* what you know. That way I can work out how best to help you. Let's start with the informant's name?"

"Not a problem. I can do that," Anton said, relishing the moment. "Fred Donovan. A hard-nosed Manchester gangland criminal, currently serving ten years on the Cat A Wing at Full Sutton Prison. Sentenced in 1995 for conspiracy to smuggle amphetamines, he's keen to get early parole. That's what he's hoping his solicitor, Patrick Gudgeon, will get for him by trading illegal firearms using Ben Harrison as the go-between with the Home Office."

Mick now looked extremely uncomfortable. He seemed shocked we knew that much detail. He stayed quiet for longer than I expected. I thought he might confirm immediately and then ask a load more questions. Instead, he reached forward and poured himself a glass of water. He sipped it slowly and deliberately, trying to present an air of calm. His expression, though, belied obvious anger.

Hesitatingly, he then offered an explanation. "Okay, yes, Donovan's our source inside Full Sutton. He's picking up intelligence from other inmates on the wing and using his solicitor to get it out to us. We filter what's relevant to our investigation and give away anything that isn't. That's on the basis it won't compromise his identity and safety. Donovan thought he could distance himself sufficiently for the information not to appear to come from him. Ben Harrison is handling him, yes, albeit through the solicitor."

"Hang on, Mick," Anton interrupted sharply, "what do you mean you were filtering out '*what's relevant*' to your own investigation? You just told us Donovan hadn't yet given you anything. So which is it?"

"Okay, yes, you're right. So far, he's only given us intel about firearms. Look, Ben Harrison thought passing that on to police was the right thing to do. We all want to get guns off the streets, don't we?"

"Yes, of course, but didn't you think to question Donovan about who's supplying the firearms?" Anton went back to challenging Mick. "Wouldn't you want to know that in case the relationship went sour? You could then go after the supplier yourselves regardless."

"No, we hadn't considered that. Look, Ben never actually got to see Donovan. Everything was done through the man's solicitor, Gudgeon. He wouldn't allow Ben to visit, because of the risk other inmates would find out. Ben never got to question Donovan face-to-face. Had he been able to, you and I might be having a very different conversation."

Mick paused while he checked whether our expressions endorsed his reasoning. Anton and I shrugged to indicate neither of us were convinced. Mick realised it and continued making excuses.

"Yes, perhaps with hindsight we did focus too much on Donovan's promise of a big drugs' job. And perhaps we thought it more important to build trust than question Gudgeon about who was supplying the guns. Look, my guidance to Ben was to use Donovan to recover the guns first. Gradually build the relationship while doing so, and then get the intel on the bigger prize. Ben's one of our best informant handlers, so I trusted him to work it all out."

"And did you ever review his methodology?" Anton asked.

"Initially, no. My focus at first was to protect the informant. I understood from Ben that Donovan was confident he could distance himself. That meant he wouldn't give us anything to help with arrests or identify where the guns came from."

Mick sensed from our looks that Anton and I were still not convinced.

"Look, Anton, losing your contraband to the police is an occupational hazard for most villains. Having your mates arrested as well will lead rapidly to revenge on the person who grassed you up. On a Category A Wing, that's likely to be fatal. We realised that from the start. It's documented in our risk assessment. That's why we'd been happy to take it slow and wait several months between each job."

"You said, 'initially no' about reviewing Ben's methodology. Does that mean you have now?"

"Yes. After the call from the Kent SIO about the Tollgate Hotel job. My first reaction was to blank her like I did the other two. But then I decided to ask Ben to meet me for a full review."

"And what did that reveal?"

"That whilst one of the finds included a few blocks of cannabis, there was no real evidence of there being a big drugs job. I thought Donovan was only ever going to give us intel on guns."

"Why do you think that was, Mick? Was it because Donovan was just using you to facilitate the Home Secretary into releasing him?"

"Okay, yes, I did suspect that's what was going on," as he said this, Mick pulled a small notebook from his outside jacket pocket.

"And what did you do about it?"

Quickly referring to his notebook, Mick answered, "I instructed Ben to stop talking to Gudgeon after the third recovery. I told him to break off all contact until Donovan gave us actionable intelligence about the major drugs job he'd promised. Ben then passed that on to Gudgeon."

"When was that?"

"Immediately after he met me to review the case. That was on Friday, March 7th."

"So, is there anything else in the pipeline from Donovan?"

"Not to my knowledge, no. Ben's had no more contact." He paused for a few seconds before asking, "so what's all this about it being a scam anyway?"

"What deal have you done for Donovan with the Home Secretary?"

"He wants early parole. Ben passed that on to Colin Murray, deputy head of the Prison Service at the Home Office."

Anton and I briefly exchanged glances to confirm this was what we had suspected.

"Colin Murray then briefed the then Home Secretary, Michael Howard. We were told he'd agreed in principle to parole. Just in principle, though, nothing in writing. I expect that's all on hold now Jack Straw is in the role. Back in January, Gudgeon sensed the Conservatives would lose the election and pressed Ben several times for a firm answer in writing."

"Well, that would explain the second and third recoveries in rapid succession in February and March. It would also explain why the guns got more interesting third time round, with the addition of the MAC-10s and a BAR," Anton commented.

"Yes, I suppose it does. But, Anton, you still haven't explained why you think it's a scam."

"One moment, Mick. Can I first check how Gudgeon knows Ben?"

"They met at some point after Donovan's arrest."

"Okay, another quick one. When did Gudgeon first approach Ben with Donovan's proposal?"

"Last year in early October." He referred again to his notebook. "Yeah, Gudgeon called him around the 4th. I was off that week, so Ben had to wait till I got back for my approval to approach the Home Office."

"And when did you give him that?"

"The following Tuesday, October 8th. I remember because it was also my wife's birthday. Ben called the Home Office the same day. He got a very positive response giving the Home Secretary's agreement in principle that Friday."

"Thanks, and what did Ben tell Gudgeon?"

"Exactly that. The Home Secretary would give him parole on the proviso he helped us recover illegal firearms hidden away by criminals."

"Did Ben tell him how many firearms were needed to secure his release?"

"No, but Ben did tell Gudgeon it had to be significant."

"So, from what he's disclosed so far, would Donovan think he's done enough to get parole?"

"It's possible, yes, he probably does think sixty-five firearms entitles him to some benefit now, for sure. So, why do you think it's a scam."

"Michael," Anton said, turning to me, "would you explain the similarities between this case and Haase and Bennett?"

Mick's face visibly paled as Anton said the names. Once again, he leaned forward to sip more water while he calmed himself in preparation for what I was about to say.

"Is Paul Cook also one of yours?"

"Yes, why do you ask?"

"What was your involvement in his negotiations to get Haase and Bennett released?"

"I approved it. You'll no doubt know they helped recover a whopping thirty-five separate caches of firearms and ammunition, one of which was connected to the IRA. It was the right thing to reward them. Where are you heading with this?"

I pressed on with how I wanted to sequence my questions, "were you able to identify the source of those firearms and ammunition?"

"No, like Donovan we focused on protecting our informants."

"So they never gave you anything to help identify their source?"

"No."

"Was it one source or more?"

"No idea. Everything Paul got came from Haase and Bennett and their solicitor Nelson."

"Did you or he make any enquiries to find out who they were talking to on the prison wing to get the information?"

"No. Again, where are you heading with this?"

"Can't you see the similarities between the two jobs? Donovan's approach to Ben is almost a carbon copy of Haase and Bennett's with Paul. And the reason for that is in 1995 Haase, Bennett and Donovan were all on the same prison wing at Full Sutton."

"Oh my God!" Mick shouted involuntarily as he recognised his failure to realise this before.

"What makes it worse," I continued, "is that Paul and Ben work together, and you're their boss, and not one of you seems to have spotted the similarities."

Trying a retaliatory defence he commented, "surely, what it shows, Michael, is there are a lot of guns out there in criminal hands that prison inmates know about!"

"Donovan and Gudgeon might have been able to claim that Mick if they hadn't got complacent with the last consignment. You see we can prove Gudgeon called Ben about that job before he'd even had the chance to visit Donovan in Full Sutton. A little due diligence from Ben by simply checking with the prison on the timings and he would have discovered that anomaly for himself."

Anton had been reading the pages from Donovan's prison intelligence file, which, for dramatic effect, he now chucked on the table in front of Mick saying, "as with the other two recoveries, Gudgeon gave Ben detailed information about where to find the guns at the Tollgate Hotel. They included the make, colour and registration of the car. As Michael just said, we know Gudgeon didn't get that from Donovan." Mick listened intently as he sipped his water. "We also know the car was bought just two days before and no one on Donovan's wing had any visits or outside communications in that time for the information to get inside. It's all been one big scam and, just like you did with Haase and Bennett, you and your NIS people fell for it hook, line and sinker."

Mick remained silent. He reached to refill his glass as a device to help him think how to find a dignified way out from our growing evidence of incompetence.

"Mick, do you now see it's a scam?" Anton said softly as he moved in for the 'coup de grâce'. "Donovan and Gudgeon have been manipulating Ben. You didn't learn anything from Haase and Bennett. Did none of you stop to think how on earth they could get such detailed information on a prison wing? For heaven's sake, Mick, how could anyone on a Cat A wing get hold of a treasure map of a Squirrel Sanctuary? They've been taking the bloody piss out of you."

Mick slumped back in his chair clearly defeated.

"Okay, so someone's misread the situation," he began contritely. "Thank you for telling me. If I'd known before, I wouldn't have allowed Ben to approach the Home Office. Shit! And you think the same thing happened with Paul Cook and Haase and Bennett?"

"Yes, but we aren't investigating that case. But you must admit the similarities with Donovan are too obvious to be ignored."

Mick nodded.

"Maybe Merseyside Police will look at them again. We're leaving their case alone for now. We're focusing on who Donovan used to supply his guns. That's because it will lead us to the same source who's arming gangs in London and Manchester. If I were you, Mick, I'd be reviewing everything about your dealings with Haase, Bennett and now Donovan ahead of a major public inquiry into your team. It's all happened on your watch, and you can bet the Home Office will want a scapegoat now it's starting to come out!"

"Okay, okay. So what do you need me to do about Donovan?"

"I was going to ask you to tell Ben Harrison to stop having anything to do with Gudgeon, but from what you've said, that's happened already."

"Yes, but I'll let you know if Gudgeon makes contact again."

"Thank you, and I'd prefer you don't tell Ben Harrison about our conversation today."

"Yes, I can do that."

"We are going after Donovan and Gudgeon to identify the source of supply. To do that, we need you and your people to step right back."

"I think I made it clear we have already."

"Good. Thank you. Michael, you probably want Mick to know about your meeting next week hosted by MI5."

"Thank you, Sir, yes. So we're bringing together the SIOs for the three firearms recoveries, the Brixton homicide, and the SIO for the Manchester shooting. We're meeting at Thames House next Thursday. I sense you'll want to be there too and share what you know."

Sounding worried, Mick asked, "are you going to tell everyone about Donovan and Ben?"

"No," I replied wanting to allay his fears in the hope it would secure his cooperation. "I don't intend to mention them openly in the meeting. We've briefed the Security Service already, as you'd expect. Can you make the meeting?"

"No, and in the circumstances, I think it's best I don't."

"What's your reasoning?" Anton asked.

"I want to avoid being drawn into a discussion and then speculation about our conduct in that forum. You seem to know everything about our investigation anyway. You don't really need us there in person. However, I'll offer you a compromise."

Sounding annoyed, Anton asked, "And what's that?"

"I'll send one of my team to observe. He won't have had any involvement with Donovan, so will take any questions on notice. He'll just observe, record, and report back to me. If I think the meeting identified something we ought to make known, I'll call you direct Anton. How does that sound?"

"It's crap, and you know it, Mick, but I understand why you want it that way. Who will you send?"

"Jack Porter. I'll get him to call you, Michael, and you can give him the meeting details. I think we're done now, aren't we?"

"Yes, we are," Anton replied, his abruptness revealing some residual anger. However, he stood up and courteously added, "Thanks for coming over at such short notice. Hope you found it worthwhile."

"Worthwhile," Mick snorted, "that's one word for it. Confronting would be a better one. Thanks for alerting me to the issues and being so frank."

We all shook hands more warmly than before. I then escorted Mick through to Back Hall and watched him leave the building.

Anton was waiting for me in the fourth-floor corridor when I returned.

"My office, please." He then walked ahead without saying a word. Pushing the door to, he indicated I take a seat. He flopped into his chair. His expression showed he was deep in thought. Finally, with a gentle brush of his hair he asked, "well, what did you make of that?"

"First, I'm delighted he came over. Clearly, it worked isolating him on our turf. I was surprised how much of a beating he took without any real retaliation."

"That's because he already knew from his own review just how much shit he's in."

"Well, we got some useful dates from him we can now flag on our chart."

"Yes, indeed. So, we also know they've got nothing more in the pipeline and have broken off all contact with Gudgeon. That means the RPGs are Donovan's only hope now of early parole. We need to exploit that alongside you working on the data."

"Well, we're making good progress on that."

"Good, as I'm hoping it will reveal how Donovan's friends and family arranged those three consignments of firearms, and the supply chain. That should identify for us who they've got doing the same for them with the RPGs."

"That's certainly one of our objectives."

"Thanks. My fear now is we can expect Gudgeon and Donovan to object to us delaying negotiations on the RPGs. I need to find you some extra resources, so we stay ahead of whatever they are planning. I just hope Donovan won't be tempted to just dump the RPGs on us and then demand parole anyway."

"How about you join us on Friday morning, Boss, for an update on the job? With the progress the team are making, we should have a lot more actionable intelligence to help you go back to the Home Office and get their cooperation."

"Yes, set that up, please, and I'll be there. Well done. Now let's get back to work."

CHAPTER 14

Small Steps

Tuesday, 6th May

The following morning, I brought our team meeting forward to 8:30, as John and I needed to be at the Lab by 10:30 to review all the Abonar exhibits with Marco. Whilst John made himself a drink using his own Earl Grey tea bags, the rest of us waited as the machine in the Fordham Suite dispensed something akin to coffee. It was similar in colour but not taste, and the punnets of UHT milk did nothing to improve the flavour. Nevertheless, it was quick, easy and, most importantly, free.

"Who wants to kick this off?" I asked.

"I do," Alice said raising her hand, "there's a problem with the BT data."

"How so?"

"Historically, they can only give us BT calls into BT numbers, so they're not capturing incoming calls from mobiles. Outgoing is not a problem. To get incoming or a 'reverse search' is a special service that BT limits to very specific enquiries, not fishing exercises like ours. They want us to provide dates and times, Mr H, rather than everything going back to October 1st."

"Who did you get that from?" I asked.

Giving me one of her now familiar disarming stares, she replied, "Pete. I spoke to him because I could tell there were gaps in our data."

"Okay, so what's the workaround?"

"Going forwards won't be a problem because we've got live monitoring now on most of them. It's just the historic ones that we have gaps for. I'm hoping, though, that once we get the outgoing calls for the BT numbers, like the TK, and it calls a mobile, we'll then pick up the incoming ones when we ask for the mobile's billing."

"Sounds good," I told her with a reassuring smile.

"Thanks, and Pete also explained the mobile CSPs are configured differently, so they capture both incoming and outgoing without a problem."

"Yes, that's correct, so let's hope our Abonar targets stick to mobiles."

John caught my expression and recognised my slight annoyance that Alice had gone to Pete direct rather than through me.

"Hope you don't mind Guv, but I saw Pete with Alice yesterday and asked him to let us have all the call data as soon as it comes in. I know you briefed him to give it to you, but I thought you wouldn't mind given the progress we're making, and you weren't available."

"Hmm, okay. I'll let Pete know I'm happy to continue," I said, rather impressed by their initiative. I chose not to say so in case they thought I was giving them licence to push other boundaries without asking.

I changed the topic, saying, "right, let me update you on what happened yesterday afternoon when Mr Baxter and I met Ben Harrison's immediate boss, Mick Burridge."

"I bet that was an interesting meeting Guv. Hee, hee, I'd love to have been a fly on the wall for that one," John said, clearly hoping Anton and I had given him a hard time.

I then recounted the highlights before giving out the resulting tasks. "Alice, I need you to look at all the calls and prison visits between March 7th and 13th. That six-day window is when Harrison told Gudgeon he was breaking off communications about the firearms and then Gudgeon came back, bypassing Customs, to go direct to Murray with the new offer of RPGs. I want to know what happened in the intervening period to set it up."

"It may also tell us who Gudgeon and the Donovan family spoke to about the firearms deal being cancelled," John added.

"Quite so, which means some detailed analysis, please."

"Sure," Alice replied, looking into my eyes as if expecting more guidance.

Embarrassed, as I had nothing to add, I looked down at my notes saying, "see whatever you can find."

"I'll look for whatever clues I can," Alice commented as she looked down to write in her daybook.

"If you would please." Then handing her a copy of the pages from my daybook, I added, "you'll see from my notes of yesterday's meeting, I've highlighted the dates for last October when Customs started talking to Gudgeon and Donovan about the firearms. Please see if that throws out any new leads too."

Taking the papers, Alice looked me sternly in the eye saying, "maybe Mark can work on that while I focus on the tasks I've got already."

Her tone had a hint of despair, and I realised I was overloading her. I reacted immediately, "Sounds like you need me to organise some reinforcements. Mr Baxter mentioned he was willing to find some."

Alice smiled, looking relieved that I had picked up on her signal.

"Yes, I was going to suggest that too Guv," John commented. "Can you ask Angela to spare us two more analysts so we can get the backlog of data loaded on to the chart?"

"Sure, I can ask. Oh, and I've got the ACPO Telecoms meeting this week. I'll be pressing on the CSPs to turn around our requests much faster. In the meantime, please keep filling out the forms and putting them on my desk. Anything else?"

John answered for everyone when he said, "no, we've got enough to be getting on with."

"Last thing from me then. I've invited Mr Baxter to join us on Friday morning at ten for a full briefing. I feel sure you'll do a great job with that."

Seeing the three of them nodding confidently, I felt comfortable with not going into any more detail just then.

As I stood up to leave, John announced, "sorry Guv, almost forgot, Merseyside sent us the photos of the firearms and other items they recovered courtesy of Haase and Bennett."

"What do they show that's useful to us?"

"Well, some bear the same TIG weld marks, which suggests at least one of the suppliers is our Abonar target." He then passed the albums across saying with a little flattery in his tone, "you were right to ask about the three silencers in the Cash Converters bag too, Guv. Whilst they weren't painted black like the ones found at the Tollgate Hotel, you'll see they're of the very same design."

"Very good. Thanks for following up. When we meet Marco later, you can ask him whether he's seen these too and can link them forensically to our Abonar ones."

"Sure, I'll add that to our list of discussion points."

CHAPTER 15

Marco

John and I walked to the Lab to meet Marco. Viewing all the Abonar firearms with him meant we'd get the benefit of his encyclopaedic knowledge from years of examining weapons. What we also needed from him was to identify any links between our guns and other investigations.

Simon, the photographer, was waiting for us at reception. He had come across from our Technical Support Unit (TSU) within the same Lambeth complex as the Lab. The receptionist phoned Marco and he met us a few minutes later. He was in his late thirties, thinning sandy-coloured hair, and glasses. He had been born in London and despite his Italian heritage spoke without a hint of an accent. He was dressed in the customary white laboratory coat, which hid his casual T-shirt and trousers beneath. As he led us through to the Gun Room on the ground floor, I could smell the distinctive odour of burnt cordite emanating from his lightly work-stained coat.

Around his laboratory were large pieces of scientific equipment. Benches lined the walls with low-back revolving metal stools positioned alongside. There were also different sized steel cabinets along the walls. Their open doors revealed some held trays of spent bullets and cartridges while others an array of firearms. Marco and his team used these to make comparisons when looking for linked crimes. The fluorescent light bulbs above, white painted walls and white linoleum flooring created an intensely bright environment. At the far end of the room was the 15-foot-long rectangular bullet-catcher filled with water. Technicians test-fired guns into this and then retrieved the spent bullets from the bottom using either a sieve on a chain or a pole with Blue-Tack stuck to one end. Firing into water meant the bullet quickly lost all its kinetic energy, without leaving a mark. The scientist would then compare the striation grooves caused by its travel along the barrel to check whether the gun had been used in a shooting for which police had previously recovered bullets. This was how Marco had linked the Brixton MAC-10 found at

Michael Senior's home to the murder of Devon Dawson. It was one of the principal functions of the Gun Room. Another was examining engineering marks and matching them to tools found in a gunsmith's workshop.

Marco had spread out all the Abonar guns and bags of ammunition on three separate benches. Helpfully, he'd written labels on each marked, 'Whitechapel', 'Plaistow' and 'Tollgate Hotel'. On a fourth, labelled 'Brixton', he had placed the MAC-10 used to kill Devon Dawson. The detectives involved had used cable ties to hold each gun to the inside of a shallow cardboard tray that was once the lid to a box of photocopier paper. They had stuck handwritten adhesive exhibit labels to each one and cross-referenced them with an entry in the 'Exhibits' Log'. Each gun was then wrapped inside a clear plastic bag held tight with a numbered security seal. All the ammunition was packaged in similarly sealed clear plastic bags.

Deciding to let him lead the discussion, I asked, "okay Marco, I know John's briefed you on Abonar, so what can you show us to help with our lines of enquiry?"

"Well, I should start by telling you we won't be test-firing any of these for crime-scene comparison," he said matter-of-factly while clasping his hands together. "Of course, we've done the Brixton MAC-10. Right now, though, firing these won't bring any value to your investigation to identify the supplier."

"Agreed, but we can have that done later if needed?"

"Yes, but you'll save me a lot of unnecessary work and yourself a small fortune in Lab fees if you don't," Marco said smiling, still clasping his hands.

Wanting to move on to something we could do, I asked, "okay, so where do you want to start?"

"First, the TIG welder marks," he announced, "as they're a common denominator. I thought you'd like to see the obliterations for yourselves." Marco then passed round a series of boxed handguns for us to view, commenting, "you can see it's the same on all of them, which suggests it's been done by the one person. The metal's been melted to the point where there's no chance of us recovering the original marks beneath."

John and I nodded to confirm the marks were all very similar. Wanting to demonstrate his knowledge, John explained, "yes, the obliterations are very obvious on these Russian Tokarevs."

"Ah, but they're not Tokarevs, John. They're military issue Chinese copies known as the 'M20'," Marco said authoritatively while John looked disappointed at being corrected. Marco saw this and quickly added, "easy mistake, as they're almost identical. Whoever is supplying these must have a load of them, as they're common to all three Abonar recoveries."

Wanting to reassert his knowledge, John quickly commented, "yes, we spotted that too".

"Now what's interesting," Marco carried on, "and you should follow this up with the London Proof House, is the gunsmith obliterated more than the serial numbers on these. I think this additional area on the slide-top, where he's also used the TIG, is to fool you into thinking these had a deactivation mark there too."

Having only limited experience of this, I asked, "forgive my ignorance Marco, but can you explain that for my benefit?"

"Okay, I'm sure these haven't been deactivated. All original parts," he announced confidently. Then taking one of the M20s, he began pointing out the features. "Here where the TIG welder has melted the metal on the slide-top, this is exactly where the Proof House stamps its deactivation mark to certify it's been done to the required standard. Alright?"

"Okay, but how do you know they weren't deactivated?"

"Let's compare them with the MAC-10s. That'll give you an idea of the work needed to reactivate a previously deactivated gun," Marco continued in his cheery manner.

"Have all our MAC-10s been reactivated then?" I asked.

"Oh yes, definitely every one of them," he announced, again clasping his hands together. "Look, I've got an original Perkins-made SF Firearms MAC-10 out to show you. You see, its barrel is rifled. All yours are smooth. That's the first clear indication of reactivation." As Marco spoke, he unscrewed the locking pin holding the frame and receiver. Having removed it, he stripped the Perkins' gun into its component parts and set them out on the bench. He then passed round the receiver with its barrel assembly.

As John and I noted the rifled barrel, Marco opened the packaging for one of the MAC-10s from the 'Tollgate Hotel' bench and stripped it down into the same parts. Passing round its barrel assembly to compare, he said, "see, no rifling grooves, it's smooth bore."

"And the next indicator of reactivation?" I asked.

"Compare the two sets of components. The Tollgate Hotel MAC-10s are the same as those for the Brixton and Manchester guns. They've all been rebuilt internally, with many replacement parts," he said, delighted at having the opportunity to demonstrate his knowledge. "New breech bolt; new feed ramp, and modified grips to accommodate the replacement Uzi magazine."

"What's that telling you?" I asked.

"Whoever did this knew exactly what he was doing. He's quite a craftsman," Marco replied, sounding almost in awe of the man. "Like the Chinese M20s," he continued, "he's also used the welder to obliterate the deactivation marks on the MAC-10s along with the serial number. He's obviously very proud of them, because unlike all the other guns you've recovered where he's left the weld-marks bare, with his MAC-10s, he's tidied them up and repainted the area to look as good as new. And he's done the same where he's removed the deactivation mark here on the receiver." Marco finished by pointing out a circular weld mark no more than 5mm in diameter next to where the serial number had been similarly obliterated under the SF Firearms address.

"Simon," I said turning to our photographer, "when Marco's done, I'll need you to take photos of all these features he's pointing out, please."

"Sure, Guv."

"Now for ease of reference, and you'll like this Michael, we're calling all these reactivated MAC-10s the 'Abonar MAC-10' in honour of your investigation to find the gunsmith doing the work."

"Wow, I like that," I told him, "and the rest of the team will too. So, Marco, to finish off, just explain why you think these Chinese M20s haven't been deactivated and then reactivated?"

"It's because there's no evidence of the same type of work as the MAC-10s." He said while opening the packaging for an M20 and then stripping it into its main component parts. Having separated the slide from the frame and barrel he handed them round for us to examine.

"As you can see," he continued, "it's an original rifled barrel. The slide rails are still intact too, as are the breech face and firing pin. They all get chopped up in the deactivation process, so these are all untouched and original."

Again, John and I nodded at our newfound knowledge.

With added emphasis, Marco concluded, "that's how I can be sure these M20s, um John's 'Tokarevs'," he added smiling, "are all original parts and have never been deactivated."

"Thank you, now I understand," I said, happy with his explanation.

"Good. So, moving on; these are interesting too," Marco said as he passed round more boxes from the three benches. "They're military issue, French-made MAB Model D semi-automatic pistols and, like the M20s, probably from the

1950s or 60s. Don't often see them. They were originally manufactured with a blued finish. Someone's sandblasted that off and refinished the frame, slide and magazine in nice-looking matt nickel-plate. He's also had the barrel and trigger re-blued. All done very professionally I might add." He pointed out each feature as he went along. "It tells me whoever did all this has access to a plating workshop too. You'll see that after the nickel-plating was done, though, he used the TIG again to obliterate the serial numbers."

"Were these MABs also reactivated?" I asked.

"No, and I would suggest your Abonar gunsmith planned to sell them commercially. That explains the very high standard of refinishing, so they look like quality modern handguns despite their age."

John and I passed the sample MAB between us to see for ourselves what Marco was describing.

"One more thing you'll notice with some of the MABs," he continued, "the gunsmith added a barrel extension with a screw-thread and cap to protect it. Remove the cap, and you can attach a suppressor. That's not factory original."

John and I carried on examining the pistol while Marco continued his narrative. "Now you need to know we've seen that exact same workmanship on a gun submitted very recently: a CZ Model 27 semi-automatic pistol. It also came with a suppressor and a screw-thread barrel extension, but no protective cap."

"Who submitted it? I asked.

He hesitated before quietly saying, "our mutual friend at Weapons Intelligence, Hamish."

"Do you know where he got it?" I asked in a similar hushed tone.

His voice now dropped almost to a whisper, "You'll have to ask him yourself, Michael, I'm not allowed to say. He won't mind me telling you, though, that it's part of a multi-agency operation and all very confidential."

"Thanks, we'll certainly ask him."

"Next up," Marco continued now at full volume, "these Smith & Wesson 'Model 10' and 'Model 36' revolvers. Same as the MABs; newly refinished in matt nickel-plating. Again, subsequent welding over the serial numbers. No evidence of deactivation or reactivation. All original." John and I looked and helped by our newfound expertise nodded in appreciation as Marco continued. "I'm assuming like the MABs, these too were redone for the commercial market but then diverted to the criminal one."

"Why would someone do that after going to so much effort to make them look good for the legal market?" John asked, clearly mystified.

"Maybe with the forthcoming handgun ban, your Abonar supplier is hurriedly disposing of all his stock to criminals. What he'll be offered for them under the Home Office's 'Buy-back Scheme' won't match what he'll get on the illicit market. There's probably £25,000 worth of firearms right here on these benches. The Home Office won't give him more than half that."

Marco then passed round more examples for us to view.

"Have you also seen the three Smith & Wessons GMP recovered a few months back in Moss Side?" John asked optimistically.

"Yes, I have John, and, before you ask, they show the same workmanship as these. GMP's MAC-10s and Smith & Wessons have all the hallmarks of your Abonar gunsmith."

Reassured, John said, "thanks, that's very helpful."

Marco then carried on his tour of the tables, "now these blue-finish Colt .38 'Police Positive' revolvers are almost certainly police or military issue. Either someone stole them, or they've come on to the market as military or police surplus."

"So where should that take our enquiries?" I asked.

"If they've been stolen, I recommend you check with INTERPOL for any reports. Hamish should be able to help too. As for what's on the international surplus market, well one of your contacts in the Gun Trade Association, John, should be able to help you with that."

"Okay, I can follow that one up easily," John replied.

"Yes, and the Belgian Police are very knowledgeable about this stuff too," Marco commented. "They tend to see these post-war guns first. That's because of the troubles they're having right now with gangs coming in from the former Soviet-bloc; especially Albania and Bulgaria, where many of these old guns ended up. There's a lot of ex-military weaponry circulating in Eastern Europe after the Balkan Wars." Marco paused, before adding, "so I suggest you get in touch with the equivalent of the 'Flying Squad' in Brussels and show them your photographs."

"I'll follow that one up too, Guv," John said eagerly.

"Now, I want to show you something very odd on these old Colt revolvers," Marco said, reaching for one in a box. "Look at this area on the left side of the frame alongside the hammer." I looked at where he pointed. "Yes, it's easier if you lift it up to the light," he told me while helping me to do just that. "You see that discolouration? Someone who knows what they're doing milled out a mark here, filled in with new metal and almost perfectly refinished it. Can you see what I mean?"

"Yes, I can," I said with some relief noting the small oval patch of different colour. "Why would our gunsmith do that?"

"Not sure, but my instinct tells me it's to remove another tell-tale mark he'd rather you not find. Hamish should be able to help with identifying what it might be."

Marco then waited until we had returned all the guns back to their respective benches before continuing. "Now what I've also done is take each of the handguns out of their packaging to remove the grips." I could tell from his voice he was excited about what he wanted to show us

"So, from the liberal coating of fingerprint powder," he continued, "I could tell the SIOs had all the guns forensicated, but I wasn't sure they'd have looked under the grips. So I did. Sadly, they've all been wiped clean. No fingerprints." And then with delight he exclaimed, "but look at this!"

He then set out on the bench one model of each of the M20s, Smith & Wessons, Colts, and MABs, with the grips removed on the left side. John and I looked on while Simon manoeuvred round us to work out how best to photograph them. I could see that someone had scratched into the metal frames a three-letter code, beginning with 'T' on what the gunsmith had also mistaken for a Tokarev; 'C' on the Colt; 'M' on the MAB, and 'W' on the Smith & Wesson, but with the letter on its side.

"Okay, have you seen those marks before?" I asked.

"Yes, but only on handguns we now attribute to your Abonar gunsmith, which includes those three Smith & Wessons recovered by GMP."

"And what's their relevance?" I asked.

"Well, they match the three-letter Cyrillic codes written on the cloths used to wrap the guns found at the Tollgate Hotel."

"Yes, but what's your expertise telling you about why it's been done?" I asked, still wanting something more from him that could help focus a line of enquiry.

"I have no idea."

Letting out my frustration at his answer, I yelled, "sugar, bloody, damn Marco. I thought with all your build-up, you knew."

"Oh, I'm sorry, Michael, no I don't have a clue." Seeing the look of disappointment on my face, he tried to be helpful by adding, "maybe it's something else you should ask Hamish."

John decided it was time for him to demonstrate his knowledge, as he asked, "what about these World War Two era guns, Marco? The BAR 30-calibre and Colt 1911s. They've all had their serial numbers obliterated too."

"These are odd, because they could actually go back to the First World War."

"Oh," John said, sounding disappointed he'd got the wrong era.

Sensing he had just knocked John's confidence again, Marco quickly added, "but you're right, these are all Second World War vintage."

John smiled with relief as Marco carried on, "I can't be certain but, to my knowledge, anything from either war is inherently hard to trace other than back to the manufacturer. Later records just don't exist."

"So why destroy the serial numbers?" John asked.

"I'd say whoever did this knew they could be traced to something very recent, such as the inventory of a dealer in military surplus."

"I'll check that with my contacts," John said enthusiastically.

"Now, the BAR was wrapped in a length of blue cloth," Marco reminded us, "possibly industrial hand towel. The four MAC-10s were wrapped in the same material."

"Yes, we saw that too," John commented.

"If you want, Michael, I can submit all the cloths to the right people in the Lab to identify where they come from. Any pollen they find in the weave will tell us which country made the fabric and where it's been since."

"Thank you, Marco, yes, please do that. Let me have the paperwork to authorise it."

Nodding, he moved on to say, "now for the ammunition." Casting his hand over the bags on each bench he commented, "nothing unusual about any of them except these". As he spoke, Marco picked up and then dropped a large bag of bullets on the bench-top, and the sudden noise caused me to glare at him.

"Sorry, Michael, I didn't mean to surprise you. Perhaps not quite the right thing to do with live ammunition."

"No, Marco, probably not, but you've got my attention. Those look to be the blue-tipped 9mm we've heard so much about."

"Yes, indeed they are. They're Israeli made, with 'IMI 9mm' stamped into the base. Again, you'll need to talk to Hamish about them."

"Okay, but what do you know?" I asked him.

"Well, prior to last year, we hadn't seen any. Now they're popping up everywhere in shootings; especially in London and Manchester. As you know, bullets just like these killed Devon Dawson."

"Okay, so what can you do with all the food bags they're wrapped in?" I asked.

"Nothing right now but bring me any rolls of them you find during a search, and we'll run a comparison. If they match, then you'll have your supplier of all this ammunition."

"Okay, well let's bank that and hope we find those rolls. What's next? What about the silencers?"

"We prefer to call them sound moderators or suppressors," he replied almost scornfully before adding, "but I'm happy to refer to them by their common term of silencer. I imagine you want to know about the ones from the Tollgate Hotel."

"Ah, yes, we most certainly do," I replied enthusiastically.

"Good," and then lowering his voice added, "they're also of the same design as Hamish's that was fitted to his CZ pistol."

I nodded back, grateful for the extra detail.

"I've stripped one down into its component parts," he now carried on at his usual volume, "professionally made in a well-equipped workshop. Imperfections in the tool marks suggest it's not a commercial factory, though. More likely a hobbyist engineer using a vertical milling machine and lathe. Nonetheless, very well put together."

"Anything unique about them?" I asked.

"Definitely. They screw together at both ends to hold the internal baffles, which requires a two-pronged face spanner. Should you identify a suspect with a workshop, look out for one as he's used it to assemble all his suppressors, sorry, silencers."

Lifting one of them to show us, he pointed out, "see these two holes on the face plate either side of the barrel port, well that's where the spanner fits. If you can find me the one that made these tiny indentations when he screwed them together, I'll prove whoever's has it made your silencers."

He then passed round a magnifying glass so we could see the tell-tale marks it caused.

"Now I should tell you; we've seen about a dozen of these," and, in a whisper added, "including Hamish's." Returning once more to his normal voice, he continued, "now, some are in bare metal, others painted black, like this one. You'll have noted, no doubt, for the Tollgate Hotel MAC-10s the gunsmith added a screw-thread to the barrel for the silencer."

"Yes, we did," John confirmed.

"Well, we've tested the combination of the Abonar MAC-10, silencer, and blue-tipped ammunition, and it's awesome." Marco's excitement seemed a little inappropriate given the devastating effect of these weapons. "Almost completely silent," he added, "except for the breech bolt recoiling and ejecting the spent case."

John took from his briefcase a photo album and passing it to Marco asked, "have you seen these three silencers in bare metal that Merseyside Police recovered in 1995?"

"Oh yes, I have. And I can tell you they were made by the same person as yours."

John and I nodded to each other.

Marco put the silencer back on the bench but kept hold of the MAC-10. "I want to give you my impression of these Abonar MAC-10s," his tone changed, now sounding more like a schoolteacher. "As you may know, the first of these was developed by Gordon Ingram in the 1960s. It's called a MAC after his company, 'Military Armament Corporation', and '10' because it was the tenth attempt at perfecting the design, albeit he started with number '5'."

I saw John nodding to show his shared knowledge, but it was mostly new to me.

"They've been copied since by multiple manufacturers. It's a formidable, easily concealed machine pistol, capable of firing over 1,200 rounds-a-minute. The only limitation is the magazine. On full-auto, you'll empty a 30-round clip in under two seconds."

Marco paused for effect to allow us to consider the devastating effect of that firepower.

"Now, as I mentioned," he said, carrying on with his lesson, "it was a British gunsmith named Christopher Perkins who set up SF Firearms in the early '90s. We know that's where all your Abonar MAC-10s originate from due to the SF markings. Perkins got the templates from another gunsmith, Guy Savage. Now Savage is well-known in the arms trade as an out-and-out rogue," and Marco's tone revealed his own contempt. "He set up 'Creative Gunsmiths Limited' in St Johns Wood, and when Perkins got a contract with a Belgian company to make a hundred MAC-10s, he asked Savage for help. However, subsequently he had serious problems with the Home Office."

Marco then turned upside down the frame of the Perkins MAC-10 he'd previously disassembled to show us a switch to the right of the trigger guard saying, "this allows you to choose either 'Safe' or 'Fire'." Flipping it over he added, "and then this lever on the left allows you to select between semi- and full-auto. For the British market, Perkins removed the full-auto option."

He then put the Abonar MAC-10 frame alongside the Perkins one. "You can see here on your reactivated Abonar MAC-10 its trigger mechanism is missing Perkins's semi-automatic sear. Its absence means there's nothing to hold the bolt back until you pull the trigger again. It's permanently set to full-auto."

As John and I nodded, Marco added, "I'm certain your Abonar gunsmith deliberately did that to make his version much easier to use in inexperienced hands and, thus, far more dangerous. On some, he's welded the switch so there's no safety either," and his tone quickly changed to one of scorn. "Without Perkins's features to worry about, with the Abonar MAC-10 you just squeeze the trigger for an instantaneous burst of fully automatic gunfire."

"Wow," I commented, shocked by the obvious consequences.

"Yes," Marco nodded, acknowledging my reaction before adding, "and this also makes it almost impossible to fire anything less than a one-second burst. That's somewhere between ten and twenty rounds; just perfect for a drive-by shooting, as in the case of Devon Dawson."

"We must find this gunsmith," I said quickly in response.

"Yes, you must!" Marco agreed.

"Hmm, so why did Perkins make his in semi-auto mode?" I asked.

"Good question; because he thought it would allow him to sell them here legally as a semi-automatic pistol, not a machine gun as he had for his Belgian client. But the Home Office told him that since he'd originally made them as a machine gun, under the Firearms Act they remain one regardless of him adding the semi-automatic sear. The Home Office classed them as 'Section 5 prohibited firearms' and Perkins didn't have the right licence. So, he was forced to either scrap or deactivate every one he hadn't already sold."

"When was that?" I asked.

"Sometime in 1995, I think. We know he sent dozens to the London Proof House for certifying as lawfully deactivated. However, for about a year now, we've been seeing them reactivated and very much live firing and on full-auto. Each one bears the same hallmarks as the Abonar ones right here."

"Marco," I asked, "do you know who Perkins sold the deactivated ones to?"

"No. Sussex Police have spoken to him numerous times. He hasn't kept any records of the sale. Perkins claimed he didn't have to, as they were all deactivated and, technically, he's right."

"So, at some point," I commented, "we need to pay Perkins a visit ourselves."

"Yes, you should. I'd say he has a good idea who's now reactivating his MAC-10s; but doesn't want to admit it. I think you'll find it's someone he knows."

"Anything else you can give us as a line of enquiry?" I asked, feeling energised by this lesson.

"Yes, there is one more. Come back to the Tollgate Hotel bench and look at the breech bolt of your Abonar MAC-10. Its design is quite unique," he said, holding it out for me to look at. "I recommend you visit the Pattern Room at the Royal Armouries, Michael. I'm sure they'll show you that none of the other MAC-10s in their collection has one like this."

"Okay, that'll make an interesting day out of the office, but how will that help my enquiries?"

"Because once you identify the workshop where these are being produced, finding just one will be like 'Superman's kryptonite' for the gunsmith making them. It'll be unequivocal evidence that he's made all of your Abonar MAC-10s."

Marco gave us a few seconds to absorb the information, before saying, "and here endeth the lesson on Operation Abonar. I hope that was useful guys," and he concluded by briefly clasping his hands together once more.

"Thank you, enormously," I told him, before asking, "and when should we expect the results of the forensic work on the cloths?"

"Twelve weeks. Sorry, we just can't do it any quicker unless you've got someone in custody."

Having confirmed with Simon the photographs we needed, John and I left to walk back to NSY.

That night I had to travel to Birmingham by train for the quarterly meeting of ACPO Telecoms at the Tally Ho Conference Centre. Before heading to the station, I spent the afternoon doing my Secretary job preparing the brief for DAC Fry. I left it for him to read whilst he travelled up by car first thing in the morning. In those papers I included an update on Abonar. I ended it with a recommendation we meet the CSPs to request their help with accelerating our enquiries. I went ahead to set that up.

CHAPTER 16

Clearing our Lines

Wednesday, 7th May

I was down in the hotel dining room for breakfast before 7am ready to meet the people from the CSPs. I wanted their agreement to stay on after the main ACPO meeting for a short briefing with DAC Fry on Abonar. One after another I manoeuvred between the tables to catch up with the heads of the 'Single Points of Contact[24]' for each of the mobile and landline companies. In my short time as Secretary, we had built a strong relationship. It helped that we were in regular contact, sometimes in the middle of the night working on a kidnap investigation. The obvious urgency of those operations, and then huge elation when we recovered another hostage safely, led to a tremendous esprit-de-corps as a joint police-industry team. By the time breakfast finished, I had everyone's agreement to stay for the additional session with DAC Fry.

Of particular interest to me amongst the law enforcement delegates attending the main ACPO meeting was Detective Inspector Jim Morton from Merseyside Police. In the coffee-break, I went over and introduced myself.

"Jim, what do you know about the former Home Secretary pardoning John Haase and Paul Bennett?"

He very nearly spat out his coffee in surprise. "Heavens, I'll need to know why you asked that? It's a sensitive subject in Merseyside."

"I'm investigating another inmate at Full Sutton who wants to do a similar deal."

"Oh God, no. Give me your card and I'll call you tomorrow. Here's mine. It'll be around eight, just before the day gets busy."

---

24 Single Points of Contact: dedicated team of people in each CSP who provide the focal point for all law enforcement enquiries.

"Perfect, thanks. Call my mobile. I can relocate to a Brent if necessary."

"I'll bear that in mind. Good to meet you."

At the conclusion of the main session, I ushered the law enforcement representatives out of the room to allow DAC Fry and I to separately brief those from the CSPs.

"Thank you for sparing the extra time," DAC Fry began. "The purpose of my asking you to stay behind is simple. I want to make sure you all know about Operation Abonar, and I would appreciate it if you'd pull out all the stops to give Michael what he needs for this job as a priority, please."

He looked around the faces to check for a positive reaction.

Paul Griffiths from '*Cellnet*'[25] spoke first, "I think I speak for everyone from the industry, Mr Fry, when I say, of course we'll help any arms trafficking investigation. What would be useful, though, is if either you or Michael can tell us more about it. We don't need to tell our staff. We just want to understand what you're up against. That way we'll know how best to use our capabilities to get you ahead of the people you're interested in."

DAC Fry turned to me, "Michael?"

I summarised for them what we knew about the suspects' use of the telephone networks, and finished by adding, "we're certain there's more serious weaponry in the pipeline. That's why we urgently need your help to identify who's involved, where they store it, and how they intend to move it. We need to be on top of them before these weapons hit the streets. Right now, it's your data that's driving our investigation."

I stopped to check for a reaction. Thankfully, everyone was nodding in agreement.

"Thank you, Michael," DAC Fry cut back in, "any questions?"

No one spoke.

"Excellent. Thank you. I look forward to celebrating another joint success."

I followed DAC Fry out of the room. "Thank you, Sir. That will make my job a lot easier."

"I hope so. A novel approach taking them into your confidence but, clearly, the right thing to do when their data has advanced your investigation so much and so quickly. Good luck. Keep Mr Baxter updated. From what he tells me, we're about to go head-to-head with the Home Office lawyers again."

---

25   Cellnet: one of the mobile CSPs at the time.

CHAPTER 17

Weapons Intelligence Branch

Thursday, 8th May

My desk phone rang at a minute after 8am.

"Michael. Jim Morton. So, Haase and Bennett. No need to switch to a Brent. What I can tell you is mostly in the public domain anyway. First, my ACC[26] wants to know whether you're reopening that investigation?"

"No, we're not."

"Good, because there'd be hell to pay if you were. It's a Merseyside job, not a Met one," he said firmly. Then changing to a more friendly tone continued, "now we've got that sorted, what's your interest?"

"There are clear parallels between Haase and Bennett and our job. We've had three separate recoveries so far totalling sixty-five firearms and a thousand rounds of ammunition."

"Interesting. Who's your informant? Can you say?"

"Yes, but he's not ours; like Haase and Bennet, he was being handled by Customs. His name is Fred Donovan, a Manchester criminal using a Manchester solicitor as the go-between. His caches of weaponry have turned up in London and Kent. No obvious connections with Liverpool, other than the same M-O[27] as Haase and Bennett."

"Okay, I'll check whether we hold anything on file about Donovan. Otherwise, my ACC is keen you leave Haase and Bennett to us. I'm sure you understand the territorial issues."

"Yes, of course, but if there is something in your files that can help, I'd be grateful for a call," I said assertively, somewhat annoyed at being told to butt-out. Wanting to sound conciliatory, though, I added, "Donovan was

---

26 ACC: Assistant Chief Constable.
27 M-O: Modus Operandi – methodology.

on the Cat A wing with Haase and Bennett. That's the principal connection between them."

"Okay, that gives me something solid to look for," his tone now suggested a mellowing in his attitude. "What I can tell you is we're investigating Haase and Bennett's finances. We're convinced Customs didn't seize all their proceeds of crime. If we can't put them back in prison, hopefully, we can hit them where it hurts most by taking away their money."

"Well, good luck with that."

"There's one final point I'll add, Michael, which will explain why you should keep well away from Liverpool. The local Labour MP, Peter Kilfoyle, has kicked up a storm about the former Conservative Home Secretary. He's alleging corruption and backhanders. My ACC will be very happy to hear you're not adding fuel to that fire by coming up here asking unhelpful questions."

"That's all fine, Jim. When will you let me know about Donovan?"

"Give me a day or so to retrieve the file. If I find his name, I'll let you know. If not, I'll see you at the next ACPO meeting."

Putting down the handset, I looked up to see Pete hovering at my open door.

"What have you got for me today, Pete?"

"I understand you and the DAC briefed the CSPs about Abonar yesterday."

"Yes, we did."

"Well, it's had something of an effect." His look of disapproval, however, told me he was not entirely happy with it. "Hmm," he continued, "so overnight they've sent through all the data you've requested." He then handed me a set of his customary A4 brown envelopes before sharply exiting my office, clearly in a huff.

Next, John, Alice and Mark appeared at my door ready for our daily catch-up.

"Guvnor, is now convenient?" John asked.

"Do you have anything new to add, or will your time be better spent on the analysis?"

"Nothing sensational, no, and yes, we could get more done without a catch-up."

"Okay, that's fine John. Anyway, you and I have a 10am with Hamish, so Alice and Mark, please crack on with building the chart."

They all looked relieved.

"Oh, and I haven't had time to look through these yet," I said, offering the latest envelopes to Alice. "Pete's just dropped them off. It's all the outstanding call data you requested."

"Thank you, Mr H," Alice said, smiling and holding my gaze as she took the envelopes.

I felt embarrassed, so looked away at John to break the awkwardness. "One more thing before you head back to your desks," I asked, "are you ready for tomorrow's briefing with Mr Baxter?"

"Yes, I am, certainly," Alice replied in her usual enthusiastic manner, again trying to catch my eye.

Feeling her stare, I stayed focused on John, saying, "great. John, book the Fordham Suite briefing room for the morning?"

"Sure."

Continuing to avoid Alice's look, I asked John, "has Simon dropped off the photos?"

"Yes, they're on my desk and I'll bring them with us."

"Good. I'll come and find you in ten minutes, and we can walk across to Thames House together."

As John and I made that walk to the north side of Lambeth Bridge, almost apologetically he asked, "is everything okay between you and Alice, Guv?"

"Yes, why?"

"Oh, she thinks you're not impressed with her work because you rarely look her in the eye."

I laughed before explaining, "I find her stares somewhat beguiling and that's not good for a professional relationship, so I'm trying hard to avoid them."

"Oh, so she does that to you too. I thought it was only me."

"No, sorry John, she does it to all of us. I think we should call it the 'Alice effect'."

"Damn. I was beginning to think she'd taken a shine to me."

"Well, I suggest you have a word with Alice to reassure her that I'm very happy with what she's doing for us. You might also like to say something about her toning down the Alice effect. Better it comes from an older, more fatherly type like you, anyway," I added smiling at his look of scorn at my remark.

The grand 1930s neoclassical exterior of Thames House befits the building's purpose as the headquarters of the Security Service, a legacy from its former life as the prestigious head office of Imperial Chemical Industries. Once inside, though, the functional security measures somewhat spoil the grandeur. John and I announced ourselves at the bulletproof security window and slid our warrant cards into the bank teller style hatch to confirm our names. The guard looked at the photos and then us. He checked the visitors' list and then passed back our IDs. The security door buzzed to our right to indicate we could go through. This led into a small waiting room with garish orange fabric-covered chairs. We surrendered our mobile phones and received a ticket to retrieve them on the way out. A few minutes later, Hamish collected us. After the usual greetings, he checked our tickets to confirm we had handed over our mobiles. "Thank you. We must check. Nothing worse than escorting a visitor through the building and having their mobile go off."

I winced, recalling my doing just that to Hamish's boss, Fiona, some weeks before. She and I were travelling in the lift with others. I excused myself saying I was on-call, which was true, but still not allowed. Fiona took me straight back to security to deposit my phone. She did allow me to keep my pager, though.

Hamish led us into his office. We acknowledged the "Hellos" from the other members of the Weapons Intelligence Branch. Scattered around the room were assorted pieces of large and small military ordnance with which one or more of the team had been associated in its seizure.

"Thank you for making the time to see us today," I said to Hamish as we took our seats, "and for agreeing to host our get together next Thursday with the SIOs."

"Not a problem. Where have you got to with Abonar?"

"Customs have now confirmed Donovan is their informant for the three firearms recoveries," I said, pleased to share this development with him. "We're now trying to convince the Home Office to let us go after his solicitor Gudgeon, but they're blocking us."

"That's not surprising given what's at stake for their reputations," he commented dryly. Then, with a hint of suspicion in his voice he asked, "have you now read the Merseyside report on Haase and Bennett?"

"We have, yes, and all its striking similarities with Donovan and Abonar. Sadly, it's obvious that Customs; the trial judge; Home Secretary and his advisors failed to recognise it was an elaborate scam and they were all completely fooled."

"Yes, indeed, in which case I needn't say anymore. You've clearly learned from their stupidity and haven't been drawn in by Donovan now attempting the same." He hesitated before asking, "do Customs know about the RPGs?"

"No, and their man Burridge assured us they've got nothing more in the pipeline."

"Good, so Abonar is now entirely a police matter, albeit a senior official at the Prison Service is the one negotiating."

"Yes, and my boss is now coaching him on what to say."

"Good. Well I had hoped to introduce you to some people here who have an interest in RPGs, but they've had to cancel due to a more pressing matter."

"Oh, that's a shame," I said disappointedly.

"No matter, all they would only have told you is we don't have any specific intelligence about them being in the country."

"Does that mean they're either on the way, or they don't exist?"

"My advice is you assume they do exist, and they are already here," he commented without showing any emotion.

"Come on Hamish, what are you not telling us?" I said, a little annoyed.

"From my experience," he began with a knowing nod, "when someone makes an offer like that, you must believe they're genuine. Proof of that is when Donovan, as with Haase and Bennett, offered firearms to trade for his release. He was confident he could do so because he'd already got control of them. He'd look pretty stupid if Customs then called his bluff and he couldn't deliver." He paused for effect before adding, "so you must assume Donovan also has control of the RPGs."

Smiling, I replied, "Okay, old friend, I'll accept the wisdom of your years."

"Good, so do you know why he's offering them?"

"We think it's because Customs broke off negotiations on the firearms, so his solicitor bypassed them and went direct to the Prison Service with the bigger offer. We assume that was in the hope of accelerating his release before the election."

"But it didn't work. Hmm, so, what have you learned about the supply chain?"

"Our analysis of the call data and prison visits suggests the Donovan family are arranging everything," John chipped in.

"Do you know who they're talking to?"

"No, we're still working on that."

"Well, I wish you luck."

"Hamish," I said, wanting to move on to our other lines of enquiry, "we spent a valuable morning with Marco on Tuesday. John's got a copy for you of the more detailed photo album we had done."

Hamish took it and casually flicked through the images as I then asked, "he suggested most, if not all, these guns are former police or military issue. Could they have been stolen from an armoury?"

"Nothing comes to mind for these types of old model handguns."

"What about the surplus market?" John asked, recalling Marco's advice.

"That would be a very good place to start, yes."

"We suspect some are from the former Soviet-bloc," John said, wanting to sound knowledgeable.

"Many were wrapped in oiled cloths marked with a three-letter Cyrillic code," I added. "Someone scratched the same letters into the frames of each handgun under the grips." Simultaneously, John helpfully pointed to the relevant photographs.

Shaking his head, Hamish commented, "I've not seen that before. I'll need to check with our Eastern Europe Desk to see if they can interpret them. The Belgian authorities are seeing a lot of former Soviet-bloc weaponry right now. You should talk to the police at the Brussels HQ."

"Marco recommended the same," I commented.

"We do tend to have similar views," he continued in his dry tone. Then with a little more animation said, "oh, and if you'd like an extra day out of the office, may I recommend you go and see Donald Manross. He's head of the INTERPOL Firearms Section in Lyon and has access to all the systems and connections you'll need to help trace the source of your guns."

"Very helpful, thanks. Now Marco recommended we talk to you about these MABs," I said, pointing to the relevant photographs. As he studied them, I asked, "he also said you've got an active interest in a CZ 27 with an identical barrel extension and screw thread plus a silencer."

"Ah, he did, did he? Well, he will have told you, no doubt, it's part of an ongoing investigation. So there's nothing more I can tell you. Sorry."

"What, nothing at all?"

"No, nothing."

He looked at the photos of the MAB pistols and then back at me. He could tell I was not happy.

"Look, I'll tell you what I'll do," his tone changed to being more conciliatory. "I'll invite the people leading the investigation to come along to your meeting next Thursday and observe. I'll leave it for them to then decide whether they talk to you."

"Thank you, that would be great."

"Yes, but be warned," he said sternly, "arrests are imminent, and we've thrown a lot of our own resources into this too. We're talking about a major target. No one will thank me if you get in the way with your Abonar enquiries."

"Okay, understood."

John had thumbed through his copy of the album to find the pictures of the Colt revolvers before asking, "Marco pointed out this area of refinishing on the frames of these. He thinks someone removed an important mark and that you might know what it was?"

Hamish looked at the images before turning to his computer and began searching the 'Talisman' photographic database.

"Yes, here you go, 'Operation Desert Storm'." Reassuringly, his tone now had a hint of enthusiasm. "Colt Police Positives seized from Iraqi soldiers and police. Each gun had an Arabic arsenal mark stamped in just that place on the frame."

John and I examined the images on his computer screen.

"Not sure what that means for Abonar," Hamish added, "but at least you now know your Colts came from Iraq. Here's what the mark looks like should you find any not refinished. I'll print off a couple of images for you to keep." He paused while deep in thought, before saying, "You know, come to think of it, after the Gulf War the Iraqis dumped on the military surplus market many of the other types of handguns you've recovered."

With that he searched Talisman again, which filled his screen with thumbnail pictures.

"There you go," he said almost triumphantly. "I think you'll find your handguns came from Iraq post-1991. Where they went to after that is anyone's guess. You'll have to speak to your contacts in the gun trade. It may well be some did reach Eastern Europe but only after the collapse of the former Soviet-bloc. These aren't Soviet era. They could all have been bought up for use in the more recent Balkan Wars."

Once Hamish retrieved the pages of photographs from the printer, I asked him more questions about what we had learned during our visit to the Lab.

"We heard from Marco about the original SF Firearms MAC-10 made by Christopher Perkins and where the reactivated ones have since turned up in the UK. Can you tell us in which other countries they've made an appearance?"

"Well, one was picked up only this month after a shooting in Dublin. I know of more in Europe where the guns have yet to be recovered but the unique marks left by the breech-face on the spent cases suggest they were fired by one of your reactivated MAC-10s. I think four murders can be attributed to them and you can expect many more until you stop the source of supply."

"Well, that's the plan," I told him. "So, how many have been recovered?"

"Hmm, in total it must be twelve now, including the one from Dublin. You need to check with the London Proof House about how many Perkins sent them for stamping with their deactivation mark. That'll give you an indication of the numbers still out there."

"It's on my list of enquiries."

"Good. You do need to identify who's reactivating your 'Abonar MAC-10'."

I smiled at Hamish's use of the same Marco had given them while he turned back to his computer screen and brought up a selection of images.

"Look here," he announced, becoming more animated, "as I said, the breech bolt is unique. It's been very well designed. We've tested it. MAC-10s are renowned for jamming after a couple of magazines." He pointed to a different variant of the machine pistol. "You see, the weakness is the feed ramp, and then the positioning of the extractor claw that ejects the spent cartridge." Changing the screen to our MAC-10, he added, "your gunsmith fixed all that, not least by moving the claw to a forty-five-degree angle instead of the standard ninety. That is unique to the Abonar MAC-10," Hamish added with extra emphasis in his voice. "Of course, you'll need to go to the Pattern Room to get an expert opinion you can use as evidence. I can't do that for you."

"Yes, Marco recommended we do that too."

"I told you we think alike. Did he also say that when you find the man with the workshop producing these breech bolts, you will have identified a very major source of guns to the criminal market?"

"He did, yes," John replied with some delight. "He said it would be like finding Superman's kryptonite."

"Did he? I hope he also told you to hurry up. Your Abonar gunsmith's become the principal source of illicit firearms in the UK, which makes him responsible for the escalation in gangland shootings."

"Well, Hamish, if your friends help us next week, we can," I snapped back, causing Hamish to frown.

"Now for the ammunition," John quickly interrupted, sensing the potential friction. "Marco suggested we talk to you about these non-standard, blue-tipped 9mm bullets."

"Yes, oh yes, I know these. They're Israeli made."

"What's with the blue tip?" I asked.

"It means they're subsonic for use with a silencer. Ideal for clandestine military operations, such as assassinations. In your case, though, they're perfect for drive-by shootings."

"Well that explains why they've become so popular amongst gangs here. Where would they get them?"

"They're made by '*Israeli Military Industries*'. You will have seen their headstamp, 'IMI', and '9mm' on the base of each cartridge."

I was pleased Hamish was now being more open with us. "We did. Would ours have been acquired from the Israeli military?"

"Unlikely. They're also sold commercially under the brand name, '*Samson*'. The distributor is '*Samson Arms and Ammunition*'. I can make a call if you like?"

"Yes, please do."

"Alright, then let me keep this album, and I'll speak to them and a couple of my other contacts."

"Of course and thank you. Right, we better get back to the Yard. As always, Hamish, you've been super-helpful." Still annoyed at his refusal to tell us more about the CZ pistol I added, "well, mostly."

Having collected our mobile phones from security, John and I headed back to the office. For the rest of the day, I worked with the team preparing the briefing for Anton in the morning.

CHAPTER 18

Briefing the Boss

Friday, 9ᵗʰ May

I walked into the briefing room fifteen minutes ahead of Anton's scheduled arrival at 10am. It was a hive of activity. Alice was going through her chart, which she had projected on to the big screen. Meanwhile, Mark and John were sorting through photo albums and other documents. The aroma of pipe smoke assured me John had done his thinking beforehand and was ready. I placed a chair for Anton at the head of the table opposite the big screen. Alice sat at a computer to the left. John and I sat opposite her at the main table. Mark put himself on a corner ready to take notes. On the hour, Anton entered without knocking.

"Would you like something that looks like coffee from the machine?" I asked.

"No, thanks. You should know me by now, I don't do compromise when it comes to a posh brew. Let's just get on." I caught him admiring Alice as he sat down and casually brushed his hair back.

"Alice, over to you and your chart," I said, wanting to get Anton's attention on the briefing.

"Okay, first the firearms' recoveries. Mr H asked me to reconstruct events by working backwards from Ben Harrison's calls to SO13 and Kent Police."

"Whoa, Alice, stop. *Mr H?* What happened to *Whizzy?*" Anton asked with a playful grin on his face.

"It's now Mr H, Boss," John replied before I could.

"If I may continue," Alice interrupted, now glaring at Anton.

"Yes, sorry, do go on with what *Mr H* asked you to do," Anton said, visibly softening under Alice's disapproving stare.

"So, by going through the call data, it's taken me right back to August 15ᵗʰ, 1996." She then circled the cursor around the corresponding event. "This is when someone took out a contract with Orange via a back street mobile phone shop in Hither Green. I'll be showing you shortly why it's so significant, as it kicks off the whole sequence of calls to arrange the three deliveries." She then paused to sip her coffee. "Had it been a one-off, I would have dismissed it, but it's the same pattern for all three. Let me now show you that on the chart, Mr Baxter," she added demurely.

Anton leaned forward staring intently at Alice and then the screen as she moved the cursor.

"We know from your conversation with Mick Burridge that Gudgeon initiated contact with Ben Harrison on October 4th. Here I've mapped their calls to confirm."

"Yes, that corresponds with the dates he gave us," Anton said impatiently. "What next?"

"Working on Hamish's assumption that Donovan would not instruct Gudgeon to contact Harrison until he was sure he had control of the first batch of firearms, I went looking for the calls which set that up."

"And?" Anton said, still sounding keen that Alice get to her point.

"I'm sorry Mr Baxter, but I'm an analyst and I work in a logical way. Please don't rush me." Alice transfixed him with one of her disarming stares and said, "I promise to get you where you want to be, but I'll do it in the right order."

Anton replied, "Sure, sure, please go on," as he visibly shrank in his chair, acknowledging the justification for her rebuke. John and I exchanged looks of admiration at Alice's cool composure with our boss.

"So, now in its logical sequence, let me explain the call pattern," Alice restarted, looking confidently at Anton. "It began in late September with the Donovans' home phone. It received a two-second call from the Orange mobile I just mentioned. In the time it would take someone to walk from their home to the phone box, erm," Alice corrected herself, "TK, around the corner, they then used it to call back the Orange mobile." She paused to circle the events with the cursor.

"The call to the Donovans' home was only the second that mobile made. The first was to 123, the BT 'Speaking Clock'. I assume to test the connection. Interestingly, the call back from the TK was the first it received. To me, that initial pattern was so unusual I needed to dig further. I found the mobile only because it turned up so regularly from calls made to it by the TK. It's such a common denominator around the timings for Whitechapel, Plaistow and the Tollgate Hotel, I realised it had to be significant." She paused again for more coffee.

"Taking things in sequence then," Anton asked sheepishly, "when was that first test call?"

"On September 30th, just over a month after it was bought."

"Okay, and what calls did the Donovans make to trigger the one it made to their home?"

"I have no idea. I haven't found anything in the data yet."

"Okay, perhaps it was just word of mouth," Anton suggested as he ended his line of questioning.

"So this initial call confirmed the firearms were available," Alice said, confident in her assessment. "We can see from Donovan's prison file, his wife then visited him two days later, and Gudgeon the day after that on October 3rd. We know from what Mick Burridge told you, Gudgeon's first call to Harrison proposing the deal to secure his client's early parole was on October 4th. And here's that call to confirm." Alice circled each event in turn before adding, "that's why I'm certain I haven't broken Mr H's 'Detectives' ABC'." She then gave me a long stare and smiled.

"Sorry, I don't understand," Anton said looking troubled, "what's that?"

Clearly amused by Anton's lack of knowledge of something she thought was fundamental to all good investigators, Alice took great pleasure in saying, "well, Mr H told me not to make any *assumptions* and dis*believe* everything until I'd *checked* and double-checked that I was right." Smugly she looked at me first and then Anton, obviously proud of showing her knowledge. Anton glared at me momentarily, slightly annoyed at being put in his place by one of my team.

Alice carried on to say, "the fact all the calls and visits followed that first one from the Orange mobile confirmed for me its significance. It's clearly the one that said the guns were available, so Gudgeon could make the offer. Using Mr H's ABC, there's no other conclusion you could draw," she ended, pleased with her logic.

Anton laughed and muttered, "*ABC*, whatever next". He paused before asking, now confident he could do so, "okay, so Alice, what do we know about your Orange mobile?".

"I'll let John answer that, if I may."

"Yes Boss," John began courteously. "I asked DC Chris Ferguson in the Computer Crime Unit to look into the subscriber details, as nothing came up on InfoS, and whoever bought it did everything to protect their identity. They didn't use it for over a month. No doubt that's because they wanted to make sure the shop had overwritten the CCTV of them buying it."

"So who's the subscriber?" Anton asked, struggling not to sound impatient.

"It's a male who used a false name, Boss, with the address of an empty flat in Eltham."

"Yes, but it's a contract phone," Anton countered, sounding annoyed, "so Orange will surely have a bank account and a name."

"Yes, they have," John reported, "but DC Ferguson found it was opened using the same bogus details a week before, with a £500 cash deposit to cover the direct debits until either they finished using it or topped it up to carry on."

"Okay, I'm determined not to give up just yet. Where is it now and what calls is it making?"

"It's dead Boss, and I suggest we let Alice explain all that when she gets to it in her sequence."

"Sure, sure, very sensible, I don't want to be told off again," Anton said, staring at Alice, who smiled back before returning to her computer.

"Thank you. In a moment I'll explain why we think the mobile was bought specifically for this job and nothing else. I think the term is a '*burner phone*'," Alice said, proud of her new-found police vernacular. "Before that, let me show you its significance in coordinating the first delivery to Whitechapel." She circled the cursor around the next sequence of calls and prison visits.

"So once Harrison reported back to Gudgeon on October 11th that the deal was on with the Home Secretary, Gudgeon called the Donovan home number." Moving the cursor to the corresponding events, she added, "what follows are a series of calls and prison visits to have the consignment of guns and ammunition ready to deliver on November 12th." She paused to make sure we were all at the same point on the chart

"The pattern finished," she continued, "when whoever had the Orange mobile let the Donovans know where the car was parked ahead of them calling Gudgeon. He was himself on his way into Full Sutton to visit Donovan, ready to make it look like that's how he got the information to pass on to Harrison. To add to their ruse, Gudgeon waited until he left the prison before he called him. Armed with Gudgeon's news of where to send the police in Whitechapel, Harrison then called SO13 to arrange the first recovery of guns and ammunition, oh, and the cannabis."

Turning sideways in her chair to face us, Alice waited for questions.

"Okay, so now show me that pattern for Plaistow, please," Anton asked.

"Certainly," and turning away she lined up the chart to begin. "So, as you can see, exactly the same as Whitechapel, culminating in a call from the Donovans to Gudgeon as he's en route to visit his client at Full Sutton. Once again, he waited until he'd seen Donovan before he called Harrison telling him to send the police to the Wickes car park in Plaistow."

"Amazing," Anton said excitedly, now combing through his hair with both hands. "That's absolutely fantastic work Alice. I'm hugely impressed."

"Thank you, Mr Baxter," she said, giving him a broad smile.

"But my problem is none of that exactly proves Gudgeon knows it's all a scam," Anton commented, sounding disappointed. "You see, if we apply Mr H's *ABC*, I feel sure the Home Office will argue it's all supposition on our part. For example, Mrs Donovan calling Gudgeon on his way in to see her husband doesn't mean she was passing on details of where the guns were hidden."

I decided to interject, "I get your scepticism, Boss, but from the pattern of calls involving the Orange mobile, the Donovans' home phone and the TK, I'm convinced there's no other conclusion you can draw."

Alice gave me a reassuring nod as she smiled supportively, which Anton noticed.

"Okay, okay. You must appreciate I need to play devil's advocate," he insisted. "After all, it's the first time I've seen your chart. You've got to convinced me there's enough in your chart for me to take to the Home Office later today and do battle with them again."

"Understood Boss," I agreed. "So, Alice, shall we go on to the Tollgate Hotel delivery, as that one clearly implicates Gudgeon knows it was a scam?"

"Sure. So the major difference we see between the patterns to set up Whitechapel and Plaistow and the Tollgate Hotel is that this time Gudgeon did not wait to see Donovan at Full Sutton. Instead, he called Harrison immediately after the Donovans called him from the TK."

"So where was he?" Anton asked brusquely.

John answered, "March 1st was a Saturday and the cellsite on his mobile placed him at home or close by. That also confirms he hadn't got to Full Sutton before calling Ben Harrison."

"And," I chipped in, "we know that call was to tell Harrison where to find the next consignment, because he then immediately rang Kent Police to tell them."

"Okay, okay," Anton said, raising his hands in surrender. "But how do you explain him not waiting to see Donovan?"

"Easy," John replied confidently, "it's because the Maestro was left unlocked in what is well known locally as a crime hotspot. The Donovans didn't want to risk the consignment being stolen before the police got there. Hence, they convinced Gudgeon not to wait, and so he called Harrison immediately."

"That does seem logical," Anton said, now sounding convinced. "But what a serious mistake for them to make. It destroys their whole story about Donovan overhearing conversations on the prison wing."

"Exactly Boss," I said, wanting to add another important point, "and, when you next brief upstairs, you can reassure the Commissioner we've got the evidence to justify not giving Donovan any benefit. It's all been a scam and, quite clearly, he controlled all three deliveries from the start."

"Can you prove that?" Anton asked. "I mean can you actually prove he knew what his family were up to on the outside?"

"Yes, we can," I said, turning now to John. "Would you take us through what you found on Donovan's prison file about his calls home. Alice, you might like to help with this too."

John began the explanation, "so, we know from Donovan's file his home number is the only one he's allowed to dial from the phone on the Cat A wing. When he enters his PIN, the system lets him dial only that number. It also records the conversation." He paused to let Anton absorb the significance before continuing. "Interestingly, when Mrs Donovan visited her husband back in early October, prison officers saw Donovan pass her a piece of paper. Security found it when they stopped and searched her on the way out. DC Overton sent us a copy." John passed the paper to Anton.

"As you can see, Boss, it's days of the week and times. Security let her have the paper back, thinking it unimportant. We didn't think anything of it either until Alice checked the dates and times against Donovan's calls home. They coincide exactly with the ones on the paper. Mr H, do you want to take it from here?"

"Sure. So, prison officers later listened to the tapes. Notes on his file record a man answered each time. When Alice checked the billing for the Donovan home number, it showed simultaneous outgoing calls to the Orange mobile."

"So, what does that mean?" Anton said, sounding confused.

"It means someone deliberately diverted the family phone to it. The paper Donovan passed his wife was for her to set up these diverts in advance to bypass the prison's security system. That means Donovan has been talking directly to anyone he pleases on whatever number his family diverted the home phone to." I waited until Anton's face told me he recognised the significance.

"Sadly," I continued, "the prison hasn't kept the tapes. Fortunately, a prison officer thought the very first conversation sounded interesting enough for him to make a note. John has a copy."

"And?" Anton asked, wanting a quick answer.

John quoted from the file, "*the man told Donovan, 'The charity can do pens and refills loose and in boxes, all types'*."

"I know this goes against the ABC, as it's pure supposition on my part," I added, "but we think '*charity*' is a euphemism for their supplier and, thus, '*pens*' are guns and '*refills*' the ammunition."

"Yes, yes, in all the circumstances, I think you're absolutely right to assume that," Anton said while nodding. "Please tell me you've now told the prison to keep the tapes."

"Yes, but only since yesterday when we discovered this. We've lost everything before then."

"Shit! Okay, at least we'll have them from now on to cover negotiations on the RPGs."

"For sure. So, Boss, to answer your question, that's how we're certain Donovan knew what his family were up to on the outside," I told him confidently.

"Yes, well that does it for me too. Well done."

"What it also tells us is whoever had the Orange mobile did not control the guns. He's merely the arranger. And that's probably a good time for me to mention, Boss, that with only Alice available to do the analysis," and I slowed to labour the point, "we haven't yet had the opportunity to find out who the Orange mobile called to supply the firearms and ammunition."

"Okay, Michael, noted you need more resources."

"Yes Sir."

"So, this Orange mobile, do you have cellsite on it to say where it was the whole time?"

"Yes, we do, Boss," John spoke up. "For most of the time it was in south-east London; specifically Eltham and Hither Green, plus occasionally in north Kent around Dartford."

"So, does Donovan have any known associates or family in those areas?"

"We're checking that, and whether Haase or Bennett had any too," John replied. "We're working on a theory that Donovan used the same person they did to coordinate the firearms' deliveries."

"Very good. Let's hope you find the connection."

I decided to interject at this point, "yes, we know from Donovan's prison intelligence file he was good mates with Haase and Bennett. We also know from the photos that some of the guns recovered in Liverpool have the same hallmarks as ours. But there's a problem. The Merseyside ACC overseeing the investigation into their finances doesn't want us up there asking questions."

"Hmm, well I don't want you making enquiries about Haase and Bennett right now either," Anton said, giving me a stern look. "You've got enough to do with Donovan and Gudgeon. I've made my own enquiries about what Customs got up to with the Home Secretary back then, and I don't want any of it tainting Abonar. If Merseyside don't get back to you, just leave them be until we've got something useful to give them."

"Then I'm happy not to get distracted too. But" I added, "it will remain an annoying loose end."

"I know but put it in the pending tray. We may get back to it once you've nailed everyone involved in Abonar, okay?"

"Sir," I said firmly to acknowledge his instruction.

"Good. Well, this has all been hugely impressive. Anything else on the firearms job before you walk me through what you know about the RPGs?"

"No," I said now turning to Alice, "would you show us what you found from the call data to inform your initial analysis?"

"Certainly Mr H. Now despite everything I said about following your ABC, I am going to start with an assumption," Alice began confidently. "Gudgeon's news to Donovan on March 11th that Customs were no longer playing caused him and his family to rethink their strategy. That meant, going bigger and better than before. Hence, the offer of RPGs."

"I'm happy so far with your assumption," Anton said while holding Alice's stare and smiling back.

"I think the speed at which they made the switch meant Donovan already had them in the pipeline," Alice continued. "For some reason we may never know, he'd chosen not to offer them before to Customs." She then paused to sip her coffee.

Anton took the opportunity to comment, "perhaps he held them back as insurance. It certainly looks like he needed something in case, as happened, his relationship with Customs ended ahead of convincing the Home Secretary to release him."

"Or accelerate matters before the election with the predicted change of government," I added.

"That too, Michael, yes, that too." Looking up, Anton spotted Alice's disapproving stare at being interrupted. He smiled apologetically saying, "sorry, Alice, do go on."

"So, between Gudgeon visiting Donovan on Tuesday and then calling Murray that Thursday, March 13th to kick things off with the offer of RPGs, there are two other calls that seem related and, possibly, a couple more."

"How so?" Anton asked.

"Well, working on the same premise as before that Donovan wanted to confirm their availability, he needed his family to call someone to check."

"And did they?" Anton asked eagerly.

With her now familiar persuasive smile, she said, "Let me take you through the call pattern and you can make your own judgement Mr Baxter."

"Okay, lead me through it," he said, bashfully now trying to hold her stare. Embarrassed by the interaction between our boss and female colleague, I was grateful when Alice at last turned away to continue.

"You can see here, immediately after the prison visit on March 11th," she advised, "when Gudgeon broke the news to Donovan about Customs calling it off, he then phoned the Donovans' home number. Almost immediately, someone used the TK to call our Orange mobile. The conversation lasted less than two minutes. Orange has since told us the mobile was then switched off and hasn't been used again."

"Which is why we now know it was a '*burner phone*' bought specifically to arrange delivery of the firearms," I added, and Anton nodded back in agreement.

"What happened within a minute of that mobile being burnt is really interesting," Alice continued.

"How so?"

"Patience, Mr Baxter, I was just about to tell you." She flashed him another disapproving look before returning to the computer. "So, the TK made another call, this time to a second Orange mobile. I think it's safe to assume, as the calls are so close together, it's the same people involved."

Anticipating Anton's next question, John decided to answer it, "and we know there's a direct connection between these two Orange mobiles, because they were bought together from the same shop and it's the same subscriber for both."

"Fucking hell!" Anton said a little too loudly. "So no chance of attributing it. Shit."

"Hmm," Alice's tone indicated her disapproval, which she reinforced with a reproachful stare at Anton before continuing, "once we get the call data, we'll be able to start working on it for you. However, Orange have already warned us whoever's got it keeps it almost permanently switched off."

"So what have you been able to glean so far?"

"I've only found one call to it from the TK near the Donovans' home on March 12th. It was a very short conversation. The following morning, someone used the Donovan's home number to call Gudgeon's mobile. As we know, it was on that day, March 13th, that Gudgeon visited Donovan in Full Sutton and then called Colin Murray. That was to make Donovan's offer to renew negotiations this time using the RPGs. It suggests the previous call to the Orange mobile was the confirmation needed that the RPGs were available to trade."

"Very good, Alice. Very good." Anton said, now sounding excited.

"Given the behaviour of whoever is using this new mobile," I commented, "we can be certain it's another burner bought just for arranging delivery of the RPGs."

"Yes, I'd agree with that," Anton replied. "So do we have any more info on who is using it?"

"Not yet," John answered. "Hopefully, whatever we develop about the first one will help us identify who's got the second."

"And I need you to authorise putting 'Toscas' on standby, Boss. As soon as that mobile is switched on again, we need to find its precise location."

"Agreed, Michael, get that done."

"Sorry, but who or what is Toscas?" Alice asked.

"It's the codename for the vehicle-based equipment we've developed in the Branch to locate a mobile phone on the ground. It's very new. It's proving far more accurate than the CSPs trying to do the same remotely from their networks using only signal triangulation."

"Wow, how very James Bondish."

"When it works," Anton said sceptically. "Okay, Alice, anything else?"

"Only the three sets of calls between Gudgeon and Murray to follow up on the initial offer we know about from his notes."

"Did Gudgeon call the Donovans each time afterwards?"

"Yes," Alice replied, "but it's led to only one more exchange between the Donovans' home, the TK and the new Orange mobile. That was on April 21st, after Mrs Donovan returned from visiting her husband. I can't tell you much more until we get the call data. That will then help me work out if there's a pattern for when it does get switched on."

"Right, anything else from your chart, Alice?"

"No, that's it, Mr Baxter, but I do need help with processing the data, please, to accelerate identifying who's actually holding the RPGs."

Alice reinforced her request with a pleading stare, and looked annoyed when Anton simply replied, "noted," before he moved on. "Well, thank you team for an excellent briefing. Very helpful for my next meeting with the Home Office."

"Would you like me there?" I asked optimistically.

"No, Michael, that won't be necessary. It's best I keep you well away from all that nonsense right now. Things might change, though, and then I will most certainly want you right there alongside me."

I shrugged in disappointment.

"Boss?" John interrupted, "may I ask how Colin Murray explained not telling Commander Jackson about his previous negotiations with Donovan and Gudgeon?"

"You can, and it's because he was mistakenly trying to protect informant-confidentiality. Hence, he thought he couldn't tell the Commander about his earlier negotiations with Customs. Thankfully, he's now confirmed it was about the three deliveries in London and Kent."

John nodded at the news.

"Right, before we finish," Anton asked, "Mr H, what will your actions be for next week?"

"Boss, there are three. First, keep processing the data on the first Orange mobile to find out who it called before and after the Donovans."

"Okay, next?"

"We need to do the same once we get the data for the second one."

"Agreed."

"Third, we're now preparing for the big meeting with all the SIOs and Customs over at Thames House on Thursday."

"Mr H, we're going to need help with those first two actions, please," Alice said, her voice clearly intended to reinforce her previous request. "*I can't do it all on my own.*"

I was pleased she focused her stare on Anton as she spoke, and I backed her up saying, "Boss, we do need more resources. I can draw some from Corporate Services, but two more of Angela's analysts would be very helpful too. Another couple of detectives from SO11 would also be great."

"I get that, Michael. Let me see what I can arrange after my meeting at the Home Office. Right, thank you everyone, fantastic work. When can I expect the next update?"

"As soon as Alice maps the data, Boss," I replied. "One point I do need to flag is that we're basing all our assumptions on the data alone. Very soon, we'll need a surveillance team on the ground, and Eltham is looking like a good place to start."

"Noted too".

"I do have a fourth action, Boss, but due to resources it will have to wait."

"What's that?"

"We need to investigate the Donovans' finances to see how they're paying for all the weapons and Gudgeon's services."

"See if you can outsource it," Anton said curtly. "Alice, I want a hard copy of those pages from your chart, please. I hope this time they will convince the Home Office of Gudgeon's involvement in misleading Customs and the Home Secretary."

"Sure, I can do that right now. The good news is you only need Gudgeon's mobile. He's had no contact with the Donovans on either his home or office phones."

"Thank you, Alice, that is helpful to know. Michael, a quick word in my office, please. Otherwise, Alice, thank you, and you too John. And Mark, I know you didn't have a walk-on part this time but thank you nonetheless."

As Mark nodded in appreciation of being acknowledged, Anton stood up and left the room.

"Well done everyone," I added as I got up to leave too. "Great job Alice."

Walking into Anton's office, I asked "Boss?"

"Wow, Alice is bloody excellent."

"Yes, she is and I'm glad you've now experienced the 'Alice effect' too. She's quite an asset to the team."

"You've made huge progress, so I wanted to tell you that I'll find the extra resources you need."

"Thank you."

CHAPTER 19

Home Office Obfuscation

I heard Anton's heavy footsteps entering the corridor after he forcefully barged open the double doors in his customary style. I had just enough time to glance at my watch and note it was 1:30pm when he stormed into my office. Closing the door behind him, he very loudly exclaimed, "Bastards. Stupid fucking bastards!"

"Boss?" I asked in a mixture of sympathy and incredulity.

"Sorry, Michael, you're the first sane person I've met since leaving Queen Anne's Gate[28]. I just had to let it out."

Almost simultaneously, Brian Mills knocked and entered. "What's happening chaps?" His manner indicating both surprise and alarm.

"I've just come from a meeting with Commander Jackson, Colin Murray, NCIS and that wanker Home Office lawyer, Smedley. Like the Belgian airline, 'SABENA', Such A Bad Experience Never Again! Sorry, I just had to release my frustration."

"Well, from my office, I thought the worst for Michael. Can I help?"

"Yes, we need to see the Director. Smedley is being deliberately obstructive in what I sense is an orchestrated effort to protect the previous Home Secretary and his own superannuated reputation."

"Okay," Brian said, trying to show empathy without knowing the full facts.

"The Home Office seem to have very real concerns about Michael's Abonar investigation," Anton continued. "They can see it leading to some officials appearing in court to explain their actions, which they're desperate to avoid. We need a strategy urgently, Brian, for how we can work around them."

"Understood. I'll talk to the Director."

"So what happened?" I asked.

"Smedley won't authorise any activity on Gudgeon's mobile in case we breach what he calls 'client-lawyer confidentiality'."

---

28   Queen Anne's Gate: another name for the Home Office due to its address being in that street.

Angrily I replied, "but that's rubbish. Donovan's not awaiting trial. He's just serving out his sentence. How can there be anything legally confidential between him and Gudgeon to protect?"

"Exactly, there isn't. And it didn't matter how much NCIS explained their role as both guardian and gatekeeper, it was like Churchill talking to General De Gaulle, we got 'Non' every time. Smedley seems to want Donovan and his cronies to dump the RPGs on us. He's not interested in helping us find out how they plan to do so."

"Bastards indeed," Brian agreed.

"They won't even approve the monitoring of either the Donovan home number or the phone box nearby!"

"Why on earth not?" I asked, now even more angry. "They're pivotal to the investigation."

"Smedley argued these would capture calls between the family and their solicitor, which would also be subject to client-confidentiality."

"That's nonsense."

"I know Michael, but Smedley argued and, annoyingly, quite convincingly that since the firearms aspect of Abonar is now over, we don't yet have sufficient *current* data to justify it."

"So we need negotiations on the RPGs to now trigger those calls," Brian suggested.

"Yes, but the Home Secretary has just told Murray to say nothing more to Gudgeon for at least two months. He wants a plausible break to distance himself from his predecessor's actions.

"Sugar, bloody, damn. Two months!" I almost shouted. "We must maintain momentum."

"I know, but it's not happening," Anton replied, also sounding dejected.

"And we can expect the Home Office to sit it out hoping Abonar goes away," Brian added.

"But if we lose the RPGs, Brian, there'll be serious bloodshed out there once they fall into the wrong hands. That doesn't seem to concern Smedley at all, though. As you can tell, I'm bloody furious."

"Okay, Anton," Brian said nodding, "I'll get a meeting with the Director."

"Thank you. In the meantime, Michael, no change," Anton said forcefully. "Keep all your lines of enquiry running. Alright?"

"Yes, of course."

Anton called me an hour later to say the meeting with the Director was scheduled for 11am on Monday. I spent the rest of Friday afternoon working through a substantial pile of telephone data authorisation forms supplied by the team. Thankfully, Anton seemed only too happy to sign them.

CHAPTER 20

Week 3 – Under New Management

Monday, 12ᵗʰ May

Looking around the briefing room once more at the start of the week, I tried to gauge the team's energy levels.

"What news since Friday's briefing, please? John, let's begin with you."

"I've put a file together requesting '*Operational Travel*' for us both to meet the Belgian police at their Brussels HQ, and then Donald Manross at INTERPOL. If you're happy, would you put the file through Mr Baxter to approve and the Director to authorise."

"Yes, of course. When do you want to go?"

"Travel Section have reserved seats on the Eurostar for us next Monday afternoon. We go to Brussels first; stay overnight and meet the police on Tuesday morning. After that, we'll take the train to Lyon. We're meeting Donald Manross on Wednesday at INTERPOL. We get home on Thursday. Back in the office on Friday."

"Very good. Thanks for organising it. Mark, what have you got for us?"

"As you know from all the authorisations I left you on Friday, I'm keeping on top of the numbers Alice flags as potentially relevant."

"Thank you. I'm in a meeting with the Director at eleven today. I'm hoping Mr Baxter will confirm then that he's got the extra resources. I'll let you know what comes of that, and I'll take your travel file with me too, John."

They all nodded and murmured their approvals.

"Right, last but definitely not least, Alice, what do I need to know?"

"Too early really to give you anything new, Mr H," she said, giving me one of her soft smiles. "I'm just waiting on that data for the second Orange mobile."

"Okay, ask Pete to chase Orange for it. So, I'm off to the London Proof House tomorrow to check their deactivation records for our Abonar firearms. But, of course, our big event this week is the meeting at Thames House on Thursday. I'll be taking John with me to let you two keep up with your analysis. If there's nothing else, let's crack on."

At just before 11am, I took a seat in the Director's outer office waiting for the previous meeting to end. Moments later, DAC Fry, flung back the door with one hand and caught it with the other.

"Michael do come in," he said, and I was grateful his voice sounded encouraging.

Brian and Anton were sitting at the coffee table with another man. I had seen him before in the building but didn't know his name. DAC Fry sensed this, and helpfully said, "Michael, this is Detective Superintendent Derek Hamilton. He's recently joined the OCG on the fifth floor."

"Sir," I said, reaching across the table to shake his hand. I was surprised by its limpness, and he quickly pulled away from my much firmer grip. I judge people on their handshake, and my first impression of Derek was that his was a 'missing strength'; a term used by an early mentor of mine. He once told me, "*Never admit to having a weakness. You have only lesser strengths. Others can have 'missing strengths', but that's not something you should ever admit to either*". Derek's handshake was a weakness. Nevertheless, he was tall and slender and wore a tailored dark grey suit with a red tie and matching pocket handkerchief. The combination gave him a far more elegant look than many of our contemporaries. He also smelled heavily of cologne, which was distinct and almost overpowering. Despite all this refinement, there was a look of vulnerability about him, which he amplified through nervously picking at his right thumb. It suggested he recognised his own inadequacies in the company of the more experienced colleagues around the table. I tried not to let it rankle me that he was possibly the same age as me and had, therefore, been able to accelerate his promotions whereas mine had stalled.

"Michael, do sit," the DAC instructed, and I took up the last chair at the table. "We've decided to hand over operational leadership of Abonar to Derek and the OCG," he continued. "It's now for them to investigate and finish." He said it so fast I heard the words but had no time to adjust to their impact. My look of complete shock at unexpectedly losing Abonar to Derek caused DAC Fry to pause for a moment before continuing more gently.

"Well, as you know, the OCG acts as our executive arm to preserve the Branch's shadowy nature. You're still on the case Michael, of course. I want you alongside Derek running intelligence-development. Angela is also giving you two more analysts until the end of the month. Take whoever you can from Corporate Services to help DC Bryan with the legwork."

I felt crushed. My first major Scotland Yard investigation had been taken away just like that. I tried not to betray the huge sense of disappointment welling inside, so I managed a respectful nod as I said, "understood, Sir."

Derek then spoke, "I've been fully briefed on what you and your team have achieved so far. Extremely impressive piece of analysis."

Remaining gracious, I said, "thank you, they're a fantastic team."

"Yes, and I'm giving you DS Roger Rowlands from the OCG. He'll act as the bridge between our two floors. I'll bring him down and introduce us both to your team later in the week. Would Wednesday work for you?"

"Yes, it would," I replied courteously. "We have a daily catch-up at 9:30. May I know what you've agreed as the priorities and objectives for Abonar?"

DAC Fry interjected, "the same as before, Michael. We need you to identify who's supplying the firearms."

"Thank you, Sir," I said, noting he had deliberately not mentioned the RPGs.

"Yes, I don't want you to stop what you're doing," Derek added. "Once you've identified the supplier, we'll take over."

"Sir," I acknowledged respectfully while still feeling angry.

"Ask Anton here for anything you need from SO11," DAC Fry interrupted, "otherwise, day-to-day you'll report to Derek. We need you to finish your analysis before the end of the month. We'll then review it all and decide what direction to go in next."

"If I may, Sir, I know my timing's not great, but would you consider this request for operational travel for DC Bryan and myself? We need to go to Brussels and INTERPOL next week to follow up on recommendations from the Lab and the Security Service."

"Yes, of course. Give the file to Sam. Has Mr Baxter seen it yet?" DAC Fry asked.

"No Sir. Forgive me, I was hoping, probably rather clumsily, to get you both at the same time."

"No problem, Sir. I'll check it first for my approval," Anton said, grabbing the file; seeming slightly annoyed I hadn't briefed him before.

"Thank you very much," I said, clasping my hands as if seeking his forgiveness. "And Mr Fry," I continued, "dare I ask about the RPGs? What do you want us to do about that aspect of Abonar?"

"Ah, now that's where Derek and his OCG team will focus," he replied.

"Yes, and once I'm ready in a day or so," Derek added, "I'll want you to hand over everything that's relevant."

"Sir," I said, again respectfully, hoping my expression did not reveal my huge annoyance at his instruction.

"One more thing, Michael," DAC Fry added, "Commander Jackson will now deal directly with Derek."

"You're still our failsafe, though, Michael," Brian added quickly, catching my eye with a reassuring look. "We've agreed if the situation merits, such as the RPGs are on the road and there's a communication breakdown, Commander Jackson will call you instead."

"Very good Sir, he's got all my numbers."

"Any questions?" DAC Fry asked.

"No, Sir. Thank you, I'm grateful for your support. Happy to be still working on getting the Abonar gunrunners arrested."

"All very noble, Michael," Anton interrupted, "but arrests aren't always the best outcome. Sometimes we choose disruption instead. That way, we leave everyone guessing while we watch a criminal enterprise implode."

As I scanned Anton's face for any hint of what that meant for Abonar, DAC Fry interrupted, "Thank you, Michael."

His tone clearly meant my presence was no longer required. I took it as my cue to leave.

CHAPTER 21

The London Proof House

Tuesday, 13th May

I surfaced from the London Underground at Aldgate East station and made the short walk along the Commercial Road to the London Proof House. This is home to both the Worshipful Company of Gunmakers and the Proof Master. Since 1637, Proof House staff have performed the task of test-firing to 'proof' the barrels and actions of every firearm manufactured in this country plus those imported from others that don't have a similar process, such as the USA. Their role is to ensure all guns are safe to use. They also inspect firearms deactivated by gunsmiths to certify that these meet the current standard, so they are no longer capable of firing a bullet and prevent reactivation. In 1675, the Proof House moved from its original location within the City of London to its new address just outside in Whitechapel. This was, in effect, a banishment resulting from an explosion in the powder store in 1649. As Masters of the Gunmakers' Company often joke, *"At least we only blew a hole in the city wall; in 1666 the Bakers burnt the whole place down"*.

I rang the doorbell and gave my name over the intercom. The electronic lock clicked and, pushing the heavy door, I entered this historically important but totally unassuming building. Most passers-by have no knowledge of the business that goes on inside. Ahead of their issue to the British military, police forces, and sport shooters, thousands of firearms take this same route across the pavement in and out of the building.

I was greeted by a smartly dressed man, "welcome, I'm Bob Pitcher, the Proof Master. Come through to my office and you can show me those photos you mentioned on the phone."

The Proof House is surprisingly compact for the volume of work done there. Bob navigated a path between various boxes and crates, each filled with assorted handguns and longarms. His office was modest in size; most of it taken up by an antique mahogany desk and chair. Looking around the walls and bookshelves, I noted the trappings of his work that included an assortment of antique firearms and memorabilia. Bob cleared a space on his busy desk to allow me to spread out the photograph albums, which I opened at the pages for the Abonar MAC10s and Chinese M20s.

"Okay, yes," Bob announced authoritatively, "this area of welding is exactly where we stamp our deactivation mark."

"Can you show me what one looks like?"

"Sure, I have a deactivated Webley revolver here for you," he said, passing it across along with a small magnifying glass and pointing to the mark on the right side of the frame. I noted its square shape was 5mm across. The impact of the stamp had left a bare metal impression of the letters 'DA' for *Deactivated* above the stylised shape of a scimitar, and below that the last two numbers for the year of certification.

"Thank you, that's most helpful," I told him as I passed the items back.

Putting them down, Bob added, "and my Proof Assistants make a corresponding entry in the annual register listing the make, model and serial number and who submitted it plus our deactivation certificate number."

"Why would someone want to remove your proof mark?" I asked.

"To me, it means one of two things: either the gun's been reactivated, and they know we can use that mark to trace it back to our register and a potential supplier..."

"Okay," I interrupted, "or...?"

"Someone's trying to trick you into believing another gunsmith has reactivated it. The extra weld is just a red herring, though, as we've not stamped our mark, because the gun hasn't really been deactivated and submitted to us."

"Yes, that's what Marco, the scientist at the Lab, was kind of suggesting too."

"Which indicates whoever is supplying them is doing so from their stocks of live-firing ones, and they know about deactivation marks."

"Hmm, it certainly appears so."

"And, of course, I can't confirm either way for you, because whoever did this welded over everything we need to check our registers."

I nodded in acknowledgement before asking, "so how many of these deactivated SF Firearms' MAC-10s did Perkins submit?"

"He sent the last of them in late 1995. I checked our records, as you asked, and found we'd marked and certified ninety-five for him in total."

Noting all his points in my daybook, I then showed Bob the rest of the photographs.

"Oh yes, we get all these quite regularly." Again he spoke with obvious authority on the subject. "After Desert Storm, the US Army dumped thousands on the military surplus market. That's because they had supplied the Iraqis with their latest US-made Berettas instead."

"Yes, so I understand, but are you seeing them now as live-firing for proof-testing or certification as deactivated?"

"Only the latter."

"Who's submitting them?"

"Well, you're most welcome to check the registers. You'll find we deal with at least a dozen businesses on a regular basis. Between them, they must have sent us around ten thousand."

"Thank you. Are you able to log me in to your system so I can make a start?"

"I can do better than that," Bob said, laughing as he reached down a set of thick paper registers. "You can simply thumb your way through these."

"Oh, still steam-driven," I commented in an attempt at humour whilst realising the amount of manual work ahead of me.

"Yes, I'm afraid so. I recommend you don't go back beyond 1995, otherwise you'll be here long enough to become part of the furniture. I'm sorry I can't spare anyone to help. You're welcome to use the photocopier if you want to take anything away."

"Thank you," I said, now daunted by the task.

"Well I'll pop back in an hour or so. Good luck."

After two hours, Bob returned to reclaim his office holding a mug of tea for me. Looking at the detailed notes I had made in my daybook, he asked, "did you find something useful?"

"Yes, and I've taken copies of every page that lists our types of Abonar guns too, thank you."

"Very good. I'm glad we could help. What will you do with it all?"

"I'll create a spreadsheet and give it to my team to work through hoping something here will match our other intelligence."

Bob showed me out of the building, and I took the Underground back to St James's Park station, and my office. I spent the rest of the afternoon putting together the spreadsheet on my computer and then copied it to disc for John and Alice to process the next day.

I got home in time to read a bedtime story to my daughter. This was something very special for us both. Sadly, the 'exigencies of duty' meant I did not get the chance to do it often enough. When I saw Rebecca struggling to stay awake, I tucked her in and turned out the light. I left the bedroom door ajar and the landing light on outside. She liked the reassurance of seeing it on and knowing her parents were still up and about until we too went to bed.

CHAPTER 22

Kidnap

Wednesday, 14th May

It felt like I had been in bed only a few minutes when my pager sounded with its irrepressible electronic ping. Grabbing it from the bedside table, I silenced the alarm and read the screen. The disapproving noises coming from Olivia on the other side of the bed warned me I needed to leave the room. Reaching for my mobile, I headed downstairs to the lounge and dialled the number given to call the Duty SIO in the OCG.

"Thanks for calling me back so promptly." I immediately recognised the Welsh lilt in the voice of Detective Superintendent Roy Richards. "We've got a kidnap. I need you to open Central 500 and call out your team. How quickly can you get in?"

"Thirty minutes with a fast-car-run."

"Good. I'm on my way in too."

Next, I dialled the number for the Information Room Chief Inspector to arrange transport. Within minutes, I was up, dressed, and sat in the back of a double-crewed police traffic car.

"To the Yard, Sir?" the driver enquired.

"Thank you, yes. I don't wish to appear rude, guys, but I'm just going to sit here and make a few calls to mobilise my team."

On the journey in, I tried not to dwell on Olivia's remarks as I left the house. Angrily she had said, "off to see your mistress again, are you?"

"Of course not. It's another kidnap," I replied, hoping the softness in my voice would sooth her unfounded suspicions. "Sorry to wake you, but I've got to go," I added in a whisper so as not to rouse Rebecca.

"Yeah, sure," Olivia answered unconvinced. I chose not to respond. I had learned that nothing I said would help and, in any event, she would be determined to have the last word.

The driver navigated his way effortlessly through the minimal night-time traffic. Occasionally he used the siren to complement the blue lights. Roy called me en route to give the information I needed to turn out my contacts in the CSPs and get them to trace, track, and monitor various mobile phones.

I jogged my way into NSY and along the corridor to Central 500. Pushing the buttons to unlock the door, I reached into the darkness for the light switches to my right and turned them on. Moving from desk to desk, I powered up all the computers and then the bank of flat screen televisions linked to the London-wide traffic camera system.

Sitting in the chair at the desk designated for the 'Green Commander' (Green) I called Roy. "Central 500 is open, Sir. I'm just waiting for my team and yours to join me. The victim's and hostage's mobile numbers are now on live monitoring. I'll give you an update as soon as I have one."

"Thank you. I'm still on my way from home. My deputy, DI Martin Hampton, is closer and should be coming through the door any minute."

I paged the on-call SO11 Negotiator, known as the 'Red Commander' (Red), inviting him to call me when ready. Tonight, it was DCI Dave Woodfield. He and his DS had set up the 'Red Centre[29]' in the house the female hostage had been taken from by the kidnappers. Her mother was now negotiating with them by phone, so was termed the 'victim[30]'. Dave's job was to covertly coach her with what to say in alignment with the SIO's strategy. His DS's role was to evidentially record all the telephone conversations between the victim and kidnappers.

Dave called me back and, as he briefed me, I typed all the information to the computer. For additional security, we used a standalone system known as 'CLIO'. This generated the log for each investigation run from Central 500. Only staff working in the room had access. It created a time and date stamped record for every entry that each team member made, which everyone else could then read as the operation progressed. From an earlier job, the whiteboard opposite still showed our kidnap protocol: '*The safety of the hostage and courier[31] are paramount, everything else is secondary*'. SO11 and the OCG held the enviable record of having safely rescued every hostage in our joint kidnap investigations. Once again, we sought to maintain it.

---

29 Red Centre: term used for wherever the police establish their hub for covertly coaching those who are communicating with the hostage-takers.
30 Victim: term for the person negotiating with the hostage-takers (coached covertly by the police), who may also be the one expected to pay the ransom to secure the hostage's release.
31 Courier: term for whoever delivers the ransom.

The two banks of desks filled quickly. DI Harry Somers, the 'Blue Commander' (Blue), sat next to me. He was in charge of the SO11 Surveillance Teams. Beyond, the OCG team took up the remaining three desks in the front row. Along the back, Inspector Vic Edmonds, had taken the seat at the end closest to me reserved for the SO19 Specialist Firearms Tactical Adviser. Sitting at the others was a mix of my own staff, including Beverly from the TIU. My principal responsibilities as Green were to manage the Covert Operations Room and act as the communications bridge between Central 500 and Red.

Shortly after 1:30am, Roy briefed us on the fast-moving kidnap.

"The hostage is a nineteen-year-old woman. The victim is her mother. Red is with her at the home address in Battersea. We have regular proof of life calls. Green, what can you tell us about the phones they're using?"

"Okay," I began in the required matter-of-fact manner Roy preferred, "so the kidnappers are letting the hostage use her mobile to call the victim. I've set up live monitoring, so we'll know if she's making any other calls. Cellsite puts the mobile in Brixton. It hasn't moved the whole time, which suggests the stronghold is in a building."

"Okay, good," Roy commented, while nodding at me to continue.

"Toscas is on another job for SO13 outside London, so we're relying entirely on the location data *One2One*[32] is getting from their network. It's not going to give us any more granularity than the block of streets in Brixton where they've already tracked the mobile to. I've added to CLIO the street names around the boundary, so you can all see the neighbourhood where we'll find our hostage."

"Thanks. Now what's the latest from Red?" Roy asked.

"The kidnappers want £10,000 for the hostage's release." I then quickly checked the CLIO screen to confirm my information before continuing, "the victim thinks it's all about a bad drugs debt. Red has coached her into negotiating an interim payment of £1,000 to show goodwill. She doesn't have access to more cash until her bank opens."

"Okay, good," Roy said in his customary calm manner.

"Red says from all her screaming, the kidnappers are torturing the hostage with increasing violence."

Any chatter in the room stopped when I said this. Continuing, I told Roy, "the kidnappers have agreed to meet the victim and collect the first instalment.

---

32 OnetoOne: another of the mobile CSPs at that time.

147

But they've refused to bring the hostage. The meet will be in a cab office in Clapham at 02:30. That's it for now, Boss."

"Thank you, Green. Right, everyone, a heads-up," Roy announced loudly. "Usual protocol applies: the safety of the hostage and our courier are paramount. Understood?"

The room echoed with, "Yes Boss,"

"Okay, good. My objective is for OCG and SO11 Surveillance to shadow the victim to the cab office." Roy then looked at Harry, "Blue, I want your team to then follow whoever the kidnappers send as their runner to collect the cash. I need you to stick to them like glue in the hope he leads us to the Brixton stronghold."

"Boss," Harry said in instant acknowledgement.

Turning to Vic at the back of the room, Roy told him, "and once we've got an address, I want you to brief me on the hostage-rescue."

"Yes Boss, I'll be here waiting," Vic replied.

"Okay, good, and that's likely to be sometime after 03:00. That's the plan. Anyone with something useful to add?" he paused momentarily. "No? Okay, good. You know my objective, now let's make it happen."

Roy came over to stand between Harry and me. I had learned this was his preferred spot in the room even though as SIO he had an adjoining office.

"Blue, what's the current status of your teams?" he asked.

"I've got one positioned in and around the Brixton streets identified by the hostage's mobile signal. I've split another, with one section outside the victim's 'H-A[33]' waiting for her to move, and the other around the cab office. Thankfully, it's got a big glass window."

"Good. Green, make sure Red tells the victim to sit in that window. We want to be able to see everything that goes on in there; especially the handover."

"Done," I said as I sent a text message to Red to call me. He did so almost immediately, and I passed on the instruction before updating CLIO.

Dave then warned me, "the kidnappers called back. I got a sense the gofer they're sending to the pay-off won't be anyone from the stronghold. There's a real risk when surveillance follow him afterwards that he won't then lead them to the hostage."

"Damn," I said, "I better warn Harry."

"Yes, but let him and the Boss know I've put in a contingency. I got the victim to convince the kidnappers to let her also pass on an item of cheap

---

33   H-A: abbreviation for home address.

jewellery of sentimental value to her daughter. It's a necklace. He's agreed to their gofer giving it to her tonight."

"Great idea," I told him in admiration at his quick-thinking.

"Thanks, it was touch and go for a moment, but our victim can be bloody persuasive. She told the kidnapper, "*One goodwill gesture on her part deserved one from him*". Fingers crossed it works!"

"Yes, indeed. Keep me informed, and I'll add all this to CLIO."

Looking over my shoulder at the update, Roy reacted saying to Harry, "Blue, would you join us, please?"

The three of us then relocated to the small SIO's office in the corner of the room.

"How do we capitalise on Red's contingency?" Roy asked. "I want to exploit this meeting between our victim and their runner to then follow him to the stronghold and rescue the hostage. I've read the logs. The kidnappers are putting the girl through hell. I'm convinced they'll kill her if either we can't get to her first or our victim can't pay in full."

"From the technical side," I advised, "we'll know from the surveillance team's position when their runner enters the block of Brixton streets where cellsite has placed the stronghold."

"Perfect. So Blue, what can you offer?"

"I recommend we get the victim to wrap the necklace in something bright that my teams will see being handed over. Make it big enough to bulge in a pocket too, so we can be sure he's got it and know when he hasn't once he's passed it on."

"Michael, brief Red. Blue, prepare your team. I'll get Vic warmed up to this too."

I sent Dave another text to call me and, again, he replied immediately. I passed on Harry's instruction, and he then helped the victim wrap the necklace in several orange plastic bags.

Central 500 was now on silent running except for Harry, who was summarising for everyone the transmissions he was listening to over his headset on the surveillance team's radio channel. Almost simultaneously, he typed updates to the log. The tension in the room was amplified by everyone's intense stares at their screens whenever someone added some new piece of complementary intelligence. The hostage's wellbeing, if not her life, now depended on the success of our tactics.

"Okay, everyone, heads-up," Harry called out, "we have the victim under our control sitting in the cab office window."

"A white male is now outside looking in... Okay, he's inside... He's now sat with our victim, so let's make him 'Subject One'. Standby."

Harry typed furiously on his keyboard to add the description of Subject One for us all to read and Vic to pass on to his team.

"Victim has passed him the envelope with the cash... She's now handing over the orange package... Okay, Subject One is now out... The victim's out too and walking away. Standby."

The room remained silent for a minute before Harry spoke again.

"Okay, the victim isn't being followed, so the OCG can pick her up and take her back to the Red Centre. Standby everyone for an update on Subject One."

Harry switched on the speakers in the ceiling so we could all now listen to the surveillance team's radio commentary. The room remained hushed as the detectives tailed Subject One on foot through the streets of Clapham and into Brixton. Eventually, he stopped outside a Victorian terraced house and looked around to check if he had been followed. Not seeing anyone to concern him, he walked up the steps from pavement level and pushed the doorbell for one of the six flats. A man poked his head out of a first-floor window and called down. Moments later, someone turned on the communal hallway lights before the same man from upstairs opened the front door.

Harry added the address to the log.

"It's not in our block of streets for the stronghold," I called out as I too updated CLIO.

Roy turned to Vic, "get working on a plan to crash through that door, please."

"On it already," he replied instantly.

"Subject One is now inside the house," a voice over the radio said. "It's a temporary loss. Standby for a description of Subject Two."

The surveillance officer gave as detailed a description as time would allow her, which Harry added to the log.

"No change, no change. Subjects One and Two are still in the hallway."

"No change, no change," broke the silence a minute later.

"No change, no change," another minute later.

The words, "Subject One is out, out," could not have come sooner. It had been an agonising wait for him to reappear on the street. "He's still got the package," was the confirmation we all wanted to hear too.

Another sporadic commentary ensued until Subject One stopped outside another three-storey Victorian terraced house several streets away. Harry quickly added the Brixton address to the log.

"It's inside our target block," I called out, while also typing my update.

Again, Roy checked my screen.

"Subject One is going down into the basement area, standby," the voice on the radio advised.

A surveillance officer on a bicycle stopped at the railings above and looked down long enough to take in what was happening at the front door of the flat below.

"2-4-6, permission?"

"2-4-6 go."

"Subject One has passed the package to another male who answered the door. Description to follow. Standby."

As the surveillance officer turned around on his bicycle to watch the gate, he suddenly added, "Subject One out, out and away north on foot again."

"Blue," Roy instructed, "keep Subject One under surveillance. I'll get the OCG to join them and make the arrest. They won't approach until you say he's sufficiently far away from the stronghold?"

"Sure, I'll let the Team Leader know."

The man was so focused on the money he had just earned, he was oblivious to the two four-door saloon cars that drew up slowly alongside him. His first realisation of danger was when two heavily built men grabbed him by the arms whilst tripping him up, causing him to fall. Moments later, he was handcuffed and being driven away in the back of what he now realised was an unmarked police car. A cheer went up in the room as this was relayed over the radio.

"Vic, over to you," Roy announced, "rescue my hostage first, then do Subject Two's address."

"In progress," Vic said with his telephone headset on and already giving instructions to his teams.

Shortly before 4am, Central 500 hushed again. A surveillance team member kept his microphone open to relay events to us live. Neighbours in the Brixton street awoke to the sounds we also heard as three 'Hatton Rounds[34]' blasted the basement front door from its hinges and then the lock. A second later, the green canister of a stun grenade sailed from the SFO's hand, with its

---

34 Hatton Round: 12-gauge solid metal slug fired from a shotgun for effective entry through doors and other barriers.

fly-off lever spiralling away with an audible 'ting'. It had a one-second delay. Next, we heard six loud bangs as it detonated. For those in the stronghold, the accompanying bright flashes and concussive shock waves completely disorientated them.

Shouts of, "Armed police. Armed police," immediately followed as the six-strong team burst in. Then we heard the most important words as one officer shouted out that he had found the hostage.

"We're the police. We've got you. You're safe now. You're safe. It's okay."

Moments later, Vic announced, "Mr Richards, my Team Leader says the building is secure. He'd like your officers to come forward, please. The hostage is safe but a little bruised. Nothing life-threatening. She'll need to go to St Thomas's for a check-up, though. Three male suspects detained. No shots fired other than the Hatton Rounds."

The room erupted with cheers. I picked up the phone and called Dave.

"Hostage safe, mate. The hostage is safe," I told him. "A few bruises, but she's alright. The OCG will take her to St Thomas's Hospital for a check-up."

I listened as he then told the mother. She let loose a mix of emotions in screams of joy and wails of overwhelming tears. It filled me with great pride at what we had achieved in only a few hours. As a parent, this moment always had a profound effect on me too, and I often had to hold back tears. For the hostage and her family, it was a very different experience, potentially, with lifelong consequences and trauma.

Thirty minutes later, Vic's team used the same decisive effects at the first address Subject One had visited to now arrest Subject Two.

"Okay, good," Roy announced on hearing the news. "No loose ends. Just how I like it. Good job everyone, thank you. For those who still can, go home."

Vic came over to my desk, "I'll say good night but before I go, I thought you'd like to know the teams found handguns and ammunition at both addresses. OCG have them now. I expect they'll bring them back here later."

Turning off the lights in Central 500, I checked my watch. It was nearly 6am. I unlocked my office and moved the chairs to create a makeshift bed. There was no point in trying to get home and back on public transport. That would take more than two hours. I had become used to this and kept a change of clothing, wash kit and razor in my wardrobe for such occasions.

CHAPTER 23

The New Order

I woke at around 8:30am to the increasing thuds of footsteps along the corridor outside my office. Yawning, I moved to my desk to phone home. From experience, I knew Olivia would still be annoyed at my being called out in the middle of the night. We had first met when she rushed up to the front desk at Shepherds Bush Police Station to report chasing two men she'd discovered trying to steal a neighbour's car. I was the Duty Inspector and left my office to find out who was shouting so excitedly at my staff. I got Olivia to explain enough of what had happened for me to then quickly radio the descriptions to patrolling officers, and a short while later they arrested both men. I then took her through to my office and arranged for tea and a '*KitKat*' to help calm her down.

I was immediately smitten by Olivia's youthful beauty. She was twenty-four; I was six years older. I must have made an impression on her too, because the next day she left a message inviting me for dinner. A year later, we had a beautiful daughter, Rebecca. Her birth affected me deeply. Becoming a father only strengthened everything I felt about the preciousness of life. It also gave me extra resolve to protect people from harm. Joining SO11 and being part of the renowned '*Kidnap Team*' made me incredibly proud each time we did just that by rescuing another hostage.

I tried to find a work-life balance, but the nature of my duties investigating serious crime made it difficult. Catching kidnappers and gunrunners who gave no consideration to their victims meant my personal life sometimes took second place: what we in SO11 called the '*exigencies of duty*'.

As the previous night's events illustrated, very often we had just hours to prevent a murder. Olivia was, however, losing patience with these frequent interruptions. She was also incurably jealous, despite my never giving her grounds to be so. It had not helped that at a '*Senior Officers' Dining Club*' dinner we attended shortly after I joined the Branch one of the other wives gave Olivia an unhelpful warning. She told her, *"You'll have to get used to it darling. They'll tell you they've been out all night on a kidnap, but for all you know they've been shagging some tart"*. Sadly, Olivia never forgot that, and my frequent absences only fuelled her suspicions.

I was desperate to make our marriage work, hoping she would finally accept the nature of my job and that I was a faithful husband. But I also had to prove my worth in SO11 to build a successful career now as a detective and finally earn promotion to DCI. Consequently I was exhausted from having to fight battles both at work and on the home front. I wanted to come home to a sanctuary from the rigours of my job, but the support just wasn't there anymore from Olivia. For our daughter's sake, I tried not to let her see how her mother's unfounded suspicions were tearing us apart. So, whenever I could, I got home in time to read her a bedtime story. Weekends were precious but could also be interrupted.

Unless you have experienced the intensity of being permanently on-call in any profession, it can be hard to understand what drives us. For my part, it was the thrill of disrupting serious criminals and bringing justice to their victims. In many ways, though, the intensity of SO11 operations was now compensating for a steadily imploding marriage.

"Hey Olivia, how are you?" I said over the phone as she answered, "I'm sorry about disturbing you this morning."

"So, where did you sleep?" she asked, her voice laden with distrust.

"I got a couple of hours in my office."

"Likely story," she huffed in disbelief.

"Don't be like that, we had a kidnap," I said, trying to be gently persuasive.

"Or you've been shagging some tart," she countered acidly.

"That's not true, and you know it. I love you," I said, desperately wanting her to hear the genuine strength of feeling in my voice.

The tone of her "yeah?" in response told me she didn't want to listen.

"I'm sorry, but you knew how I was when you married me. This is my job. It's what I do. We just rescued a young woman and got her safely back to her mother. Imagine if that had been Rebecca. Surely, you'd want me to do the same for her."

"Yeah, well I've now got to get Rebecca to nursery," and with that, she hung up. I sat for a moment with the dial tone still buzzing in my ear. Once again, I was disheartened at my failure to convince her that these *'exigencies of duty'* were very much a critical part of both our lives.

Not wishing to dwell on the call home, I grabbed my wash kit and razor and went into the fourth-floor toilets to freshen up. The only shower facilities available below the rank of Assistant Commissioner, who each had en suite bathrooms, were in the gym on the ground floor. Right now it would be filled with sweaty colleagues who had just cycled or jogged into work, and I didn't have the appetite for such an encounter. Thankfully, the facilities on our floor were enough. I had learned to function after very little sleep and got myself ready for the daily catch-up with the team. The overnight kidnap was typical of how all the senior officers in SO11 were expected to juggle multiple responsibilities in addition to keeping on top of our day-jobs and, for me, also running Abonar.

My desk phone rang. It was Derek to confirm he and DS Rowlands would join us at 9:30am.

As I walked along the corridor, John, Alice, and Mark were already going into the Fordham Suite. They had been joined by the two other analysts, Emily and Natasha, and I caught them up before the door closed.

"Very quickly," I told them, "we've got two guests joining us from the OCG. Derek Hamilton, a Detective Superintendent, and his bag-carrier, DS Roger Rowlands. I'll let them explain their roles. If you don't mind, we'll hang on until they get here before we start."

"Oh, does that mean reinforcements?" John asked.

"Kind of. Oh, and John, there was a kidnap last night. The OCG recovered some handguns with ammunition. Can you get a look at them and check whether they're connected to Abonar?"

"Yes, of course."

Almost immediately, Derek knocked and entered with DS Rowlands. I spent a moment introducing everyone before he took over. I was amused to see Alice sniffing the air, having noticed the heavy scent of Derek's cologne.

"Great to meet you all. I'm responsible for serious crime investigations with the potential to embarrass government," he began. "Roger here is my go-to man. He's hugely experienced in major crime investigations, so you'll find him a great asset on your team."

For reasons I don't remember, I had deliberately left it to Derek to break the news of a change in Abonar's leadership. Hence, I quite understood the team's looks of confusion. Derek noticed them too and continued cautiously saying, "Abonar has progressed rapidly thanks to your hard efforts. As a result, we're able to move from an SO11-led intelligence gathering exercise to a live OCG operation. Consequently, DAC Fry has asked me to take over."

Now the looks on my team's faces turned to shock, and Derek saw them too.

"As you know, we prefer to keep SO11 separate from arrests and prosecutions," he asserted, trying not to sound overly defensive. "That allows the Directorate to continue operating in the shadows. It also protects the covert techniques you're using that we'd rather not expose in court."

He looked around their expressions and realised nothing he had said so far allayed any of their concerns. My team also stared at me to judge my reaction. I remained attentive and indicated by pointing at Derek that they do the same.

"I've asked Roger to work with you now full-time," Derek said, trying again to placate them. "His focus will be on converting, where possible, your intelligence into evidence we can use without betraying your methodologies. As and when we get to the point of making arrests, I'll bring in more resources from the OCG to work with you. Any questions?"

John spoke first, "so will tomorrow's meeting with the SIOs still go ahead at Thames House?"

"Yes, it will. I understand it's to further the reactive investigation into who supplied the Abonar firearms. My focus is the proactive operation to seize the RPGs, so I don't need to be there. Michael will still lead it. DS Rowlands will be there too, but only to observe on my behalf."

"And will we still be able to go to Brussels and Lyon next week?" John then asked.

"Yes, of course. I see those lines of enquiry as essential to our intelligence gathering."

"Mr. Hamilton," I asked, "I hold this meeting every morning. Will you be leading it from now on?"

"No. I'll pop in perhaps once a week. I'll take over when you tell me you're ready for us to start making arrests."

"And the RPGs?" I asked.

"I'm taking it all upstairs," he replied bluntly.

The sudden intake of breath from my team as they expressed their surprise was very audible.

Wanting to avoid any upset between our new leader and the team on the first occasion they met, I interjected, "okay, Alice and John, maybe now is a good time for you to walk us through your latest findings?"

"Certainly Mr H," Alice said with a hint of petulance in her voice. "There are only two new things of note. First, an interesting development. GMP believe Donovan has an associate living in Eltham. This came up in their original drugs investigation. Sadly, like us, all they had were calls from TKs in the area, so no name or address yet."

"Damn. And the second?"

"The calls to purchase the three cars for Whitechapel, Plaistow and Gravesend were all made from one TK in Eltham High Street."

"Okay, that reinforces our need to deploy surveillance there once we've got a clear target for them to follow."

"I drive through Eltham on my way into work every day," Roger followed up helpfully. "I'll make a detour and pop into the local nick and find out what they know."

"I can let you have the e-Fits we've got for the three purchasers of the cars," John added. "The only common denominators are they each wore grey hoodies and were white men in their 20s. Whilst it's likely they're all the same person, the E-fits don't offer enough similarities to confirm that."

"Thank you," Roger replied, and I was pleased with this promising indication of collaboration.

"Yes, but whatever Roger finds must come to me first," Derek interrupted, "and I'll then decide whether you need it too. Okay?"

"Boss," Roger responded, looking at me too for a similar positive reaction. I gave a shrug in recognition of the demarcation line Derek had now so clearly drawn.

Quickly, I changed the subject by asking Alice, "is there anything else?"

"No, that's it for now. I'm still processing the data for the two Orange mobiles," and she then tried one of her persuasively demure looks on Derek but, troublingly for her, he ignored it.

"I'd like everything about them to come to me," was his cold reaction. "I'll be taking Emily and Natasha upstairs to work on this from now on, so please hand over to them all the relevant data."

"Mr Hamilton," I interjected, "we also need that data to check for patterns and links to what we've mapped so far. The calls made and received on the first Orange mobile are critical to identifying who then supplied the firearms."

"Okay, take a copy for the first mobile for Alice to work on. I want Emily and Natasha to build me a separate i2 chart using all you've learned about the offer of RPGs. And I want everything about Donovan, Gudgeon and Murray in terms of the RPG negotiations deleted completely from your chart. Understood?"

Looking around at Alice, John, and Mark, I could tell they were not at ease. I decided to pick this up with them privately later.

"Okay, Sir, we'll make that work," I said respectfully. "If I may, Mr Hamilton, I'd now like to go over the purpose and agenda for tomorrow's meeting."

"Yes, carry on."

"Thank you. So, the purpose is to enable everyone to meet and compare notes on the firearms they've recovered. This will be the first time they've all met. Our objective is to find the common links to help identify the source of supply."

"Will you mention Donovan?" Derek asked hurriedly.

"No. Mentioning him won't get us get very far. We know that trade is now over, and it was a scam. The end-user was, of course, the Home Secretary. I don't want to turn this into a beat-up for Customs. My focus will be on identifying the links between the Manchester and London gangs who are also being armed with the Abonar MAC-10s and handguns."

"Good. And what about the RPGs?" Derek asked impatiently, nervously picking at his thumb.

"No, not a word. For reasons of operational security, we won't be discussing them."

"Good."

"My principal hope is the people MI5 are bringing along will provide the breakthrough we need."

After a pause Derek said, "well, if there's nothing else, I'd like Michael to wait behind with Roger. Good to meet the rest of you. Emily and Natasha, I've arranged desks for you upstairs in the OCG Main Office. If you'd like to collect the data from Alice, I'll be up to brief you shortly."

Once the others left the room, Derek continued. "Let me explain my rationale for how I'm going to run Abonar from now on," he said, his tone deliberately asserting his authority over me. "I've been brought in, principally, to develop the operation to recover the RPGs. For me, identifying the supply chain for the firearms is secondary."

I felt unable to do much more than nod in recognition of his different priorities to mine.

"Now Roger's job is to be an extra pair of hands for you. He's got the skills and experience you don't otherwise have on your team."

"I'm grateful, but my team have clearly demonstrated their abilities."

"Yes, but none of them has any real experience of serious organised crime. I understand you're learning on the job too as a 'Branch Detective'." I felt the sting in his words and his next comment only compounded it. "I know it's galling having me step in and take over your job, but that's how it is. It's also how we all fit into the established chain of command."

Begrudgingly I nodded, accepting I sat two ranks lower down it than him.

"Look, your bosses, mine on the fifth, and above on the eighth all want to make sure we get these RPGs. The Commissioner doesn't want anyone blaming Scotland Yard for whatever political fallout might follow if we don't. Hence, he wants a top team of experienced detectives. You've already proved your worth, which is why the DAC wants you running the firearms strand of Abonar until we reach the arrest phase. Then I will take over. Clear?"

"Yes Sir."

"Also, you'll appreciate we might not invite you to certain meetings even though you've developed the intelligence. Therefore, your job is to keep me very well briefed."

"Sir."

"Good. As Anton hinted, we may choose a different outcome. That's another reason for keeping a firewall between what you and I are doing. I'm now running Abonar as two parallel strands that may never meet. Upstairs, my focus is on the strategy and tactics to recover those RPGs. Downstairs, yours is on identifying for me the source of the Abonar firearms and their supply network. Clear?"

"Perfectly." I then turned to Roger to ask him, "since we'll be working together, I expect you'd like to say something about this arrangement too?"

"Thank you, yes. I'd like you to see me as your wingman." His voice sounded comforting after the abruptness of Derek's. "My job is twofold, Guv: one, advise Mr Hamilton on the potential to make arrests, and two, give you the benefit of my experience. My forte is covert investigations into serious organised crime gangs. As Mr Hamilton said, I'm here to fill a gap in your team's capabilities. Please see me as a bit of a mentor too if that's okay with you."

"Of course, having you alongside will be helpful. Thank you. However, DC John Bryan remains my Number Two on the firearms job. I'm sure you won't have a problem with that. He's a recognised expert in this specialist field. Okay?"

"Yes, and I won't intrude into your leadership of the team. In fact, I'm sure I'll learn a thing or two. I'm going for promotion this year, so this will be useful preparation."

Sensing Derek wanted to finish the meeting, I said to him, "If we're done Sir, I'd like to hold on to Roger to go through what we've identified so far."

"Yes, carry on."

At that, he got up and left. Roger and I then spent the rest of the morning reviewing our lines of enquiry. It was helpful to have his fresh perspective. He was a career detective, having done more than 15 years in the CID, and much of that in SO. Now in his early 40s and still a DS, I understood why he wanted promotion to gain a greater leadership role. He wore thick black rimmed glasses that gave him an earnest look. They added to the sense of gravitas I felt he wanted to convey by way of confirmation that he was a safe pair of hands who could also be trusted with greater responsibilities through higher rank.

By lunchtime, we were done. In one way I was grateful he had not found any gaps in our investigation. In another, I had hoped he might have an epiphany and find something monumental we had missed, but he didn't. Our meeting at Thames House was, therefore, going to be critical.

John knocked as Roger and I finished.

"Guv, thought you'd like to know, I've seen the two handguns OCG recovered from the Brixton kidnap. They're two of the Colt Police Positive revolvers with that refinishing mark Marco and Hamish showed us."

"Interesting, were they loaded?"

"Yes, standard '*38 Special*'. Oh and there were five of our blue tipped 9mm bullets too. Looks like they've had access to one of our Abonar MAC-10s, but it wasn't recovered. Maybe it's another of those 'dial-a-guns' the Lab thinks are going round."

"What's that about?" Roger asked.

"'Op Fordyce'" John replied. "Marco at the Lab is analysing every shooting in London. So far, he's looked at thirty-four involving a mix of fourteen guns, which suggests two things. One, there aren't as many guns out there as people might think and, two, given the spread of where they've been used, someone must be hiring them out, hence dial-a-gun."

CHAPTER 24

The Thames House Meeting

Thursday, 15ᵗʰ May

The room Hamish chose for our meeting at Thames House was perfect for the impact I wanted. The dark oak panelled walls emanated the seriousness of the business done in that space. I needed everyone to have a sense of awe upon entering. From its upper floor vantage point overlooking the River Thames, the large windows offered magnificent views across to Lambeth Palace. The centre of the room was dominated by an impressive mahogany boardroom table that could seat twenty. It was complemented by chairs in the same wood around it. There were half-a-dozen more for observers against the back wall opposite the door. A similar but smaller rectangular table took up the space opposite the windows. This was set with the refreshments for each delegate to pour from assorted dispensers. Hamish had also laid on biscuits that came in individual packets of three offering the usual Custard Creams, Digestives and Bourbons.

The room filled gradually. I stood with Hamish at the door to greet everyone. Most seemed more interested in being directed to the coffee and tea than engage in small talk. John and Roger had strategically placed themselves over at that table to listen in on the conversations.

"Hello, I'm Jack Porter. Customs."

"Welcome Jack," I replied as he entered.

"You know I'm here just to observe?"

"Yes, your boss made that clear when I met him."

"Ah, Michael, let me introduce you to two people not on your guest list," Hamish interrupted, pulling me away gently as two more men entered. "You'll find them far more useful than talking to Customs," he added in a hushed tone.

"It's my pleasure to introduce you all," Hamish said enthusiastically. "Michael, this is Detective Superintendent Don McGregor from Strathclyde Police and his bagman Detective Sergeant Craig Campbell."

"Thank you both for coming," I said. "You'll understand I'm intrigued by you being here."

In his broad Scottish accent, Don replied, "aye, I imagine yae would be."

"This meeting must be important to your investigation. May I ask what you'll be able to contribute?" I asked.

"Not a lot, laddie, but I'm looking forward to hearing what yae've got to say nonetheless."

"You know we can match your CZ pistol to our Operation Abonar?"

"Aye, Hamish told me as much. As I said, we're here to listen, that's all I can promise."

"We've done some digging into that CZ pistol Sir," I said, wanting to get something useful from our initial chat. "My DC found it was recovered with a silencer by BTP[35] at Preston Railway Station in January. It was in the possession of a passenger on the Glasgow-bound train."

"He's done well to find that out. Look, I'd like to help yae, laddie, but I cannae risk my operation," and for a moment his face took on a more serious look. "Hamish has told yae to be patient, I believe. I will tell yae all when I'm ready to. I understand we can help yae with your investigation, and yae may well be able to help with mine." Then changing to a genial smile, he continued, "once we've taken out the main target, there'll be others we won't be interested in, but I know yae will. If all goes to plan, yae and I will be talking again and very soon."

"Okay. Here's my card. Let's keep in touch, Sir."

"Aye, I'd like that. Right now, we're going to sit at the back and watch."

"As Don said, just be patient," Hamish added in his hushed tone as the Scotsmen moved away.

Don McGregor was the epitome of the TV detective 'Taggart', he even looked like him. His hard-edged manner was very similar. His 'bag-carrier' was older, and I assumed a career DS, potentially close to retirement.

Once John confirmed everyone on our guest list had arrived, I decided to start. Wanting to appear collaborative, I chose not to sit remotely at one end of the table. Instead, I took a chair in the middle with my back to the windows. The seven SIOs had each brought one subordinate as their traditional bag-

---

35 BTP: British Transport Police.

carrier. I called the room to order and invited everyone to join me at the table. Our colleagues from Scotland remained against the back wall.

Just as I was about to speak again, a woman entered and acknowledged Hamish. Spotting the two Scotsmen, she joined them at the back. Looking round the table, I saw more factions had formed. Each SIO and bag-carrier had left a sizeable space between them and the next. I sensed encouraging collaboration would have its challenges.

After the usual tour-de-table introductions, John and I gave a presentation on how the Lab had confirmed the hallmarks left by the gunsmith indicated all the firearms seized in London, Manchester and Kent originated from the same source of supply. I finished by explaining that Eltham High Street had also become a common denominator, and John passed round the E-fits of the three car-buyers.

This triggered some healthy dialogue between all the parties but not enough to generate a new lead.

"So, I see we've got someone from Customs here," the Kent SIO said rather abruptly. "How about you tell us, Jack, where your information came from?"

"I'm really sorry," he began falteringly.

Sensing his discomfort, I intervened, "we're investigating all that in conjunction with Customs. You'll appreciate as it's informant-led, we're unable to discuss more than what we've shared so far."

I noted the murmurs of discontent coming from the two Met SIOs. "What can you tell us then?" demanded DCI Jenkins from Plaistow.

"The reason we're here is to identify the source and stop the supply of firearms. To achieve that, MI5 and my own team need three things from you to take away and check against your case files."

"And what are they?" DCI Jenkins asked in a manner that warned he was unconvinced that anything I wanted would be worth his while with following up.

"First, do you have any suspects with connections to either Eltham or Hither Green?" I persevered.

"We've checked already, and no," DCI Jenkins said impatiently.

"Okay, well I'm asking everyone here to do that too, please. Second, how many other firearms have you recovered with the same Abonar hallmarks?"

"Surely you know that from the Lab," DCI Jenkins countered.

"Sadly not. By way of example, until we asked you to submit yours, Guv, they were languishing in the station property store. The same with

Whitechapel's. There must be more similarly sitting in stores elsewhere, with no follow-up action because they too were recovered without an arrest."

"What if we find them?" he again pushed back.

"You need to tell us, please. We'll arrange for the Lab to make a scientific comparison."

"And you'll pay for that, will you?"

"If needs be Guv, yes, but this is meant to be a joint investigation."

"I hope the minutes will show you agreed to pay," DCI Jenkins added, looking around the table at the others for support. "And what's the third thing you want from us?"

"Go back to the people you've arrested in possession of these types of Abonar-related firearms and ammunition, and ask who supplied them?"

"Why? Don't you think we haven't done that already?"

"No," Hamish interrupted with perfect timing. "In my role here in Weapons Intelligence I get to read all your reports about firearms' recoveries." Then, in a schoolmasterly tone he added, "very rarely do you ask someone you've arrested with a gun where they got it. You seem much happier to just charge them with unlawful possession, which means you're failing to identify their supplier." He paused to let the SIOs think about their own experiences before continuing. "So, Michael and I need you to think more strategically. We want you to start asking everyone you arrest with a firearm who supplied it. That will help us assist you in finding the sources whether it's the Abonar gunsmith or someone else."

"Thank you, Hamish," I said, hugely grateful for his intervention. "We need your help to pool knowledge about the market from end-users back to their suppliers and everyone in between."

"We'll do what we can in Manchester to help, Michael," the GMP SIO spoke supportively. "We've got first-hand knowledge of the devastation these guns are having on our streets. It's only by good fortune we haven't lost one of our own."

"And the same for me," the Brixton SIO now spoke up. "We've got plenty of experience in south London of young men who are only too happy to shoot indiscriminately. I'd be happy to help you find out who's arming them."

I looked around the other faces at the table and was relieved to see them all now nodding in support of those who had just spoken, including Don McGregor sitting at the back. Begrudgingly I thought, DCI Jenkins submitted to the peer group pressure and signalled his support too.

"Right, John will circulate the minutes with those three action points," I told everyone. "We'll follow up with you in two weeks. Thank you. Before I draw this to a close, does anyone who hasn't spoken yet have anything new to add?" Looking at Don, I asked, "anything Sir from a Scottish perspective?"

He smiled saying, "nae, but thank yae for asking."

People mingled for a few minutes more before being escorted by members of Hamish's team out of the building. I chose to stay on and speak to Don and his two companions. Artfully, the woman manoeuvred around to the opposite side of the table and left the room. I moved to block the others before they could do the same to avoid me.

"Something I said?"

"Nae, she's from the MI5 team working directly on our joint investigation. It's just the way she is. Nothing personal."

"That's a relief."

"I'm sorry we could nae say anything today, Michael. I heard your frustration with the others. I've been there myself. In a wee while, when we're done, I'll call yae. We can meet, and I promise to be much more forthcoming about the connections between our two investigations. Okay?"

"Thank you, yes. I look forward to your call."

Jack Porter joined me as the two Scotsmen left.

"Useful meeting Michael, thanks. Oh, and John mentioned your trip next week. I think it would be useful for us to take advantage of meeting the Belgian Police and INTERPOL as well. Do you mind if I tag along?"

"That's fine with me Jack, but we've already made our travel plans. Speak to John and he'll give you the details."

CHAPTER 25

Wrapping Up Week 3

Friday, 16th May

Walking into the Fordham Suite once more for our daily catch-up, I was looking forward to the latest from Alice. Following the meeting at Thames House, Roger had spent the afternoon overseeing Emily and Natasha as they created the second i2 chart that Derek wanted. Alice had quickly deleted all references to the RPG lines of enquiry from ours. I had gone back to Derek to try and persuade him to keep a master chart for '*intelligence purposes only*' that combined both, but he refused. He was adamant the two be kept separate.

"So, Alice, having now sanitised your chart, what did you have time to process yesterday?" I asked.

"Well, I had quite a good day. I've nearly finished the first Orange mobile." With that she projected her chart on to the big screen. "As you can see, I was being frustrated by an anonymous pager," and she highlighted the outgoing calls to an 01459 number.

"There's another pager later in the sequence that has brought my research to a stop, though," and she highlighted a second 01459 number. "Fortunately, I've been able to do something with the first."

"Okay, show us?"

"Straight after the calls between the Donovans and the Orange mobile to set up Whitechapel, the mobile messaged the first pager. Now, cellsite puts the mobile in Eltham, but I'm told we can't get location data for pagers."

"No, but we can get their messages," I offered.

"Oh, well that would be wonderful, but I fear all that'll give us are the numbers to call back."

"Well, let's see once we've got them. The two you've found are on the 'Vodapage' network," I commented, as I noted their numbers in my daybook.

"I was at a loss as to where to go next. But then I had some luck," Alice continued, sounding more upbeat. "In the lead up to Whitechapel, I found the mobile received a number of calls from one of three TKs around Dartford."

I nodded as she showed us each one.

"I then found the same pattern for Plaistow and the Tollgate Hotel, so I requested the billing for each TK. That was my lucky break, as the data revealed when the mobile messaged the pager, minutes later, a Dartford TK called one in Eltham. From the mobile's cellsite locations, I could see it was very close to whichever Eltham TK the Dartford one had called back."

Again, I nodded as she showed us the pattern.

"I don't think I'm pushing the boundaries of the ABC, Mr H, when I tell you this means whoever had the Orange mobile was in Eltham."

"I'd say you're right looking at your chart."

"And the Dartford TK data is telling us whoever had this first pager was someone calling back from there."

"Agreed."

With added confidence, she continued, "I think this call pattern is telling us three things, Mr H. First, whoever was using the mobile is the Donovans' friend coordinating everything from Eltham."

"Yes."

"Second, this person in Eltham didn't hold the firearms, that's someone else. And the person in Dartford with the pager is also another middleman. I know I'm right because why else would the contact in Eltham page them immediately after talking to the Donovans?"

"Okay, that works for me. And third?"

"The person in Dartford then messaged someone with a second pager. I'm certain this will prove to be the one who did actually control the firearms. Fingers crossed he controls a lot more and is our Abonar gunsmith who's still arming the gangs."

"Explain your logic?"

"Because, Mr H, when that person replied to their pager messages by calling the Dartford TK, it closed the loop. All the calls and messages thereafter go back in the opposite direction for each of the three recoveries. I can follow the loop all the way round and back to the Donovans. Therefore, whoever has this second pager is our Abonar supplier."

"Okay, just show me one of those loops, please?" I asked.

"Sure, I'll take you through it in sequence. So, when the conversation between the middlemen in Dartford and Eltham reached the point of finalising a delivery, the person in Eltham used the Orange mobile to call the Donovan home number. Look."

I nodded at the sequence Alice picked out with her cursor.

"As you can see," she continued, "the call from the mobile to the Donovans' home lasted only a couple of seconds. I think that was to tell them to go to the TK near their home. I'm sure of that too, because, in the time it would take them to walk there, someone used it to call the mobile back for a longer conversation." She then paused to check I was following and nodding in agreement at her logic. "As we've discovered," she continued, "someone then used that same TK to call Gudgeon to let him know what to tell Harrison about where to find each of the three recoveries. Look, it's the same pattern every time in the build-up to Whitechapel, Plaistow and the Tollgate Hotel."

"Fantastic work, Alice," I said in awe at her capacity to assimilate the information so readily.

"So, let me now take my theory forward a few more steps, Mr H. I think the Donovans and their friend in Eltham were happy to call each other openly because both the mobile and Manchester TK were anonymous and unattributable."

John interrupted, "um, can you explain that for the rest of us, please Alice?'

"Sure. Look, it didn't matter, for example, when the person in Eltham made a two-second call to the Donovans' home number asking them to phone back from the Manchester TK. That's because the mobile was unattributable. Similarly, when the Donovans called back, they thought we couldn't connect their local TK to them. It means the Donovans in Manchester and whoever is using the Orange mobile in Eltham think they've been super clever at anonymising their communications."

As John now nodded, I asked, "What else? What about the second pager you found?"

"Well, the billing for the Dartford TKs shows what happened after the calls with their contact in Eltham. Whichever Dartford TK had been used then called either one of two Brighton 01273 numbers, or it messaged the second pager. I'm sorry to say, but his one has me stumped. Like the first, it doesn't have a registered subscriber."

"What about the Brighton numbers?"

"Oh, they're both TKs. I haven't had time yet to request the call data."

"Okay, we need to get that done. I've got the two pager numbers noted and will work on a solution for you to identify who's using them. Anything else?"

"No, nothing more from me. I'm hoping before you and John get back from your trip, I'll have all the call and location data mapped. I'll then be very close to showing you the entire Abonar communications network."

"Okay, Alice, thank you. Roger, over to you. What can you share from your work upstairs on the RPG job and the second Orange mobile?"

"Hmm, well since that first call from the Manchester TK, it's been almost permanently switched off. However, someone turns it on at 8pm every Tuesday. On two occasions, almost immediately, it's had a call from our Manchester TK. Straight after those, it messaged another anonymous 01459-pager before being switched off. Each time cellsite puts it in Eltham. Whoever's using it is, once again, being super careful to minimise our ability to trace and track it."

"And if no one calls it?"

"It's switched off after two minutes."

"Okay, recommend to Mr Hamilton he tasks the TSU to deploy Toscas in Eltham ready for next Tuesday's 8pm switch-on. Hopefully, they can pinpoint its location over a number of Tuesdays."

"Okay, I'll mention it, thanks."

"I also made a note of your anonymous pager, so I'll do some work on that too."

"Actually, Guv, if you don't mind, Mr Hamilton tasked the team upstairs with that already."

"Fine, no problem. Okay everyone, Monday is the start of week four of Abonar," I announced. "And whilst John and I are away, Mark and Alice, I have an important job for you. I need you to go through all the call data again, please. I want you to check whether our Abonar suspects made a mistake."

"How so?" Alice asked looking surprised.

"Well, as you explained, they think they've all been super clever. I want you to check in case one of them broke out of that secure network. It might be just a single call when they contacted a device we can attribute to a named subscriber. Are you okay with that?"

"Sure," Alice replied instantly, obviously thrilled by the task. "I'll get Mark to help me."

I thanked them all before heading back to my office. John caught me as I reached the door. "A word if I may, Guv?"

"Sure, come in. What's on your mind?"

Pushing the door shut he said, "we can all see how gutted you are at losing Abonar to the OCG, Guv, but on behalf of the team, I just wanted to say we're all still behind you 100 percent. We wouldn't be this far ahead if you hadn't gripped the job and run with it so quickly. That's all."

"Thank you, John. I appreciate you telling me. Let's hope Brussels and Lyon give us something more."

CHAPTER 26

Week 4 - Brussels

Monday, 19th May

The train journey to Brussels was uneventful. Jack Porter joined us at the Waterloo Eurostar terminal and immersed himself in a novel for the whole trip. The French and Belgian countryside appeared identical as we dashed between the hedgerows, towns, and villages. We arrived at Gare de Bruxelles-Midi in the early afternoon. John had arranged with the British Embassy for their '*Drugs and Crime Liaison Officer*', Bob Fitzgerald to meet us. He was on secondment from Merseyside Police. He would also be our interpreter with the Belgian Police. As we gathered our bags, John called Bob to agree where to meet.

After the usual introductions, Bob led us to his car outside the station. "Right, I'll get you to your hotel to freshen up. Our meeting with the Serious and Armed Crime Squad is at 9am. I'll pick you up at 8:15am from your hotel. Remember, we're an hour ahead of London. So, in your language, I'll be picking you up at the equivalent of 7:15." He paused to make sure we understood. "Okay, so between now and then, to help you acclimatise, I'll come by your hotel at 7pm and take you to a local bar."

Bob met us as agreed and took us to a venue popular with the diplomatic corps. It was packed and noisy, with loud 90s pop music, forcing us to hold conversations at full volume to be heard.

Bob had left the car at home, which was just as well, as he outdrank me by a mile. Whilst I stuck to one gradually warming glass of white wine, he was back and forth to the bar for another beer. Our conversation was, therefore, rather stilted. Increasingly, the combination of loud music, his slurred voice and heavy Merseyside accent made it almost impossible for us to understand him. After two hours, the alcohol took its effect. Bob's head dropped and he fell into silence. John and Jack were clearly getting along very well and were chatting animatedly. I could not hear what they were saying, so I made do with a smile and shrug whenever they turned to me for a reaction.

At around 10pm, I shook Bob gently to wake him. He was leaning at an angle away from me. I felt some responsibility; especially as he had been so generous with his off-duty time.

Waking and looking embarrassed he said, "Sorry, I need to get home. See you all in the morning."

He got up unsteadily and then meandered through the other patrons towards the exit upon which his gaze was firmly fixed. I was pleased to see him make it without incident. I stood up too and readied the other two to leave. Reaching the street was a huge relief, as my ears reaccustomed to normal volumes. I had hoped we would head straight back to the hotel, but John had other ideas.

"I went for a walk earlier and found a great little bar close to our hotel. They even allowed me to smoke my pipe inside. One for the road?"

Eagerly, Jack replied, "absolutely."

"Okay," I resigned myself, "I'll join you, but just for one."

John walked ahead leading the way to a small bar in the same street as our hotel.

"Right guys, the first one's on me. I won't have more than one anyway," I told them.

"As we're in Brussels," John announced, "I fancy Belgian beer."

"So do I," Jack responded enthusiastically.

Just as I got comfortable at a corner table, John demonstrated the old rivalries between the Metropolitan Police and HM Customs were very much alive.

"I bet you Jack," he challenged, "I can drink all those bottles on the top shelf from the left and reach the middle before you can do the same from the right."

"You're on," Jack replied enthusiastically.

I looked up and counted the bottles. They would both have to consume five to reach the middle and one more to achieve their goal. Each had a different label and, undoubtedly, varying strengths in alcohol. Having reconciled myself that one or other of them would concede after only a couple, I let them enjoy building their friendship.

The conversation between us was genial as we began to appreciate each other's company. Jack felt comfortable enough to confide in me about another outcome of Mick Burridge's review into their handling of Donovan.

As a result of Abonar, he had re-deployed Harrison to be their *'Drugs Liaison Officer'* in Asia, and so kept him well away from any repercussions.

I realised after an hour that my companions were taking a little too much advantage of being away from the office, so I stayed to keep an eye on them. They continued with their testosterone fuelled ritual of trying to outdo each other whilst determined to fly the flag for their respective organisation. I chatted with the bar owner, instead, who spoke reasonable English whenever my French failed. He was clearly amused by the adventure John and Jack had embarked upon and only too happy to accept their cash in the process.

Looking at my watch, I realised it was past midnight. John and Jack had reached their limits well short of their target, and both had fallen asleep at the table. Neither of them had got closer than three bottles. I declared the competition a draw. However, now they could not stay awake for longer than it took to open and close their eyes. They were both too heavy for me to carry. Jack in particular was a big man weighing over sixteen-stone. Helpfully, the bar owner organised a taxi and, a few minutes later, one pulled up outside. It was now pouring with rain. The driver helped me lift John and then Jack and carry them to the car. Having got the two safely on to their beds, I reminded them of the 8:15am pick-up. By the time I reached my own bed, it had gone 1am. I set my alarm for seven.

I did not welcome the shrill sound when it woke me. I had finished breakfast by 7:45am anxiously hoping the others would soon join me. When neither of them appeared, at 8am I asked the hotel receptionist to telephone their rooms. Their voices told me everything. Both were in a state of regret and getting themselves dressed and presentable was a greater priority than breakfast. I wrapped in paper serviettes a couple of 'pain au chocolat' from the breakfast bar before returning to wait in reception.

John and Jack appeared fifteen minutes later dressed and shaved with their bags packed. Outwardly, they looked respectable. The fact neither of them spoke indicated that inside it was a far unhealthier picture. Almost immediately, Bob joined us. "Let's go," he said to me, oblivious to the fragile condition of his other two passengers. Handing them each a serviette with the pastry I said, "breakfast? Hopefully, the Belgian Police will give you coffee. How are you?"

"The beer was off," Jack replied.

"More than likely," John confirmed. "I don't normally react like this to English beer." Looking at my breakfast offering, he added, "thanks, Guv," and eagerly took it.

173

They were otherwise silent during our journey to the Belgian Federal Police Headquarters. Bob sensed it had been a late night. "May I recommend, Michael, you and I do the talking. It's probably best that Jack and John sit this one out."

We were greeted at the police building by three plain clothes detectives. None of them spoke English, so Bob interpreted everything. When I could, I dropped in some words from my modest French vocabulary. The first, as soon as we sat down in their office, was to arrange the coffee, "*Merci, café au lait pour mois, et noir fort pour mes deux amis* [Thank you, white coffee for me, and strong black ones for my two friends]."

John opened his briefcase and, without speaking, handed me the albums of Abonar photographs. I pointed to the features evident in each image, which Bob translated. Our Belgian Police hosts graciously took their time to study every one.

Bob interpreted my request, "so, have you seen any of these types of firearms and this method of obliterating serial numbers here in Belgium?"

"Non."

"And these three-letter Cyrillic codes?"

"Non."

Within minutes, Bob and one of the Belgian detectives escorted us out of the building. Having expressed our gratitude for the meeting, we were then abandoned on the street. Bob had to be elsewhere and pointed us in the direction of the railway station and, with that, left.

I was now annoyed we had gone to the trouble of coming to Brussels. We could have saved ourselves the time and effort by sending a copy of the photo album. John sensed this too and kept quiet. Picking up our bags, we set off to catch the train to Lyon. John had the tickets for us both, which he presented to the guard at the platform gate. Jack then announced he was not coming with us. We were surprised. He had not mentioned this before. Instead, he was meeting his wife for a short break in Brussels. He then bid us farewell and left the concourse.

CHAPTER 27

INTERPOL

Tuesday and Wednesday, 20th and 21st May

Thankfully, the train journey to Lyon was as straightforward and uneventful as our one to Brussels. John caught up with his sleep for the first couple of hours. I had to wake him for the change at Lille. We were booked into the *Sofitel Hotel* in the city centre and took a taxi there. By the time we checked in, it was just after 4pm. Having agreed to meet again at 5pm for a walk ahead of finding somewhere for dinner, I took advantage of the spare time to make some calls. The first was to Roger.

"Well, I hope INTERPOL is more productive, Guv," he commented after I briefed him about Brussels. "By the way, I spent a couple of hours yesterday at Eltham Police Station. I'm sorry to say there's no one in their Collator Records with a connection either to Donovan or Manchester."

"Damn. I was really hoping you'd have some luck. What about getting Toscas for tonight?"

"Yup, that's all organised."

"Great, well good luck with that."

Finishing the call I was pleased at his keenness to be a part of the team, and I was growing to like him. Next, I phoned home to speak with Olivia and Rebecca. Sadly, the conversation did not go well. Olivia let her usual jealousy take over and questioned whether I was really travelling with a male colleague before she hung up. I could hear Rebecca in the background wanting to talk to her Daddy, so the abrupt end upset me. When I called back, it went to the answerphone. I left a message hoping Rebecca could hear me even if her mother would not pick up.

It was now 5pm. I grabbed my jacket and took the lift to the hotel lobby. After a very pleasant walk around the city centre in the balmy spring weather,

John and I found a restaurant for dinner. I was grateful he did not have the appetite for a repeat of Brussels, and we were back in our rooms by 9pm.

The following morning, John joined me dutifully for breakfast. An hour later, we were in a taxi heading to the International Criminal Police Organisation (INTERPOL) on the Quai Charles De Gaulle. On the way there, I tasked John with re-booking our return tickets. I wanted to be back in the office after lunch on Thursday rather than Friday morning.

Donald Manross met us in reception. He was a US Department of Treasury Special Agent of the 'Bureau of Alcohol, Tobacco and Firearms (ATF)', and in the final year of his secondment. His title was *'Specialized Officer, General Crime Branch, Firearms and Explosives'*. It had become a tradition for the ATF to fill the post. That was due, in part, to their significant financial investment in it. The main reason, though, was more fundamental. It was because many of the weapons Donald's section was asked to trace were manufactured in America. He was in his early fifties, greying hair with a thick moustache, and unmistakable Philadelphia drawl. He exuded welcoming geniality. This was a pleasure after the rather perfunctory manner of our Belgian hosts. I could not have imagined then how much I would owe Donald later in shaping my future career, but that is another story.

As with so many detectives blessed with having their own office, Donald had decorated his with souvenirs from an interesting career and travels. We performed the usual swapping of 'war stories' and I then gave him the customary item of Scotland Yard memorabilia. He really appreciated the cufflinks depicting the MPS armorial crest. Reaching into his desk, he reciprocated with a cased bronze ATF *'challenge coin'*. It is a tradition of US law enforcement agencies that when standing at the bar and someone challenges you to *'Produce the coin'*, failure to do so means you buy the next round.

John took from his briefcase the Abonar photograph albums. Donald looked at each image as we pointed out the unique features and hallmarks.

"Okay, we get to see these types of firearms all the time," I was grateful to hear him say. "Tokarevs, M20s, Smith & Wessons, Colts. All of them. MAC-10s too, but none with these obliteration marks. I don't see how I can help you make a link for you today with a potential supplier."

Donald saw my look of disappointment, so added, "okay, here's the deal. Once you've identified and arrested whoever is supplying these, send me the details. I'll post them as an *'Orange Notice'*. It'll go to every INTERPOL member country. If their law enforcement agencies have a match, I'll let you know. That'll help you build the case against your supplier and help illustrate the full extent of their trafficking operation."

I left grateful we had at least achieved something positive.

CHAPTER 28

Clone Pagers

Thursday, 22nd May

Our return to London on the Eurostar went smoothly. John and I were back at NSY by 3pm. Derek had set up a meeting with the team for us all to catch up an hour later. I had my head down checking the correspondence from my pigeonhole when I heard footsteps stop at my doorway alerting me to a visitor. It was Trevor from our TSU. He had earned the nickname 'Clever Trevor' due to his many innovations in our electronic surveillance capabilities. He was responsible for Toscas along with other equipment installed in our covert fleet of vehicles and aircraft. We had become firm friends from working alongside each other in Central 500. He and his team of civilian engineers operated from a discreet building in south-east London. The site was a former Second World War radio listening post. It seemed only right we continue that legacy as the Directorate of Intelligence.

"Good trip?" he asked.

"Yes, but disappointing in terms of no suspects for Abonar. Made some useful contacts for the future, though."

"Well, this will cheer you up. I brought you a couple of gifts."

He produced a padded envelope from his briefcase and tipped the contents on my desk. It was two pagers, identical to the one I carried for my SO11 duties. "Here you go," he announced, "the '*clone pagers*' you wanted."

"I've marked this one with 'A' and the other 'B', with their actual numbers on the back. From your report, A is the one messaged by the Orange mobile and Eltham TKs. I'm sorry to say, the billing suggests it's now dead. No one's messaged it since mid-March. I'm letting you have it just in case it comes back to life."

"What about Pager B?" I asked hoping for better news.

"Yes, it's very much alive. This is the one called by the Dartford TKs."

"Trevor, thank you. Fantastic service, as always."

"No problem. Let me know how you get on. Be aware you're getting messages at the same time as your suspects. They won't know that unless you react too soon and tip them off by turning up to something they've organised that you couldn't possibly know about otherwise."

"Sure. Tell me, did you clone one for Derek Hamilton too?"

He smiled saying, "I'm sorry, but I'm not able to talk about that," and in a hushed voice added, "Yes, of course I did."

"Any more gifts?"

"Oh yes, I nearly forgot." Rummaging again in his briefcase, he produced two brown A4-size envelopes, one much thicker than the other, and handed them over smiling. Opening each one I discovered why he looked so happy. They contained the historic messages for each pager going back to 1st of October 1996, as I had requested.

"Trevor, this is bloody amazing. Thank you."

"I knew you'd be pleased. Right, I'm off to see our boss."

I quickly scanned the thinner collection of messages for Pager A. Exactly as Alice had predicted, each was just a phone number, no explanatory text or name. Almost certainly, the pager-user would know from the local dialling code who was messaging them to call back. I spent half an hour going through the list noting each number. I recognised three as our Eltham TKs. There were six more, each beginning with 01273, indicating somewhere in Sussex. Two of these Alice had found before from the billing for the Dartford TKs. I typed up the authorisations to request the subscribers, and then separate ones for the billing up to the current day. I also asked for live monitoring going forwards.

By the time I finished it was close to 4pm, so I could not do the same for Pager B. I dashed into the TIU to task Pete with getting the CSPs to provide the subscribers. I then tucked the other authorisations and the two envelopes into my daybook and rushed down the corridor to the briefing room. When I walked in, Derek was already sitting at the table along with Roger, John, Mark and Alice, but not Emily and Natasha.

"A wasted trip, then?" Derek said somewhat critically as I sat down. I looked across at John, whose shrug of his shoulders indicated he'd already explained what had happened.

"No, I think it will prove to our advantage," I responded, wanting to sound positive.

Sceptically, Derek asked, "How so?"

"You see, while we were on the train coming back, I thought about everything we know so far. The reason our counterparts in Brussels and INTERPOL haven't seen these Abonar hallmarks is because our source is homegrown."

"What evidence do you have to support that?" Derek asked, still unimpressed and sensing my comment was a rapidly contrived excuse.

"Well, we've now processed a massive amount of call data and we haven't found any international numbers. Everything is London, Manchester and home counties based. I get the feeling our firearms and ammunition were here already. There is no smuggling operation."

"What about the Cyrillic codes?" Derek demanded.

"They're on old firearms that my visit to the Proof House indicates were already in the country. They were imported by UK businesses dealing in military surplus from the Gulf War six years ago."

Derek shrugged, looking nonplussed, "okay, we'll bank your theory for now and see if the broader intelligence picture confirms it later."

"Of course, I'm mindful of the detective's ABC, so I'm keeping an open mind too, Sir. Just thought it helpful to share my thoughts on one positive outcome from our trip."

The room stayed silent, so I decided to take the initiative and continue. "If I may, Sir, I'd like to hear from Roger about what he and the team achieved in our absence?"

He nodded to Roger.

"Okay, well the major news is Alice and Mark found that mistake you hoped for. The one where a suspect made a call that broke out of their closed network. Well they did."

"Great. What does it tell us?"

"The Orange mobile called a Dartford landline for just a few seconds before they realised their error," Roger said rather pleased with his news.

"And do we have a subscriber?

"Oh yes, and his address. It's a Kieran Walshe living in Dartford."

"And is he known to us?"

"Yes, and to Kent. Right now he's a major target in a Flying Squad job, 'Operation Bridge'."

"Does that help us?" I asked, crossing my fingers under the table that it did.

"Yup, he's suspected of multiple armed robberies on banks, building societies and cash in transit vans. All of them in and around south-east London. He's just the sort of person who'd know how to get hold of firearms."

Before I could comment, Derek cut in, "and there's no need for you to kick off another line of enquiry down here Michael, because I've made him an OCG target upstairs."

"Perfect," I said encouragingly, whilst ably disguising my annoyance. "Alice and Mark, great work finding that call. No others then?""

"Unfortunately no," Alice said, giving me one of her encouraging stares.

"And the billing for the Brighton TKs, how did you get on with that?" I asked quickly, trying to avoid my growing sense of awkwardness.

"We didn't get time, but it's on our list of things to do," Roger answered.

"Okay, that's fine," I replied, wanting to sound supportive before turning to Derek. "Sir, may I ask what you can share about the RPGs? What about Toscas?"

"There's nothing that'll help with what you're doing down here," he replied curtly. His continuing off-hand manner surprised me, so I made a mental note to ask him about it afterwards. As I pondered on it, there was a knock at the door. Derek motioned for John to see who it was. It was Pete wanting to speak with me. Having sought forgiveness, I went out into the corridor, closing the door behind me.

"Here are the subscriber checks you asked for." Giving me his usual warning by glaring at me over his glasses, he added "I'm going at 5pm, so if you need anything else, you'll have to be quick."

As he walked away, I scanned through the results. Each was for a phone box in the Brighton area. Rather than return immediately, I went instead into Central 500. Opening the cabinet used by Blue, I took out the street atlas for Sussex. Systematically, I checked the index and then the map for the location of each phone box. Bringing everything with me, I returned to the briefing room.

"Sorry about that Sir. I'd asked Pete to run some subscriber checks and, knowing they were urgent, he was keen to let me have them straight away."

"Anything useful?"

"Yes, and if I may, Sir, while I brief you, would you mind signing these billing authorisations and requests for live monitoring too, please?"

"What are they for?" he asked testily.

"Six Brighton phone boxes. They're pivotal to where we go next with Abonar." I took the prepared forms from my daybook and slid them across.

"Okay, so what else have you got?" Derek asked, still sounding annoyed.

Taking Trevor's two gifts from my belt, I placed them on the table. "I've got these clone pagers. 'A', here in my left hand, is the one Alice identified last Friday that the Orange mobile called for the person in Dartford. This other one, '*B*', is the next in the sequence that generated calls back from the Brighton TKs."

Alice looked mystified as she asked, "Um, what's a clone pager, please?"

"Sorry, Alice, it's another one of our SO11 tricks. The TSU can programme the signalling code for the real one into a spare we hold to mimic it and thereby create its clone. We then receive the messages at the same time as the suspect does on theirs."

"Oh, that's so James Bondish. I love it," she said.

Smiling, I commented, "yesh Mish Moneypenny," giving my best impression of Sean Connery. Continuing, I explained, "so, after last Friday's meeting, I asked Clever Trevor to set these up. Being the good chap that he is, he also got Vodapage to send us the earlier messages. As you predicted Alice, every one of them is just a phone number."

I passed the pages of messages across to her while adding, "so, before this meeting I quickly went through the ones just for Pager A. As you'd expect, many of them are to call one or other of the Eltham TKs. Sadly, it's been dead since March 11th, which means it's another burner used just for delivering the firearms. It may well have been discarded by now. I've got its clone, though, just in case it does come back on-line."

Giving me a smile, Alice mischievously commented, "so a bit of sugar, bloody, damn then".

"Quite so, thank you Alice, but all is not lost, because the messages identified the six TKs in the Brighton area."

"And?" Derek interrupted.

"Well those billing authorisations I've just given you are for them. If you can sign them now Sir, Pete can ask the CSPs to start working on getting us the data before he leaves at 5pm."

"Okay, fine," and he hurriedly signed each one before handing them to Mark, telling him, "take these to Pete with my blessing."

Opening the Sussex street atlas, I continued, "I just took a moment to do some research so I can show you where these Brighton TKs are on the map. We know from Alice's work that after the calls between the Donovans and the person in Eltham, the latter used a local TK to message Pager A. That resulted in a call back from a Dartford TK. We also know from the Dartford TKs' billing that they then messaged Pager B and, on a number of occasions, also called one of these Brighton numbers."

"And?" Derek asked impatiently.

To my delight, John stepped in saying, "it means, Sir, we now know what happened next in the sequence. After Orange mobile messaged Pager A, and then the people in Dartford and Eltham had a conversation, the person in Dartford messaged Pager B. He then got a call back from someone in Brighton. So, we now know that's where we'll find the last person in the Abonar supply chain: the gunsmith."

Nodding to him approvingly, I said, "precisely, John. Thank you."

"And that means the person in Dartford doesn't control the guns either. It's whoever is in Brighton," Alice added.

"Got it in one. Yes." I said, triumphant in my team being on message.

"Show me the Brighton TKs on the map?" Derek now demanded still sounding irritated.

"Certainly Sir." I decided to take it slowly by explaining, "the three TKs used the most are in an area known locally as Bevendean," and showed him their proximity to each other on the map. "The others are more towards Hove, just here on this page."

"Very good. So, what does that mean for your priorities for the rest of the week?" Derek asked, trying to regain some control of what he had intended to be *his* meeting.

"Well, Roger, I need you to babysit Pager A, please. It shouldn't give you any trouble unless it does come back to life."

"Sure Guv, happy to do that."

Just then, Mark returned to the room. "Good timing Mark," I said, "as I need you to help Alice and John repeat the process I did for Pager B, and collate the messages, dates and times for A." I then passed him the envelope.

"Do you want me to take Pager B as well, Guv?" John asked.

"No, not at the moment. I'm going to hold on to it for now. Alice, I need you to add to your chart the messages for both pagers along the timelines for Whitechapel, Plaistow and Tollgate Hotel, please."

"Sure. They should now complete the entire Abonar network end-to-end."

"Well, I'm looking forward to seeing it."

Derek seemed disinterested, choosing instead to draw the gathering to a close.

As he stood up to leave, I asked, "Sir, could you and I have our own catch-up now, please?"

"Yes," he said tetchily, "follow me up to my office."

I followed his trail of cologne and, as we reached the empty staircase, I decided to begin the conversation there. "Sir, I hope you don't mind me saying, but I got a sense I've done something wrong. You seem angry with me."

Turning to face me, he quickly said, "because I am!" His curtness surprised me. "Look, I get you're passionate about this investigation and the team like the way you run things, but you need to temper that by being more challenging with them. You also need to recognise you're not here to upstage me."

Momentarily he studied my expression, which gave away I didn't know what he meant.

"Look, I know I was supportive of your European excursion," his choice of terminology sounded deliberately disparaging, "but it's clear from the outcome you didn't have a good enough reason to go. While you've been away, Roger and I have been doing your job. That's not what I'm here for. From now on, I expect you to be more challenging with your staff; especially when it comes to any major expenditure, such as travel."

"As regards the trip, yes Sir, I'll be more circumspect in future. I still say it helped eliminate smuggling from our lines of enquiry."

"Well I'm still not yet convinced of that. And then just now you showed me up by springing on us your clone pagers."

"That wasn't deliberate."

"Before you do something like that, show me the courtesy of letting me know first and not try to undermine me. I'm leading Abonar, not you. Is that clear?"

"Of course, Sir. I'm sorry you took it that way. It wasn't my intention."

"Is that all you wanted to get cleared up?"

"Yes Sir."

"Good. I'll get back to my office and suggest you head to yours," and he started to go up again.

"Now we've cleared the air, Sir, do you fancy a pint once you're done?"

He stopped and I was relieved his face broke into a smile. "Another evening, Michael, yes, I'd like that. We really should get to know each other better. I'll let you know when it's good for me."

Returning to the fourth-floor corridor, I found Roger and John deep in conversation.

"Roger, what happened about the clone pager for the RPG enquiry?" I asked. "I know you got one, so I'm surprised it didn't get a mention just now."

"Because, like Toscas, Mr Hamilton doesn't want you knowing what's happening upstairs."

"Are you getting any intelligence from them?"

"No, not a thing. Toscas couldn't get a location for the Orange mobile in time and the pager's dead. We just hope they both come back to life once someone tells Gudgeon and Donovan the Home Secretary is ready to negotiate."

"Well, as you know Roger, we're all happy to help, if Mr Hamilton will allow us."

"Yeah, I know that, but he won't."

"Guv, we're going for a pint if you'd like to join us," John then asked.

"I'd love to, but I haven't been home in three nights, so I should make that a priority. You might want to do the same."

"How about just a quick one, then?" Roger added.

"You go ahead guys. I'm in deficit with bedtime stories. Oh, and John, let's not have a repeat of Brussels, please."

He laughed whilst Roger looked on mystified.

"What happens on tour, Sarge, stays on tour," John told him.

CHAPTER 29

Blowing Away the Smokescreen

Friday, 23rd May

The next morning John was waiting for me as I entered the fourth-floor corridor.

"I thought you'd want to see this straight away. Mark's been through your spreadsheet of companies that submitted deactivated firearms to the Proof House, and he's had a eureka moment."

"What did he find?"

"Well, 'Foresight' is one of the companies."

"Yes, I remember."

"Their registered address is 30 Baden Road, Brighton. I think it's more than a coincidence it's right in the middle of the plot for those TKs around Bevendean."

"Wow, well you better get on to Sussex and make some discreet enquiries. Start with their Special Branch. They'll know to be sensitive."

"Sure, Guv."

"I'll update Mr Hamilton and Roger once you've got more background. Let's skip this morning's meeting and make Foresight our focus for the day."

"Right-o."

"I sense Mark and Alice have enough to do with those pager messages without me distracting them too."

As I unlocked my office, the desk phone was already ringing. It was Hamish at MI5. Twenty minutes later, he was escorting me through security at Thames House. Just short of reaching his office, he broke off and diverted me into a large meeting room.

"I thought it would be easier if we met here. Take a seat while I phone a colleague to join us."

Minutes later, a woman in a smart navy-blue business suit entered the room.

"Hello, I'm Linda from the East European Desk," she said after Hamish had introduced me. "Hamish asked if I could interpret the Cyrillic script on the Abonar firearms and wrappings."

"Great, what can you tell from them?"

"I've copied these pages for you from one of my reference books on the Cyrillic alphabet to help explain my theory." As I studied them, Linda surprised me with her statement, "the three-letter codes are all an elaborate hoax. Almost certainly scrawled by someone with a modicum of knowledge of the Cyrillic alphabet, but certainly not the phonetic sound of each letter."

"And that's because?" I asked cautiously.

"The most obvious is the letter 'C' on the Colts. Whilst the letter certainly exists in Cyrillic, its phonetic sound is 'S', as in School. The correct letter would be 'K'."

"What about the 'T' for Tokarev, 'M' for MAB, and 'W' on its side for the Smith & Wessons?"

"Well, yes, they're partly correct, but alongside the other two in the code they don't make sense in any language using the Cyrillic alphabet."

"And you're sure of that?" Hamish asked.

"Oh yes, absolutely. I'd say you're looking for an English-speaker, probably living here, who thinks they've cleverly created a smokescreen to make you focus enquiries elsewhere."

"I think that's also confirmed by their mistaken use of 'T' for Tokarev when in fact the pistols are Chinese M20s," Hamish commented.

Linda continued her explanation saying, "almost certainly the person who did this wants you to think these firearms are the proceeds of some smuggling operation from the former Soviet-bloc. They want to throw you off the scent because the source is much closer to home."

"Thank you, Linda, I had reached the same conclusion, and you've just confirmed it. Thank you."

"Good. Glad I could help save you some wasted enquiries. Oh, and if you need someone outside MI5 who can give you a statement, I can let you have the details of an Oxford language professor."

"No, I don't think that will be necessary but thank you anyway," I said as she left the room.

"I'm sorry you had to come and hear that in person, but I thought it best you did," Hamish said as we re-entered the corridor.

"I'm glad, as it will now convince Mr Hamilton I'm right that we start looking for a homegrown supplier."

"Well, how are you getting on with that?"

I explained the huge progress we had made with the call data and Mark identifying the relevance of Foresight.

"Foresight, you say. Come into my office and I'll run it through our box of tricks too."

As we reached his desk, Hamish commented, "you know I'm also pretty good without using our systems. Foresight... now that name does ring a bell in a very recent enquiry I ran. Sorry, I've been so busy on the Scottish job it's slipped my mind."

He immediately began to rummage through some handwritten notes. Finally, he let everyone in the room know he had found what he was looking for.

"Eureka! Well, here's another useful lead for you, Michael. I knew I'd been given the name Foresight. It's the largest commercial buyer in the UK of the blue-tipped IMI 9mm ammunition."

Excitedly I asked him, "who's behind the company?"

"Foresight is run by Anthony Mitchell, a Brighton based Registered Firearms Dealer. He buys the ammunition direct from Samson. Their records show he's had fifteen thousand rounds of your blue-tipped and copper jacketed 9mm since 1995."

"Wow, wow, wow! Hamish, that's fantastic news. Do you also have any intelligence on Mitchell?"

"We didn't before, but with this latest information we now have both him and Foresight flagged."

"Can I get a statement from your Israeli contact to confirm this?"

"Yes, but we're more likely to get you something evidential from Samson."

"What else have your enquiries produced?"

"You should talk to Ralston Arms in Leeds. A contact suggests they bought up thousands of military surplus handguns coming out of Iraq after 'Desert Storm'. With the post-Dunblane handgun ban now imminent, they're offloading all of it now for deactivation."

"That confirms what I found at the Proof House. Ralston was one of the companies submitting those types of guns for certifying and stamping as deactivated."

"Very good. Remember what I told you, almost every gun on the illicit market was once on the legal one. I think Abonar will prove that maxim true.

Sounds like between Ralston, Foresight and Mitchell you're going to find the point where all your firearms and ammunition came from."

"Thank you, Hamish, wise words, as usual. Oh, and what news on Don McGregor's job?"

"Imminent is all I can tell you. Remember, *patience is a virtue, virtue is a grace…*"

"Yes, Hamish, and '*Grace was a little girl who wouldn't wash her face*'. Hardly relevant, but I'll be *patient* a little longer. However, as you know, every day risks another load of firearms reaching gangs in Manchester and London. We had two more last week used in a kidnap."

"I'm well aware of that. You also need to look after yourself."

"That's an odd thing to say, Hamish. Am I in danger?"

"Physically, no, career-wise, yes. We know in this building what's going on behind the scenes politically with your Operation Abonar. There are forces at play and, as you're close to the bottom of the hierarchy of power, you're the most likely to get hurt. Watch out for the Home Office. They're looking for someone to carry the can over Abonar as well as Haase and Bennett. Make sure they don't make you the scapegoat."

On returning to NSY, I went to find John in the Main Office. He was at his desk with Roger, Alice and Mark standing next to him.

Roger saw me approach and, as I reached them, asked, "the Reserve said you'd dashed over to Thames House. Something urgent?"

"They confirmed our source is certainly homegrown. The Cyrillic letters are a smokescreen. Oh, and we're right to be looking into Foresight too."

"Good, because while you were out, I asked John to phone Bob Pitcher at the Proof House and check some details."

"And?"

John couldn't wait to say, "I ran some checks, Guv, on the man Foresight uses to deliver and collect their deactivated firearms. His name is Robert Bown. Bown has a conviction with a suspended sentence from July last year for possession of an unlicensed firearm. It was a Smith & Wesson Model 36 snub-nosed revolver just like the ones we've seen in Abonar. His address is in SE12, a stone's throw from Eltham."

"Fantastic, sounds like he'll be our first target for surveillance."

"Yes, and we've started developing a profile on him," Roger commented.

"Good. And John, have you spoken to the Sussex Special Branch yet?"

"Yes, Guv, first call I made."

"And?"

"Nothing on Foresight as a company, but its owner is Anthony Mitchell. Interestingly, he was a Special Constable until he got busted in 1993 by Customs at Gatwick for illegal possession of ammunition. He convinced his force it was an administrative misunderstanding, so they didn't also revoke his RFD authority. Consequently, he's still in business."

"Well, with what Hamish told me, that puts Mitchell and Foresight at the very top of our list of targets. Since 1995, Mitchell has bought fifteen thousand of those IMI 9mm bullets, both the blue-tipped and copper jacketed types."

"Good God!" John shouted before apologising to others in the office for his loudness.

"Yes, indeed, and Hamish also recommended we look at Ralston Arms as the potential source of our surplus military handguns. He thinks that's where Mitchell gets them from. I suggest we pull this all together and brief Mr Hamilton and Mr Baxter on Monday. I'll alert them now to what we know and book a slot in their diaries to meet us."

"Sounds good," Roger said.

"Oh and Roger, I appreciate your divided loyalties, so I suggest you and I see Mr Hamilton first. He's already told me he hates being upstaged. Is he in the building?"

"He is Guv and I'll be happy to join you."

Turning to Alice, I asked, "how are you getting on with mapping all those pager messages?"

"Just fine. I'll have it done by close of play today," she answered looking over her glasses in her usual disarming manner.

"Anything new, though?"

"No. Be patient Mr H, you shouldn't expect there to be anything more until next week when we'll get the billing back for all those Brighton TKs."

"Okay. Roger, let's go and brief Mr Hamilton."

Roger and I were glad to find Derek in his office with the door open. The aroma of his cologne in the corridor confirmed where he was. Respectfully, Roger let me lead.

"Astonishing work. Put a presentation together. Given everything else that happens on a Monday, let's get everyone together in the Fordham Suite at 2:30pm. That'll also give me enough time to meet with Anton and agree what resources we'll need."

CHAPTER 30

Brockwell Park

It was just after midnight when the two 5 Series BMW saloons pulled into Arlingford Road, leading to Brockwell Park in south London. Three men got out of each and walked together through the park gates and over to the partly illuminated adventure playground. As they did, a third BMW pulled up in front of theirs from the opposite direction with its lights off. Two men got out and walked towards the others who had now spaced themselves out in a line watching their approach.

"Hey bro, you brought the money?" asked the eldest of the six.

The taller of the pair, a young black man, who used the street name "Squeako" replied, "yeah, you got the blow?" He then gently raised the small gym bag he was holding in his left hand and shook it. The others took the gesture to mean it contained the money they wanted.

With that, a skinny twenty-year-old man in a baggy purple shell suit stepped forward from the others. He was holding a *Sainsbury's* carrier bag. The tautness of the plastic indicated the contents was the half kilo of cocaine Squeako and his associate had come to buy.

"Let my bro have a butcher's, then we'll do the trade," Squeako shouted.

"We want to see the money first, then you can look," the skinny man called back.

Squeako opened the gym bag to reveal rolls of used banknotes. As he did, the man with the cocaine turned towards his friends looking for a signal. The oldest of the group, a man in his thirties, nodded, and so the shell-suited man let go of one handle for the buyer to inspect the carrier bag's contents. This was a young black man who used the street name, 'Pinkie'.

"I need to be sure it is what it is, bro," Pinkie said, looking behind him momentarily at his associate. Squeako nodded back. With that, Pinkie took out a small pocket torch and shone it into the bag being offered.

"Easy my friend," the skinny man said harshly.

"You can't expect me to buy without checking the quality, bro," said Pinkie, now reaching in to touch the white powder contained in the partly open sandwich bag inside.

The other five moved forward protectively.

"Easy, easy," Squeako said, now feeling exposed. "We're cool. We're cool," he said. "Just let my bro confirm the blow is good and you can have your money." Again, he shook the gym bag to show goodwill.

Pinkie gently poked a finger into the powder before lifting it to his nose. He sniffed sharply leaving a crescent of white around one nostril. Turning back to Squeako, he said softly, "we're cool."

With that, Pinkie, moved suddenly to the right and dropped to the ground. Squeako let go of the gym bag and swiftly reaching behind him with his right hand, pulled a MAC-10 from the back of his trousers. Raising it to chest height and turning the gun on its side, he squeezed the trigger. The gun jerked violently in his hand as it sprayed bullets. Squeako swept it in an arc of fire from right to left ensuring every one of the six men opposite was hit. A stream of spent cartridges flew upwards and then fell away to the right. The intensely bright flame from the barrel illuminated the men's looks of contorted horror as the 9mm bullets tore into their torsos, necks and faces. Smoke drifted away as the final echoes of gunfire faded. Faint groans accompanied by the writhing bodies of two of the six now sprawled on the wet grass indicated they were still alive.

Moving quickly, Pinkie got up, ran back to where the carrier bag of cocaine had fallen and grabbed it. Squeako picked up his gym bag and walked over to where his victims had fallen. Pointing the MAC-10 at one of the two now groaning, he squeezed the trigger, but the gun just clicked impotently.

"Leave 'em!" Pinko shouted. Reluctantly as he realised the gun was empty, Squeako turned and sprinted away. Catching up with Pinko at their car, he stuffed the now hot MAC-10 into his gym bag. As the two of them drove away, the only sense of alarm was the sound of dogs barking in the neighbouring properties.

Rolling over in bed I reached for my pager to silence it. The familiar expletives uttered by my unsympathetic wife warned me once again to leave the room. Grabbing my mobile, I went downstairs as usual to call the number displayed on the pager screen.

"Chief Inspector Information Room," announced the voice on the phone.

"Sir, you paged me, CAD 2-3-7 of today."

Thirty minutes later I stepped from the marked police traffic car that had collected me from home. I told the driver to wait. The dew was glistening in the dawn light and a faint mist slightly obscured the police activity ahead of me around the adventure playground. The number and variety of marked and unmarked police vehicles foreshadowed the crime scene I was about to encounter. As I reached the Constable guarding the cordon at the park gate, I produced my warrant card and gave her my name for the Crime Scene Log. Lifting the blue and white 'Police Do Not Cross' tape she pointed to the SIO standing just outside the large police forensic tent. I put on a pair of forensic overshoes and carefully walked the path marked out with red and white 'Police Inner Cordon' tape, so as to avoid stepping on any footprints left by the suspects. A short distance from the tent, a police photographer in a full forensic outfit was working his way around the yellow crime scene evidence markers placed on the grass. I stopped to check the black numbers on each looking for the highest that would tell me how many spent cases had been found.

Seeing my approach, DI Greg Turner walked to meet me. He had been a DS at Shepherds Bush when I was there as an Inspector.

"Hello Guv, I was told to expect you."

"Not Guv to you anymore, Greg. Good on you for getting promoted. I understand there's been a shooting with a machine gun."

"Yes, we've got four dead and another two at St George's Hospital. One was able to tell uniform what happened. As for the other, it's touch and go whether he'll make it."

"Did you recover the firearm?"

"No, but from the shell cases I can tell you it was a 9mm."

"How many have you recovered? I saw '29' on a marker."

"Yes, twenty-nine. That's one hell of a burst, but I suppose it's what you need if you want to take out six people in one hit."

"Any bullet fragments?"

"Yes, the paramedics retrieved a few from the victims' clothing. My Exhibits' Officer has them in the tent. You're welcome to have a look."

"I would, but without contaminating your crime scene."

"Don't worry, you won't. The world and his brother have walked over that already. The shooter stood over there," and he pointed to where the photographer was busy filming. "Follow me," he then said, leading the way along the short pathway of metal stepping plates. His forensic team had laid these up to the tent to prevent people walking on anything evidential in the grass.

Pieces of clothing, empty packaging and wrappers for dressings and other medical equipment discarded by the paramedics marked out the area where they had treated the two wounded men. The grass was stained deep blood-red where each had fallen.

The tent door was slightly open as we approached, starkly illuminated by an internal floodlight. Greg called out, "Frank, can you let the DI here from SO11 look at those bullet fragments you've got?"

The DS opened the tent door fully. Like the photographer, he was dressed in a white disposable forensic suit over his own clothes, with blue plastic overshoes, and purple latex gloves. The combination of white hood, mask and goggles made him indistinguishable. I took this in whilst focusing more on the scene of the massacre now exposed inside. There, contorted and motionless on the bloodstained grass were four men, ranging in age from early twenties to mid-thirties. It was clear from how their legs were unnaturally tangled; each had died instantly. The paramedics had cut open their upper clothing to check for vital signs, and then left them finding none. I stared briefly at the exposed bodies, each with bloody bullet holes in their abdomens, chests, and necks, and one with his face almost completely torn away wearing a now ripped purple shell suit. It was an horrific sight.

The DS looked at me briefly and reached into the white plastic crate just inside the tent to retrieve two clear plastic exhibit bags that contained the bullet fragments.

"May I?" I said taking them. Gently, I rolled the fragments between my thumb and forefinger while shining a torch to examine each one through the clear plastic. Enough was left for me to see they had blue tips. There were no obvious striation marks, which indicated the gun had a smooth bore barrel.

"I'd like to see the spent cases too, please."

"Sure," and turning to the photographer Greg called out, "Phil, would you bring a couple of those spent cases over here."

He picked up two evidence bags and walked across another line of stepping plates to reach us.

Taking them, I rolled the cases in the bags to look at the markings on the base. Both had the distinctive "IMI 9mm" stamped into them. They also had the tell-tale crescent shaped indentation from where the unique Abonar breech bolt had struck them.

"Thank you, that's all I needed. Do let me know if you get a suspect and recover the firearm, Greg. I'm certain it will turn out to be a reactivated MAC-10 stamped: SF Firearms, with an address in Tunbridge Wells."

CHAPTER 31

Week 5 - It Finally Makes Sense

Monday, 26ᵗʰ May

After attending the scene of the shooting, I decided to spend the rest of Saturday and most of Sunday in the office. I wanted to pull together Abonar's many strands ready to brief Anton and Derek on Monday. More data for the Brighton phone boxes had come in over the weekend, so I had plenty to work on. Once again, the exigencies of duty took precedence. Early in my time with SO11, Brian Mills had advised me that to be successful in the Branch, I needed a home life that put the Directorate first 'whenever necessary'. Given the quadruple murder that had also left two young men fighting for their lives, my working this weekend was such an occasion. I would have asked John and Roger to help but, due to Anton's restrictions on their ranks earning overtime, and mine not being eligible anymore for that extra payment, I worked alone. Olivia was convinced otherwise, despite the frequent calls from my desk phone to reassure her where I was. In one, I got the chance to talk to Rebecca and promise I would be home in time to read her a story before bed. I was glad on both nights that I did. I hated letting her down.

I was back in the office on Monday at 8am. My first job was to take upstairs to Derek the billing authorisations my research had generated. He was not at his desk, so I left them in his pigeonhole.

On my return, I saw Roger and John approaching from the lift lobby.

"Gentlemen, may I buy you a posh brew?"

"Thank you, yes," they said almost in unison.

We took our seats in a quiet corner of '*Caffè Grana*' in the arcade at St. James's Park station. Arguably, this was the best local coffee shop near NSY. The downside was that anyone passing could see through the glass frontage to observe who was talking to who. Consequently, when I wanted a more discreet meeting, I chose one of the local hotel bars. Over a welcome coffee, the three of us caught up on our weekends.

"So, Guv, you think the Brockwell Park shooting was one of our Abonar MAC-10s?" Roger asked.

"Yes, I'm convinced. It makes our going after Mitchell an even greater priority. When we meet later with the bosses, I want your help with pushing for surveillance this week."

"For sure. A quadruple homicide with two more in critical condition will have the very big bosses' attention too," Roger replied, shaking his head. "They'll be asking questions about how to stop the slaughter, and 'Operation Abonar' is the perfect answer."

"Absolutely," I told him.

"So Guv, I assume you didn't earn any points with your wife this weekend," John then asked.

"No. She's not terribly supportive of my wanting another try for promotion."

"Not sure we can cut you any slack, Guv, the way things are right now," Roger said sympathetically.

"Yes, and running Corporate Services is full-on too," I told them. "Then we have to drop everything in response to whatever Central 500 brings in. My problem is that the day-job involves such exciting goings-on I don't want to miss out by being away."

"Remember the old adage, Guv, '*You may love the job, but it doesn't love you back*'," Roger warned. "Oh, and there's another you should think on, and that's '*Graveyards are full of men who thought they were indispensable*'."

"Maybe so Roger, but right now, after what I saw at Brockwell Park, I need to get the job done on Abonar."

"So you don't have any leave planned?" John asked, wanting to show some understanding too.

"No, and I couldn't possibly take any until Abonar's over."

"Well, with us identifying Mitchell and Bown," Roger said, sounding upbeat, "I'd like to think the bosses will now agree to surveillance. That'll resolve Abonar very quickly and you can take a week off or two in June."

"Perhaps," I replied, hoping that might be possible.

I let them walk ahead to the Main Office while I diverted to check my pigeonhole. I was delighted to find Derek had returned the paperwork all signed. On handing it to Pete, he reciprocated with an envelope containing the results to the subscriber checks I had faxed to the CSPs on Sunday.

As I headed back to my office, I found Trevor loitering outside.

"Do you come bearing gifts, again, my friend?" I asked.

"I do, but not everything you wanted," he replied apologetically. "Programming two more clone pagers for you was easy, but Vodapage can't get you the messages until tomorrow at the earliest. Sorry. What they did confirm is that these two are very much alive."

"Okay, well thank you for turning around your bit so quickly."

"It's simple when you know how. I also realised the urgency when I saw you'd sent me the request on Sunday afternoon. Do I assume you worked the whole weekend again?"

"Most of it, yes. Someone shot six people on Saturday: killing four and leaving two critical. The shooter used an Abonar MAC-10, so, yes, we need these pagers urgently. They should get us much closer to the source and his supply chain."

"Glad to help. Right, I've labelled them 'C' and 'D' and written their numbers on the back as usual. I'll leave you to sort out which tone you want them to play."

When we reconvened for our daily meeting, I handed Alice the discs I had worked on over the weekend for her to load on to the i2 chart. "I'm sorry to give you more of these," I told her, "but this latest batch should prove critical to finally identifying everyone in the Abonar supply chain. The good news is the data answers your question about what happened next after the call to the Brighton phone box. It called back the one in Dartford."

With confidence, I then summed up for them what I had learned from my research. Concluding it, I explained, "the data confirms your theory Alice, that Mitchell is clearly at the end of the communications' loop and he's our supplier. He may also be the Abonar gunsmith. That also means Brighton is where we'll find his store of guns and ammunition."

"All this data; it's never-ending Mr H. Anyway, I'm hoping this is the last of it," Alice said crossly while giving me an uncommonly angry look.

"Emily and Natasha aren't busy, Guv. I'll get them to load it for Alice," Roger offered.

"Thanks, as long as that doesn't put you at odds with Mr Hamilton."

"No, and I'll deal with that if it does."

"Thank you," Alice said, looking relieved.

"Good, can you get them to add these subscribers to go with the billing?" I said handing Roger the envelope from Pete.

"Sure."

"Now, Alice, I did help you out over the weekend. I found you hadn't processed the messages for Pager B, so I did them for you."

With another stern look she commented, "that's very kind, but I don't suppose you added them to the chart."

"No, sorry, that's beyond my skill set. Hopefully, Emily and Natasha can do that for you. Roger?"

"Sure, I can ask them to do that too."

"I want to put some markers down," I then announced, " so we can start giving our suspects names. For the Donovans' contact in Eltham, in the absence of identifying them, for now, I propose we call him or her '*Eltham*'."

I was glad to see everyone was nodding.

"And the middleman in Dartford with Pager A, we're comfortable that's now Kieran Walshe. Agreed?"

Again, everyone nodded.

"And we're now attributing Pager B and the Brighton TKs around the Foresight business address to Anthony Mitchell. Everyone still happy?"

"Yes, that's correct," Alice agreed.

"Good, so over the weekend, I went through the call data for those Brighton TKs and found two significant parallel channels of communication. First, Mitchell messaged what is now '*Pager C*'. John, present for you," I said, sliding across the table to him one of the devices Trevor had just given me. "I don't yet know who this belongs to. What I can tell you, though, is that Mitchell messaged *C* at times that coincide with the build-up to the deliveries to Whitechapel, Plaistow and the Tollgate Hotel. I think this will prove to be his courier."

"Did you work out where he's based, Guv?"

"Yes, he paged Mitchell with 01634 numbers, which is around Rochester in Kent. As we don't yet have a name, let's call this suspect '*Rochester*'."

"And you did all that without using an i2 chart?" Alice said with a mischievous giggle.

"Yes, Alice, and when you're next in my office, you'll see my whiteboard is one massive mind-map with different coloured lines for each of our suspects. What it also threw out is 'Pager D', and here you go, John, another gift. I need you to babysit this one too, please," sliding the second device over.

"Sure," he said, trying to look appreciative of this extra task.

"I'll explain what to do when they go off afterwards. Vodapage advise that *C* and *D* are very much alive."

"So where do we start looking for whoever is using Pager D, Guv?" Roger asked

"I'm coming to that. So, as I said, I found two parallel channels of communication. Pager C, aka Rochester, is tied in to our three firearms recoveries. Pager D is not. Mitchell calls him or her at other times and frequently. That indicates this second channel is used for his other business."

"Have you also located Pager D?"

"Yes and no. I went through Mitchell's messages and Brighton billing to work out the pattern. That led me to a single TK in Marvels Lane, Grove Park, in south-east London. But I can't tell you yet who's using it."

"No way!" Roger shouted excitedly. "I know who it is. Who's got the *Geographia London Street Atlas*?"

"There's one here," I said, passing it to him.

"Yes, yes, I knew it," he said, staring at the map. "Right, Marvels Lane is in Grove Park. It's SE12. Which of our named suspects also lives in that postcode?"

"SE12 is Eltham, isn't it?" John suggested.

"Yes, but Grove Park isn't anywhere near the Eltham TKs, so it's not our suspect 'Eltham'." Annoyingly, Roger continued his game, "it's someone else we identified at the end of last week."

"Come on Roger, we can all see you're dying to tell us. Who is it?" I asked.

"Robert Bown," he announced with obvious glee. "Look on the street map. He lives here at 9 Balder Rise, SE12. If he walks out his front door to the end of the road, that's Marvels Lane. The TK is on the corner. I know this because Grove Park was my old ground as a PC."

"Wow, fantastic. What a result! Good local knowledge, Roger," I said, delighted with his news. "If we now accept Pager D and the Marvels Lane TK are Bown, I can explain why he is so important to my theory of parallel channels."

"You're clearly on a roll, Guv, best you keep going," John said, now quite animated.

"When you did that digging, John, into the CZ pistol that Don McGregor didn't want to talk about, what date was it recovered?"

"January 18th."

"Yes, and interestingly, Mitchell received three messages the day before from the Marvels Lane TK. Mitchell called him back each time. What if that was Bown wanting to know when Mitchell would deliver the gun for him to give to whoever was travelling by train to Scotland the next day?"

"Mr H, I'm surprised at you," Alice smiled, "you've just broken your ABC," and then laughed.

"Yes, that is quite a long-shot Guvnor, even by our standards. How did you jump to that conclusion?" Roger asked.

"Well, Marco as good as confirmed the MABs and CZ were worked on by the same gunsmith." I looked around confident that I could change their sceptical expressions. "Look, I know I've had the advantage of spending the weekend staring at the data, but I can tell you there's more to back up my theory about this being Bown and Mitchell sorting out the CZ. Oh, and Alice, you'll also find a London number paged Bown at the same times. Can you research that too?"

"Of course, Mr H."

"We're with you Guvnor," John commented, his tone suggesting he was not yet convinced, "but you'll need something far more solid when we brief the bosses later."

"Yes, I know. My annoyance is we don't yet have the messages for the two new pagers. However, what I can see from Mitchell's and his use of the Brighton TKs is he's not the one organising business with Bown. It's Bown who's paging him first to call back. The trigger is that London number that messages him beforehand."

"And the earliest we can expect those is tomorrow?" Alice queried.

"Sadly, yes," and I paused for a moment before moving on. "Right, now I need to give you my agenda for this afternoon. Alice, I want you, please, to take us through the end-to-end sequence of phone calls and pager messages for our three firearms recoveries."

"If Emily and Natasha have loaded the data by then, I can," she replied pointedly.

"Okay, well, if not, I'll have to bring everyone into my office and do it from the whiteboard. What we need to show is the loop that begins with Eltham messaging Walshe who messages Mitchell, who then messages Rochester, and then back again all the way to the Donovans in Manchester."

"And then to Gudgeon and Harrison," Alice added.

"Exactly."

"I better come and look at your whiteboard, Mr H."

"Please do, Alice. Right, Roger, I want you to lead on what we know about Bown."

"Sure."

"John and Mark, please add everything we've learned about Foresight and Mitchell, including what we got from the Proof House and the links to Bown and Foresight."

"Yup, we can do that."

"Very good. Right, please meet me back here at 2pm. My door is open if you need me."

Operation Abonar

CHAPTER 32

Convincing Our Bosses

That afternoon, Alice did a magnificent job walking Derek and Anton through her chart and highlighting what we knew. Roger and John added more details from their knowledge to corroborate it. Other than a couple of questions to confirm their understanding, our bosses were happy with the presentation and hugely impressed with what the team had achieved.

"So, if I may, I'll now summarise who we need to target," I began. "By 'we', I'd like to recommend a joint SO11-OCG surveillance operation."

"Okay," Anton said abruptly, "Derek and I will let you know who's doing what a little later once we've had our own separate chat about your briefing."

"Of course, Boss. First, I'm going to take the unusual step of saying who we're not going after in phase one, and that's the Donovans' family friend we're calling '*Eltham*'."

"Why?" Anton said, not even trying to hide his surprise.

"Other than our assumptions about what the call data indicates, we've got nothing to identify them. We'd also burn up valuable surveillance time watching a bunch of phone boxes when we can go after the big prize, Mitchell, right now."

"Okay, I can see your logic. So this person Eltham still remains a target for later?"

"Yes, absolutely. It may be once we show Mitchell how we broke into his closed communications network, he'll give us the name anyway. He may also give us the Donovans."

"Hmm, what risks do we take if we do delay?" Anton asked, sounding dubious.

"With the firearms job, none," I replied confidently. "But Mr Hamilton may think differently, as Eltham could also be your suspect for the RPGs."

"Let's keep the two separate," Derek interjected sharply. "I can take the risk of delaying surveillance to identify Eltham while the Home Secretary continues to defer negotiations."

202

"Fine, then I can go with that too," Anton said nodding, and then smiling added, "any others you want to discount, *Mr H?*"

"Yes, I'd also like to leave Kieran Walshe alone for the same reasons. The call data suggests he's simply the arranger and may not lay hands on the firearms and ammunition himself. If we arrest him now and he blanks us in interview[36], then we've got nothing solid on him about his involvement. I doubt the call data alone will be enough."

"And he'll know everything to then alert the others," Roger helpfully added.

Derek concurred, "yes, and with the Flying Squad's Operation Bridge looking promising, I'm happy to let Walshe keep running too. Again, Mitchell may give him up along with the others."

"Okay, that all seems sensible," Anton smiled. "So, *Mr H*, tell us about Mitchell and Bown?"

Looking at my team with pride I said, "Anthony Mitchell is our number one target. Number two is Robert Bown. We know they're involved in this together. That's confirmed by their communications. I recommend we put them both under surveillance."

"What about the suspect '*Rochester*'?" Anton asked.

"With the Customs' job now over," I replied, "that connection is quiet compared to Mitchell and Bown. I'd recommend we sweep him or her up after the other two in the hope they give us the name."

"Okay, to go after Mitchell and Bown will require extra resources if it means doing them together, which I think is the best approach," Anton commented. "Bown being in London won't be a problem, but Mitchell in Brighton will stretch us. I'll need to talk to the Regional Crime Squad at Crawley."

"Yes, we should call a meeting with them for later in the week," Derek added. "I'd also like to see the i2 chart finished beforehand to be certain we've tidied up all the loose ends."

"We're on to that already," I replied to reassure him.

Anton stood up and, nodding to the team said, "brilliant work. Who'd have thought you could get this far from nothing more than analysing call data and some educated guesswork. Not sure you've stuck to your ABC *Mr H,* but well done."

We all laughed as Anton added, "I can see Corporate Services being used for more jobs like Abonar. Derek and I will get back to you on next steps once

---

36 In interview: colloquial police term rather than say 'in an interview'.

we've organised a meeting to arrange surveillance. We can also discuss your support for the next phase of this SO11-led OCG operation."

Derek visibly flinched at that remark.

"Well Derek, it is SO11's intelligence that's been leading your OCG operation," Anton said with pride as the two of them left the room.

CHAPTER 33

Pager Messages

Tuesday, 27ᵗʰ May

Almost immediately after I unlocked my office door to start the day, my mobile rang. The screen displayed a number I did not recognise.

"Good morning. Hope all is well with yae."

I immediately recognised the Glaswegian voice and accent.

"Detective Superintendent Don McGregor, I assume."

"Aye, indeed, it is I. I've got a meeting this morning at Thames House. I thoroughly recommend yae join me. I can now tell yae all about our involvement in your Abonar job. I expect yae'll want to hear what we know."

"Yes, absolutely."

"Good, very good. It may well be that I can hand over some aspects to yae, as I promised. That way I can focus on the job that matters to me in Glasgow."

"Sounds great. What time, Sir?"

"Say 9:30, is that good for yae, laddie? It'll go on for most of the morning and maybe a little into the afternoon. That way the Security Service can buy us all lunch too. Can yae make it?"

"Yes, of course. Can you book me in, or should I call someone there to sort it?"

"I can do that for yae. It's best you come without your team. Sorry, but there's some sensitivities about what we'll be discussing and the people yae need to meet."

"Sir, if I may, I should bring my Detective Superintendent. He'll be very lumpy if I come without him. Can I call you back to confirm?"

"Aye, alright. Call me back on this number."

John and Roger appeared at my door.

"Sorry, guys. Give me a minute while I clear my lines to get permission for something. Fancy another posh coffee when I come back?"

They both nodded as I headed swiftly to Anton's office. Thankfully, he had just got in too and was still gathering his thoughts before starting the day in earnest. I explained the call I had just received.

"Thank you for remembering to seek permission rather than forgiveness. Sorry, I can't make it. Derek's leading Abonar anyway. I recommend you ask him."

I rushed up the fire escape stairs and found him in his office in a fog of freshly applied cologne moving papers around his desk. Again, I explained the meeting invitation.

"Okay, I can make it for the morning, Michael, but if it goes into the afternoon, I'm not so sure. Have to play it by ear. Let Don McGregor know I'll be coming with you."

I called Don back and gave the details for Derek and myself.

Returning to my two coffee companions, I checked my watch. There was enough time to treat them and get to Thames House.

On our way back from *Caffè Grana*, Pete called my mobile to say he had put several envelopes in my pigeonhole. We stopped off at the Branch Office for me to collect them. I was delighted to also find two from Vodapage. Grabbing them, I handed the lot to John. As I did, I heard an unfamiliar ringing tone and quickly realised from the accompanying vibration against my left hip that it was Pager B.

"Hang on guys, it looks like Mitchell just got a message."

John and Roger stopped while I checked the screen. "It's Bown wanting Mitchell to call the Marvels Lane phone box. Let me call BT Special Services."

The BT Duty Manager went through the standard verification process to confirm my authority before agreeing to page me with the details of the incoming number calling the Marvels Lane phone box. A few minutes later, my own pager sounded. The screen showed one of the 01273 Brighton TKs. By now we were all standing around Alice's desk and I showed them the message.

Just then, John flinched as he realised Pager C was vibrating on his belt. He unclipped it to view the screen while I redialled BT Special Services.

"It's Mitchell leaving a message for Rochester to call him on the same Brighton TK you got Guv," John said, clearly pleased that he recognised the connections.

A few minutes later, my pager screen lit up giving an 01634 Rochester number and I showed it to the others.

"That's one of the three Rochester TKs they've used before," Alice advised. "The fact the person called Mitchell back so quickly suggests it's very close to where they either live or work. That confirms '*Rochester*' is in that town."

"Yes, indeed," I said encouragingly. "I've got to dash over to Thames House now with Mr Hamilton. John, I need you, please, to call back the Duty Manager in BT Special Services and request all the incoming and outgoing calls for the past 24 hours for the Marvels Lane phone box. Similarly, the next ones made to and from the Rochester one." John nodded as he wrote down my instructions.

"BT have had both on live trace since yesterday morning," I continued, "so they should be able to give you the numbers straight away. If it's anything significant, page me. Alright?"

CHAPTER 34

The Glasgow Connection

Once Derek and I cleared security at Thames House we were met by the woman who had arrived late for my meeting on May 15th. Shaking my hand, she said, "Good to see you again. I'm Felicity from T6. I'll take you up to the meeting room."

"May I also introduce Detective Superintendent Derek Hamilton from the Organised Crime Group."

"Yes, I head the executive arm of Abonar," Derek announced rather too pompously I thought; especially since he was riding on our coattails. He sensed my annoyance and tried to compensate with, "I'll be leading the surveillance operation now to arrest the suspects identified by Michael's team."

"That's useful to know," she commented courteously, "as we'll be getting into the division of labour at the meeting."

Derek and I exchanged glances and smiled at the news of this promising development. Felicity led the way to the same dark oak panelled meeting room we had used for ours. The room was abuzz with the voices of those already gathered. There was a group of men and women getting themselves teas and coffees at the refreshments table. One of them was sorting through the biscuit assortment, picking out the chocolate ones and placing his choices on an extra saucer. Felicity resumed talking with Hamish, who acknowledged our arrival and came over.

"Hamish, I'd like to introduce you to Derek Hamilton from the OCG. He's now leading both strands of Abonar."

"Delighted to meet you," Hamish said but his tone suggested indifference, possibly due to Derek being unknown in the world of MI5 Weapons Intelligence.

I noticed Hamish was holding an album of photographs opened at the page of an image of a CZ Model 27 pistol and silencer. "It's the one recovered at Preston Railway Station in January," he explained seeing my stare. "Thought you'd like to see it," and he handed it over for me to study.

Don McGregor and his DS, Craig Campbell, were deep in conversation with three men over by the window. They were all in very good spirits, with laughter interspersing almost every point of their conversation. I began counting the heads to find we totalled twenty in the room.

"Better grab a coffee and some biscuits, Sir, and then work the room," I said quietly to Derek.

"Good idea. Do you know many of these characters?"

"You've just met my opposite number in MI5. Those two are from Strathclyde Police. That one is, Detective Superintendent Don McGregor. Alongside him is his bagman, DS Craig Campbell. I recognise at least one of the three they're talking to. May I suggest we chat to them first?"

"Lead on."

"Mr McGregor, DS Campbell, may I introduce my boss from the Organised Crime Group, Detective Superintendent Derek Hamilton."

"Michael, good to see yae again," Don said enthusiastically shaking my hand.

"And Derek, glad yae could join us too." He seemed surprised by Derek's limp handshake and released his grip quickly. He paused for a moment before courteously saying, "I'm chairing the meeting and will get everyone to introduce themselves, so yae know who's who. Please, grab a seat."

We took up two in the middle opposite Don. "Let's get cracking," he announced loudly as we did so. "Everyone, please grab a seat.

This time, no one chose to sit away from the table. The introductions usefully identified who else was in the room. They included other members of MI5 with responsibility for countering serious organised crime. Some were involved in technical and conventional surveillance, others with analytical roles. Also of note were three detectives from the South-East Regional Crime Squad (SERCS), Detective Superintendent Barry Gough, Detective Chief Inspector Marcus Bagshaw, and Detective Inspector Arthur Wilton.

"Right, now we all know each other, let me bring yae up to speed," Don began eagerly. "I'd like to start by thanking our MI5 colleagues and SERCS for such brilliant help with arresting Paul Ferris. Now we need to ensure 'Houdini', as he's known in Glasgow, goes down at court," he said with extra emphasis on his last four words.

I looked around at the knowing nods and smiles from the others.

Derek looked as perplexed as I, and Don sensed this.

"Okay. Sorry. For those of yae not engaged in last Friday's phenomenally successful operation, let me explain. We have Paul Ferris, aka Houdini, in custody. That's what we call him due to his incredible ability in the past to escape justice."

I nodded in appreciation of the explanation.

"With him were Arthur Suttie and Constance Howarth, also from Glasgow, plus John Ackerman from Islington here in London. We've nicked them all for unlawful possession of firearms. Derek and Michael, of particular interest to yae will be three MAC-10s, six Uzi magazines, a hundred rounds of your blue-tipped 9mm ammunition and fifty rounds of the copper-jacketed variety. There's also three silencers and a detonator, although, we have no idea why they had that last item."

"Fantastic result, well done," I said excitedly.

"Aye, and from the photos yae shared with me at your meeting, Michael, I can tell yae these all tie in with your job at the Tollgate Hotel in March, and the others in Brixton and Manchester."

DS Campbell slid an album of photographs across the table to us.

"Thank you. And what about the man who supplied them?" I asked.

"Dinnae despair, I'll come to him shortly laddie. Now, when we arrested Ackerman and searched his Islington address, we recovered a MAB pistol. Yae'll recognise that one too, Michael."

While Don kept talking, DS Campbell indicated the photograph we should look at in our album by showing us the corresponding one in his.

"Craig, would yae like to explain the connection between Ackerman's gun and the Abonar ones," Don asked him.

"Sure, Sir. Yae'll see it has the same features as yours. Under the grips there's the same three Cyrillic letters scratched into the frame. There's also a threaded extension to the barrel for a silencer. I know it dinnae appear on all the Abonar MABs, but it's the same workmanship as the MAC-10 barrels. And the silencer with Ackerman's MAB is like those with the MAC-10s. It's also the same workmanship as the CZ pistol we recovered at Preston Railway Station."

He smiled at me as he said it, and I nodded back my appreciation at finally getting confirmation.

"Thank you," Derek said, "great result. How did you know when and where to make the arrests?"

"If I may, Derek," Don took over again, "for the benefit of not boring everyone else with a story they already know, I'll brief yae privately afterwards. I wannae focus now on next steps and who's doing what to tie up the loose ends. Is that okay for yae Derek?"

"Yes, of course. Please carry on."

"Thank yae. Right, forgive that brief interlude while I brought our friends from the Yard up to speed. Let me focus now on the two main purposes of this meeting. First, to make sure we have the evidence really tight. I wannae be sure nae jury will let Ferris walk away this time," Don raised his voice to assert his expectation. "I know it sounds personal, and that's because it is, but I want to prove he's nae longer a successful escape artist."

It was clear from the murmurs around the table that the others shared his annoyance at whatever had gone before.

"Second, to divide up the work that's fallen out of these arrests. I want your agreement before we leave today on who'll lead the operation to make the arrests, and who'll take charge of the intelligence-development to support it."

Again, the others nodded, and I noticed Derek was doing the same. It had become so infectious, I found myself doing it too.

"As far as Subjects One and Two, Ferris and Suttie, are concerned, they're claiming Subject Three, Ackerman conned them. They thought he was handing over a box of counterfeit £20 notes and the plates to print them they'd come to collect, all for the £4,000 we found in Ackerman's home. They're claiming not to know about the MAC-10s. We recovered them from a box their girl, Constance 'Connie' Howarth, our Subject Four, was taking back to Glasgow for them. Ferris and Suttie dinnae know about the evidence we've built around them. In particular, that they've been planning for months to buy guns in London to settle a gangland feud in Glasgow. Right now, they're nae cooperating."

Don paused to look at his notebook.

"And with regard to Subject Four," he continued, "Connie's having none of it either. She claims her friend, Suttie, simply asked her to take a box back to Glasgow. She dinnae know about the contents. When we told her we'd had her under surveillance since April along with Suttie and Ferris, she decided to make no comment. Yae'll recall April 9th is when the three of them originally came down to London to meet with Ackerman and arrange the deal to buy the MAC-10s."

Again the others nodded showing the benefit of their knowledge that Derek and I were only just learning.

"So, we cannae expect Connie to be much help. With any luck, though, since she got remanded in custody yesterday and is now banged up in Holloway[37] for a wee while, we can have another go at getting the truth once reality kicks in for her."

---

37   Holloway: HMP Holloway – all-female prison in London.

Don reached for his coffee and took a gulp before continuing.

"Moving now to Ackerman. He's become an evangelist I understand. He can't stop talking to SERCS. I think he's on his tenth taped interview. Am I right Barry?"

Barry Gough nodded.

"So, to summarise, Ackerman's telling the whole gunrunning story he's been involved in since the late 80s. He's identified his source of supply, how the network operates, and he's named the courier delivering the guns to him."

Don paused again, as others expressed their appreciation by gently banging the table in applause. "Very good, very good," he continued. "So, this is where your own hard work on Abonar will pay off for us now, Michael," Don added, looking at me kindly. "Yae can help close some gaps in our knowledge."

"Sure," I replied, and nodded back in eager anticipation.

"So, my proposal is this. Now that Ackerman's remanded into police custody, Barry, I'd like SERCS to continue debriefing him. Bleed him for everything he knows about Ferris first, and then the other gunrunners in the supply chain. Can yae do that for us, Barry?"

"Yes, of course, Don. We'd be delighted," he replied. "From what I understand, other than the Scottish dimension with Ferris, many of Ackerman's clients are based in the south-east anyway, so it's right he stays with us."

"Excellent, thank yae."

"Oh, and I'll also need to talk to the North-West Regional Crime Squad," Barry added. "Ackerman's talking about links to gangs in Merseyside and Manchester."

"The more yae can bring in to help the better, Barry," Don said smiling.

"What about the man Ackerman named as his supplier? Do you want us to take him on too?"

"Gimme a moment, Barry, before we move on to that character. Let me just finish off with what we'll do about Ackerman first. So, from a Scottish perspective, and I think our MI5 colleagues will agree, we've achieved our mission by getting Ferris locked up." He looked momentarily at the MI5 officers sitting to his right and got a nod from them. "Good, so I need to focus my efforts now on making the case stick against him and then Suttie and Howarth. We've also got to finish off connecting McAuley's arrest directly to Ferris for that CZ pistol."

"If I may Sir," DS Campbell interrupted, "for the benefit of our Scotland Yard colleagues, I think we should share what we know about the communications that went on behind McAuley getting the CZ pistol?"

"Aye, you're right, thanks for the reminder. I'm sure yae'll find that helpful, Michael. Lead them through it, please, Craig."

DS Campbell was glad to do so and began, "from our schedule of telephone calls between Ackerman's landline, McAuley's mobile, Ferris's mobile and messages on his pager, there's a very strong inference to support each of them being connected with the CZ pistol." He paused to show everyone their equivalent of Alice's chart. "As you'll understand, we need to do some work now to make it all evidential and avoid exposing how we knew what they were talking about. What's particularly important to you, Mr Hallowes, are the calls on 17th January. These are between Ackerman and the man who delivered the gun to him, and between that man and the one who supplied it."

"Would you be able to share with us their phone numbers?" I asked.

DS Campbell looked sideways at his boss, so I focused my stare on him too.

"Aye, we can give yae the numbers now," Don said smiling, "and I feel sure Craig can fax you down our schedule of calls once we're back in Glasgow."

"Thank you very much," I replied gratefully. "Can you also share the names of the men who supplied and delivered the CZ pistol?"

I noticed DS Campbell had already started writing on a pad of paper. He stopped and looked up due to the continuing silence from his boss, who seemed to deliberately delay answering my request.

"Aye, we can do that for yae too, Michael," Don eventually announced with a huge smile after his unnecessarily long pause, which I took to be his attempt at humour.

With huge faith in my team, I took a chance by asking, "can you confirm the supplier is Anthony Mitchell and his courier is Robert Bown?"

"Aye, Michael, they are. So now yae know why I could nae share with yae what we knew before. I could nae risk yae compromising our golden opportunity to catch Ferris with his hands well and truly dirty."

Nodding, I replied, "yes, I quite understand."

"Aye, as yae have no doubt worked out for yourself laddie, it was Mitchell who gave Bown the CZ pistol to deliver to Ackerman. There was a delay, hence the calls between Ackerman, Bown and Mitchell to get it sorted. Ferris was leaning on Ackerman, who put pressure on Bown, and that led him to page Mitchell. As yae know, the gun got to Ackerman in time for McAuley to collect it as planned on January 18th."

I sat back in my chair, exhilarated by this major confirmation of the success of our own analysis.

Leaning forward I asked, "and can you also confirm the same arrangement between Mitchell, Bown and Ackerman for getting the MAC-10s to Ferris?"

"Aye, I can do that for yae too. What I dinnae think we can help yae with today is how Mitchell supplied the guns recovered in London and Kent. We'll have to ask SERCS to work that one out."

"Thank you, we'd be delighted to work with SERCS on that," I offered. As I spoke, I felt Derek tug at my arm reproachfully. When I turned to look at him, he just stared straight ahead. I was then distracted as DS Campbell slid the paper across on which he had written the names and phone numbers.

"So, where was I?" Don seemed lost in thought for a moment before continuing, "aye, so I'm very happy to leave everything to SERCS that Ackerman tells yae about people and events south of the border. Is everyone else happy with that as an outcome?"

They all nodded in their usual manner.

Don looked at Derek and me. "Well, that's all good then. Derek, is that alright with yae? SERCS take on Mitchell and Bown?"

"Yes, I'm happy for SERCS to take over that aspect of our investigation too."

I was dumbfounded. After weeks of intense work, in an instant he just had given away our chance of being involved in the arrests of our principal Abonar suspects.

While the others continued their discussion, I consoled myself by quickly scanning through DS Campbell's list to compare them with ours. I noted we did not yet have the mobile and home numbers for Bown and Mitchell. This reinforced our supposition that because these were directly attributable, neither had used them for what went on with Abonar. I waited for a moment when the conversation lulled to check this.

"Mr McGregor, if I may, I've just been comparing your list of names and numbers with ours. May I ask how you came by the ones for Bown and Mitchell?"

He turned to DS Campbell to reply.

"Aye, until Ackerman's arrest, we only had their pager numbers. We didn't know any names or other numbers until SERCS searched Ackerman's address."

"Yes," Barry Gough added, "we found Ackerman kept an address book. He also had them in the contacts on his mobile."

"Thank you, that's very helpful," and I nodded to show I had finished my line of questioning.

Suddenly, I was very conscious of the fact I had Mitchell's clone pager right there in the room clipped to my belt. I prayed it did not go off. I needed time to work out what leverage I could gain from having it and Bown's, plus the so far unattributed Pager C for '*Rochester*'. Since Derek seemed all too happy to be giving away our involvement, I hoped these would give us something of a stake in what SERCS did next. That prompted me to say, "Mr Gough, if I may, I'd like to suggest one of your team spends a day with mine. I'd also be very happy to join you when you crash through Mitchell's and Bown's doors. We can put an evidential package together, so you know what we're looking for."

"Thank you, that's a great suggestion."

"Let's not get ahead of ourselves, please," Derek interrupted while looking at me sternly. "Barry and Don, you were talking about a division of labour, with SERCS taking the lead."

"Aye, I was. Are yae agreeing to Michael's offer to help with the intelligence-development to arrest Mitchell and Bown?"

"I'll need to check with the Director of Intelligence before I can commit to that," Derek replied somewhat falteringly. Regaining his composure, he quickly added, "of course, I'm happy to share with SERCS the intelligence picture we've built so far."

"Very good, very good," Don responded. "For a moment there Derek, I thought yae were walking away completely. Right, everyone, shall we take a fifteen-minute comfort break? I'd like to resume by reaching agreements on what we can and cannot use in evidence. We've employed a fair few covert techniques that I suspect need expunging from what we're prepared to disclose in court."

Again, the gathering nodded in agreement and their voices grew louder as the formality of the meeting was overtaken with more genial conversation.

Derek turned to me. "I have to get back. You're welcome to stay but understand this. I don't have the resources to commit to your strand of Abonar. I've got enough to do with the RPGs. Quite frankly, I'm bloody relieved SERCS have taken over. You're not to say anything about the RPGs, though. Is that clear?'

"Of course, Sir," I said, trying not to sound overly obsequious whilst feeling particularly let down by his easy surrender of Abonar to SERCS.

"Good. By all means let SERCS have a package for when they execute their search warrants, but that's where your role ends," he added firmly. "You don't need to be involved in the arrests. You can now happily walk away knowing you and your team did a great job. And I'll be telling Anton that when I see him later. Okay?"

"Sir, of course," I said, but as I began working out an alternative approach, he interrupted my thoughts.

"Good. Remember, from now on you're here just to observe. I understand the protocol is you move to the back of the room."

With that, he walked around the table and spoke to Barry and Don. In doing so, he pointed in my direction. They looked across at me briefly and then watched Derek leave the room.

Hamish came over. "Are you alright? You have a face like thunder."

"No, I'm not. This may sound ridiculous, my good friend, but Abonar was my first major Scotland Yard investigation. The team's worked flat-out for a month to the point where we were just days away from arresting Mitchell and Bown ourselves. Now Derek expects me to hand it all over to SERCS and walk away. I'm just not wired that way to give up my investigations."

"Yes, and I can see that. Some might say it's one of the perils of being an intelligence officer. Yours is not the glory to be had. That's for the operational people who act on your guidance. Nevertheless, SERCS would be foolish not to take up your offer. That may work to your benefit."

I sat there pondering a similarly painful experience as a Trainee Detective on the Divisional Crime Squad in 1983. I had spent days identifying and then tracking down the suspect for an armed robbery. He had slashed a shopkeeper's ear clean off with a carving knife when he refused to open the till. The awful thing was police had actually stopped the suspect nearby because he matched the description. However, they forgot all that when he came back as 'wanted' on the PNC for a breach of bail. They took him to the police station where he remained in custody for court in the morning. The officers hadn't searched him properly, because he then paid the fine with the money stolen from the robbery. He had kept that hidden all the time in his underwear. A week later, I tracked him to an address in the City Road. I was all ready to make the arrest when my boss told me to go home as he couldn't afford the overtime. I had to hand over what was a very good job to colleagues who knew nothing about it, and that hurt. The experience so early in my career was now hardwired into my character not to let it happen again. So, it was doubly painful to see it being played out now with Abonar.

Don and Barry came over to join us. Barry was the first to speak.

"Michael, I think we've met before somewhere."

"Yes Sir, my office is next door to your old colleague, DCS Brian Mills. You and I have often passed in the fourth-floor corridor. I'm sure I've encountered DCI Bagshaw there too."

"Of course, yes, that's where I know you from. You're the married man with the baby next door!" he added laughing.

"I'm keen to forget that, actually."

"Look, we can all see the tension between you and Mr Hamilton. He wants you to hand over what until now has been your job. I get it you'd like to hold on to something of the reins." Barry's tone sounded reassuringly sympathetic. "So, let me make you an offer. I'll talk to Brian. I'll ask him to agree to you helping us prepare for Mitchell's and Bown's arrests."

I nodded as he set out his plan, very happy to still be involved.

"We came into this cold ourselves when Don asked us to assist with arresting Ferris and Ackerman. Before last week, we knew nothing. I could really do with your help navigating a path to sweep up Mitchell and his entire gunrunning network."

"Aye, that's only right, Barry," Don added. "I know what it's like when a job like this gets personal. Now, I've also promised Michael, I'll tell him the whole story. If we can wrap this up shortly, how about yae join us for a pint? Would that suit yae, laddie?"

"Thank you, it would."

CHAPTER 35

A Scottish Tale

Don was very gracious. He insisted I remain at the table and did everything he could to make me feel part of the meeting. The story he told later explained the enormity of Paul Ferris's gangland violence in Glasgow, and why arresting him had become so personal to Don.

In March 1992, following an extensive Strathclyde Police investigation, and after the longest criminal trial in Scottish history lasting fifty-four days, involving more than three hundred witnesses, Ferris walked free from Glasgow's High Court. The jury failed to convict him on all seven counts that included murder, possession of a firearm, and supplying drugs. This was due mostly to one prosecution witness who proved to be hugely unreliable. It must have influenced the jury significantly because they chose to disregard all the hard evidence, including forensics, that seemed to connect Ferris to the crimes.

That experience made Don determined to catch Ferris next time with his hands dirty. He wanted to make sure it was for the serious gangland violence he knew Ferris was actively orchestrating. Thus, he needed the evidence to be so overwhelming no jury could acquit him again.

Ferris was running a company, 'Premier Security Services'. His violent gangland activities allowed him to expand the business. Very quickly, he had become 'public enemy number one' in Glasgow. The rivalries he caused with other gangs escalated to the point where he needed heavier weaponry in his arsenal to settle feuds once and for all. Because of this, he wanted the CZ pistol and the MAC-10s plus the ammunition and silencers.

Knowing he could be under police surveillance and fearing there may be informants amongst his associates, Ferris distanced himself from all visible acts of criminality. That was why in January he arranged for one of his more trusted lieutenants, Joseph McAuley, to travel by train to London and collect the CZ pistol, silencer and ammunition from Ackerman. However, MI5 had McAuley under surveillance the whole time. Their objective was to put him into a situation where he would be arrested on his way back to Glasgow.

It was late on Friday, January 18th, when McAuley collected the package from Ackerman and headed back to Kings Cross Station where he boarded the overnight sleeper to Glasgow. In the buffet car, he was delighted to be befriended by two men who generously bought him drinks. It did not take long for McAuley to cross the threshold and become an aggressive drunk. His two drinking companions deliberately goaded him about his Scottish heritage. Alarmed by McAuley's behaviour, the train guard telephoned ahead to British Transport Police, requesting they board at Preston. Uniformed officers arrested McAuley for being drunk and disorderly and found the pistol with its ammunition and silencer when they searched his bag. The following day, McAuley's drinking partners debriefed their colleagues at Thames House on the success of their mission to trap the man.

Furious at McAuley's incompetence, Ferris contacted Ackerman again. This time, he would come to London and do the deal in person. On Wednesday, April 9th, MI5 surveillance officers followed Ferris, together with Arthur Suttie and Constance Howarth, all the way from Glasgow to meet with Ackerman at his Islington address on Highbury Station Road. MI5 let the three Scots return home. They already knew Ferris's purpose that day had been simply to build trust and then wait for Ackerman to confirm the MAC-10s were ready for collection.

Around lunchtime on Friday, May 23rd, more than 60 officers from Strathclyde Police, SERCS, and MI5 plotted up around Ackerman's home.

"Subjects One and Two, with Subject Three, out, out," the surveillance officer reported over her radio. She was watching Ferris (Subject One) and Suttie (Subject Two) leave with Ackerman (Subject Three) from the latter's home.

"Subject One is carrying an Opal Fruits box. Repeat, Subject One has the package," she continued.

"I have[38]," said the next officer in the team, as he picked up the group and took over the commentary, following the trio on foot to the junction with Liverpool Road. "Now into the 'Duchess of Kent'," he added moments later. "All three subjects into the public house on the corner of Ellington Street and Liverpool Road."

"5-1-7, go in and observe," the Team Leader instructed.

Another surveillance officer's radio broadcast the noises of people talking inside the pub followed by her hushed voice, "Subject One is on the phone at the bar."

"5-1-7 received. Subject One on the phone. Standby," the Team Leader relayed more loudly to everyone.

---

38 'I have': surveillance term to confirm they have the subject in sight.

"From 2-1-6, Subject Four is two minutes away, just ended a call on her mobile," reported the second surveillance Team Leader. She was heading south in the Holloway Road. Her team had been following Constance Howarth since she left Glasgow early that morning driving a blue Vauxhall Nova hatchback.

"From 5-1-7," she said quietly again, wanting not to be overheard, "Subject One is now waiting at the Liverpool Road door with the package."

"From 2-1-6, Subject Four is now pulling into the car park in Ellington Street."

"Subject One out," 5-1-7 said quietly, "towards the car park now."

"From 2-1-6, I have them both. Subject One has handed over the package to Subject Four. Package now in the boot. Package is in the boot of the Vauxhall Nova.."

"From 5-1-7, Subject One now back into the pub."

"Okay, from 2-1-6, Subject Four away. Standby for direction."

"5-1-7, are you still inside the pub with Subjects One, Two and Three?" enquired the first Team Leader. "Thank you. Three clicks received for yes."

"From 2-1-6, Subject Four now northbound, A1 Holloway Road. I'm going to let her run for a mile then bring the car to a hard stop."

"2-1-6 received."

"5-1-7 sitrep[39]?"

Again, her radio broadcast the sound of voices from inside the pub.

"Nothing received. Are all three subjects still together?" and then when confirmation followed, "Thank you, three clicks received for yes."

Every few minutes, one of the surveillance officers reported, "no change, no change".

Suddenly, another officer advised, "from 5-1-5, Subjects One, Two and Three out, out. Liverpool Road. Standby".

The surveillance teams parked up around the Islington streets waited.

"From 5-1-5, Subjects One and Two away north on foot. Subject Three away south on foot."

The first surveillance team followed Ackerman back to his home. A third now kept up with the other two as they got into a Ford saloon, with Ferris driving and Suttie his front seat passenger.

Constance Howarth was frustrated at her slow progress in heavy traffic. "What the fuck are you doing?!" she screamed at the man driving the white Ford Transit van as it now overtook her car and then cut sharply in front. Furious, she braked hard to avoid a collision and yelled hoping its driver or a passenger would hear

---

39 Sitrep: Situation Report, meaning update.

her protests. As she glanced in the rear-view mirror, she saw with horror as the dark grey Range Rover behind shunted gently into the back of her car blocking all movement.

"Fuck, fuck, fuck," she screamed as plain clothes detectives from SERCS wrenched open the front two doors of her car and one pulled the keys from the ignition.

"Constance Howarth?" the detective asked.

"Yes."

"Police. You're under arrest for unlawful possession of firearms and ammunition."

From the boot of the Vauxhall Nova, another detective wearing forensic gloves had already removed the heavy Opal Fruits box. Inside, he found the three MAC-10 submachine guns, six 30-round Uzi magazines, three silencers and one hundred and fifty rounds of blue-tipped and copper-jacketed 9mm ammunition.

"From 2-1-6 to all units, Subject Four detained. Package recovered. Confirm we have the firearms and ammunition," she reported over the radio.

Ferris and Suttie were travelling along Upper Berkeley Street in Marylebone when they were suddenly overtaken by two non-descript police cars. Before they could fully comprehend what was happening, Ferris braked hard to avoid a collision with the first, which had now cut in front. The second boxed them in on the off-side, whilst parked cars prevented any escape along the other. Six casually dressed men jumped from the two vehicles wearing black baseball caps with chequered bands embroidered with the word 'Police'. Two grabbed Ferris through the open window and forcibly pulled him out. He had no chance to resist. Suttie's removal was only slightly more dignified as the detectives opened his door first before wrenching him out.

Shouts of, "armed police! Get down on your knees! On your knees! Show us your hands!" accompanied both extractions.

Ferris and Suttie dropped to the ground and put their hands on top of their heads.

"Paul Ferris? Arthur Suttie?" one detective asked.

Both men nervously replied, "yes."

"You're under arrest for unlawful possession of firearms and ammunition," and the detective continued with the caution.

While this was happening, Ackerman was laid on his sofa at home, wondering where he could exchange the £4,000 in Scottish £20 notes he had just received from Ferris. Hearing a noise at the front door, he tucked the money back into its envelope and slipped it between the sofa cushions. A second later, the sounds of splintering wood and shattering glass were followed immediately with shouts of

"Armed police!" Two police officers dressed all in black, wearing balaclavas and Kevlar helmets burst into his front room. Both pointed their Glock pistols directly at his torso. Ackerman was taken totally by surprise and, before he could even grasp what was going on, the officers had forced him down on his knees. Like prisoners of war he had seen in the movies, he automatically put both hands behind his head. The roughness of the cable ties used to handcuff him cut into his skin, but he soon realised that was the least of his worries.

"John Ackerman?" one officer asked.

"Yes."

"I'm arresting you for conspiracy to supply illegal firearms and ammunition."

When the officers searched his home, they found the cash and his nickel-plated MAB Model D pistol with its silencer.

Following his arrest, Ackerman agreed to cooperate fully with the police. He made twenty-four taped interviews telling the detectives about his ten-year involvement in unlawfully supplying firearms and ammunition. These would become the foundation for how SERCS approached the next stage of Operation Abonar.

CHAPTER 36

Breaking the News

Wednesday, 28th May

The next morning, within minutes of my arrival at NSY, Anton walked through my door and pushed it shut. "It won't surprise you that Derek saw me yesterday," he began. "He was concerned about what you thought your role would be now that SERCS have taken over Abonar. Barry Gough also called Brian."

"What did you decide?" I asked, unable to hide my uneasy apprehension.

"Clearly you and DC Bryan have the specialist knowledge SERCS need when they arrest Mitchell and his two cronies. I can see sense in you both being there as technical advisors. That is, provided you don't end up being the Exhibits' Officers and having to appear in court. It does happen but I prefer it didn't. If you can keep a low profile, Brian and I are happy for you to continue. Okay?"

"Thank you, of course, yes. As you know, Abonar is my first major investigation. I'm still hoping it will help towards a rite of passage to becoming a fully-fledged DI and then, maybe, DCI."

Anton laughed as he turned to leave but stopped just before opening the door. "Oh, and I should let you know that I'm taking time off in June. I'm studying for the Chief Superintendents' promotion boards. If you need anything and Derek can't help, go to Brian instead, alright?"

"Yes, thanks. Good luck. Oh, if I may ask one more kindness, would you please authorise these requests for call data? They're for the numbers we got from yesterday's meeting."

"One more kindness! You spent too long working for the AC. Yes, alright. I'll get them done."

My desk phone rang as he left. "Michael, DI Arthur Wilton from SERCS, Crawley. We met yesterday at Thames House."

"Yes, I remember. What can I do for you?"

"I'm taking up your offer to brief one of my team. DC Clive Philpott would like to come up and see you tomorrow. Is that alright?"

"Yes, of course. I'll meet him in reception at 10."

The team were more energised and excited than I had anticipated when I briefed them about the latest Thames House meeting. They were keen to get cracking on linking everything I had learned with our own data. Alice quickly checked the new numbers provided by DS Campbell with those on the Abonar database before exclaiming, "Bingo!"

"What have you got?" I asked.

"This is really exciting," she said, projecting the relevant section of her chart to the screen for us all to see. "While you were away yesterday, we added all the outstanding call data. Sorry, I still can't give you Rochester's real name. But look, here's the new suspect, John Ackerman, using his Islington home number repeatedly to page Bown about the CZ pistol on January 17th."

"Well that confirms I didn't break the ABC rule after all."

"Yes," she smiled, "and what's also interesting is that until December, Ackerman was paging Mitchell directly. He left him the number for the payphone inside the Duchess of Kent pub close to his home to call back."

"Wow, so what do you draw from that?"

"Well," Alice said, thinking out loud, "could it be that Ackerman and Mitchell fell out, and ever since he's had to go through Bown to get guns from Mitchell?"

"Anything to back that up?"

"Well, why else would Ackerman put Bown under so much pressure to get the CZ when he could have gone to Mitchell direct?"

"Good point Alice. It's certainly a useful dynamic to test their allegiances in interview. I'm dying to read the transcripts of Ackerman's tapes."

"Oh yes, they will be amazing. But, Mr H, I can't see any connection between Ackerman and our three firearms recoveries. His communications happen in complete isolation to them."

"But we do have Bown and Mitchell as common denominators?" I pointed out.

"Yes, but as you told us on Monday, Bown isn't connected at all with Whitechapel, Plaistow and the Tollgate Hotel. The only common denominators for them are Mitchell and Rochester."

"Guv," Roger interrupted, "if you want to keep SERCS happy about us being involved, then we'll need to focus on identifying Rochester for them."

Before I could respond, Mitchell's pager sounded again. Everyone stared at me while I checked the screen before telling them, "Mitchell's got to call an 01634 number I don't recognise."

I read it out and Alice checked our database, pushing her glasses up the bridge of her nose as she did. "Nope, it's not here."

"Damn. Mark, would you do me a huge kindness, please? Run this number down to Pete and ask him for the subscriber. Tell him it's urgent and I'll get the authorisation to him shortly."

"On my way, Guv," Mark said as he headed out the door having noted the number in his daybook.

When he walked back into the room a few minutes later, Mark held aloft like a trophy the faxed subscriber result before reading it out loud, "it's a woman living at 122 Clandon Road, Chatham, Kent. Does the address mean something to anyone?"

"I'll check it with Kent Police," John said, taking the paper from Mark while picking up a desk phone. We listened trying to make sense of his conversation, but it wasn't clear. So when John finished, we were all anxious to know the result. "So folks, do you want some good news or some *really* good news?" he teased.

"Either way it's going to be good, John, so what is it?" I asked impatiently.

"122 Clandon Road, Chatham, is the address Kent Police have registered for a member of the Tudor Gun Club. Their members shoot at the Stone Lodge Range in Cotton Lane, Dartford."

"So?"

"Well, I bet you can't guess who it is?"

"Rochester?" Roger offered.

"No."

"A member of the Donovan family?" Mark suggested.

"Alright John, who is it?" I said tersely. "It wasn't much fun when Roger played this game."

"Yes, but if you'd got his question right, you'd get mine right too. It's Robert Bown."

"Wow. I wonder why he's calling Mitchell from there and not the Marvels Lane TK," I pondered.

"I may be able to explain why," Alice chipped in.

"Please do."

"Well, yesterday, I spotted repeated calls from the Marvels Lane TK to what you learned from SERCS is Ackerman's home number. As each lasted no more than a few seconds, I assume they went to his answerphone. We now know that's because he's been in custody since Friday. I just parked it along with all the other loose ends somewhere in my head until something made sense. Now it does."

Annoyingly, Alice chose this moment to pause and sip her coffee.

"Alice, please do me a kindness and tell us."

"Sure, sure. Look, I know it's free, but this machine coffee really is rubbish. Okay, so you'll remember the flurry of pager messages between Bown, Mitchell and Rochester yesterday, just before you left for Thames House, Mr H?"

"Yes, I do."

"Well, they all came after Bown made one final call. I ambushed Mr Woodfield again to authorise the subscriber check." Alice then moved her chart to show us its place. "It was to someone at 62 Highbury Station Road."

"And who's that?" Roger asked impatiently.

Alice smiled at Roger's inability to make the connection she'd made in an instant. "Ackerman lives at number 60, so Bown had phoned his neighbour. I think that's how he learned of Ackerman's arrest. That's why he then called Mitchell to warn him. Moments later, Mitchell called Rochester to alert him too. Anyway, that's my theory. It would also explain why Bown is now at the Chatham address, probably lying low."

"Alice, that's bloody amazing. There's little to corroborate your theory, but I'll go with it. Working with you is ruining my reputation for preaching the ABC." I held her stare for a moment and winked. Turning back to the others, I added, "and John, find out what you can about the membership of these gun clubs."

"Sure, Mark and I will get on to it."

"Very good, I want to tie up all our loose ends. Tomorrow morning we've got DC Clive Philpott joining us for a briefing. He's coming up from the SERCS Branch Office at Crawley."

"Okay," John said, sounding hesitant, "I suppose you want us to make friends with him so we can be there for Mitchell's arrest?"

"Yes, John, I do. But remember, no mention of the RPGs. We can talk about Donovan and Gudgeon, the Home Office and Customs, but nothing, please, about the OCG's investigation. Okay?"

They all nodded in agreement.

"Thank you. Now enough of this shilly-shally. Back to work folks."

That night at just before 11pm, Mitchell's pager woke me up. As usual, the message was just a phone number. It was the one for Clandon Road again.

CHAPTER 37

Online Enquiries

Thursday, 29th May

I was back at NSY by 7:30am and went straight to the Main Office. It was time to get DC Chris Ferguson involved in Abonar. He was an absolute genius at using Internet data for investigating serious crime and the ideal choice for running the Computer Crime Unit. Chris did this for me with great panache aided by one member of our civil staff. Their principal role was trawling through dozens of 'Suspicious Activity Reports' submitted daily by London's financial institutions. They checked them against our intelligence systems looking for a crossmatch with names, addresses, and telephone numbers. If they found one involving a current serious crime investigation, they forwarded the report to the relevant SIO to follow up. Chris had set up covert electronic access to multiple open sources on the Internet in such a way he did not leave an electronic 'footprint' to reveal his visit. He complemented these with other capabilities to support his due diligence enquiries about people that accessed databases run by businesses and government agencies. These all helped us exploit intelligence we would not otherwise get access to. Chris knew I was in awe of his skills, and he took advantage of it with a level of familiarity others might not get away with.

"Good morning, Guv, what can I do you for? Perhaps you have one of your kindnesses for me?"

I laughed saying, "let me buy you a hot chocolate my friend. We can then discuss whether it's a kindness or just part of your job description."

He grinned. "Okay, that's very kind."

Chris was short and slightly stocky, with sandy-coloured hair, and wore glasses with thin gold rims. He preferred to come into the office in casual clothes. That was unless he had a meeting with more senior officers or visitors when he dressed smartly in a blue suit. Today was not one of those.

He was a practicing Mormon, which meant he neither drank tea nor coffee, and he hated anything decaffeinated. He did, however, welcome a good hot chocolate. We crossed the fourth-floor bridge into the canteen and, having paid for our drinks, I led him to the seating area on the left, away from the other diners.

"The kindness I need from you," I told him, "is to run a financial profile on a suspect, Fred Donovan. He's an inmate at Full Sutton Prison. I'll give you his details when we get back to the office. He's the kingpin in an investigation of mine. I need to prove either he or his family are buying dozens of off-ticket[40] guns from a Sussex-based Registered Firearms Dealer. He then has them deposited around London and Kent for police to recover as part of a scam to secure his early parole. I'd like to know how they're funding it. I suspect he and his family have undeclared assets they're liquidating into cash. I also want you to find out what you can about his Manchester-based solicitor, Patrick Gudgeon. He's acting as the go-between with the Prison Service."

"Okay, let me have their details and I'll see what I can do. What will you do with the information?"

"If you identify how the Donovans are raising the money then, when I'm ready, I'll pass it on to GMP to follow up. The original drugs case that put him inside was theirs, so they should be interested in what they didn't find first time round. Right now I don't want to upset Donovan. Instead, I want whatever mischief you can find out about him, his family and his solicitor in my back pocket ready for the day I do."

"Okay, understood. I'll tread carefully. Is there anything else you need?"

Remembering the message to Mitchell's pager from the previous night, I looked in my daybook to check the name and address of the subscriber to the Chatham number.

"Yes, there is. Would you do me another kindness and work your magic on this woman and her address. Speak to John Bryan too. He may have more."

"Sure, I can do that. Many thanks for the drink."

As we then walked back, I described the key features of the Abonar investigation and its principal suspects. On reaching his desk, I copied into

---

40 Off-ticket: common term for firearms that have been 'lost' by a Registered Firearms Dealer who no longer has them correctly recorded in their register of what they hold in stock.

his daybook the details I wanted him to research. Next, I went to tell John about my tasking Chris and for the two of them to liaise.

"Sir?" Pete called out. "Um, you asked BT to put a live trace on a Chatham number. They've just sent through the data," he said, handing me another of his sealed envelopes before hurrying away.

I sat next to John and loaded the disc into his computer. We then went through the call records.

"Right, there we are," I said pointing at the latest entry. "Last night, Michell's pager went off with a message to call the Chatham number. What I find surprising is that Bown's using a phone with a named subscriber. It goes against the rule of keeping their communications anonymous."

Just then, the alarm for Rochester's pager sounded. John and I looked at the message.

"I'll be blowed," John said, recognising the digits for one of the Brighton TKs. "It's Mitchell messaging Rochester again."

Immediately, I called the BT Duty Manager to ask for the number that called Mitchell back. Within minutes she confirmed it was one of the Rochester TKs we had already on live trace, so nothing new to help identify the man by name. Just then Chris joined us.

"Okay Guv, I ran a search on the woman in Chatham. She's Robert Bown's sister. The address is her marital home. Does that help?"

"Good Lord, Chris. That was quick work. Fantastic. Yes, it certainly does. Thank you."

"Easy when you've got my box of tricks Guv. I've also brought over the Kent street atlas. You might find it useful to look at the address and whether any locations nearby are relevant."

Reaching to take it, John asked, "while you're here, Chris, can you also run some searches on a couple of Dartford gun clubs? I'm hoping you can work your magic and access their membership records from Kent police?" He then handed over his notes on them.

"Yup, that should be straightforward," Chris replied before heading back to his desk.

I ejected the disc from John's computer and then walked with him to find Alice in the Fordham Suite. She was at her regular desk and happily took the new disc to load into her computer. Very quickly she spotted one number with a Rochester dialling code that wasn't on our Abonar database. Walking swiftly back to my office, I completed a subscriber authorisation and took it down the corridor to Pete. When I got back, John was fully absorbed in checking the map of Chatham.

"Got it!" he announced suddenly, "that explains why Bown broke the rule".

"What does?" I asked.

"There's no phone box anywhere near the Chatham address. Look, not one. He's too lazy to walk or drive the half-mile to the nearest one that's here," and he pointed to the map symbol for it.

"Well, we can bank that for when SERCS interview him," I suggested. "They can point out how he broke their anonymity rule. Maybe exposing his stupidity will encourage Bown to give them names, dates and places."

"And on that point, Guv, right now you're meant to be meeting DC Philpott," John advised.

I checked my watch. He was right, it was 10am. "Damn, yes. I'll take him for a coffee in the canteen first. Have everyone ready in the briefing room for 10:30, and I'll bring him through."

"Sure. I'll get that done. Oh, are you going to tell him about the clone pagers?"

"No, and we're hanging on to them. I daren't risk something crucial falling through the cracks while SERCS play catch-up. They also give us leverage when it comes to being in on the arrests."

"Ah, Guv?" Chris called out to me as I was heading down the corridor.

"Yes."

"Here you go. Courtesy of Kent Police. A complete list of members of the Tudor Gun Club who shoot at Stone Lodge. Recognise any names?" he said wanting to pass the pages to me.

"Sorry Chris, I've got a visitor to meet. You better give it to DC Bryan to check. He's in the Fordham Suite. Thanks."

CHAPTER 38

DC Philpott

I took the lift to the ground floor and walked through to the Back Hall reception. DC Philpott was the only person waiting there. I studied him for a moment before introducing myself. He wore a crumpled dark grey suit in a manner suggesting he would be more comfortable dressed less formally. He seemed to begrudgingly carry his briefcase, but at least it made him look purposeful. From his greying dark brown hair and thick moustache, I guessed he was 15 years older than me in his late 40s. He was also shorter and carrying a bit more weight. To be fair, it's a challenge keeping it off as a detective. Much of our time is spent sitting, whether that be in an office, the interview room or on surveillance. Having gone through to greet him, I quickly led the way back to the fourth-floor canteen where we sat and chatted over coffee.

"Mr Wilton sends his apologies, Guv. He hopes to see you in the next couple of weeks," Clive said, giving away his south coast accent.

"Not a problem. Tell me, which is your home force?"

"Sussex. Crawley Branch Office is mostly Met, Kent, Surrey, and Sussex. As Mitchell lives in Brighton and that's my old ground, the bosses put me in charge of intelligence-development."

"When do you think you'll be ready to start surveillance?"

"Not for a few weeks. We've got to clear the decks with Ackerman first. Mr Wilton will be running this job. He's got a couple of others to finish first, though. We have a DI from the Met too, but he's got a big job on right now too, so he can't help us move any sooner. I think it will be July before we start."

"Well by then, we should have identified a third target for you."

"Okay."

"But there are two things I need you to take back to your DI, please. First, every day we don't take out Mitchell and his associates risks them putting more guns on the street. I hope, like me, your boss is keeping a '*Decision Log*' to record why he can't go sooner."

"I'll let him know Guv."

"Please do. And second, let him know my team will keep on developing the intelligence until he's ready to take over."

"Well, that would be good, as it's just me for now and I've only had the job since yesterday."

"Okay, so let's meet the team who'll be helping you."

We walked quickly through the canteen and across the bridge to the SO11 offices. When we reached the Fordham Suite, Roger, John and Mark had the table set up with folders of documents and photograph albums. As usual, Alice was at the computer projecting the i2 chart on the big screen. For the next two hours, we gave Clive a very thorough briefing.

As we finished, I commented, "so, as you can see, once you're ready to move, we can come down to Crawley, do the same for your team, and be there to support you with the arrests."

"Great, thanks. I must say, Guv, it's very impressive work for what's mostly a desktop investigation."

John scowled at Clive whilst huffing noisily. I glared at him as I reacted more positively to Clive's remark, "yes, my Corporate Services' teams are pioneering the art of such techniques. We're proud of what we've achieved with Abonar. So, what'll be your next step once you're ready?"

"It'll be the same as you'd planned; put Mitchell under surveillance."

"And the others?"

"From what you've shown me, it's Mitchell who's supplying the guns. We'll focus everything on him first. Once we've got a clear picture of how he operates, we'll decide whether there's value in going after Bown and anyone else, like Rochester."

"Value?" I said, now as deeply annoyed by his dismissive attitude as I could see the others were too. "All three are part of one major conspiracy to supply firearms. You must go after them all." I looked sternly at Clive as I continued. "And I'll be making that very clear to DI Wilton. In the meantime, we'll carry on monitoring them."

"Okay Guv, but like you, we've only got limited resources," Clive pushed back defensively. "We may only widen the net beyond Mitchell when and if the evidence justifies it and competing priorities allow. What I'm trying to tell you, Guv, is that arresting Mitchell, and possibly Bown, may be where our operation ends. That's just how it goes. Sometimes the ones we can't pick up first time round come again later."

"I appreciate that, Clive, but I'll be pressing on your boss to arrest all three. I've seen for myself the horrors of their gunrunning enterprise. We need to take out everyone involved in the supply chain. No one must be left behind, otherwise they'll just re-group and keep going."

"I hear you, and I'll feed it all back to Mr Wilton, Sir."

"Please do. And remember, Clive, John and I are coming along for the searches. We have the specialist knowledge you need, so you don't miss anything. I doubt you have anyone with our expertise."

"No, no, we don't," he said and then paused for a moment before continuing. "Guv, as you know, we're getting a lot of information from Ackerman. Your analysis mostly confirms what he's told us. Perhaps we can use that to go after Mitchell and, possibly, Bown, and then you won't have to disclose your techniques. What I'm saying is we may not need your intelligence to get the job done anyway."

I bristled at his remark. Unwittingly or otherwise, he had just dismissed everything we had achieved. Evidently, Clive held more worth in being given the job on a plate by Strathclyde Police.

"My team and I see it *differently*," I told him, with added emphasis on the last word. "Don't dismiss so easily what you call a 'desktop investigation'. Remember, if Ferris gets to Ackerman, and he withdraws his cooperation, you'll need everything we've just shown you. I understand you've got nothing else evidential against Mitchell."

"No, we haven't Guv, and yes, you're right of course. I'll pass that on too," his apologetic tone indicated he had registered my annoyance.

"Okay, I think we're done, Clive," I said, trying not to show I had lost patience with him. "If everyone else would like to wait behind for our daily catch-up, I'll show you out."

CHAPTER 39

Going Away

"Desktop investigators! Is that all he thinks of us? Arrogant bloody carrot-cruncher from the sticks!" John was saying loudly as I returned. "I bet I've nicked more armed robbers than he's had hot dinners!"

"He's an old school detective," Roger responded more calmly. "He's been brought up on informants and surveillance as the only way to run investigations. He's not used to the new art of data analytics."

"I prefer 'Desktop Warriors' anyway," I interjected. "Oh, and John, if we're to hang on to any chance of joining SERCS on those searches, I need you to stay friends with them. Understood?"

"Hmm, okay. Oh, and thanks for sticking up for us Guv. I hope you can get his boss to accept your advice about arresting everyone. They must dismantle the whole supply chain."

Roger interrupted, "um, getting back to the job in hand if I may Guv. As you left to meet Clive, DC Ferguson tried to give you the membership list for the Dartford gun club. You need to look at it. I think it'll cheer you up after what we've just been through with DC Philpott."

Roger handed me the sheets of paper and I quickly scanned down the names and addresses.

"Wow. Would you look at this rogues' gallery," I said in amazement. "Ackerman, Bown, Mitchell, Perkins and Walshe. They're all members."

Passing it to Alice, I said, "shout if you spot anyone else connected with Abonar."

"Sugar, bloody, damn," she commented after rapidly scanning it too, clearly having fun with using my expression. "I hoped there'd be only one with a Rochester address, but there's a few."

"No problem," John commented, "we can check them against the Kent street atlas. Hopefully there's only one living near the TKs."

"Sure, and, sadly," Alice added, "there are no members with an Eltham address."

"I think a visit to the gun club would be helpful," Roger proposed. "If we can contrive a reason for doing so, that is."

"Not right now," I countered. "We can't risk our appearance tipping them off that we're interested in their members. I've got another idea, and I'll come back to you later if it's a goer."

"Okay, Guv, you've got me intrigued."

"Right, before I wrap this up, I'm conscious, Alice, we need to hand you back to Angela tomorrow as it's the end of the month. What can you do for us over the next 24 hours?"

"I'll carry on as before. I think Angela will be happy for me to carry on, though, and do a couple of hours here and there when you need me."

"Thank you. That would be excellent."

"There is one person I do want to focus on today and tomorrow, Mr H, and that's Bown." As Alice said this, she determinedly held my stare. "He's the weakest link in the Abonar network. I mean, he uses a TK only yards from his front door and the phone at his sister's place. I'd like to concentrate on who else he's calling. It might just be he'll help us finally identify Rochester, perhaps, even Eltham."

"Please crack on, Alice. Thank you everyone. Plenty still to do while we wait to hand this over to SERCS next month."

Brian was coming out of my office as I approached it. "Good timing," he said. "My office, please."

Not knowing what to expect, I pushed the door shut and sat down taking in the aroma of stale cigarette smoke as I did.

"I've got some good news. A place on the next DI's Course is unexpectedly available due to a late cancellation. I've told the Detective Training School you're taking it."

"Thank you. When?"

"Monday. You'll need to clear your desk. It's a four-week course and when you return, you'll be a fully qualified Detective Inspector."

"Thank you, Sir, but Abonar is at a critical stage. I can't be away right now."

"Nonsense. Delegate it to DS Rowlands. He seems a safe pair of hands. I'll talk to Derek about making him the Acting DI. He could do with the experience."

"Maybe Sir, but these next four weeks are critical to an effective hand-over to SERCS," I added in earnest. "I'd like to turn down your kind offer and take the next course when it comes. I could also do with a few days' leave to repair things at home."

"Got anything planned?"

"No, Sir."

"Well then, this takes precedence. Anyway, I wasn't offering, I was telling you." The tone of his voice made clear this was not negotiable. "You'll find I've left the joining instructions on your desk."

"Thank you, Sir," I said, respectfully accepting his decision.

CHAPTER 40

CHIS

My head was reeling with this unwanted development. The joining instructions made clear there would be no time to slip back to the office during the course. I needed to write myself off for the whole of June.

It was now close to 2pm and I needed to phone David. He was one of my best contacts in the gun trade and both a keen shot and Registered Firearms Dealer. I had known him for years and enjoyed his company. He was a fantastic cook and bon viveur. He smoked heavily and drank only neat vodka. From a professional perspective, I welcomed his vast knowledge of how the grey areas of the gun trade operated on the fringes of legality. Consequently, I had registered him as a Covert Human Intelligence Source (CHIS), an '*informant*' in old language.

"Dear boy, how wonderful to hear from you. *Come sta* [how are you]?" he added, breaking into Italian, as he usually did in every conversation.

"*Non ce male, grazie* [Not too bad, thank you]," I replied with one of the few expressions I knew from the phrase book. "I may have a mission for you, my friend. What do you know about the Tudor Gun Club and the Stone Lodge Range in Dartford ?"

"Den of iniquity," he replied instantly in feigned disgust. "However," he continued less disparagingly, "I must confess to being a member myself. In fact, I'm going there later."

"What, today?" I asked in disbelief at my good fortune in calling him today.

"*Si, amico mio, oggi* [Yes, my friend, today]!"

Well that is a happy coincidence. Look, I need you to do something for me while you're there."

"Then, I think we should meet beforehand, say 4pm at our usual watering hole?"

I used the intervening time to complete the paperwork for authority to deploy him into the gun club. Brian briefed the SO10 Commander on my behalf and then sent me down the corridor for his signature on the docket. As I passed by

Brian's office with it all signed, he called me in. "Good luck with your friendly[41]. Don't let him take any risks or you and I will both be in the smelly stuff."

"Of course. Oh, would you be able to do me one more kindness, Sir?"

"Don't you use that bloody awful expression with me!" he laughed. "I get enough of it from the big boss himself. I expect you want me to update Derek."

"Yes, I do. I don't want him thinking I tried to arc him."

"Yes, that's fine. I'll call him in a minute."

Returning to my office, I found Roger loitering outside. "Thank you for allowing me to act-up in your absence," he announced to my surprise. "I promise to take good care of Abonar and the team."

"News travels fast! I was hoping to brief you personally myself. Yes, I can't say I'm entirely happy about being away for a month, but so be it."

"But you should at least get the weekends off."

"Yes, but it's a residential course and my wife's got a problem with my sleeping away from home."

"Yes, I can see how that wouldn't be helpful. Do you have time now for me to update you on the RPG job?"

"I do, and then I've got something I need your help with."

"Okay, well this morning Murray told Gudgeon that the Home Secretary won't be available to consider Donovan's early parole for two months. When he does, though, he wants proof the RPGs exist. He wants a sample. Gudgeon has just booked a visit for next week to tell Donovan. Upstairs are now monitoring the phone lines to see what happens."

"Sugar, bloody, damn, that's another reason why I don't want to be away."

"Guv, if I may be so bold, from my experience over many years of working in SO, you need to get over your '*FOMO*'."

"My what?"

"'*Fear Of Missing Out*'. It happens a lot. You start a job; it takes on a whole new dimension, which means someone else steps in, and then it's not yours anymore. You may also never get to hear what happened. I appreciate Abonar is your first, and you've now lost both strands to SERCS and the OCG. But don't worry, I'll keep you updated."

"Thanks Roger, I'd appreciate that."

"Yes, and I'll keep reminding SERCS about you and John being there for the searches. You need to think of me as your '*LAMA*' man."

---

41   Friendly: police slang for an informant (CHIS).

"My what? Are you full of acronyms?"

"A few, yes. It means '*Look After My Arse*'. It's what I'm doing for you anyway with Mr Hamilton, and I'll do the same with SERCS."

"Thanks, Roger, that's most kind. Oh, and please recommend to Mr Hamilton he talk to DC Overton about covertly monitoring Gudgeon's visit."

"What does it involve?"

"He'll need to get the Prison Service and Home Office to agree but, in the circumstances, that shouldn't be a problem."

"I'll let him know. Now what was it you wanted my help with?"

"I need you to meet a CHIS at 4pm. We're going to deploy him into the gun club today."

"Good heavens, that was quick work. Okay, I'll do some prep. Where are we meeting?"

"St Ermin's Hotel, Caxton Street, in the bar."

CHAPTER 41

David

Roger and I left NSY 15 minutes ahead of the appointment with David and separately carried out our 'fieldcraft'. This involved taking a circuitous route, with frequent stops and doubling back, to make sure neither of us was being followed. It concluded with us both walking through the rear service area of the hotel and into the bar. I led Roger over to my regular seat at a corner table towards the back next to the window overlooking the front entrance. David would undertake similar manoeuvres too but come in through the front. I watched as he entered reception from the driveway. He then sat in an armchair where he knew I could watch him from my vantage point. After five minutes on his own, he got up and joined us. I made the introductions and, instinctively, the two of them exchanged business cards. Since the bar was empty, I went out to reception to ask the staff to organise coffee and biscuits.

Returning, I was delighted to find my companions deep in conversation. I had learned the best way to build a relationship with a CHIS was to spend ninety percent of the time talking about anything other than what you wanted them to do. David was telling Roger some amusing tale about his real day-job. He was on commission to various harbour authorities around the world seizing ships for them when their captains left without paying the required port fees.

"So, dear boy, what's my mission?" he said, coming to the end of his story.

"What did you mean by calling the club a '*den of iniquity*'?" I asked.

"I think in your parlance you'd say some of its members are '*well-dodgy*'."

"How so?"

"I shoot at Stone Lodge every Thursday, sometimes on the weekends too. Have done for years, so I know what goes on. Now I haven't seen this for a while, but if you need ammunition on the sly, the pistol range is the place to get it."

"How?"

"Oh, you fire only some of the rounds allocated, and then walk away with the rest in your pocket. It's been rumoured for years that's how London criminals have been getting theirs."

"We can pick that up another time," I said curtly, somewhat annoyed he hadn't brought this to me before. "Today, we need your help with a specific group of members," I continued. "Do you know Anthony Mitchell?"

"Oh, Blondie. Yes, I know him. Complete '*Walter Mitty*'."

"What makes you say that?"

"Well, he and his two mates get all dressed up in black to look like ninjas. They're all wannabe police SFOs. I think Mitchell is the only one who's in the police, but only a Sussex Special. The others aren't anything to do with the force. That doesn't stop them, though. They head off to the US and, I think Eastern Europe too, quite regularly posing as British cops." He paused to sip his coffee before saying, "they compete in tactical firearms competitions with genuine cops. They've even won some trophies. There are photographs of them in the clubhouse. They call themselves something ridiculous like, um, um, the 'Black', oh what is their damned name? *Mi dispiace* [I'm sorry], oh yes, 'Shods', that's it, they call themselves the 'Black Shods'. As I said, ridiculous bunch of wannabes."

"Who are the other two in the group?"

"Ah, let me think. Um, I don't know their full names. One of them is Bob and the other is… Andy. Yes, Bob and Andy. They're also friends with quite a few of the other regulars."

"Do you also know a chap called Kieran Walshe? Is he in their group?" Roger asked.

"Kieran. Hmm, that's a rather popular name round those parts. Everybody tends to go by first names. Mitchell's such a weirdo I decided to find out his surname. Other than my own shooting comrades, I don't know many members by their full names."

"Would it help if I show you some photographs?" Roger asked as he took an envelope from inside his jacket and spread four images face-down on the table. "I got these from the DVLA, Passport Office, and our own files," he explained as he turned over the first one.

"That's easy, it's your man Mitchell, aka Blondie."

"And this?"

"Another easy one. That's his 'Black Shod' compatriot, Bob."

"And do you recognise *him*?" Roger asked as he revealed the third.

"Yes, he's a member, but I don't think we've been introduced. Who is he? Walshe?"

"No, it's a man named John Ackerman. He's banged up right now, so you won't be seeing him for a good while. Well, not unless he's friends with the former Home Secretary, of course."

"What?"

"Sorry, inside joke on the team," Roger said, smirking at me before turning over the fourth and asking, "How about this last one?"

"Yes, I know him too from the club but, forgive me, again, I don't know his name. Who is he?"

"This is Kieran Walshe."

"Okay, where's your photo of Andy? The other Black Shod."

"The name Andy hasn't come up before," I told him.

"Well, if Blondie and Bob are up to something, Andy will be in on it too. They're inseparable. I'll see if I can get his full name when I'm at the club later."

"That would be very helpful," Roger replied.

"If not, I'll try and sneak into the secretary's office and have a rummage for a name and address."

"David don't take any chances, please," I warned.

"*Mio caro regazzo* [My dear boy], I know the rules of engagement. Leave it to me. I'll be careful."

"I know you will. So, while you're there, this is what we'd like you to do," I said, to begin the actual briefing. "Keep a look out for Blondie, Bob, Kieran, and their friend Andy. If any of them turn up, work your usual magic, and ingratiate yourself into their conversation. Is that possible?"

"Yes, that should be easy enough. They know me already. It won't be out of the ordinary if we have a chat. I'll watch out for any associates not in your deck too. I assume you'll want car registrations?"

"That would be great, yes, if you can do it safely," I replied, looking at him sternly.

"*Splendido* [Splendid], *splendido*, I'll get that done for you, dear boy."

"Good, then let's use this evening as a reconnaissance mission."

"Might I ask what I should be looking for?"

"Of course. I was about to get to that. We suspect they're supplying firearms and ammunition. Handguns mostly. Smith & Wesson and Colt revolvers; Chinese M20s that look like Russian Tokarevs, French MAB pistols, plus some off-ticket

Second World War stuff. Colt 1911s and once even a BAR. More worryingly, they're supplying a homemade Ingrams-type MAC-10 with silencers."

"Handguns like those do turn up on the pistol range. I'll look out for them, but the rangemaster wouldn't let anyone shoot those other guns there."

Nodding, I said, "also, look out for blue-tipped and copper-jacketed 9mm ammunition stamped with 'IMI 9mm' on the cartridge base."

"I can check the spent cases for sure. If I find them, what would you like me to do?"

"Collect some samples and get the name of who's firing them. Okay?"

"*Assolutamente* [Absolutely]. And to engender a conversation with your targets, I'll take along a couple of my own World War Two era handguns."

"Fine, do whatever you think will make them happy to talk to you."

"Anything else?"

"We don't want you to do anything more than get into conversation at this stage," Roger added. "Your mission is just research. We need to know who's mixing with who amongst our target group, what they do together, and where they go at the club."

"Yes, and if it works to our advantage, would you be available to go back next Thursday?" I added.

"*Assolutamente caro ragazzo* [Absolutely dear boy]! And every Thursday thereafter if necessary."

"Thank you. We won't send someone with you today," Roger advised. "Depending on what happens, we may ask you another time to take me along as a guest."

"All understood. I'll just conduct an initial recce to scope out what might be feasible in future. *Splendido*, this is going to be an interesting mission."

"Good. The usual rules apply," I said, taking over. "You're to call to let me know you've arrived safely. Then do the same once you're home. Please make it no later than 11pm. You can then debrief me over the phone. Agreed?"

"All received and understood. I better get going. Ciao, ciao."

David called me at 6:30pm to say he was about to arrive at the club. I sat up waiting for his second call when I got home. It came at 10:45pm.

"The dachshunds are in the long grass," he said.

"And the bluebirds are over the Volga," I replied.

This was our good-humoured way of confirming the security of our conversation.

"*Come sta*?" I then asked.

"*Bravissimo caro ragazzo* [Very good dear boy]. Just got home. Interesting evening. No sign of Blondie, but both Bob and Andy were there. Andy didn't stay long. Neither of them went on the range, so no spent cases. If you've got a pen and paper, I can give you their car registrations."

I had my daybook ready and recorded the details as he dictated them.

He followed up with a surprise question, "are you ready to strike now?"

"Why, what happened?"

"Well, I waited to make sure everyone left before I did. And, as I sat in my car, I noticed Bob's was still there parked behind the club house. I watched as he collected a cardboard box from behind the bins and put it in the boot."

"What size box?"

"Oh, like a big squarish shoebox, maybe slightly larger. No idea what was inside, but whatever it was, he didn't want anyone else to see him moving it. Clearly, he'd waited till he thought everyone else had gone before venturing to retrieve it. Whatever was inside must be contraband, wouldn't you think?"

"Certainly sounds it the way you describe his behaviour. Tell me more about the box?"

"Brown with some brand name on it, but it was too dark to read. He was definitely up to no good, that's why I asked whether you're ready to strike now."

"Not based just on that. I daren't risk a much bigger prize by moving too early. Did he say anything when you spoke to him to explain what he was doing?"

"No."

"What about Andy?"

"Oh, *perdonami, ho quasi dimenticato* [forgive me, I nearly forgot]. He arrived after Bob. The two chatted briefly for maybe thirty minutes and then Andy left. Both seemed very anxious about something. From what I overheard, someone they knew had been arrested, possibly very recently. Could that be your third man, Ackerman, maybe?"

"Maybe. So, did you get Andy's full name?"

"*Sì, caro ragazzo, sì* [Yes, dear boy, yes]. It's Phillips, Andy Phillips. I found it on the Black Shods group photo with Tony Mitchell and Bob Bown. I couldn't sneak into the office and get you his address; sorry, the secretary wasn't in. Unhelpfully, he'd left the door locked. I'll try and get it next time, but Andrew or Andy Phillips is his name."

"Excellent, thank you. I'll get my team to check him out in the morning. Anything else?"

"*No, è tutto* [No, that's all]."

"So quite a productive evening, thank you."

"*Prego* [You're welcome]. Lovely coincidence I was going there anyway."

"Indeed, indeed. Once again, David, you're an absolute star. We'll want you to keep going, please, but I need to leave you in Roger's very capable hands. I'm away for a month."

"Going anywhere nice?"

"No, Hendon, on a course."

"Oh, not so nice. Well, *buonanotte* [Good night]. Ciao, Michael, ciao."

"*E lei* [And you], David. Ciao, ciao."

I turned off the lights downstairs and headed up to bed.

CHAPTER 42

Hand-over

Friday, 30ᵗʰ May

I left home shortly after 6:30am. As I reached the garden gate, from the main road some 100 yards away to my left there came the unmistakable sound of tyres skidding accompanied by sharp braking. Many motorists misread the bend in Sandy Lane, and it was notorious for catching out a few. I had not witnessed an actual accident but had come home to find the debris from many. This time, though, I was surprised by the sound of the impact as two vehicles collided. I ran from the gate to the junction and saw a blue Ford Fiesta embedded in the front of a forty-seater coach. As I reached the scene, some of the tourists aboard had already got off and were taking photographs. I pushed through them to check on the driver of the Fiesta. He was a casually dressed young man in his early twenties.

Opening the car door, I asked, "Are you okay? Are you injured?"

"Nah mate. I'm okay. I got to go. Can't hang around," and he tried to push me out of the way. Sensing something was wrong, I blocked the doorway.

"You're going to have to stay and exchange names and addresses," I told him forcefully.

"Nah mate. Can't do that, I got to go. Someone'll call the police and I can't be waiting for them."

"Why's that?"

"Cos I just nicked the car, mate. So, I got to go. See? Now get out of my way!"

"Well, you're in luck *mate*! I am the police, and you're under arrest."

"Shit, shit, shit!" he exclaimed.

I reached into the side pocket of my black canvas briefcase and whipped out a set of handcuffs. I was relieved he did not resist as I snapped them on.

Pulling him out of the car, I made him sit cross-legged on the verge while I called the police on my mobile. After escorting my prisoner to Twickenham Police Station, I phoned John to let him know the reason I would be late.

"Some excitement this morning, I hear Guv," Roger said as he saw me in the corridor unlocking my office door. "Always good to keep your hand in. Don't want you losing the art of arresting people, even if our bosses preferred you did," he added smirking.

"Not the usual start to my day, Roger. Can you get everyone together in the Fordham Suite, that is if there isn't a job on in there?"

"There isn't. I'll gather them up for you. Oh, and by the way, Mr Hamilton followed up on your recommendation. Unfortunately, he got a solid "*No*" from the Home Office. He's furious about it. Apparently, they gave him a real hard time. He may call you."

"He hasn't yet. Those bloody Home Office lawyers are hopeless. Whose side are they on?"

"Not ours, obviously. How did your friendly get on?"

"He got Andy's surname for us but not his address. It's Phillips. Ask Alice and Chris to run him through their systems, please. Oh, and I've got two car registrations to check as well."

"Goodness, that has been a productive first visit. Well done, Guv."

"David also saw Bown remove a box from the bin area behind the clubhouse and put it in the boot of his car. No idea what was in it. I'll make an entry in my Decision Log to say it's not enough to risk the investigation now by getting a warrant."

"Agreed, right call, Guv. I'll see you shortly in the briefing room."

Moments later, Derek called my desk phone.

"Sir," I answered, "I've just had Roger tell me the news."

"Stupid bloody Home Office lawyers, and I told them so. They're now threatening to complain to the Commissioner about my attitude. I was forthright, yes, but not rude. Anyway, I asked; they refused, and I've documented it all. Thought I'd let you know."

"Thanks for sticking your neck out for us, Guv. Shame we won't know what Donovan and Gudgeon talk about during next week's visit."

"Yes, I think someone in the Home Office is deliberately working against us. It seems that Abonar has them seriously spooked. Oh and, thank you, Brian called me about your friendly. How did he get on?"

I briefed him on what I had just told Roger.

"Okay, very good result. Yes, right decision not to go after Bown. Can't go chasing shadows when there's much more at stake. If I don't speak to you before, enjoy your course."

"Thanks."

I made it through the door to the briefing room at 10:30 saying, "I'm so sorry about having to reschedule." Before I could continue, Mitchell's pager sounded. Looking at the screen I told the team, "It's Bown using the Marvels Lane TK. He's back home."

"Probably Bown wanting to let Mitchell know he collected something from the gun club last night," Roger suggested. "I've updated everyone on the outcomes of your friendly's visit already, Guv."

"Okay, so Bown removing that box last night suggests he's having a clear-out following Ackerman's arrest. So, what have you lot got for me?" I asked, looking around the room.

"We've some more good news for you Guv," Chris said, sounding excited. "That name your friendly gave you, Andrew or Andy Phillips lives in Rochester. We're now sure he's the man you've been calling '*Rochester*'. He's Pager C too, no doubt."

"That's bloody fantastic. So, Chris, are you now working on developing his profile?"

"I am. Once I've put it together, I'll brief the team. As you're going away, Guv, you'll get to see it when you're back. Unless you want me to disturb you during the course that is."

"No, I can wait, thanks."

"Your friendly did good then, Guv," John added.

"Yes, and Roger will keep him going back to the club until SERCS can start arresting our Abonar conspirators. Anything else to share with me?" I asked, looking around the room, again, but noted they all shook their heads.

"Good. Well, as you already know, Mr Mills has put me on the DIs' course. I'm back on June 30th. Hopefully SERCS will be ready by then to start surveillance and I won't have missed anything."

"You'll be back in time, Mr H, don't worry," Alice said, giving me one of her reassuring smiles.

"Right, so Roger is the Acting DI while I'm away, and he knows what I'm expecting. You've all done an exceptional job as 'Desktop Warriors'. In just five weeks we've cracked Abonar. Thank you. Oh, and John, here's another pager for you to babysit while I'm away; it's Mitchell's."

"Thanks Guv, Mrs Bryan is going to be even more unimpressed if this one goes off at night too!"

"Much the same for me, as my wife has made abundantly clear several times. Tell Mrs Bryan it's called '*exigencies of duty*'. Maybe you'll have more luck explaining what that means than I have with Mrs H."

I paused to detach my mind from the thoughts of a faltering marriage that had suddenly distracted me.

John sensed it too. "You okay Guvnor?"

"Not doing so good on the home front, John, but thanks for asking."

"You're not a nine-to-five copper, Guv. Like us, you want to get the bastards responsible for Abonar. We're all happy to put in the extra hours if you can't." Looking at Roger to confirm, John continued, his tone expressing sympathy and support, "we're with you all the way Guv. You can rely on us."

"Thanks, John, and I really appreciate everything that every one of you is doing. Now, that just leaves me to invite you all to the 'Old Star' at 5pm for a well-earned drink before I disappear for a month. No excuses, it's my shout."

CHAPTER 43

A Difficult Kidnap

Saturday, 31st May

Rebecca hugged me before I walked to the police traffic car waiting at the gate outside our house. My wife had already expressed her opinion on another family lunch being ruined, so she didn't come and see me off. So much for spending the weekend with them before starting the residential course. Once again, I was paying the price for the juxtaposition of an exciting job butting up against a crumbling home life. From the back seat of the car during the blue-light run, I made the usual series of calls to turn out the team to join me in Central 500 for another kidnap. The traffic officers dropped me at NSY, and minutes later I was powering up the systems once again.

I felt the draught on my neck as the door opened behind me. I looked over to see it was Roy Richards, his deputy, DI Martin Hampton and, to my surprise, DI Greg Turner.

"Ah, Michael, thank you for turning out as Green, again. Do you know DI Greg Turner from 'AMIP[42]'?" Roy asked.

"I do. What brings you in on a kidnap, Greg?"

"The hostage is my main suspect as the shooter for those murders at Brockwell Park: Claude Belvoir, street name 'Squeako'. We went round to his girlfriend's today at 5am with a full SFO team looking to arrest him, only for her to tell us he'd been kidnapped two hours earlier."

"Do you know who by?"

"Yes, members of the '*Mozart gang*'. They're 'Yardies[43]' and the people he and his mate Cecil White, aka 'Pinkie', ripped off for a half-kilo of cocaine.

---

42   AMIP: Area Major Incident Pool, which consisted of experienced detectives available to assist divisional, station based detectives in the investigation of major crimes, such as non-domestic murders or those that crossed the boundaries of divisions.
43   Yardie: common term for a gang member with Jamaican connections.

Like us, they've been hunting for them ever since. We've been trying to nick them before the opposition could exact their revenge. Now it looks like they're going to do that with Belvoir."

"Okay, so how has this become a kidnap?" I asked.

"The girlfriend got a call two hours ago from someone in the Mozart gang. They're offering to release Belvoir if she can now get Pinkie to meet them. If he gives back the cocaine and pays them a £10,000 penalty, they'll let them both go. The money is what Belvoir and White should have paid for the cocaine. That was the deal they set up for their meeting at Brockwell Park."

"I doubt they'll let Belvoir and White go with just a telling off and a fine."

"No, for sure they'll kill them. They'll want to send a message to any other gang that might be thinking of double-crossing them."

"What's Belvoir's girlfriend said about all this?"

"She's totally traumatised. The kidnappers pistol-whipped Belvoir in front of her. She's willing to help us secure his release and is happy to try and convince White to meet her to make the pay-off."

"That could be dangerous. Did Belvoir have the MAC-10 with him when he was kidnapped."

"The girlfriend didn't see a gun, but said he brought a gym bag to her place, and they've now taken it."

"Then we must assume they've got it now."

"I fear so."

Roy interrupted, "so now you know the story, Michael, I need you to fire up your whizzy tricks for me once more. I'm relying on you to find my hostage and Greg's second murder suspect."

"Sure, give me all the mobile numbers they're using, and I'll get cracking."

Three fraught hours later, Roy called us together for an update. Harry was back in his usual chair as Blue, and Vic in his as our Firearms Tactical Advisor. Dave was once more on the ground as Red. "Listen up everybody, I want facts not speculation," Roy said forcefully. "Tell me only what you know. I don't want speculation about what you think or believe. Green, I'll start with you. What have you learned from Red?"

"He's been coaching the girlfriend, our 'victim' and, so far, she's got hold of White's sister, Monique. Monique is our only means of contacting him. From monitoring their call data, we've now got both hers and White's mobile numbers. I've put them both on live trace. As regards organising the pay-off, the kidnappers will call back at 7pm, which gives us twenty minutes."

"Okay, so that's a heads-up for everyone," Roy repeated loudly, "next proof of life at 7pm."

He checked for nods in acknowledgement before asking me, "how's the victim getting on with the sister?"

"She's got Monique to pass on the message to White. He's agreed to a meeting, but only with his sister at 10pm outside Westbourne Park Station. He'll bring whatever cash he can raise along with what's left of the cocaine. He's then going back into hiding. Monique has agreed to meet our victim after that and hand over whatever White's given her. She's too scared to get involved in paying off the kidnappers. She's leaving that to our victim."

"Right, Blue and Vic; start working up a plan for being there too when they meet at Westbourne Park Station," Roy instructed. "I want Monique and White contained and arrested. You can be sure he at least he will be carrying for his own protection."

"On to it now, Boss," Vic replied in his usual matter-of-fact manner.

"We'll do a recce now, Boss," Harry similarly responded.

"Good. We must make this meeting work to our advantage. It doesn't sound like we'll have a second chance."

"Thanks, so Green, where are Monique and White right now?"

"Cellsite puts her mobile in Hammersmith and his in Stepney. These locations don't match up with the subscriber details for their registered addresses, so I'm relying on the CSPs to triangulate their positions on the networks."

Sounding irritated, Roy commented, "that's not much help to me, though."

"Well, at least they'll confirm ahead of 10pm whether our two targets are on the move towards the meeting place," I offered as reassurance.

"I've got photos of both Monique and Pinkie," Greg interrupted, passing them round, "so you need to get these to your teams, Harry. White will be 'Subject One' and Monique 'Two'."

"What about locating the stronghold?" Roy asked, looking at me.

"This 7pm proof of life call is the first when we'll have live monitoring on the victim's phone. The kidnapper blocked his number previously with 1-4-1, so I've got Vodafone on standby to get it this time."

"Well, Whizzy, we're relying on you as usual. Anything else?"

"One more Boss. I've got Toscas on standby at Paddington nick ready to start work on locating the kidnapper's phone if it's a mobile. I'm assuming since he's a member of the Mozart gang, he'll be somewhere on his turf in either W9 or W10."

"Good idea. Does anyone have anything to add?" Roy asked, looking around the packed room of faces, but no one spoke up.

"Well then, we really are in your hands Whizzy, or is it now Mr H, I understand?" Roy said, looking at me smiling.

"Thank you, Mr H does seem to be what everyone's using now, Boss."

"Yes, but I gave you the name Whizzy, so I kind of prefer it," he replied, smiling mischievously. Turning away to look around the room, he then directed, "okay everyone, let's stay focused on getting our hostage back."

He took up his preferred position alongside my desk to wait for the 7pm call. I looked at the wall clock and noted we had just a couple of minutes, so I placed my mobile on the desk next to me. Putting my headset on, I used the desk phone to call Ray at Vodafone and waited for his live monitoring to give us the number.

"Here you go," Ray said, "It's another one of ours. I'll fax you the details."

Suddenly, my mobile pinged with the incoming text from Red, "*POL now.*"

"Heads-up everyone, we've got proof of life and the kidnapper's number. I'll put everything on CLIO in a moment." I stood up and stretching the headset cable reached for the fax to grab the incoming message and add its details to the log.

"Michael, you still there?" I heard Ray asking over my headset.

"Yes Ray, sorry, I had to put myself on mute for a moment while I updated the room."

"Okay, you'll see from my fax the subscriber and cellsite details. We can put the mobile in the area between Harrow Road, W9, Kilburn Lane, NW6 to the north and west, and Fernhead Road, W9 to the east. The centre of the 300-metre radius around where it's registering on our network is Lancefield Street, W10. Sorry, I can't do better than that."

I thanked him, and then immediately called Trevor.

"I need your Toscas kit in Lancefield Street, W10," I said as soon as he answered.

"Okay, that's not far from where we are now. Text me the mobile number for the stronghold and we'll go looking for it. It'll be fifteen minutes max to get up there and then maybe another 60 before we've narrowed it down to the street and, maybe, a door number."

"Thanks, and I'll call you if we get any intel here to help narrow it down for you."

Roy looked down at my screen to read the transcript of the conversations he'd overheard me having with Ray and Trevor.

"Very good. Very good," he said nodding before looking up and calling out, "Greg, can you come and read this too."

As he joined us, Roy asked him, "Does any of this match your own intel?"

"Only that Lancefield Street is in the middle of the Mozart gang's turf," Greg replied.

Once he finished reading from the screen, I opened a new log entry to take the call from Red.

"Confirmed proof of life," Dave said. "The kidnappers are torturing the hostage. He's doing a lot of screaming. Very distressing for our victim. She did very well, though, to build in a delay. They'll call her next at midnight. From the voices in the background, there's at least two other males and a female in the stronghold."

"That's helpful. I'll log that for Vic. What did our victim tell them about Pinkie paying the ransom?"

"She told them that *Friends had got hold of him and he's agreed to pay back what he owes*. She persuaded the kidnapper to wait until she hears back from 'Pinkie's friends' about when and where he'll meet them. The man wasn't happy, but our victim managed to persuade him to wait."

Roy and Greg read the update as I typed it. Roy spoke first, "well, the victim's bought us some time, thank God."

"Yes, I'm relieved Boss," Greg added. "At least we can now focus on securing White and his sister, Monique, before rescuing Belvoir."

"Vic?" Roy shouted across the room, "make sure your armed officers around the Red Centre stay alert. There's always a risk the kidnappers might go back there."

"I'll call their Skipper[44] now Boss."

I saw a new entry pop up on the CLIO screen. My on-call TIU team member, Beverly, who was at the back of the room, had added all the numbers now being called by the kidnapper since we put his mobile on live trace.

Walking over to her desk I said, "thanks for adding those numbers. When this is all over, DI Turner and his AMIP team will want them and everything from White's mobile to help identify and dismantle both gangs."

"Mr H?" DC Chris Edward's familiar voice whispered from the adjoining desk, "I've just added something to CLIO you and Mr Richards should look at."

"Okay, come over to my desk and explain."

---

44 Skipper or skip: colloquial term for a Sergeant.

As I checked my computer screen with Roy looking on, Chris told us, "the woman registered as the subscriber to the kidnapper's mobile is known to police. She's the girlfriend of a Jasper Beauchamp. He was arrested for drugs when the locals raided her address at 6 Caird Street, W10. That's right in the middle of the plot where Toscas is searching now for the stronghold."

"Boss," I said turning to Roy, "from my time as a Sergeant at Harrow Road, this area around the Mozart Estate is a frontline for police. I'd like to put the 'TSG' on standby."

"Yes, good idea," he said. "Didn't I hear you say you'd been with that mob once yourself?"

"Yes, in '95. I was on 1 TSG at Paddington. I had one of the best callsigns, '*Uniform 1-1-1*'."

"Well, call whoever's the Inspector now and get them to a forward position at Harrow Road nick. They're to join up with Vic's lot from SO19. They'll be just where we need them too for Westbourne Park Station if it all kicks off round there at 10pm."

"Sure, I'll brief them."

The light on my console flashed to alert me to another call from Trevor.

"The stronghold's in Caird Street, on the north side. Another couple of sweeps and we'll have a door number for you."

"Excellent. Our intel on the kidnappers suggests the same street and it could be number six."

"Okay, we'll check anyway, and I'll call you back once we're certain."

"Boss," I said, wanting Roy's attention. "Toscas has confirmed Chris's intel. The stronghold is in Caird Street. Trevor is just checking whether it is number six. I'll now add it all to CLIO"

"Okay, good." Then raising his voice, Roy shouted out, "Vic, you're reading this too, I hope?"

"Yes Boss, on it already. I'll have the hostage-rescue plan for you shortly."

"Looks like you might have done it again Whizzy! Thank you."

The light on my console flashed once more with a call from Ray at Vodafone.

"Your target in Stepney is now on the move," he advised. I looked up at the wall clock; it was just after 9pm.

"Where to?" I asked.

"He pinged on our network around Whitechapel, so looking at the Tube map I'd say he's got on the Hammersmith and City Line and is heading west."

"Heads up everyone, Subject One is on the move. Potentially on the Underground, heading towards the RVP at Westbourne Park Station."

Anxiously, Roy asked, "Vic, Blue, have you got all your bases covered?" Both nodded back.

A few minutes later Ray called again. "Your second target is now on the move. I'd say she's also on the Hammersmith and City Line heading east. She just pinged at Goldhawk Road Station."

Roy read my screen, "Okay, good," he said in his familiar calm manner before raising his voice to add, "heads up everyone. Hopefully, we're about to get hold of Subjects One and Two. Blue and Vic, the show is yours."

Almost immediately, Harry called out, "silent running everyone and listen up."

No one spoke as I took control of the traffic camera above Westbourne Park Bus Garage and moved it remotely to look down on the RVP. I switched the system to broadcast the imagery live to the TV screens at the front of the room so everyone could watch the events.

We were all transfixed waiting for Blue's update, and it came very quickly. "We have Subject One, White aka Pinkie, Tavistock Road outside the pub next to the station entrance, south-side. Standby for an update on Monique, Subject Two."

I zoomed in with the camera to view White. He was holding a blue Adidas sports bag and nervously looking all around him.

"Boss," Vic called out as quietly as he could to Roy, "we're ready in Woodfield Road at the back of 'Delta Romeo[45]' with 1 TSG, now rolling slowly towards the RVP."

Blue interrupted him, "Subject Two coming up to street level from the eastbound platform. She'll appear any moment."

I zoomed the camera out a little just as White answered his mobile. The TV screen was now showing his position to the left, with the station frontage in the centre.

Greg announced excitedly, "that's her! The woman on the mobile. That's Monique, Subject Two. She's obviously talking to White."

We watched in silence as White hugged Monique before handing her the sports bag. She looked inside and they spoke briefly before he turned away having spotted a passing cab. He hailed it and walked into the middle of the

---

45   Delta Romeo: callsign for Harrow Road Police Station.

road to get in as it stopped. Monique watched for a moment as the cab pulled away to head south in Great Western Road towards Westbourne Park Road. She then returned to the station while putting the strap of the sports bag over her shoulder.

Monique walked through the ticket hall towards the stairs leading down to the westbound platform. She hadn't paid any attention to the man and woman reading the Tube map, so was surprised when they called out her name. She froze. Looking over her right shoulder, she realised her escape back to the street was now blocked by two men whose eyes were firmly fixed on hers. Coming up the stairs was another man looking right at her. She went limp as the detectives explained they were arresting her for drugs offences. Checking the sports bag, they found cocaine and rolls of banknotes.

"*Who the fuck do you think you are, Emerson fucking Fittipaldi,*" the cab driver shouted at the Range Rover driver as he sped past and cut in front of him just before the Zebra Crossing at the T-junction ahead. He braked so sharply to avoid rear-ending the car that his passenger shot forward and hit the dividing screen hard. Seconds later the expletives from the cab driver were joined with shouts of "Armed police, armed police! Show us your hands!" White was now aware the doors on both sides had opened and everything around him was illuminated by dazzling torch lights. Suddenly, he was moving. Someone was roughly dragging him out of the cab by his legs and his next sensation was the cold dampness of the road surface as his face was pressed into it. At the same time, he lost control of his hands as they were brought together behind his back and then bound with cable ties. He lay still, his heartbeat pulsing in panic as he was forcibly rolled one way and the other while being searched.

"Gun!" the SFO shouted as he felt the handle of the revolver tucked into White's waistband. The torch lights steadied on White as the officer carefully removed it. Next, he was lifted to his feet. For the first time he could take in the scene; a dozen or more uniformed and plain clothes police were standing around him illuminated by multiple flashing blue lights. The road was blocked off by three TSG 'Carriers[46]'.

"Cecil White, aka 'Pinkie'?" a detective asked him.

"Er, yeah man."

"I'm arresting you for conspiracy to murder, and possession of a loaded firearm."

---

46 Carriers: term used for the large Leyland DAF armoured police buses.

Watching all this on the CCTV caused us all in Central 500 to cheer. Greg shook my hand amid his own euphoria.

I then noticed the light flashing on my console once again.

"Okay," Trevor said, "confirmed, the door number you need to go crashing through matches your intel: it's number six."

The first SFO fired three Hatton Rounds in quick succession to remove the front door. The sudden loud noise got everyone's attention, both inside the house and elsewhere in Caird Street. As the door at number six splintered away from its frame, the double 'tings' of the flyoff levers from two stun grenades warned there was more to come. Twelve dazzling flashes with simultaneous and disorientating bangs completely overwhelmed everyone downstairs.

Shouts of "Armed police, armed police!" followed as the SFO team moved rapidly through the lower floor. They met no opposition as they manoeuvred in pairs into every room. Then, as one SFO raised his Heckler and Koch MP5 Carbine to allow its torch to illuminate the stairs up to the first-floor landing, a man appeared at the top. The beam picked out the Colt 'Police Positive' revolver in his right hand. He froze pointing it downwards.

Calmy, the SFO said to him, "Drop the gun mate. Drop the gun if you know what's good for you.' And then with force shouted, "Drop it now! Drop it!"

The man had screwed up his eyes, dazzled by the torchlight. He may not have realised it was fixed to the MP5 carbine pointing at his chest.

Regretting he had rushed from torturing the hostage in the bedroom to find out what was happening downstairs, the man hesitated as he considered his options. Two gunshots were the last sound he heard as the SFO registered the sudden upward movement of the revolver in the man's hand. The gun clattered to the ground, as the man's body recoiled backwards. His face hit the wall leaving a descending bloody trail as his epitaph.

"Boss," Vic called out. "The hostage is safe, but we've shot dead one of theirs. He was armed. Sounds like the SFO had no choice."

No one said a word as we all looked at Roy.

"Okay, well… that's always to be expected," his face revealing deep sadness. "Thank you everyone for doing your jobs. Best we tidy up here. Then for those of you who can, please go home and hug the ones you love."

I called Harry to let him know the outcome but did not stay on the line this time to hear the victim's reaction.

As I closed down Central 500 and cleared the last of the debris from the desks, Greg called my mobile from Belvoir's bedside at St Mary's Hospital.

"Sorry, Michael, no MAC-10 for you. All we got is one unfired, blue-tipped bullet stamped IMI 9mm. It was in the bag Belvoir had when he was kidnapped, which we also found in the stronghold."

"Damn. So where did the MAC-10 go?"

"He says he borrowed it for Brockwell Park and then gave it back. He's not yet ready to tell us who's got it now."

"Damn."

It had gone 3am on Sunday when I finally got home to re-join the family. That left me only a few hours to be with them before starting the residential course that night. '*Exigencies of duty*' once again I reminded myself. Olivia had other words for my absence. She reminded me once more of the increasingly painful contradictions of my wanting to become a respected Scotland Yard detective and her failure to support me with achieving that ambition.

CHAPTER 44

False Start

Monday, 30th June

After four weeks' absence it felt slightly odd to be walking back into NSY. I was grateful not to have been disturbed during the weekends, as I had some precious time at home. Sadly, not enough to rebuild much of my relationship with Olivia, but Rebecca was happy to see me. We spent the daytime exploring Bushy Park, which was opposite our house.

Someone had created a mock-up of a name plate, 'Detective Inspector Michael Hallowes' and pinned it to my office door. I smiled and decided to keep it there for the morning at least. I watched through my open door for my staff making their own returns after only a weekend away. Getting back into the Monday morning routine, I began reading the weekly updates from each of my unit heads.

Roger was the first to appear. "Congratulations on being elevated to a real DI," he smiled on seeing the sign. "Don't forget to have your warrant card amended to show it too."

"'Elevated' hmm, not sure my uniform Inspector colleagues would agree. What news on Abonar?"

"Well," he began, pushing the door shut behind him. "Let's start with the pagers. I've been babysitting them while John's had a couple of days off."

"And?"

"Mitchell's has been silent the whole time. We reckon Ackerman's arrest really spooked him."

"I'm sure it did."

"Bown's has been very active, but all domestic. We've identified he's got a mistress. She's the one leaving all the messages. Usefully, we can now tell whether he's at home or in Chatham from the return calls to her number. We've got it on live trace too."

"Where was he over the weekend?"

"Chatham, as usual. At first, we thought his wife had kicked him out. But we've since worked out he goes back home during the week."

"And we've got an address for the mistress just in case he goes there to lie low?"

"Yep, all in the file Guv, which I'll give back to you later."

"Anyone else calling him?"

"No, none of his previous contacts. Both he and Mitchell are using their mobiles though, but subscriber checks haven't thrown out anyone with a criminal connection."

"And Phillips? What's happening with Pager C?"

"Like Mitchell's, silent."

"Okay. So what news from SERCS?"

"Well, on Friday, DI Wilton called to say they'd start surveillance today."

"Excellent, I'll call him in a few minutes to see how it's going. I hope they're looking at all three of our targets."

"So far, he's only committed to looking at Mitchell. Although he did say they'd check out Bown's and Phillip's addresses as an initial recce."

"Have you told him about Bown's movements between Grove Park and Chatham?"

"Oh yes."

"Good, and how's David doing at the gun club?"

"He's drawn a blank. He's still going there, but none of our targets have returned since that first time. He's happy to keep going if we want him to."

"Yes, and right up until SERCS start making arrests."

"Sure. Will you call David, or should I?"

"You can, Roger. I'm happy to leave him to you for now, or until he reports something significant. Oh, and what more do we now know about Phillips?"

"Nothing. He's a complete cleanskin. No previous and no intel with Kent Police. The address we had from the gun club is for his mother's place. The car David saw him driving was a hire car, and the address on his licence also came back to his mother's. We got his actual H-A from calls Bown made to it from Chatham and Grove Park, just as Alice predicted."

"Well that also proves her point that Bown is the weakest link. How have we confirmed it's the same Andy Phillips who's the 'Black Shod'?"

"SO11 Surveillance loaned us a photog[47] for the day and he got some

---

[47] Photog – slang for police surveillance photographer.

excellent pictures of him wandering around Rochester. David recognised him as our third man immediately."

"Excellent, excellent. Sounds like you kept the team busy while I was away. Thank you. Let's have a proper catch-up with John and Mark at 9:30. Oh, and would you ask Chris to join us too?"

"Sure, I'll let them all know."

"One more thing, Roger, what about Mr Hamilton's job with the RPGs? Where's that got to?"

"Nowhere really. After Gudgeon saw Donovan in Full Sutton, Mrs Donovan visited too. Mr Hamilton then had her under surveillance for forty-eight hours. Sadly, she didn't do anything other than confirm she uses the Manchester TK, as we thought. So, he's cancelled everything except the live monitoring of the two Manchester numbers. Nothing useful yet on them either."

"Damn. I thought it would have progressed much more than that by now. And Toscas trying to locate the second Orange mobile?"

"Couldn't get a precise fix again. It had one more call from the Manchester TK on the Tuesday after Mrs Donovan's visit to Full Sutton, but has stayed off since. We assume that's because she told the Eltham contact nothing's going to happen until the Home Secretary gives the green light to restart and Donovan's ready to give us a sample."

"Surely Donovan and Gudgeon must realise that's going to expose they're running another scam?"

"Maybe, but they've agreed to provide one. We're exploiting what Donovan must now realise is his only hope of getting early parole. That's why he doesn't seem bothered to play along with us. Right now we can't risk losing the opportunity to trade the RPGs."

"Well, no one else will want them."

"Maybe so. Certainly using an RPG in London would be a first. Like you, I can't see any criminal gang needing them. Possession would earn a minimum sentence of ten years; using one probably life."

"That's my thinking too. I imagine Mr Hamilton is tearing his hair out with all this delay."

"He is, and that's why I've spent most of my time down here avoiding him. I suppose now you're back on deck, I'm no longer the Acting DI and a DS once again."

"Yeah, sorry about that. You should be alright with the promotion process in a few weeks, though, and then you'll be a substantive DI."

"Oh, I do hope so."

"And thank you for looking after Corporate Services, Roger. Judging by these weekly reports you've kept them all running smoothly too. I appreciate it, thanks."

"It was a pleasure, Guv. Right, I'll see you with the team at 9:30."

Soon after he left, my desk phone rang. Intuitively, I looked at my watch to check how much time I had before the meeting: forty-five minutes. The caller was DI Arthur Wilton.

"Now you're back, I thought you'd want to know we started on Abonar this morning," he said, but his tone sounded less than cheerful as he continued. "And I've called you on the GTN, so we can talk freely."

He then recounted the events from when he and his team started their day at 5:00am with a briefing at the Crawley Branch Office…

"Good morning, everyone, settle down. Lots to get through."

Using his laptop and a projector on the adjacent desk, Arthur displayed on the big screen behind him photographs of Anthony Mitchell, his Brighton home address, and then his red Ford Mondeo car.

"Right, this is Subject One. Anthony Mitchell, aged 44, registered firearms dealer and former Sussex Police Special Constable."

He waited for the groans to die down amongst his audience. They came from the Kent, Surrey and Met officers to the annoyance of their Sussex colleagues.

"Intelligence tells us he's the principal source of illegal firearms getting into the hands of organised crime gangs in London, Glasgow, Liverpool, and Manchester. Our job today is to use surveillance in the hope he'll take us to where he stores them. He may even have a workshop where he's reactivating firearms. Today, I want to start developing a profile while we plan for his arrest: the times he gets up and goes to bed; the places he visits; who he meets, and how he operates. When I'm done, I'll hand over to Myles to brief you on your deployments. Then Clive will give you some context from the intel."

DS Myles Hurst and DC Clive Philpott acknowledged him with a nod.

Arthur then moved the slideshow on to show photographs of Robert Bown, his addresses in Grove Park and Chatham, and then his car.

"Right, this is Subject Two, Robert Bown, aged 46. Previous conviction for unlawful possession of a firearm. Employment status unknown. SO11 and our own intel says he's the principal courier used by Mitchell to deliver guns to Ackerman."

Arthur paused to give the Team Leaders time to finish making notes before recommencing.

"Next up, the third man in our conspiracy, Andrew or Andy Phillips, aged 45. He's Subject Three. No previous convictions. Employment status unknown. Address in Rochester. SO11 has intel he's the courier who delivered three consignments, totalling sixty-five firearms and a thousand rounds of ammunition recovered in London and Kent. We have no intel of our own on this man. Ackerman never mentioned him. For now, be aware of Phillips and Bown in case either of them turns up on the plot for Subject One. Today, neither of these two are our priorities."

The audience nodded as Arthur continued. "There's no intel about our subjects being armed themselves, so, I'm not authorising firearms today."

A chorus of disappointed groans filled the room.

"Look, the bosses won't go for it unless the risk assessment says otherwise," Arthur responded angrily. "If you spot anything to change that, then I'll reconsider. So, in the best traditions of 'Hill Street Blues', 'Let's be careful out there'."

Once the groans died down again, Arthur invited Myles and then Clive to complete the briefing.

At just after 6:15am, the white Ford Transit used by SERCS as their primary observation vehicle, callsign 'O-P', reversed into a parking space on the brow of the hill some 50 yards away from Mitchell's house. Other vehicles tucked into parking spots in adjacent streets. It was already daylight and people were leaving their homes.

"O-P to all units," the radio suddenly announced, "Subject One, out, out. Green parka, blue jeans, white trainers, nothing in his hands. Standby."

The surveillance team members then eagerly waited for an update. They did not expect what happened next. Mitchell walked around the block of streets surrounding his house quite deliberately checking every vehicle with someone inside in case it might belong to a police surveillance team. Consequently, he disrupted their ability to keep him under control. Rather than risk jeopardising the whole operation on the first day, Arthur radioed his team telling them to withdraw to the pre-agreed rendezvous point and standby. A few minutes later, Arthur updated the team from the back of the van that he hadn't been able to move while Mitchell was still about.

"O-P to all units, Subject One is now back at the H-A. Standby."

In the cramped space Arthur commented to DS Hurst sat next to him, "you know, Myles, for a former Special Constable, Mitchell's bloody good at counter-surveillance."

"Yes," Myles replied, somewhat disillusioned, "but I get a sense he does this every day regardless of us being here."

"Well, time will tell. I don't think he's spotted the van, so let's just wait and see what he does next."

Minutes later, Mitchell came out on to his doorstep and looked up and down the street. The white Ford Transit now stood out, as all the vehicles previously parked in front of it had left. Mitchell walked up the hill and stopped next to it. First, he felt the bonnet for residual heat. Next, he put his ear against the side nearest the pavement. Arthur and Myles sat motionless holding their breaths. Mitchell looked at the builders' materials strapped to the roof rack but did not spot the embedded miniature cameras that provided three-sixty-degree vision of the surroundings, including him. The detectives were transfixed in silence watching their CCTV screens as Mitchell reached into his pocket and took out a cheap plastic biro. He walked to the rear of the van and wrote on the palm of his left hand the registration number. Walking around to the windscreen, he checked the tax disc. It was a printed version rather than handwritten. Walking back to his house, Mitchell nodded as if to acknowledge that meant it was probably part of a fleet and not privately owned.

Gasping, due to the shallow breaths he'd been taking, Arthur was the first to speak, "Holy, fucking shit. The bastard almost certainly made us[48]. Call up 4-5-4. Get her to drop off 4-5-3 and drive us out of here. There's no way one of us can jump into the cab. That's the end of watching Mitchell for today."

An hour later, Arthur and his team were back at the Crawley Branch Office debriefing.

"So, Michael, not exactly a good first day for us," Arthur said, finishing the story. "We'll try again on Thursday. That'll give Mitchell time to relax, and I can rethink how we redeploy. He's way too surveillance conscious, which makes it difficult with a conventional team."

"Yes, I wouldn't have expected that from him. It suggests he's got something serious to hide."

"Agreed, and I look forward to finding out what it is."

"Do the next two days now give you an opportunity to look at Phillips and Bown?

"Yup, maybe."

"Okay, then you need to call me beforehand so I can tell you whether Bown is in Grove Park or Chatham."

"Yup, of course."

---

48 'Made us': short for 'made us out to be the police'.

CHAPTER 45

Getting Reacquainted

As I headed down the corridor towards the Fordham Suite, the daylight shining in from the Victoria Street side indicated Anton's door was open. That meant he was back too. I had missed him heading to morning prayers due to Arthur's call, which meant he did not have my reports. I sent him an apologetic text. I must have looked rather sheepish when I walked into the briefing room a moment later because John saw my expression and asked, "everything okay, Guv?"

"Yes, yes. Sorry, mind elsewhere. I may need extra copies of the Sunday papers down the back of my trousers to soften a beating. I didn't get Mr Baxter his weekly updates in time." Then, more cheerily I said, "right, I'm back and raring to go. Roger's already given me a complete update on everything I've missed, so anything extra from you John?"

"Well, we've now got a real DI running the show," he announced, causing everyone to laugh.

"I suppose it was one of you who kindly mocked up the sign on my door." They all laughed again.

"Just wanted everyone to know we've got a real Guvnor leading us now."

"Anything relevant to Abonar you'd like to comment on John?"

"Um, yes, of course. Those three actions you gave the SIOs when we met are starting to pay dividends. Marco says the three handguns sent to him so far have all the hallmarks of our Abonar gunsmith. When you next come by my desk, I'll show you the photos."

"Excellent, let's hope they find more. Any intel on who supplied them?"

"No, nothing yet."

"I'm hoping, Chris, you have something to tell me about Donovan's finances?"

"Yes, and I've pointed GMP to where they'll have the greatest success. He's got properties he didn't declare at the asset confiscation hearing. There's as much as half-a-million hidden away."

"Wow, good work. How did GMP react?"

"They're delighted. I've told them to go slow until you tell them they can start knocking on doors."

"Thank you. Yes, we don't want them upsetting Mr Hamilton's job. So what have you learned?"

"Since last October, the family disposed of £50,000 in assets. No doubt most went into buying the guns from Mitchell and the RPGs. Sadly, it's all untraceable cash transactions thereafter."

"Very good. Have you added that to the Abonar file for when Roger lets me have it to read?"

"I have, yes."

"Good. What about Gudgeon's finances?"

"That's less clear-cut. We don't know exactly what services he's providing the Donovans, so we can't tell whether his fees are reasonable or not. The Donovans are paying the Manchester law firm direct and not him. Of course, they might also be privately bunging him envelopes of cash."

"Yes, quite possibly. Excellent work. Roger, when can I have the file?"

"It's on my desk. Sorry, I'll get it for you after this."

"Thanks. Anything more about the Brockwell Park shooting?"

"The two survivors are off the critical list," John advised. "They've been very lucky. One may never walk again, though."

"And the MAC-10?"

Shaking his head, John reported, "AMIP are still crashing through doors mopping up after that kidnap using all the call data it generated, but no trace of the MAC-10 yet."

"Damn. Okay, we'll just have to be patient."

"Yes, the intel they've generated suggests it's another dial-a-gun. I spoke to Marco about it too. He confirmed from his own Op Fordyce, the marks left by its breech face on the spent rounds indicate this MAC-10 has been used twice before Brockwell Park, but nothing since."

"How many murders?" I asked.

"Only the four at Brockwell Park," John replied. "There's a chance it's now been dumped. No one will want to be nicked holding it and risk being charged as an accessory to those murders. Marco knows to call me either if it turns up in a fresh shooting, or it gets recovered."

"And news on the Colt revolver recovered at the stronghold when SO19 shot the kidnapper?"

"Yup, it's one of ours. At least we can add that one to the conspiracy once Mitchell's arrested."

"What did White aka Pinkie have in his waistband when arrested?"

"Not one of ours. It was another '*Brocock*' air pistol converted to fire .38 Special. Just shows how ingenious gangs are getting when they can't get hold of a real gun."

"Yes, indeed, and we can expect a lot more of that once we disrupt the Abonar source of real guns. Right, I better update you on the call I had earlier from SERCS."

CHAPTER 46

More Challenges

Thursday, 3rd July

My mobile rang just as I was having a conversation with DS Alan Murphy in the Crimestoppers office. Arthur's number showed on the screen. "Arthur, hang on, I'm just heading to my office so we can talk."

"No problem, Michael. I'll call you back on your desk phone using the GTN."

Unlocking the door, instinctively I noted the time on my wall clock: 11:15am.

"How have you got on?" I asked, immediately after picking up the handset.

Arthur hesitated, so I asked, "you didn't call me to confirm Bown's whereabouts on either Tuesday or Wednesday,"

"Yes, that's because we've left him and Phillips alone. As for Mitchell, well, given I'm calling you now rather than at the end of the day should be an indication that he's defeated us again."

"What did he do this time?"

"He drove like a madman. Any attempt to follow him, and we'd have shown out immediately. We're going to have to wait until our TSU can put a 'lump'[49] under his car and track him remotely ."

"When can they do that?"

"It's booked for Sunday night. We'll have another go at him on Monday."

"Okay, did something spook him today?"

"No. I'm certain we didn't. Everyone was off the street until he left the house just before 8:30. He did his usual walk-about, and we just let him go. I had the streets around him plotted up with our teams for when he got back. Once in his Mondeo, he shot off like a bat out of hell. As I said,

---

49 Lump: under-vehicle covert electronic tracking device.

if we'd tried to keep up, he'd have made us. He's proving a very challenging surveillance target."

"Let's hope the lump does the trick. While you wait, will you now look at Bown and Phillips instead?"

"No, my boss wants us to focus on Mitchell."

"Why's that? Sounds like you've got nothing else to do."

"He's concerned if we blow it with either of them, they'll compare notes and realise they're all under surveillance."

"Well we'd see that immediately from what we're doing here. I can tell you right now they're not talking to each other."

"Maybe so, but the boss says no."

"Sugar, effing bloody, damn Arthur!"

"Look, I've got to go Michael. I'll call you on Monday or Tuesday with another update."

CHAPTER 47

A Change of Plan

Monday, 7th July

On Monday I was understandably eager to hear from Arthur and was relieved when he called my desk phone just after 5pm. He was much happier to explain what had happened…

"All units from the O-P, standby. Subject One out, out of the H-A. Now right on Baden walking north towards his red Ford Mondeo. Standby."

"From the O-P, brake lights on. Reminder, the vehicle is facing south. Standby. Okay, he's off. At speed now south in Baden towards Coombe. Turning right on to Coombe and it's a total loss on visual. Going to tracker. Standby."

All the detectives readied themselves in eager anticipation. The lump constantly updated the map on the computer screen in the replacement observation van, a pale blue Mitsubishi 'Express'.

"Left into Mafeking towards Ladysmith Road. Now left, left into Ladysmith. Back towards Baden. Standby."

If they had not done so already, the surveillance team drivers started their engines and waited for the tracker to give them an indication of Mitchell's real direction. So far, he had just gone round in a circle. As before, he was looking out for anyone following him.

"From the O-P, it's a stop, stop in Ladysmith at the junction with Coombe. Standby… Okay, he's off again, now east on Coombe and right, right into Bevendean Road, and now a left into Bear Road at speed. Standby."

"O-P from the DI, permission?"

"DI wait. Target turning right, right into the cemetery. He's now stationary in the middle of the cemetery. DI, go."

"Yeah, O-P and all units from the DI, remember, just let him run and let the O-P track him. DI out."

"He's still in the cemetery," the O-P continued the commentary. "Looks like he's waiting to be sure no one's followed him in there. Standby for an update."

Seconds later it came, "from the O-P, we're on the move again. He's heading for the exit into Hartington Road opposite Bernard Road. Standby."

"Subject One is out and heading west on Hartington Road. Looks like he's now keeping to the speed limit. I think he's decided it's safe and he's not being followed."

"O-P from the DI, permission?"

"DI, go."

"All units start heading west but keep off the streets Subject One is using. 4-2-7 follow him but hold back and keep him on a long-eye. DI out."

After some 20 minutes, Mitchell slowed at the turning into Bellingham Crescent, Hove.

"All units from the O-P, Subject One's stopped at the Knoll Business Centre off the Old Shoreham Road; access is via Bellingham Crescent, standby."

"O-P from the DI, permission?"

"DI, go."

"4-2-7 get close enough to see where he goes in there."

"DI from 4-2-7, I'm at the entrance to the car park. Premises appear to be an old school converted into workshops. Subject One is unlocking the door with keys from his parka pocket. Standby for the unit number."

Everyone waited, eager for his next update.

"Okay, all units from 4-2-7, he's gone into Unit W11. Appears to be on his own. There's no business name above the door. To get your bearings, his unit is next door to 'Lizzies Wholesale Bakery', 4-2-7 over."

"All received by the O-P."

Arthur then took over on the radio, directing the surveillance team to park up around Mitchell's location and wait for further instructions. The Mitsubishi van arrived a short while later and parked in a space in Bellingham Crescent. This gave an uninterrupted view of Mitchell's car and the door to his industrial unit. Other than requesting the occasional comfort break to use a toilet, the detectives stayed in their positions for the next five hours. No one else went into Unit W11. At just after 4pm, Mitchell came out and locked the door. He looked around the car park and up towards where the Mitsubishi van was now positioned but took no notice of it.

"All units from the O-P. Subject One is out. Standby."

The other detectives, many of whom had slouched in their car seats, sat up. Rather like airline passengers readying themselves for take-off and landing, they adjusted their seats to the upright position and waited.

"From the O-P, Subject One is having a walk around the car park. Standby... Okay, he's now back in the red Mondeo."

The surveillance team kept their distance, relying instead on the tracker. Arthur assumed Mitchell was so convinced by the success of his manoeuvres earlier he had become complacent. He had failed to consider that police could follow him technically rather than conventionally, which was evident from him not using any counter-surveillance measures on the return journey.

"That's excellent news, Arthur. Good job." I said as he finished.

"Oh, and my boss is here and wants a word too."

"Michael, DCI Bagshaw. I need to update you on a development since we last spoke," his tone forewarned me he was about to share bad news.

"What's happened, Sir?"

"I've been reminded Arthur's operation is principally to investigate the supply of firearms and ammunition to Ferris. That begins with Mitchell, through Bown to Ackerman, and then to McAuley and Ferris."

I could tell what was coming, so protested, "but concurrent to that, we know Phillips was the courier Mitchell used for the three consignments recovered in London and Kent."

"Maybe, but Ackerman knows nothing about them, and our priority has always been to corroborate his story to support Don McGregor's case against Ferris. That means we're only after Mitchell and Bown now. Sorry, but that's just how it goes. Phillips is no longer our target."

"Who made that decision and why, Sir?" I said, knowing full well I sounded disrespectful.

"It came down from on-high this morning. I've been told to ignore your Abonar job. Our objective is to get Mitchell for supplying the MAC-10s to Ferris. I'm also to get Bown for delivering them. I'm sorry but your investigation into the three consignments is no longer part of that."

"Holy, fucking shit," I said, before pausing to recover my composure. "Sir, apologies. I don't often swear, but this is crap and, what's worse, you know it is too. So you're just going to ignore everything my team has worked on?"

"That's the nub of it, yes," he replied curtly. "I've said my bit, so I'll hand you back to Arthur."

I waited for a moment and then asked, "Arthur, can you be overheard?"

"No, why?"

"When Mr Bagshaw said this came from on high, who does he mean?"

"Who probably doesn't matter. It's all got very political here. We and the other Regional Crime Squads are under threat of another structural reorganisation courtesy of the new Home Secretary. My bosses want to minimise any damage they can do to us. Hence, they consider continuing with Abonar presents a risk we should now avoid. It's not about you and it's not about your team. Sorry, it's just small 'P' politics."

I wanted to swear again, but stopped myself to ask, "what about us being there to help with your searches?"

"I don't know, Michael. I just don't know anymore. Sorry."

I dropped the handset back on its cradle. Sitting back in my chair, I thought about how I was going to break it to the team. I reconciled myself by reading the Abonar file. I then updated it with the latest from SERCS before leaving it on Anton's desk to read and then hand to Derek.

CHAPTER 48

More Unwelcome News

Week beginning Monday, 14th July

Sitting in my office a week later, having heard nothing more from Arthur, I was now especially anxious for him to call. At midday, I dialled his mobile number. It went straight to voicemail, so I left a message. At 6pm, having not had a reply, I tried again.

"Michael, sorry, I can't talk for long," he answered, sounding rushed. "We're planning on this week for the arrests and searches. As soon as we've finalised which day, I'll call you. Sorry, got to go. Cheers."

His next call came late on Thursday afternoon, July 17th. "Thought I should call and give you the news personally," he began, his tone immediately hinting at more unwelcome news. "Yesterday, we nicked Mitchell and turned over his house and workshop."

Furious I asked, "What? I thought we had an agreement, Arthur. You were supposed to call me beforehand. What changed that?"

"Politics, Michael, pure politics. My bosses decided not to involve SO11."

"Sugar, fucking bloody, damn, Arthur! How could you let this happen?"

"Wow, you don't normally swear."

"No, I don't. It's what I'm calling the '*effing SERCS-effect*'!"

"Look, it's nothing personal," he replied defensively. "As I told you, it's not about you or your team. Our bosses wanted this to be an exclusive success for SERCS. I'm really sorry."

"This is shit, Arthur. So much for collaboration."

"I get why you're angry, but don't take it out on me. Neither of us can change what's happened. Look, I need to get on."

"Arthur wait, please. I don't want you to hang up. Can you at least tell me what you found?"

"Yes, of course. I suppose I owe you that. Oh, and before I talk about Mitchell, I should tell you we also tried to get Bown. But he wasn't at home."

"Grove Park or Chatham?"

"Grove Park."

"No, he wouldn't have been, Arthur. He's been replying to messages from his Chatham address all week. If you'd frigging well called me, I would have told you that."

"Shit, the guys told me they'd checked with you on Tuesday night."

"Well, they didn't, so you better ask them who they think they spoke to. What a shame, Arthur. What a bloody shame."

"Look, all is not lost. We did get some gear from his address."

"What?"

"A deactivated MAC-10, and a silencer amongst other things from his bedroom."

"An Abonar-type silencer?"

"No, and it was a dummy to go with the deactivated MAC-10."

"So nothing of value. Anything else?"

"Yes, he had a black nylon bag with another three silencers, and they are your Abonar-type."

"Well, that's some good news. Anything else linking him to our investigation?"

"Three Uzi magazines and a MAC-10 shoulder stock. None of the Israeli ammunition, though."

"Any live firearms?"

"No, none."

"Where are the items now?"

"At Crawley while we decide what to do with them."

"Let me know when you do. I'd like to come and have a look. What about Mitchell, what can you tell me about him, or do politics prevent that?"

"No, I can tell you about his arrest."

Arthur then recounted the events of Wednesday morning…

It was a couple of minutes after 6am when Arthur stood on Mitchell's doorstep at 30 Baden Road flanked by five other detectives. Taking the paper search warrant from inside his jacket, he thumped loudly on the door. Mitchell was dressed in pyjamas and cautiously unlocked the door, opening it sufficiently to allow only his head to be exposed. With the rest of his body he leaned heavily against the door to stop it being opened further. Arthur held up his warrant card saying, "Mr Mitchell, police…"

Before he could finish, Mitchell responded with, "Ah, but I've had my annual visit from Sussex Police Firearm Licensing Unit. You need to talk to them." As he finished, Mitchell began to close the door.

DS Myles Hurst pushed Mitchell back forcibly into the hallway, followed by his colleagues, saying, "We're not from Sussex Police, Mr Mitchell. We're from the South-East Regional Crime Squad. We've got a search warrant for illegal firearms and ammunition."

"There must be some mistake," he answered, sounding flustered before regaining some composure saying, "I'm a Registered Firearms Dealer. I'm allowed to keep firearms and ammunition on my premises. You won't find anything illegal here. The Firearms Licensing people will tell you that. I'm not due another visit till next year."

"That may be so, Mr Mitchell, but I'm DC Philpott from SERCS and I'm arresting you on suspicion of conspiracy to supply illegal firearms and ammunition. You do not have to say anything, unless you choose to do so, but it may harm your defence if you fail to mention when questioned something you later rely on in court. Do you understand?"

"A conspiracy? Who with?"

"We'll deal with all that back at the station. In the meantime, where's your gun room?"

"It's through there, but it's locked as you'd expect. I haven't started work yet."

"Well, in that case, unlock it and we can get on with our job."

"Fine, I'll get the keys. They're in the safe upstairs." With that, he turned around to go up.

"Not so fast," Arthur said. "Given the nature of our enquiries, you'll need to let us open it. I'm going to handcuff you too. You can get dressed later. Is anyone else in the house?"

"Yes, my girlfriend, Naomi. She's in bed upstairs or was until you lot started thumping on the door."

"Right, I'll go on ahead and you can follow," Arthur told him as he went in front with Clive. Myles followed behind Mitchell now handcuffed at the front. Naomi met them on the landing.

"What's going on, Tony? What the fuck is going on? Who are these people?"

"Police," Arthur told her bluntly.

She looked at Mitchell's hands now cuffed in front of him. "Why's Tony in handcuffs? What the fuck is this all about?"

"We've got a warrant to search your house, Miss," Clive advised her. "We're looking for illegal firearms and ammunition. Do you know anything about that?"

"No, no, of course not. That's crazy. Tony's business is all about guns. He's legit. He's an authorised dealer. He wouldn't have anything to do with illegal firearms."

Having been shown by Naomi how to open the bedroom safe, Myles found only passports, some cash, and a bunch of keys. Arthur and the others then led Mitchell back downstairs.

Looking at the various keys, Myles knew it would take him an embarrassing minute or two to work out which ones fitted the gun room door. "You better show me which of these I need, Mr Mitchell," he asked, "and then stand back."

Mitchell pointed out the correct ones and Myles then unlocked the heavy steel-plated door and turned on the lights. Mitchell followed him and Clive into the twelve-foot square room. A third detective, Mick, followed filming the search with a video camera. Another, Terry, had been appointed as the Exhibits' Officer. He came in too with a large plastic crate that contained all he needed for his job to record and package every item of potential evidence. Arthur waited in the hallway, as there was no room for him as well.

"Right, Mr Mitchell," Clive began, "You sit there on the stool while we search around you. First up, what can you tell us about these?" He had spotted an open cardboard box on the floor and could see it contained MAB pistols. He recognised them from the photographs John and I had shown him only a few weeks before. He tipped them on to the workbench and counted forty-three in total. Each one was still fully activated and in its original blued finish but in a heavily used condition. None had its serial number obliterated.

"I'm in the process of deactivating them for a client," Mitchell commented, hoping the detective would take no further interest. But Clive had already spotted another open box. This one was on the workbench, and it contained assorted component parts for MAB pistols. They included barrels, magazines and frames. Two of the latter had been nickel-plated with the same matt finish he had seen in the Abonar photographs.

"And these, Mr Mitchell, what about these?" Clive asked.

"Just spare parts, I'm about to get them scrapped," he replied, feigning disinterest.

Clive reached under the workbench and pulled out two heavy unbranded cardboard boxes. He placed them alongside the other two and opened the first. It contained another inside branded 'Samson' with the label describing the contents as 'Loaded Center Fire Cartridges Small Arms Ammunition MFD By Israeli Military Industries Ltd'. Clive lifted the lid to find unopened blue and white boxes of 9mm ammunition also bearing the brand name 'Samson'. He opened one. It held fifty rounds. He immediately recognised their blue tips as matching those in the Abonar photographs. Taking one out he read 'IMI 9mm' on the base. He counted sixty of these the individual boxes of fifty bullets.

Looking now at Mitchell, Clive asked him, "What exactly do you do as a Registered Firearms Dealer?"

"Principally, I'm a gunsmith. I take a gun to see how I can improve it. Other than that, my main business is deactivating firearms here in the workshop."

"Then why do you need three thousand rounds of this 9mm ammunition?"

Mitchell did not respond. Instead, he looked on as Clive opened the second large box. As before, it contained an inner one and inside that were another sixty blue and white 'Samson' branded boxes. These were of the copper-jacketed type without the blue tip.

"There are another three thousand here, Mr Mitchell. That's six thousand rounds alone just in these two big boxes. If your main business is gunsmithing and deactivation, why have you got so much ammunition?"

"I have nothing more to say."

"Really, why's that, Mr Mitchell?" Clive challenged him.

Again, he did not reply and just stared back defiantly without blinking.

Clive broke away from his gaze to tell DS Hurst, "Skip, you better ask Mr Wilton to get the Sussex Police Firearms Licensing people over here now to look at all this while we carry on."

"Good idea, Clive. I'll get the DI to call them."

"Terry, get this all logged, bagged and tagged, please," Clive told his colleague. "Oh, and don't seal the bags tight just yet. I need them open so the licensing people can see what's inside."

Terry took the stool Mitchell had now vacated over to the workbench and sat on it to begin cataloguing everything found so far.

"Right, Mr Mitchell," Clive said, "I suggest we do the rest of the house. Let's go back upstairs to your bedroom and see what else you've got in there."

Naomi came to the lounge door to try and reach the hallway as Mitchell passed through.

"Not now Miss," Clive said robustly. "Go back in the lounge and wait with the other detectives, please."

A woman detective had joined the search team and ushered her back into the room.

Upstairs in the bedroom Clive and Myles began systematically checking every possible hiding place. Another detective now stood guard over Mitchell who looked on, again feigning disinterest. Myles had instructed him to sit on the corner of the double bed. From the wardrobe, Clive removed a black zip-up nylon bag. Lifting it, he knew immediately the contents were heavy enough to hold another firearm. Unzipping it, he looked inside. From the Abonar photographs he recognised it immediately as a MAC-10 submachine gun. However, this one was stamped with 'C.G. Ltd M10 9mm Pistol'.

"Don't get excited," Mitchell said in his now familiar defiant tone. "It's deactivated."

"Really, who deactivated it?" Myles asked.

"The guy I bought it from. Another RFD."

"Who's that?"

Mitchell shrugged his shoulders.

At that moment, Arthur entered the bedroom.

"The Sussex Firearms Licensing people are in the gun room. When you're done up here guys, you better bring your new-found friend down to speak to them."

The detectives carried on their search of the upstairs rooms and then the loft. Not finding anything that might be relevant, they brought Mitchell to the hallway. Myles and Clive conferred with their colleagues who had searched the downstairs rooms, and they too had not found anything of interest.

"Right, all that needs to be done now is for you to speak to the Sussex Police Firearms Licensing Officers," Arthur told Mitchell.

The two plain clothes police officers from Sussex were looking through the contents of the exhibits' bags in the gun room. Both were in their late forties. Their indifferent manner immediately annoyed Arthur. He could tell they had long since lost the rigour expected of officers entrusted as guardians of the firearms' legislation.

"Ah Tony," said the younger one, "bit surprised to find you've got all this ammunition you haven't told us about. What's the story with all this, eh?"

"It's all recorded in my Firearms Register."

"And these handguns and component parts, Tony. What's with them too?"

"They're all recorded in my Register."

"Where is your Register then?" Myles asked, sounding annoyed. "We've searched the whole house and not found it. What does it look like?"

"It's red and A4-size," the licensing officer replied, trying to be helpful.

"No, we haven't found one like that," Myles told him.

That prompted Arthur to say, "Maybe Mr Mitchell it's in your other workshop."

"I can vouch for Tony," the licensing officer interrupted, "these are his only registered premises, Sir," he told Arthur in a perfunctory manner. "His RFD authority prohibits him from having anywhere else unless he's told us. I've known Tony for years, if he had another premises, he'd have told us."

"What a cosy relationship you seem to have," Clive commented.

"It's all about trust, Sir. Now, Tony, when did you last see your register? If we're to help you, you need to help us find it."

"That's enough," Arthur interrupted angrily. "I'm just a little concerned with all this overfamiliarity. Mitchell here is a suspect for arms trafficking. Right, Mitchell, I want you to show us your real workshop."

"As these Firearms Licensing Officers just told you, I don't have another premises. I do everything here," he replied defiantly.

"Well, that's not true, is it?" Arthur snapped back. "You said your business is deactivation. I can't see any tools here for doing that."

Mitchell just shrugged and looked away.

So Arthur then enjoyed asking him, *"what about Unit W11 at the Knoll Business Centre in Hove? What do you use that for?"*

Mitchell's paling complexion betrayed his shock, which he tried to disguise by arrogantly replying, *"Don't know anything about it. Where exactly is this place?"*

"I tell you what, we'll drive you there, shall we. Only, unlike you, we won't go via the cemetery, and we'll keep to the speed limit, if that's okay."

Mitchell's face now revealed his full horror as he realised that somehow the police had followed him to his otherwise secret workshop.

"Right, let's get you dressed Mr Mitchell," Clive said.

When the unmarked police car carrying Mitchell and the three detectives pulled up outside his unit at the Knoll Business Centre, two others from the team were already standing guard outside. Clive helped Mitchell out of the car, almost dragging him by the handcuffs, and led him to the door. Arthur was ahead of them holding the exhibits' bag with the bunch of keys from Mitchell's safe. *"It'll speed things up if you show us which of these fit the locks."*

Begrudgingly, Mitchell pointed at the two needed. On entering, the alarm system gave off a warning 'beep' to cancel it before the external siren would sound. Mitchell used the keypad to enter the code. Clive made a mental note of the four digits, and then wrote them in his notebook at the first opportunity when Mitchell wasn't looking. Terry and Mick followed behind the others. Having seen how complex the search was going to be, Arthur brought in Myles and two more detectives to help. Coming inside, Bob and Ginger along with the others already in there quickly understood the scale of the task ahead.

Mitchell had equipped his workshop with the sophisticated engineering tools he had brought from Longley's Builders' Merchants in Crawley, where he once worked as a highly skilled engineer and welder. He had installed a lathe, vertical milling machine, sandblaster, welding equipment and an array of other specialist tools. He also had a large workbench in the middle, plus almost floor-to-ceiling metal shelving around the walls. On one to the right, he had stacked pieces of steel in various lengths and sizes.

Clive spotted the electric TIG Welder at one end of the workbench and pointed it out to Myles. He recalled this could be a crucial piece of evidence.

"Mr Mitchell, I need to remind you that you're still under caution. Do you understand?" Myles asked.

Mitchell nodded.

"So, do you now accept this is your workshop?"

"No comment."

"And all the equipment and everything in here is yours?"

"No comment."

"Don't be like that. I just want to give you an opportunity to clarify that everything here belongs to you. So, what about this TIG Welder. What do you use this for?"

"No comment."

"How about removing the serial numbers from guns?"

"No comment. Look, I'm entitled to a solicitor, you know. If you want to interview me here rather than at a police station, then get me a solicitor. Otherwise, it's no comment. I know my rights."

"Fine, if that's how you want to play it, carry on," Myles said, looking Mitchell squarely in the eyes. "Clive, keep an eye on your prisoner while I get this search organised," Myles added just as Arthur went outside to make a call on his mobile.

"Terry, first up, I'll need that TIG Welder, please," Myles instructed, and Terry put a fresh plastic crate of forensic packaging on the workbench and pulled up a stool to work from.

"Right, Mr Mitchell, you stand here with my colleague while the rest of us work our way round to see what we can find. Bob and Ginger, start there," Myles said pointing at the closest rack of shelves, "Go through it all. Anything you think might be connected to manufacturing firearms; Mick will video in situ first. Once that's done, bring it over here for Terry to log, bag and tag. Okay?"

The two detectives moved to the first line of shelves and, using Mitchell's stepladder, worked systematically from the top downwards and right to left. In the meantime, Myles examined what Mitchell had on his workbench. Unsure of their potential relevance, he asked Mick to photograph each item. He called out its description and where he had found it to Terry, who made a corresponding entry in his log. Once he had finished writing, Terry then handed Myles the exhibits' bag to sign.

"Okay, nine thick black pins with screw heads at each end. Centre of the workbench." Myles announced. "Next, a blue plastic box containing an adjustable spanner thing."

Under the workbench he found rolls of cloth. He knew from Clive's briefing about the Abonar guns being wrapped in materials like these and thought they could be relevant. He passed samples to Terry. Remembering the Abonar cloths had handwriting on them, he also gathered up all the pens lying on the bench. He did the same with a roll of brown packing tape thinking it might have been the one used to wrap the BAR. Mick kept up with him taking photographs, and Terry with exhibiting them.

Flicking through an untidy stack of papers on the workbench, Myles hoped these might produce the missing Firearms Register. However, it didn't, so he dismissed it all as scrap and left it there.

Bob and Ginger brought items over to Terry to log once Mick had photographed them. In particular, a cardboard box branded 'Emerald Margarine' that contained blue and yellow plastic bags.

Rolls of clear plastic food bags were the final items Myles wanted exhibiting. He then walked around the room checking with the others that they had done a proper job of searching everywhere.

"No guns then?" Clive said to Mitchell, trying not to let his disappointment show. "For someone who claims to be a specialist gunsmith, I'm not seeing any guns in your workshop. Where do you keep them?"

Mitchell could not stop himself from smiling as he replied, "clearly, you've made a mistake. I don't know who you've been talking to, but they've obviously been lying to you."

Myles ignored him saying, "right, let's get this all packed up and away."

"Which nick are we going to? Brighton?" Mitchell asked.

"No, Gatwick. We thought we'd spare your blushes by keeping you away from where you once worked as a Special," Myles told him pointedly. "And Gatwick is more convenient for us."

As they reached the door to leave, Mitchell said, "I need to set the alarm".

Clive positioned himself again so he could see the code and confirmed the previous numbers.

Two hours later, Clive and Myles walked Mitchell from his cell to the interview room at Gatwick Police Station. His solicitor was waiting. "We'll need a few minutes of privacy gentlemen," he asked politely.

As they stood outside in the corridor, Myles looked at Clive and sensed his disappointment.

"Penny for them?"

"Does it show that much?"

"Yes," Myles told him, "You've got that moody, dispirited look we detectives get when things don't go our way."

"Well, I thought from what Ackerman told us, and SO11 have been working on with Abonar, either the workshop or his gun room would be stacked with evidence. You know, MAC-10s and the like all ready to go. Especially after Mitchell's counter-surveillance."

"Yup. I think while we were messing around trying to follow him, he's taken the opportunity to move it elsewhere."

"Maybe," Clive responded, resigned to the fact their vain searches confirmed that. "I think we're just going to have to call his bluff in interview. Hopefully, when we tell him what Ackerman said about his gunrunning, he'll want to give his side of the story."

Mitchell's solicitor opened the door and let Myles and Clive know his client was ready. They walked back into the room and set the tape machine to record. Having reminded Mitchell he was still under caution, Clive began, "let's start with your missing Firearms Register. Where is it?"

"I was doing a stocktake this week, which your arrival interrupted. In all your moving things around, you obviously knocked it somewhere where neither you nor I can find it."

"We searched your home quite thoroughly, didn't we?"

"You searched my home, yes, 'thoroughly' I can't comment on."

"Have you recorded in your register the serial numbers of every MAB pistol we found, as required, and where you got it from?"

"Of course."

"And where did you get them?"

"I don't remember. Without my register I don't want to give you the wrong information and waste your time," he said in his arrogant tone. "I get hundreds of handguns from multiple clients who want me to deactivate them. You can't expect me to remember each one."

"I think you'd recall who sent you forty-three pistols, Mr Mitchell."

"Well, I don't."

"Look, I put it to you, what we found at your home today was forty-three off-ticket handguns and spare parts, which means you're holding them illegally. What have you to say about that?"

"No comment."

"The regulations require you to keep a register. I put it to you that you haven't done so."

"That's your supposition."

"So, tell us where you got the MABs?"

The solicitor interjected, "my client gave you an adequate explanation. Your line of questioning is tantamount to bullying. If you've nothing factual to put to Mr Mitchell about those MABs, may I suggest you move on."

"Okay, how were you planning to dispose of them?"

"Once I had deactivated them, I would have sent them to the London Proof House for certification. I'd then either sell them wholesale to militaria dealers or return them to my client for retail. I'm not required to keep records of such sales."

"How do you get the guns to the London Proof House?"

"Courier."

"Who?"

"No comment."

Then let me help you with his name, Robert Bown. Bob to you, I believe."

Mitchell's expression changed for a moment before he regained his composure.

"I can tell from that look, Mr Mitchell, you know him. So, how do you know him?"

"No comment."

"Mr Mitchell, we know that you and Bown, along with several other of your associates are members of the Tudor Gun Club. You all shoot on the ranges at Stone Lodge in Dartford. That's confirmed by the membership register. I understand there are photos of you and Bown in the clubhouse. You're members of the Black Shods. So, you do know Bob Bown, yes?"

"No comment."

Clive decided to try a new line of questioning, "okay, so how badly will your business be hit by the impending post-Dunblane handgun ban?"

"Like everyone else, the market for handguns has gone in the UK. That's why I've diversified into deactivation."

"So, would you say you've got the skills also to reactivate firearms?"

"I don't do that," Mitchell sneered back.

"But you do have the gunsmithing skills and we've seen you've got all the right tools for doing so. Yes?"

"I… don't… do… that," he said, pausing between each word for added emphasis.

"So, let's look at what we did find this morning. Please account for you having six thousand rounds of off-ticket 9mm ammunition, blue tipped and copper jacketed?"

"No comment."

"Really? No comment?" Myles now challenged Mitchell, finding it hard to hide his disbelief at the man's refusal to explain.

"No comment," Mitchell repeated defiantly.

"Alright, let's try another tack," Clive cut in, again, wanting to move on. "We're investigating a conspiracy, going back ten years or more, where you have been supplying illegal firearms and ammunition to criminals across the country." Mitchell looked away, once again feigning disinterest. Clive raised his voice to get the man's attention back, "the ammunition we found in your gun room matches the types recovered in shootings and police seizures in London and Manchester. These include homicides." Then forcefully Clive asked him, "so, how long have you been supplying ammunition to criminal gangs?"

Defiantly, Mitchell turned back to look at Clive as he answered, "no comment."

"How do you know John Ackerman?" Myles fired back, hoping to unnerve him.

"No comment."

"Come off it," Myles's voice revealed his increasing frustration, "you and he are also members of the Tudor Gun Club. Is that correct?"

"Which? That I know John Ackerman, or we're members of the same gun club?"

"Both."

Mitchell turned to his solicitor and had a brief exchange in hushed words.

"No comment."

Myles then asked, "so, what's your business relationship with John Ackerman?"

"No comment."

"Well, he says," and Myles's voice changed to reveal the relish with which he was about to ask the question, "you supplied him with the three MAC-10s he was arrested for supplying on May 18th."

"Is that a question?" Mitchell asked mockingly.

"He also says you supplied him with three silencers and six Uzi magazines plus 150 rounds of the same blue tipped and copper jacketed 9mm ammunition we found today in your gun room."

Myles paused for a reaction, and not getting one continued, "he says you sold them to him for £3,500. So, what would you like to tell us about that transaction?"

"No comment."

"So, he's telling us the truth?"

"No comment."

"Ackerman's also told us you've been supplying him with illegal firearms and ammunition since the late 80s. Is that also true?"

"No comment."

Clive looked sideways at Myles and the glance they shared acknowledged there was little point continuing with this line of enquiry. However, Myles wanted to clarify a few more points.

"*Today, we searched Bown's address in Grove Park.*" *Myles's voice was now calmer.* "*We recovered a deactivated MAC-10. In a black nylon zip-up bag, just like the one we found at your home, we found three silencers of the same manufacture as the ones you sold Ackerman. We also found three Uzi magazines; again, the same type as you sold Ackerman.*" *Myles paused to study Mitchell's face for a reaction before asking, "did you make the silencers we found at Bown's address?*"

"*No comment.*"

"*Did you supply these Uzi magazines to Bown?*"

"*No comment.*"

"*Today, we searched your workshop at Unit W11, Knoll Business Centre in Hove. Do you accept these are your premises?*"

"*Yes.*"

"*Does anyone else work there with you?*"

"*You've obviously had me under surveillance,*" *Mitchell retorted, "so you know I work alone.*"

"*So, everything we found today in your workshop belongs to you?*"

"*Yes, but you didn't find anything relevant to your enquiries, did you?*"

"*We'll let the forensic scientists decide that, shall we?*"

Mitchell sat staring straight ahead without responding.

"*Mr Mitchell,*" *Myles tried again, now with irritation in his voice again, "I'm giving you the chance to tell us your side of what others say you've been up to. So how about you do that now?*"

The solicitor interrupted, "my client is exercising his right not to comment. Unless you've got some evidence to put to him, other than this conjecture and hearsay, once again, I suggest you move on."

Myles shot back in response, "I think it's only right and fair to your client that when John Ackerman has been so explicit about Mr Mitchell's criminal activities over ten years, we give him the chance now to set the record straight, if he can?"

Mitchell stared defiantly at Myles and paused before finally saying, "no comment."

Deciding to try a different, less confrontational approach, Clive asked, "What do you use the workshop for?"

"*Engineering.*"

"*What type?*"

"*I do freelance work for Longley's.*"

"*And did you transfer your equipment from there into your unit at the Knoll Business Centre?*"

"Yes."

"So, what about your trade as a specialist gunsmith? Do you do that too at Unit W11?"

"No comment."

"So where do you carry out that type of work?"

"At my registered address, 30 Baden Road."

"But we didn't find any engineering equipment there. So how can you do gunsmithing there?"

"No comment."

"Do you accept that your workshop at the Knoll Business Centre is where you actually carry out your trade as a gunsmith, including deactivating firearms?"

"No comment."

"To point out the facts, Mr Mitchell," Clive now let his irritation show too, *"unless you've got another premises that you haven't yet declared, the only place equipped for your trade as a gunsmith is the Knoll Business Centre. Am I right?"*

"No comment."

"Do you have another workshop, then?"

"I rent a garage at the back of Portland Road where I keep motorbikes. You're welcome to check there."

"Is that also a workshop?"

"No."

Letting out a frustrated sigh before he spoke, Clive tried again. *"Why did you not declare to Sussex Police you had a premises at the Knoll Business Centre?"*

"No comment."

"I put it to you, Mr Mitchell, you did that deliberately to hide the fact you were illegally reactivating firearms."

"No comment."

"Alright then," Clive was now making his irritation very evident, *"what engineering work do you carry out with the TIG Welder we found on your workbench."*

"Just welding."

"What in particular?"

"Metals."

Clive quickened the pace of his questions. *"And that includes components for firearms?"*

"Yes, when it's part of my deactivation business," Mitchell fired back.

"So you admit using Unit W11 as your business premises for deactivating firearms?"

"No comment."

"And you should have notified Sussex Police about that?"

"No comment."

"What about your use of the TIG Welder to obliterate serial numbers on firearms?"

"No. No comment."

Slumping back in his chair and turning to Myles, Clive announced, "I'm done."

"In that case," Myles confirmed, "interview concluded at 16:42 on Wednesday, 16ᵗʰ July 1997."

Later that day, Myles charged Mitchell with all the irregularities identified with how he ran his registered firearms business. The Custody Sergeant released Mitchell on bail to appear at Crawley Magistrates' Court, and then returned to him the bunch of keys taken from his safe.

On finishing his story, Arthur said with no real satisfaction in his voice, "so, Michael, that's what happened yesterday with Mitchell."

"Would politics get in the way if I offered now to come down and look through what you've recovered?" I asked optimistically. "I may spot connections to Abonar your team missed."

"I don't see any harm in that. Let me clear it with the DCI and get back to you."

"Thank you, Arthur, thank you."

Putting my mobile down on the desk, I said, "Sugar, fucking, bloody, damn," as loudly as I dared to get some benefit from releasing the huge anger I had subdued throughout the call.

Looking up, I saw Brian in the doorway. "Everything okay?" he asked with genuine interest. "I heard you from next door. Somewhat unusual for you to swear like the rest of us. You're working late again, I see."

"Sorry. I just needed to vent my exasperation at the stupid political rivalries between us and SERCS. You're obviously working late yourself, Sir. If you have a couple of minutes, I'll explain. If not, tomorrow."

"Now is good. I'm due at a dinner at 7:30, so I've got time. But what's going on at home, Michael? Why aren't you there?"

"Pretty crappy just now, Boss, but thanks for asking. I suppose I'm using the excuse of exigencies of duty to avoid going home before everyone's in bed. That way I don't have another fight with Olivia the moment I get in the door."

Brian looked at me sympathetically as he said, "been there Michael, been there. I had something similar with my wife when I was on the Flying Squad. Like you now, I wasn't keeping regular hours."

He studied my face and could tell I was getting emotional.

"Look Michael, somehow you and Olivia have to find a bearable compromise. If you want a career in SO11, then I need you on top form." He looked at me directly as if to question my commitment, and I nodded back again.

"Okay, so how about you tell me what SERCS have been up to?" As he spoke, he pushed the door shut and sat down. I then recounted the call from Arthur.

Brian nodded sagely throughout before declaring when I finished, "seen it all before. Doesn't make it right, though. Anton told me to expect as much after he'd read your file. I'll come up with a plan and get back to you." Looking at me kindly, he then announced, "now go home. If you're quick, your daughter might still be awake."

He passed me his keys, and smiling said, "take my car, I won't be driving tonight. It'll be quicker for you than public transport."

CHAPTER 49

Staying in the Game

Friday, 18ᵗʰ July

The next morning, the shapes of Roger and John filled my doorway at one minute before 9am.

"Come in guys. Take a seat."

I broke the news to them about SERCS. Throughout my retelling of the call from Arthur, John kept saying either "Shit" or "Fucking bastards". Roger was more sanguine and just nodded. He only spoke once I finished. "So, Guv, what are you planning to do if SERCS won't let us sort through what they found?"

"I'm hoping to make us so indispensable to their investigation they will."

"Okay, that doesn't seem to have worked so far," Roger replied sceptically. "So what do you think will make a difference this time?"

"Okay, so in addition to monitoring Bown to identify where he's hiding, there are two more lines of enquiry we've not followed up," I announced, wanting to sound positive. "That's because, until now, the risks have been too great that the people would tip Mitchell off. Now SERCS have nicked him, it doesn't matter. So, I want you and Roger to get these done, and quickly."

"Okay, who are these people?" John asked, sounding interested.

"First, Christopher Perkins of SF Firearms fame. Get a statement from him. I want to know precisely how many MAC-10s, deactivated or otherwise, plus component parts he sold Mitchell and when. I want him to describe everything he did in manufacturing his guns." I grabbed the album from my desk and added, "show him the Abonar MAC-10s, and get him to document what Mitchell's changed to reactivate them. I'll leave it to you and Roger to use your powers of persuasion."

"Sure, Guv. That should be fun," he replied before asking, "and the second enquiry?"

"I want you to visit Ralston Arms in Leeds. Contact the local Police Firearms Licensing Unit, or whatever they call themselves up there. I want you to go with them for a spot check on the company's records."

"Okay, that should be fun too," he said, relishing the idea.

"Go through their registers. I'm certain you'll find that's how Mitchell got his guns. Find out what sort of business arrangement they had with him. We need to know what types of firearms they got him to deactivate, in what quantities and when. According to the Proof House, Mitchell has put hundreds through them. Do a comparison between the records I copied and Ralston's. I'm certain you'll find anomalies."

"Let's hope so," Roger added, also quite enthused by the idea.

"If you find irregularities, use them as leverage. I want a statement from someone at Ralston about Mitchell."

John answered swiftly, "right, I'll get on to West Yorkshire Police straight away."

"Good, and I want a surprise visit, mind."

"Sure, Guv, I'll make that clear," John said as he left my office.

Roger remained checking his daybook for what he had planned for the week, before asking, "When do you want these two enquiries done by Guv?"

"As soon as you can."

"Okay, well, while you were away on your course," he said, now taking a stack of documents he had between the pages of his daybook, "DC Philpott sent these through. They're extracts from the transcripts of their interviews with Ackerman. They make interesting reading."

"Anything helpful to Abonar?" I asked, taking the documents.

"Well, they reinforce why we need to arrest Bown. Ackerman said Mitchell used him as the main outlet into the criminal market for his reactivated MAC-10s. He said Mitchell supplied him with 20, all delivered by Bown."

"Okay, well let's use Bown's pager and call data to our advantage. Maybe we can arrest him ourselves and get back in the game that way."

"I'll talk to Mr Hamilton about putting a team on standby from the OCG," Roger suggested.

"Please do."

He had been gone only a few minutes when Roger was back at my door with John. Excitedly, Roger explained, "Guv, there's just been a flurry of pager messages. Mitchell's been calling Bown and Phillips. I expect he wants to alert them to his arrest."

"Where was Bown?"

"Chatham Guv, still lying low. Do we need to let SERCS know?

"No, not right now," I told them, trying not to sound annoyed by the very thought of doing anything to help SERCS at this juncture.

CHAPTER 50

Ralston Arms

Monday, 21st July

I spent most of Monday distracted by the day-job running Corporate Services and attending various SO11 meetings. It was, therefore, welcome news when Roger phoned to update me on his visit with John to Ralston Arms.

"Interesting developments, Guv. West Yorkshire Police have referred Ralston Arms to the CPS[50] to decide what to do about the irregularities we found with their record-keeping. As the manager was super-helpful about our Abonar enquiries, I'm hoping he'll only get a warning."

"Okay, I'm intrigued. What did you discover?"

"Since 1991, Ralston have been letting Mitchell collect hundreds of firearms, and I mean hundreds, for him to deactivate on their behalf." He paused to read from his notes. "We can see from their registers the guns came in as military surplus but no record of them going out specifically to Mitchell. All they've done is write 'Deactivated' against each one. They have, though, added the deactivation certificate number from the Proof House that Mitchell gave them."

"Have you checked those with Bob Pitcher at the Proof House?"

"John has, yes, and they tally with those Mitchell submitted under the name, Foresight."

"So how did Ralston explain not having the names of Mitchell or Foresight on their register?"

"The manager said it's because Mitchell was in effect an extension of their business. Thus, they hadn't seen the need to show an actual transfer to him."

"Did Mitchell return every gun he deactivated?"

---

50   CPS: Crown Prosecution Service, the independent prosecuting authority.

"No, and that's another irregularity. Around 1995, Mitchell stopped returning some of them. He asked if he could keep a few to sell himself as part-payment for his work. Mitchell did, however, continue sending them the relevant deactivation certificate numbers."

"How many guns are we talking about?"

"He's kept for himself in excess of six hundred handguns. Many are of the exact types we're interested in for Abonar, plus a load of World War Two machine guns. Thompsons, Brens, and the like. He also kept some more recent Soviet era ones. He had a couple of BARs too, one of which almost certainly turned up at the Tollgate Hotel. That's why he obliterated all the serial numbers, because he knew we'd trace them back to Ralston's inventories and then to him."

"Excellent."

"Yes Guv, and once we pointed this out to the Ralston manager, he was only too happy to give us a statement."

"So, let me get this straight. Ralston Arms used Mitchell to deactivate their guns, and he then syphoned off six hundred or more to sell on the criminal market?"

"That's exactly it, Guv."

"What's the manager like at Ralston?"

"He's genuinely shocked. He and his staff didn't suspect Mitchell for a minute. The irregularities with his record-keeping are simply down to him not asking the right questions. That's because he got complacent after years of what was otherwise a good business relationship with Mitchell."

"Okay, and you've got all this written down?"

"Oh yes, West Yorkshire Police did it for us under caution. Of course, the manager could be a hostile witness if the CPS decide to prosecute. Whatever happens, though, at least we've confirmed how Mitchell got these types of firearms to then arm criminal gangs and supply the three for Donovan."

"Very good. That's an excellent day's work. Anything else?"

"Oh yes, Ralston also let him have half a dozen CZs too. There's a good chance Joseph McAuley got one of them. John's still on the phone to the Proof House checking."

"Very good."

"You know, Guv," Roger continued, obviously giving some thought to his words before commenting, "I think we'll find Mitchell was supplying Haase and Bennett too."

"That would be fantastic if we can prove it, Roger. You and John have done a great job. Will I see you in the morning, or are you seeing Perkins instead?

"We'll have to leave Perkins until Wednesday. You and I need to meet our friendly, David, tomorrow. He called to say the gun club was busy on Sunday with appearances from all three Black Shods."

"That would explain the pager messages on Friday. What time tomorrow?"

"2pm, usual place."

CHAPTER 51

A Friendly Catch-up

Tuesday, 22nd July

I had positioned myself in my regular seat in the St Ermin's Hotel bar to observe the others arrive. Having completed their fieldcraft, first Roger and then David joined me at the corner table. The waiter brought us a pot of coffee with milk and packs of biscuits.

"*Caro ragazzo*, how are you? Seems ages since we last met."

"It has been a while, David, yes. I trust Roger has been taking good care of you."

"Oh, he's been wonderful, *ma non parla Italiano* [but he doesn't speak any Italian]."

"Not everybody does. I understand there's been a development."

"*Si, assolutamente!*" he replied excitedly. "I've been going to the club regularly hoping one of our subjects would be there. But for weeks, nothing. Then on Sunday, all three Black Shods turned up around 4pm. Blondie was very agitated."

"Could you get close enough to listen?" I asked hopefully.

"It's a small clubhouse, dear boy, so it's very easy to overhear conversations. The trick is not to be obvious about it. Blondie did most of the talking. Said he'd been raided by the police, but they'd not found anything. He'd only been charged with licensing irregularities, so he only expects to get a fine."

"Really?" I commented in disbelief. "How did Bown and Phillips react?"

"Bown said he'd been raided too but had been out. They'd missed him. He mentioned the police finding silencers and magazines, and that got Blondie very angry."

"What did he say?"

"He warned Bown to keep his mouth shut if the police come back. Bown then told him he was going away for a while. I didn't hear where to."

"What about Phillips?"

"I got a sense he found it all rather amusing. He hadn't been raided and so didn't appear bothered. Blondie warned him, though, to keep his mouth shut too."

"He could have done this over the phone and avoided the risk of being seen with them," Roger commented.

"Oh for sure, but maybe it's made Mitchell really nervous," I suggested. "After Ackerman grassed on him, he would have wanted to look Bown and Phillips in the eyes and get them to promise they'd keep quiet. 'Black Shods honour' and all that crap."

"Yes, that could be it," Roger nodded. "Kind of helpful they did get together in person, as it confirms their association with Abonar."

"What else, David?" I asked.

"Blondie said the police hadn't found what 'John' told them would be at his place. I assumed he meant John Ackerman after our previous conversations. Blondie said he'd moved it all beforehand. Does that make sense to you?"

"Oh it does, yes. Sadly, it makes perfect sense. Did he say where he'd moved it to?"

"*Mi dispiace*, no."

"Okay, well thank you, David. You've confirmed very nicely that the three Black Shods are our Abonar conspirators. Sadly, we can't risk putting you in the witness box to say so. We'll have to rely on reconstructing the meeting through their call data, if we can. You've also revealed that Mitchell is seriously rattled, which means, of the three, he's got the most to lose."

"What would you like me to do next?" David then asked, still animated by the thought of going back to the club.

"Unless Roger thinks otherwise, I recommend you keep on shooting at the club as you wish, but there's no longer a need for you to go there just on our behalf."

Roger said, "I agree. You've done a great job, David. Thank you."

"It's been my pleasure dear boys. Let me know when you need me again. Ciao gentlemen, ciao."

Roger and I stayed to compare thoughts on this development.

"Interesting Mitchell didn't invite Walshe along to that meeting with Bown and Phillips," Roger commented.

"Yes, but that may be because he wouldn't be so intimidated by him. It could also be that Mitchell would be scared to let him know of his arrest in case he gets silenced himself."

"Maybe, maybe."

Back in the office, my mobile rang, and the number displayed told me it was Arthur calling. "I have some news of sorts," and, once again, his tone forewarned I wouldn't like it. "My bosses still aren't keen on SO11 poking around our investigation. Sorry, but they just don't see the need for you to review the exhibits."

"That's fucking crap, again, Arthur, and you know it," I told him, unable to control my anger.

"Maybe, but that's what they've decided. It didn't help that your boss had a go at mine over this too. I think it makes perfect sense we get your input. But it's not within my gift."

Calming slightly I asked, "could that change?"

"Not sure. There's stuff going on at HQ that's got my DCI somewhat distracted. I sense it has something to do with Abonar and Mitchell's arrest."

"Look, Arthur, as I've said before, I don't want to fall out with you, but not using our expertise, even if it's only to sift through your exhibits, is fucking shit."

"Wow, you really are suffering from your 'effing SERCS-effect!'."

"Yes, I am, and it only started once you lot got involved in Abonar."

"I sense that and, genuinely, I'm sorry."

"Thanks but this episode with your team has changed my outlook, and not for the better." I took a breath to let myself calm down completely before adding, "look, we both want the same two outcomes. First, get Mitchell and all his cronies nicked bang to rights for the totality of their crimes and, second, stop the supply of Mitchell's illegal guns and ammunition."

"Agreed. And that's the second reason for my call. I don't think you're going to like it any more than my first. Have you seen the fax from Rupert Smedley, one of the Home Office lawyers? I can see he sent copies to your bosses at SO11 and the OCG."

"No, not yet. It will have gone to the SO11 Reserve."

"Well, I've got a copy here. He's asking to meet Anton Baxter and Derek Hamilton, along with DCI Marcus Bagshaw and myself on Friday. Says he wants to 'review the evidence found at Mitchell's premises and how it relates to Operation Abonar'."

"Review what in particular?"

"He doesn't say. DCI Bagshaw's not around for me to ask. He called just now from HQ to tell me to submit a full report on Mitchell's arrest ahead of the meeting. I doubt I'll see him beforehand."

"Okay, well call me once you know something useful that I can pass it on to my bosses."

I went to retrieve the fax from the Branch Office, but the staff told me Anton had collected it already. Walking towards his office, I was glad to hear his voice coming through the open doorway. I loitered outside while he carried on a phone call. He looked up and saw me. Waving his free hand, he ushered me in and indicated I sit. He then passed me a copy of the fax to read. The invitation was just as Arthur had described. Once he finished his call, Anton seemed more upbeat than usual.

"If you're about to ask, Michael, yes, I've just heard I passed the Chief Superintendents' process. I'm off to Kennington as their new boss in a couple of months."

"Congratulations, Sir. Fantastic news." Standing up, I shook his hand enthusiastically.

"Thank you. Unfortunately, it means I can't make this meeting at the Home Office on Friday. I've got other things to do. Brian's going instead."

"What about Mr Hamilton?"

"No, Brian wants just you there. He'll update Derek afterwards."

"Okay," I said, my voice giving away some uncertainty about Brian's reasoning.

"Smedley has complained about Derek once already, so Brian doesn't want him there and risk another one. Brian knows he's reached his own 'final rank', so he won't care if he upsets either Smedley or SERCS." I smiled as Anton added, "I'll let you make your own judgements about Rupert Smedley. Personally, I think he's an absolute wanker. He's done his best to obstruct us in every way with Abonar. I'm glad Brian's going, as I might say something that would jeopardise my promotion too. Look, my advice is take detailed notes and follow Brian's lead."

"Do you know what Smedley wants to review?"

"No doubt to find out what Mitchell's arrest means for the former Home Secretary and his own superannuated reputation as his adviser. I bet he's very nervous about what Mitchell told SERCS."

"Yes, that may well have something to do with it. Anyway, many congratulations."

"Thanks. Can you imagine me in uniform again?"

"Hmm, let's hope the old one still fits, Sir?" I said cheekily as I headed out the door.

CHAPTER 52

The 'Abonar MAC-10'

Wednesday, 23rd July

Whilst Roger and John went to see Perkins, I took the train to Nottingham. I was spending the morning at the National Firearms Centre. This is also known as 'The Pattern Room' and home to the Royal Armouries. King Charles 1st began this in 1631 as part of his initiative to standardise the purchase of British military equipment and weapons. The collection has grown over the years to now include, potentially, one of every firearm manufactured worldwide in calibres up to 40mm. It is arguably the most extensive and varied of its type. Of interest to me was that it included the world's most complete set of all variants of the MAC-10. I needed to inspect them to confirm evidentially that the 'Abonar MAC-10' was unique in its design.

I had called ahead to make the appointment with its curator, Herbie Woodend, MBE. He was both the custodian and 'defender' of the collection. He had stopped the Ministry of Defence from dumping it all into the 'North Channel'. In the 1980s, officials had wanted to dispose of it after they assumed it was of little value and too expensive to maintain. 'Beaufort's Dyke' was its intended burial ground. This deep-sea trench is where the British military has for years dumped tens of thousands of tons of unwanted munitions and ordnance. Thankfully, Herbie saved the collection not only for posterity but also for my benefit investigating Abonar.

Herbie took me through to a room lined with smart, shallow-drawered gun cabinets set out in neat rows along the walls. There was also a cloth-covered workbench in the middle. On this, he had set out the complete collection of MAC-10s ready for my inspection. The room was lit very much like the Gun Room at the Lab, with strip lights creating a stark, bright white effect.

"We've got the original Ingram version here," Herbie told me, "and then all the subordinate variants here."

"And the one I'm particularly interested in, please, Herbie?"

"Here," he said picking up two; one in each hand. "You can thank your friends in the Security Service for submitting these. I understand you know Hamish."

"Indeed, I do, a top man."

"Yes, yes, he is. So, this one here in my right hand is your Abonar MAC-10. The other is the original live firing version manufactured by Christopher Perkins in 1991. I'll now strip them both down so you can compare their internal component parts."

"Thank you, but there's no need. Marco at the Lab did that for us when we first started our Abonar investigation."

"Well, in that case, all I need tell you is the breech bolt on your Abonar MAC-10 is quite unique compared to all the others in our collection. I know that because I've examined them for you."

"That's just what I wanted you to say, Herbie. Thank you."

"Good. So I've prepared a statement to explain this and some other key points that differentiates the Abonar MAC-10 from all the others."

"Thank you, that's most helpful."

"Yes, and as Marco probably told you too, if you can catch the gunsmith red-handed making one of these breech bolts, then you've got the man responsible for all your Abonar MAC-10s."

I nodded smiling, delighted at the prospect of doing just that, but not sure how I could make it happen.

CHAPTER 53

Perkins and Savage

I was relieved to be back in the office by early afternoon and eager to know how Roger and John had got on too. It was shortly after 5pm when they appeared at my open door.

"Come in, come in and rest your weary legs. You do look rather pleased with yourselves," I said, noting their smug smiles.

"We should be Guv, because it's been a difficult but, ultimately, successful session with Perkins, and we got a statement," Roger said, passing me the document.

"And," John chipped in, "on Perkins's recommendation, we also saw Guy Savage and got a statement from him too." Roger then passed me that one as well.

"Seriously? You went to see Savage?" My tone let them know I wasn't happy. "He's a dangerous player in the British gun trade, and a very unpleasant person to boot."

Roger and John looked at me hoping I would explain my reasoning. Instead, and rather dismissively I told them, "I'll read the statements later," as I tossed them on my desk. "Just give me the headlines for now, please?"

"Sure. First up, Perkins," John began uneasily, "he confirmed that back in 1991, he got help from Guy Savage to make his SF Firearms MAC-10 by copying the design from Savage's. You'll recall they're the ones stamped with 'C.G. Ltd M10 9mm' after his company 'Creative Gunsmiths'. Otherwise, they're identical."

"Yes, but I'm more interested in what he told you about Mitchell."

"I'm getting to that Guv," John replied defensively. "I thought you'd also like to know Perkins confirmed what Marco told us. You know, about his battle with the Home Office over whether he could legally manufacture MAC-10s."

I nodded to show I recalled the conversation.

"So, in late '95," John continued, "Perkins surrendered to Sussex Police about four tons of live-firing and unfinished MAC-10s; along with component parts; steel plates from which to press the receivers, and tubing for the barrels. The Home Office compensated him under the post-Dunblane Buy-Back scheme, but clearly not to their full value."

"I'm still not hearing where Mitchell fits into this," I said impatiently.

"That's because there's a bit more of the story to tell you first, Guv," he struggled to say respectfully.

Realising I was being rude, I said, "okay, sorry, I promise not to interrupt anymore."

"Thank you. So in the middle of last year, Sussex Police started asking Perkins why his SF Firearms' MAC-10s were turning up used in crime. He told them he thought someone must have got hold of the live-firing ones he'd surrendered before they reached the smelter."

"But we know from Marco all ours have been reactivated."

"Precisely Guv, but no one ever told Perkins that."

Then Roger interjected saying, "and it was only when we showed him the photos today of the Abonar MAC-10 that the penny dropped for the first-time. That's when he realised all the guns police had been asking him about were reactivated."

"Yes," John cut back in, "so he took a very keen interest in the photos of the Abonar component parts. We didn't say anything to prompt him. He recognised for himself the breech bolt wasn't his, and neither was the feed ramp. When he saw the weld mark over the deactivation stamp, he knew for sure what had happened."

"But that's also when he decided to clam up," Roger added. "It was clear he'd realised who'd done the reactivation work and didn't want to tell us."

"So how did you persuade him?"

"I asked about Mitchell and, initially, he denied knowing him. Then I pointed out both his and Mitchell's names are on the members' list at the gun club. I told him he was lying, and he could end up being charged with the conspiracy." Then with a wry smile, Roger added, "after that, and a little more encouragement from John, he told us the whole story and gave us a statement."

"So what is the truth?"

"As you found out from the Proof House, to make some extra money, Perkins deactivated ninety-five MAC-10s prior to calling in Sussex Police to collect the scrap along with the live firing ones. He gave Mitchell the opportunity to get in first, though, and let him take all the deactivated ones. He also allowed him to pick through all the unused parts."

As Roger paused for breath, John added, "from those spare parts alone, Perkins thinks Mitchell might be able to assemble another ten to fifteen guns."

"That's very useful evidence against Mitchell guys," I commented, now much happier.

"And, Guv, the scrap Mitchell took away included smooth bore 9mm steel tubing and lengths of square steel from which he could easily machine his breech bolts."

Fearing a possible oversight on their part, I quickly asked, "can you be certain Perkins didn't make the Abonar MAC-10 breech bolts himself?"

"Yes, Guv." Roger replied confidently. "Perkins was adamant the only bolts he sold Mitchell were in the deactivated guns. He'd already cut them up. Given he'd copied his design from Savage, and his bolt is very different to the Abonar one, I'm certain Perkins didn't make them."

"Hmm, I can see that being troublesome at court if Mitchell tries to blame Perkins. So, when did Mitchell buy all this stock from Perkins?"

"Christmas '95, which ties in nicely with when the Abonar MAC-10s first appeared in mid-96. It would have taken Mitchell a few months to perfect his design," John replied confidently.

"Fantastic. Well done. And that's all in Perkins's statement?"

"Yes, Guv, it is," Roger replied, pointing at the document I had tossed on my desk.

"So why on earth did you decide to then go and see Savage?"

"John asked Perkins whether he thought Mitchell had the skills to reactivate his guns. He told us, "Not without help from Guy Savage". He said Savage and Mitchell were partners in crime selling off-ticket firearms."

"Did he offer any evidence of that?"

"Sadly not," Roger added somewhat gloomily. "He just had a hunch based on his knowledge of them both. He said they're well known in the trade for pushing the legal boundaries with their gunsmithing modifying firearms."

"So that's why we decided to go and see Savage," John interrupted, "to find out what he had to say. We also needed to ask him how one of his deactivated CG MAC-10s had turned up in Mitchell's home."

"Before you tell me what Savage said, let me just say he won't ever be a credible prosecution witness," I warned them. "After Marco's comment about Savage being 'an out-and-out rogue' in the arms trade, I did my own research. First, in '94 he was banned from trading in guns after police seized a collection of prohibited automatic weapons from his St John's Wood address." I paused, momentarily before telling them, "and second, he's not a very nice person. Last year, he blamed the families of the Dunblane massacre victims for ruining his firearms business."

"Blimey, I didn't know that Guv. Did you John?" Roger said, sounding appalled.

"I knew we'd busted him in '94, but not about the Dunblane families."

"Now you know my feelings about the man, please convince me it was worthwhile seeing him."

"Well," John began, once again uneasily, "I showed him the photos of the Abonar MAC-10s. He was able to point out all the features that had changed from the design he gave Perkins."

"But, John, we know them already. Why did you think we needed to get that from him too and, potentially, have him give evidence against Mitchell?"

"I just thought it would be good to have the man whose design Perkins copied give his expert opinion on the reactivation work done by Mitchell."

"And he's given you a statement to that effect?"

"Yes."

"Well, I hope this doesn't result in Savage thinking he can reingratiate himself back into favour."

"I understand your misgivings, Guv, but I do think his statement is useful," John pleaded.

"I'll read it and let you know. Roger, anything else from you?"

"No Guv, that's our news. How did you get on at the National Firearms Centre?"

"Herbie confirmed if we can prove Mitchell manufactured the breech bolt for the Abonar MAC-10, then we've got him for every shooting and homicide where one of his MAC-10's has been used. That, gentlemen, remains our mission either with or without SERCS. It means we must find Mitchell with the rest of Perkins' MAC-10s, either deactivated or live-firing, and the Abonar breech bolt."

"We're up for that, Guv."

"I thought you would be, John. Right, how about a drink before we all head home? You can buy me one as punishment for seeing Savage."

CHAPTER 54

A 'Shocker of a Meeting'

Friday, 25ᵗʰ July

Brian and I walked the short distance between NSY and 50 Queen Anne's Gate for our meeting at the Home Office. On the way, he smoked a cigarette while I took the opportunity to update him on the latest developments. When we arrived, Arthur and DCI Marcus Bagshaw were already sitting in reception wearing their passes.

While Brian and I got ours, I took a moment to study the two men for the first time. Marcus was on temporary secondment to SERCS from the MPS. He had an energy that set him apart as a leader. In his early 40s and short in stature, he had been spared the perils of middle-age spread, which indicated he did something active to kept fit. His neatly cut dark brown hair was beginning to grey. This added to an air of easy authority based on hard-earned experience as a career detective in SO. When he spoke, I was surprised by his hard south London accent. From his meticulously clean-shaven face and smartly pressed dark blue suit, I had expected something less abrasive.

I knew from my telephone conversations with Arthur that he had grown up somewhere along the Sussex coast before joining the local police. His accent also gave it away. He too was on secondment to SERCS. He was slightly younger than his boss and taller, with straight ginger hair, but with a similar physique that indicated he too kept fit. Alongside Marcus, though, he adopted an air of subordination, which was more than deference to his boss's senior rank. I sensed it was also that he recognised his own lesser experiences from working outside the intensity of policing in London.

Since Brian knew Marcus of old, I only needed to introduce Arthur. We exchanged pleasantries until a young man ushered us through the security doors and then into the lift to the eighth floor. Our escort wore a light grey suit seemingly one size too big for him. It suggested either he'd lost weight or bought it cheap hoping one day he might grow into it. Someone involved in the layout of the Home Office had named each of its work-areas according to colours. I was amused by the irony when our escort led us into the one signposted '*Grey Zone*'. He opened the door to a meeting room painted in a drab shade of off-white, with a large, rectangular oak veneered boardroom-style table in the middle and ten chairs round it. A side table had the customary pots and jugs for making tea and coffee.

"Please, feel free to help yourselves to refreshments. I'll let Mr Smedley know you're here," the young man said before leaving us.

I made myself a coffee and grabbed an individually wrapped packet of three Bourbon biscuits. The others did something similar before we all took our seats. Despite there being four chairs on each side, Brian and I sat together, with Arthur and Marcus opposite. We left the two narrow ends for our host to choose which he preferred. In predictable style, Smedley was late. When he finally joined us, he was as I had imagined: overweight and in his early fifties, with a pasty, unhealthy complexion. He wore the type of round-framed spectacles I associated with academics who relied more on theory than practice. His supercilious, dismissive manner quickly confirmed my assessment. He would prove typical of some government advisers I had met. They have little understanding of the operational practicalities and consequences for those they then rely on to implement their 'advice'. His tired looking plain dark grey suit seemed entirely appropriate for a person working in the 'Grey Zone'. He took the seat at the end of the table closest to the window. I smiled. My experience of civil servants was that it was all about window-positioning. In a shared office, seniority was defined by the proximity of your desk to the window. The man who brought us to the room sat on the same side as Brian and I, but a few feet away. Like me, he had a notebook open and pen in hand ready to record the meeting.

"Thank you for waiting," Smedley began without any apology for his 15-minute delay. His voice and tone belied a sense of self-importance verging on arrogance.

"Some introductions would be in order, I think. I'm Rupert Smedley, from Legal Advisory here at the Home Office. This is Charles Wheeler, my executive assistant. Which one of you is Brian Mills?"

I saw Brian bristle with annoyance as he replied, "Detective Chief Superintendent Brian Mills, OCU[51] commander of the Directorate of Intelligence, SO11."

---

51   OCU: Operational Command Unit.

"Thank you, Mr Mills but I think we can dispense with long titles."

"Detective Inspector Michael Hallowes, and I work for DCS Mills," I announced.

"Ah, yes, Mr Hallowes, your name has been mentioned several times in this matter. And who do I have on my right?"

"DCI Marcus Bagshaw, South-East Regional Crime Squad, head of the Crawley Branch Office, and this is Arthur Wilton, one of my DIs."

"Ah yes, Mr Wilton, thank you, I've been reading your most illuminating report on Mitchell's arrest."

"You've asked for a meeting to review Operation Abonar," Brian said, getting straight to the point and obviously still irritated. "What aspects do you want to look at?"

"Yes, indeed. My purpose is to find out what you propose to do next, Mr Mills." His voice sounded almost scornful. "You'll understand with the change of government, we not only have a new Home Secretary but one of a very different persuasion and, if I may say, more challenging character than his predecessor. I propose to advise him that the unfortunate episode that became Operation Abonar is now closed."

"'Unfortunate episode', Mr Smedley, how so?" Brian continued to let his annoyance show.

"Perhaps the wrong turn of phrase. Forgive me, but the matter is, nonetheless, closed. I think we all agree?" he said, ignoring Brian and I, and instead staring at Marcus and Arthur opposite, who nodded back.

"Not at all," Brian said firmly, wanting the attention back on him. "What gave you that impression?"

"Mr Mills, we're all very much aware that Abonar's original purpose was to identify the source of supply for the firearms and ammunition deposited by a criminal gang around London and Kent."

"Yes."

"And, thankfully, those weapons never reached the streets. That was because of HM Customs' diligence in notifying the police where to find them before any could be used in crime."

"That's hugely disingenuous," Brian quickly countered.

"What matters," Smedley continued with his voice now raised, "is Abonar identified Anthony Mitchell as the supplier and Mr Wilton here has now arrested him."

"Yes," Brian replied, his uncertain tone reflecting he wasn't sure where Smedley was heading.

"Sadly, however, Mr Wilton and his SERCS officers did not uncover any evidence to charge Mitchell with supplying illegal firearms. They have, though, been able to use what they did find to put him out of business. Thus, I plan to tell the Home Secretary that Abonar has successfully closed down the source of supply."

"That's not enough," Brian fired back angrily. "Abonar isn't over. Yes, I agree SERCS did a great job arresting Mitchell, but charging him with only some minor firearms licensing irregularities isn't where it ends." Sitting back in his chair and glaring at Smedley he concluded, "no doubt, Mitchell will get a slap on the wrist at court and be quickly back in business."

Smedley dismissed Brian's protest, saying emphatically, "I totally disagree."

"Fortunately, Mr Smedley it's not up to you," Brian shot back. "We must establish how Mitchell obtained and supplied the firearms recovered in London and Kent. That's because he's done the same to arm gangs around the country. We can attribute five homicides to the Abonar MAC-10s made by Mitchell." Then with increased fervour in his voice, he added, "so, in SO11, we're going after him as an accessory to those crimes and we plan to seize his remaining arsenal of illegal guns."

"Most laudable Mr Mills, but likely to be fruitless," Smedley replied in a patronising tone. "I think it really is time to stop and move on to more pressing investigations."

"More pressing?" Brian was now incandescent with rage. "Right now, Mr Smedley, I can think of nothing more so than Abonar." He reinforced his point by banging his right hand on the table before looking across the table for support. Marcus quickly looked sideways, wanting to avoid his stare.

Smedley again responded dismissively, "Mr Mills, I hope to convince you today there is absolutely no benefit operationally with you continuing, and you'll be distracting yourself and SO11 from other more fruitful serious crime investigations."

Brian shot back, "well you won't convince me, and I determine SO11's priorities." Again, he looked at Marcus hoping for his support, but he wasn't offering any.

Smedley now turned to Arthur, "Mr Wilton, maybe if you could help me with the facts, we can both try and convince Mr Mills. As I understand from your report, the searches of Mitchell's premises recovered the last of his stock of firearms: forty-three MAB pistols, and the last of his ammunition, some six thousand rounds. Did I get that right?"

"Yes, that's all correct," Arthur replied.

"Perfect. And Mr Wilton, did you find anything else to indicate Mitchell had any capability beyond those to enable him to continue his illicit business?"

Arthur avoided my gaze as I tried to read his face before he spoke. "No, Mr Smedley we did not."

"Perfect, again. So, now you've now charged him with offences relating to how he conducted his registered firearms dealer business?"

"We have, yes."

"And, as a consequence, Sussex Police have revoked his firearms certificate?"

"Yes."

"And the Home Office Firearms Licensing Unit have sent him a letter to advise that the Secretary of State has revoked his Dealer's authority, which means Mitchell is permanently out of business. Am I right?"

"His lawful business, yes," Brian interrupted, "but we have no way of stopping his unlawful activities unless Abonar continues."

"That's all supposition, Mr Mills. The facts as we have just ascertained from Mr Wilton are that SERCS found no evidence Mitchell can continue either way. Congratulations Mr Bagshaw on an excellent and thorough job done by your team."

"Thank you," Marcus replied.

"So, Mr Mills, you see, I can tell the Home Secretary the supply of illicit firearms has been stopped. I think the very fact the Customs' source has been unable to offer anything since March also confirms no more are available. Surely you must see that too?"

"No, I do not," Brian said angrily, pacing out each word to reinforce his rage. "Just putting Mitchell out of business was never our objective. Michael and his team very ably identified him as the person responsible for supplying the guns and ammunition used in multiple shootings, including a murder in Brixton and, potentially, four more at Brockwell Park. Our objective remains to charge him with all those offences."

"But where is the prima facie evidence of that?" Smedley replied, seeming determined to carry on goading Brian. "According to your colleagues here, it doesn't exist. Whatever firearms and ammunition Mitchell had were all seized last week. On that basis, putting Mitchell out of business should be sufficient for you too Mr Mills. Disruption rather than prosecution. It's a perfectly good outcome, and one your Directorate is well practiced in too, am I right?"

"Good God, that's not relevant in this case," Brian replied leaning forward, now completely exasperated. "I have a duty to protect Londoners regardless of whatever politics are being played out in this room." And once again he glared at Marcus. "We must recover the remaining MAC-10s in Mitchell's possession. My reason for attending today was to review how we do that together. Not capitulate, thinking that putting Mitchell out of business makes it all go away." Brian sat back in his chair glaring at Smedley and then looked across, again, at Marcus and Arthur for support.

Smedley calmly replied, "well, I will be recommending the Home Secretary considers the matter closed. I will also advise him not to give any benefit to the man Customs used as their source, and to write to his solicitor saying much the same."

Brian angrily responded, "you will do no such thing! You know we are in the midst of highly sensitive negotiations with that same source." Once again, he held Smedley with his stare. "You'll appreciate I can't say anymore in present company unless, of course, you'd like my colleagues opposite to leave."

"That won't be necessary. The other matter doesn't come into this conversation at all, Mr Mills. I'm surprised, given the sensitivities, you even hinted at it."

"Then why did you say you'll be telling the source he won't be getting any benefit for the Customs' job," Brian shouted back. "You know very well the strategy we're working to is to say nothing until *after* we know the outcome of the second matter."

"Of course, you're right, Mr Mills."

"Good, so you won't be saying anything to anyone until and unless I say so?"

"Well…"

"No, Mr Smedley, don't prevaricate. It is my command running this intelligence operation, not you and the Home Office," Brian added fiercely. Then in a hushed, almost menacing tone he continued, "You've been nothing but obstructive throughout Abonar. I warn you now, if you jeopardise my ability to achieve our objectives, you'll be putting many innocent lives at risk. And I'll make damned sure the Home Secretary knows exactly where the blame lies if that happens. Do I make myself clear?"

"I hear what you say, Mr Mills," Smedley replied defensively. "I can, of course, recommend to the Home Secretary that he defers giving his decision."

"Good, Michael's minute of this meeting will show you gave a firm agreement to delay. Michael, have you got that?"

I had been writing furiously to make as close to a contemporaneous note of the conversation, and had just caught up when I replied, "yes, Sir."

"Good. Another point, Smedley, and I'll wait until Michael is ready to note this too." Brian paused, now watching my pen.

"Mr Hallowes, there really is no need for you to keep a separate minute," Smedley protested. "I can assure you Mr Wheeler here is keeping the official record and we can let you have a summary afterwards."

"I've asked Michael to keep detailed notes and that's exactly what he's doing," Brian said angrily.

"Well, if you must. Quite frankly, I would have thought he had more to contribute than being your notetaker."

"Should you jeopardise my investigation, I will be relying on his detailed notes for the public inquiry and not your summary," Brian told him pointedly. "Now, let me explain why Operation Abonar is not closed. Michael, how many deactivated MAC-10s did Mitchell acquire from Perkins?"

"Ninety-five plus components for maybe fifteen more."

"When SERCS debriefed John Ackerman, how many MAC-10s did he say Mitchell had supplied to him?"

Looking directly at Arthur, I answered, "twenty," and Arthur nodded back.

"And how many of those have police forces around the country recovered?"

"Twelve, including one recovered by An Garda Siochana[52] after a shooting in Dublin."

"So, that leaves a potential eight still out there that passed from Mitchell to Ackerman," Brian said assertively. "According to our intelligence, therefore, Mitchell has as many as ninety MAC-10s still available to the criminal market." Then with renewed anger in his voice, he concluded, "so Mr Smedley, that's why we're not stopping until we find every one before Mitchell can offload them too."

"Again, a most laudable ambition, Mr Mills. The problem with it is this." Smedley countered, while I listened, unable to believe the arrogance of the man as he dismissed everything Brian had just said. "As we just heard from Mr Wilton, those MAC-10s aren't in Mitchell's possession anymore. As I said previously, continuing to pursue him hoping to find them is fruitless." Then, turning to Marcus and Arthur, he commented, "so may I recommend you follow your colleagues' example, Mr Mills, and move on."

Angrily Brian looked directly at Marcus and asked "Move on? Marcus, what does he mean?"

---

52 An Garda Siochana: the full name of the Irish police, also known by the shorter title of Garda.

Marcus looked embarrassed as he said, "we've agreed to close the file, Sir. As Mr Smedley explained, not only have we put Mitchell out of business, but between ourselves and Strathclyde Police we've also got Ferris and Ackerman bang-to-rights. That's two major gangland figures now out of circulation." He paused knowing his next words would anger Brian, so he cautiously added, "that's good enough for us, Sir. My ACC has instructed me to move on to other jobs."

With his top lip tightening across his teeth showing intense anger, Brian replied, "Marcus, I appreciate this isn't your decision, but a chat beforehand would have been appropriate. Has this got anything to do with the Home Office's threat of another reorganisation?"

"It's a factor, Sir, yes, I can't pretend it isn't. We need to keep bringing in the results. That means more quick-win investigations. I have a backlog that need actioning. Consequently, my ACC wants me on to the next job right away, and the next one after that. I'm sorry Sir, but that's my reality."

"I need to escalate this to my Director," Brian responded. "No doubt, he'll want to take it up with the Commissioner and then your Director General."

"Now, now, we don't need to escalate anything Mr Mills," Smedley rudely interrupted. "I feel sure that between us we can agree on a sensible pathway forward."

"Well mine remains to escalate this," Brian said emphatically. "By the way Smedley, what was your involvement in the original discussions between Michael Howard when he was Home Secretary and the Customs' source? Was it you who recommended early release?"

"I'm not in a position to say. My advice is and shall always remain confidential."

"But there is an official record of it here in the Home Office?" Brian asked. "Yes, of course."

"Would you just confirm," he persevered, "that the previous Home Secretary asked for your expert advice? I assume you didn't delegate such an important matter to someone more junior."

"Yes, he sought my advice."

"And, on that basis the Home Secretary gave an agreement in principle to release the source in return for the firearm recoveries."

"Naturally, because that is what happened, albeit the Minister had already made up his mind and simply asked for my endorsement."

"And did you give him similar advice in respect of releasing John Haase and Paul Bennett in 1996?" I asked.

Brian looked sideways at me in surprise. Since Arthur and Marcus knew nothing of the context, they had now become bystanders and looked on uncomfortably.

Smedley seemed uneasy too, especially as Brian and I had taken away his control of the meeting. His expression confirmed he was not happy at being challenged over facts he clearly preferred we did not expose.

Falteringly, he replied, "the Department gave its best advice based on what it knew at the time."

I decided that was not enough, so continued my attack, "and that was despite warnings from police and prison officers it was all a scam to hoodwink the Home Secretary?"

Clearly angered, he quickly repeated, "the Department gave its best advice based on what it knew at the time."

Brian squeezed my arm firmly to stop and allow him to speak instead. "And that's precisely why you want Abonar closed down, isn't it? You know if we continue, we'll expose your naivety. The media will be all over this when it goes to court too. That's what's going on here, isn't it?"

As Smedley opened his mouth to protest, Brian was in no mood to let him interrupt and he carried on. "Let me be clear, my reasoning for continuing Abonar is to recover the firearms Mitchell supplied and the ones he's still got in the pipeline. We're also determined to see him brought to justice for all the victims' sakes! If the media wants to hold you to account for your stupidity at being so easily hoodwinked by career criminals, well that's your problem, not mine, and not Abonar's."

"That is all pure conjecture Mr Mills," Smedley said, now beginning to regain his composure. "There is nothing in Mr Wilton's report to say anyone has been hoodwinked. The facts are these. Ackerman says Mitchell supplied him with the three MAC-10s, silencers and ammunition later seized from Paul Ferris. The Forensic Science Service can prove those MAC-10s and silencers are of the same manufacture as the ones recovered at the Tollgate Hotel." Then with obvious pleasure in his tone he commented, "the problem for your Abonar investigation, Mr Mills, is that Ackerman will not now to give evidence against Mitchell. Mitchell has made no comment to all the relevant questions." He paused to let that sink in before continuing, "and, since there is no actual evidence to prove he manufactured them, it means any theoretical connection you've made between Mitchell and the MAC-10s is nothing more than conjecture. You have no evidence to prove it. Those are the facts, as I understand them, which means continuing with Abonar will be a waste of effort. Trying to link the former Home Secretary to any scam Mitchell might have been involved in will, therefore, be baseless."

Brian remained silent while Smedley carried on, "yes, so the context in which, for example, the Tollgate Hotel guns were found is, therefore, completely irrelevant to any trial envisaged for either Ackerman or Mitchell. Ackerman will be tried for unlawfully transferring three MAC-10s to Ferris, and Mitchell for irregularities with his registered firearms dealer business. As these will be separate court appearances, neither will provide a vehicle to include evidence about the other."

Again, Smedley paused, but he was still not inviting anyone to interrupt.

"I do hope, Mr Mills, you can now see the wisdom of the agreement already reached with your SERCS colleagues that Abonar really is closed. You should all be congratulated for what you've achieved."

Brian sat listening intently but remained silent for a moment before responding between clenched teeth, "let me be absolutely clear, Operation Abonar is not closed. SO11 will continue its investigation. We will find those missing MAC-10s either with or without your continuing attempts to frustrate us."

"Mr Mills, we haven't sought to frustrate your investigation. We've always tried to be realistic and pragmatic and lend whatever support we can that's within our gift and lawful."

Brian stood up announcing, "right, I'm done. Nothing more to say on my part. Michael and I need to be back at the Yard."

Noting the time in my daybook, I closed it before following Brian out of the room. We navigated our way back unescorted to the lifts and out into the public reception area.

"I want to hang on for the others," Brian told me, still sounding angry. "I want a word with Marcus. He owes me an explanation." As if to illustrate his exasperation, he took out and immediately put back into his pocket a pack of cigarettes clearly wanting to smoke one. Just then the others came through to the reception area. On seeing us, Marcus looked uneasy. He knew what was coming.

"Marcus, a word," Brian called out. The anger in his voice was unmissable.

"Not here, Sir, can we find somewhere more discreet?"

"Don't like being ambushed, eh Marcus? Well, apparently this building seems as good a place as any for that. What you did to us is unforgiveable. You had plenty of time to warn me beforehand, even while we were waiting down here earlier. Clearly, you've known about this for days."

"I'm really sorry, Sir. Actually, I didn't know until this morning when my ACC called to tell me to close the file on Mitchell. I thought you of all people would appreciate the knock-on effects on a small team of a protracted investigation. It causes everything else to back up. I just don't have the resources to keep pursuing this one. I've already moved on to the next job."

"In that case, I'm going to recommend to DAC Fry we go it alone and do a proper job on Mitchell. As Michael said, we've got ninety or so MAC-10s to find."

"Yes, I understand of course, Sir, but how?"

"First, you're going to let us review what you recovered from Mitchell's and Bown's premises," Brian said forcefully. "You're going to give Michael access to everything."

"Fine, yes, I suppose we can agree to that," Marcus at last capitulated. "Arthur, get that sorted and fix a date for Michael to come down."

Arthur and I exchanged looks. His was reassuringly friendly.

"Sir, what is the 'second matter' you referred to in the meeting?" Marcus then asked.

"Absolutely nothing I can possibly share with you! It doesn't affect SERCS and has nothing to do with Mitchell. There's just a potential crossover further upstream. That's all. Okay?"

"Sure, if you say so."

"Right chaps, we're done. That was a shocker of a meeting, Marcus. Don't ever put me in such a position again." With his now hallmark menace in his voice he warned, "remember you're only on secondment to SERCS; one day you'll be back in the Met. So, let's have a lot more collaboration and cooperation from now on. Agreed?"

"Sure, I look forward to hearing from Michael about what he discovers from reviewing our evidence."

"If I may," I interrupted, "given Smedley is determined to close down Abonar, I recommend we're all extremely cautious about who we tell about me doing that."

"Fair point, Michael," Brian added. "Once we know what the forensics tell us, we should get together again to decide how to proceed. Until then, Marcus, tell your bosses the matter is closed pending whatever the Lab comes up with. Agreed?"

"Yes, agreed."

"Right, Michael, let's get back to the Yard."

Out of earshot of the others he added, while lighting a cigarette, "You better put that last conversation in your notes too. Photocopy the pages and give them to the typists. I want a hardcopy for my own records."

CHAPTER 55

The Bunker

Thursday, 31ˢᵗ July

Arthur arranged for DS Myles Hurst to meet and show me round the SERCS exhibits' store at its discreet location in Ashdown Forest. I drove to the agreed rendezvous point where he was waiting. I then followed him in his car to a short driveway off the main road where we stopped at the end in a small car park. A few yards away, I could see a concrete dome set into the hillside covering a large steel doorway big enough to allow a mid-size truck to enter. The tree canopy obscured the view from above of this once secret location. In its former life during the Cold War, this bunker formed part of the UK's network of shelters from a nuclear attack. At first, Myles looked surprised when four of us got out of my car. He had expected I would come alone. Nevertheless, he shook everyone's hands as I introduced him to John, Marco and Hamish.

I had immediately warmed to Myles during our conversations on the phone to arrange this visit. First and foremost, he was respectful, which always made a positive impression on me. His manner told me he was a diligent and experienced detective. He had confided in me that he was hoping for promotion to DI in the next Sussex Police selection process. Meeting him now, I guessed he was in his mid-thirties. He still had a full head of neatly cut, thick dark brown hair, and a similar stature to me at 6' 2" and medium build. His smart suit added to his professional bearing. I imagined that when he appeared before a promotion board, his easy confidence combined with a string of successful SERCS investigations under his belt would instantly give him a competitive edge.

Myles led us to the bunker door and pressed an intercom button. A security guard opened it and examined our identifications.

"Sign here, please," he said gruffly.

"Do we need to hand in our mobile phones?" Hamish asked.

"No Sir. You're going down five floors into a concrete and steel reinforced bunker. It's like a Faraday Cage, so you won't get a signal down there anyway." Hamish acknowledged the advice with a shrug and Myles then led the way into a lift and pressed the button for the bottom floor. When the doors opened again, we were greeted by stark white fluorescent lighting.

"This way," Myles said, going on ahead. Our footsteps echoed around the concrete walls and floors. Subconsciously, the four of us who had learned to march in our police and military careers quickly got into step to enjoy the rhythm of our collective footfall. Having had no such former life, Marco did not join in. "Oh, please," he said, "I feel like the condemned man being led to my execution."

We laughed and had to stop anyway, as Myles had come to a halt at a steel door. Unlocking it, he reached in, flicked on the light switch, and then announced, "this is it. This is our exhibits' store."

As the thick steel door swung outwards, I paused to take in the drab grey painted walls and mid-blue carpet tiles of the room we were about to enter. Stacked on multiple rows of metal shelving were an assortment of sealed crates and individually bagged items. Labels with handwritten alphanumeric codes identified to which investigation each belonged. Myles walked over to the shelves allocated to their investigation into Mitchell, Bown and Ackerman. Together, we lifted down each crate and bag and put them on a set of sturdy tables against one wall. Myles brought across the Exhibit Logs and the Exhibits' Store Register.

"Wow," I said, "there's more here than I expected. From what DI Wilton explained on the phone, I thought you'd found only a handful of items."

"We seized everything we thought relevant from Bown's and Mitchell's addresses. That's why I really appreciate you being here to sift through it all today and tell me what's important."

"Let's start with what I hope is the easiest," I suggested, "the items from Bown's Grove Park address."

I passed round a box of latex gloves that someone had helpfully left on the table, and we each pulled on a pair. Hamish took out a camera for his own records. Marco did the same. John spread out the collection of Abonar photograph albums as a reference point. Myles picked up a pair of wire cutters and snipped the security seal on the first white plastic crate, saying, "this all came from Bown's Grove Park address."

I lifted out three separately sealed bags and put them on the table.

"If at all possible," Marco asked, "can we not open the bags here. I want to preserve the contents as found, please. It will reduce the paperwork for Myles too."

The first bag contained a MAC-10; the second, three silencers, and the third, three Uzi magazines. Eagerly, Marco lifted each one to examine its contents through the clear plastic.

"Right," he started, "this MAC-10 is still deactivated. It's got the same SF Firearms markings, plus the serial number and deactivation mark haven't been obliterated. John, you'll need to check with the Proof House to confirm it comes from the batch of ninety-five Perkins then sold to Mitchell. You'll need Bob Pitcher to give you a statement making that point."

Next, Marco examined the three Uzi 30-round magazines before saying, "and I'll include in my statement that these are of the same type recovered with the Abonar MAC-10s."

Marco carefully checked the three silencers before saying, "and I will also say these are of the exact same manufacture as the ones recovered with the Tollgate Hotel MAC-10s and the ones Ackerman sold to Ferris. I'll need to take them back to the Lab, though please, to make a proper comparison. They're certainly of the same design externally as the others. You can see where the gunsmith used a two-pinned face-spanner to screw them together."

"What does that look like?" Myles asked.

Marco drew an illustration on a scrap of paper. "There, like that."

"I've got one of those from Mitchell's workshop."

"Fantastic," Marco responded, "if you've got that and, forensically, I can match the tool marks, then that's another piece of kryptonite that'll destroy Mitchell for sure. Where is it?"

"I'll get it once we move on to the crates from his workshop."

"Good, I can't wait."

Hamish then took the bag of silencers to check its contents too before saying, "Marco, would you also compare these and the spanner, when we get to it, with the silencer for the CZ pistol? The one seized from Joseph McAuley. It would be good to make that connection with Mitchell too."

Marco nodded saying, "so Myles, best you show us your spanner next."

Myles opened another crate and rummaged amongst its contents before triumphantly holding up a bag. "Here it is. Could this be what you're looking for?" he said, handing it to Marco.

"I'm going to have to open this one, if you don't mind?"

"Go ahead. I'll update the register."

Marco snipped the seal around the neck and spilled its contents on the desk. He opened the blue plastic box and took out the adjustable metal tool inside. Reaching into his pocket, he took out a small magnifying glass.

"This is Mitchell's kryptonite folks," Marco announced excitedly. "I'll need to package it more carefully to protect the teeth. At first glance, though, I'd say this is exactly the type of two-pin face spanner Mitchell used to screw together his suppressors-come-silencers." Looking again through his magnifying glass, he said, "As I told you before, Michael and John, if I can match the position and marks caused by twisting this tool in the face plates, then I'll give evidence that Mitchell made every silencer you've recovered."

"Fingers crossed," I said as I noted everyone's excitement. "Better add that to my shopping list for forensic work, please."

Marco was already rewrapping the exhibit. Having finished, he passed it back to Myles to record the new seal number, before he then put it to one side with the silencers and magazines.

In the meantime I had been rummaging through the crate looking at the contents of the other bags when I came across one that immediately got my attention. It held nine two-inch long black locking pins of the type used to hold the MAC-10 frame to its upper receiver.

"Myles, where did you find these?"

"They were on Mitchell's workbench lying loose. As I said, we picked up anything that looked like part of a gun. Are they important?"

"I believe they are. John, would you pass me our Abonar photos, please?"

I flicked through the album until I found the pictures of a disassembled MAC-10 with this locking pin removed.

"There, that's the same pin as these. What do you think Hamish?"

"I'd agree absolutely, Michael. I'd say that confirms Mitchell's been working on MAC-10s in his workshop. They're also the only evidence I've seen so far that he's had MAC-10s. It's a shame you didn't find any complete guns or other major component parts."

"Yup," I continued, "and these indicate Mitchell has at least nine MAC-10s somewhere disassembled. He'll need to replace these pins by making new ones on his lathe, so he can put them back together. They're kind of crucial. Marco, what can you do with these?"

"Well, I can do the analysis to confirm they match the ones we've got already for all the Abonar and SF Firearms MAC-10s."

"Excellent. Please add them to my shopping list too."

"I'd like to see the MABs next, please?" Hamish asked.

"Okay, they're in these crates from Mitchell's home," Myles said as he tapped his right hand on the lids of the relevant crates. Again, he snipped the security seals.

Hamish opened each in turn and peered in before pulling out the bags he wanted. He examined the two nickel-plated MAB pistol frames before handing them to me.

"Those aren't factory original. They should be blued like these ones," he said pointing to the bags that held the forty-three found in the gun room. "Does Mitchell have a sandblasting machine to strip off the original finish?"

"Yes, there was one in his workshop," Myles said confidently. "We didn't bring it with us, though. It was way too big."

"Myles, I'll need you to make a statement about that if you haven't already," I asked.

"I haven't yet. I didn't think it was relevant at the time. We took loads of photos of the workshop anyway, so that's not a problem for me to add the sandblaster in a supplementary statement."

"Great, can you send us copies of those photos too?"

"Sure Guv, I'll get them in the internal despatch to you."

"What else, Hamish?" I asked.

"These two MAB frames look identical to the ones recovered at the Tollgate Hotel, don't they?"

Myles looked on as the rest of us nodded.

"Hmm, but no Cyrillic letters on them," Hamish continued. "I would think Mitchell was probably close to reassembling them prior to another off-ticket disposal. Myles, did you find a nickel-plating kit? It's a heated bath with electrodes, brushes, and bottles of nickel electrolyte solution."

"No, nothing like that."

"That means Mitchell gets a specialist to do it off-site." Hamish commented before asking, "did you find an address book with his business contacts?"

"Sorry, no. He had loads of paper stuffed around the place. Too much for us to go through."

"Hmm, that's a shame, Myles," I now commented, trying not to sound critical. "If we'd been invited to help with the searches, I would have seized every bit of paper and had the team go through it systematically back in the office."

"Yeah, sorry. I suppose we were looking for guns and ammunition rather than bits of paper, Guv."

"That's a lesson learned. *Nil desperandum.* John, when we get back, would you go through the Abonar database of subscriber checks for everyone Mitchell called from his landline and mobile. Something's niggling me. I'm sure there's a plating company amongst them."

"Yup, leave that with me, Guv."

"Ackerman had a nickel-plated MAB too, with a silencer, didn't he?" I asked.

John went straight to the relevant photo album and flicked it open at the image before handing it to me.

"Yup, thank you, that's it. Just like the ones found at the Tollgate Hotel with the barrel extension and screw thread. Marco, we'll need you to compare the spanner marks with the silencer for Ackerman's MAB too, please."

Marco nodded.

"Can you also arrange for Metallurgy to compare the nickel-plating across all the guns and parts recovered? If we can connect just one of them to Mitchell, such as the MAB frames from his gun room, then we've got him for all of them."

"That's a lot of work, Michael. I hope you've got a budget for all this," Marco warned.

"Let me worry about that. We need it doing. If we don't, we risk failing to convict Mitchell of everything we know he's been up to."

Hamish interjected, "can we see the 9mm ammunition now?"

Myles reached for the relevant crate, snipped the seal, and pushed it over to Hamish. He reached in and lifted out the first bag of sixty blue and white Samson boxes. Through the plastic bag he managed to open one and slid out the cardboard tray. Fifty rounds of blue tipped bullets fell into the bottom of the bag. He looked at one carefully, taking particular interest in the markings stamped into the cartridge base.

"Yup, that'll do. They're not rare, but the combination of items I've seen so far would be the tell-tale hallmarks I'd be wanting to find to link Mitchell to Abonar. The other bag of three thousand copper-jacketed type just helps to confirm he's the armourer."

"Yes," Marco confirmed, "individually they might mean very little, but together, well, you're building a pretty strong case against him."

"Indeed," I chipped in, "the combination is as unique as a fingerprint. We just need a jury to realise that too."

"And the Home Office," John added.

I was still holding the album of photographs of Ackerman's MAB pistol and flicked through the images before stopping at the one I wanted. It showed the gun had been wrapped in a blue plastic bag. I had also seen the same amongst the images from the Abonar finds.

"Myles, did you find any rolls of plastic bags; blue ones perhaps?"

"Er, yes, in his workshop. Loads of them."

As Myles looked for the relevant exhibits' bag, Hamish asked, "I see you didn't find any other calibre bullets than these 9mm ones. I take it you didn't find evidence of him having another storage place?"

"Yes and no," Myles replied ambiguously.

Slightly annoyed, I asked, "which? Did you, or didn't you?"

"He mentioned a garage in Portland Road where he kept his motorbikes."

"And what did you find there?" I asked.

"We didn't look. I assumed because he gave it up so easily, he wouldn't be so stupid to keep anything incriminating there."

"So, you didn't go and check anyway?"

"No Guv."

"Another lesson learned," I sighed. "Mitchell must have a third premises where he stores everything, because what I was hoping you'd find is mostly missing from what's here." Myles avoided my gaze as I added, "it's a shame Myles, as I would have checked his garage. It would be worth getting a search warrant now and doing a proper job."

Hoping to distract me with good news, Myles announced, "here's the box of bags you wanted, Guv."

"Oh my goodness," I said as he passed the sealed bag containing a brown cardboard box branded, '*Emerald Margarine*'. "Where was this?" I asked excitedly.

"On a shelf. He had loads of them. They come from the bakery next door. Why?"

"Some of the guns recovered at the Tollgate Hotel were packaged in them. I want you to add this to your supplementary statement too, please Myles."

"Sure, Guv. Inside, you'll see this one contains the rolls of plastic bags you're looking for."

As Hamish had done, I manoeuvred the box around until its contents fell into the bottom of the bag. "Marco, when we saw you at the Lab, you said something can be done with the bags of ammunition if we could find the rolls they came from. Well, here you are. What do you think?"

"That's hours of microscopic analysis, Michael. It's feasible, yes, but will take weeks. What you've asked for so far could take a couple of months."

"Okay, but I want it done, please."

"Sure, but it will blow any budget figure you might have been thinking of."

"Let me worry about that. As I said, if we're to convict Mitchell of everything we suspect him of, we need the forensic work done thoroughly." Marco nodded as I continued, "from his behaviour during interview, we know he's unlikely to admit any of it, so we'll need to rely on the forensics being what you call his kryptonite."

"Of course. I wasn't saying no, I just wanted to make sure you've got realistic expectations about the time and work involved for our scientists."

John then chipped in, having noticed the electric TIG Welder in a large crate. "Marco, what can you do with this?"

"Not sure, but I'd like to take it back to the Lab. At best, the Metallurgy Department can prove it's of the type used to obliterate the serial numbers. They may also be able to say something about its use in welding the parts to reactivate the MAC-10s."

"Like what?" I asked.

"Well, the seam weld to accommodate the new feed ramp."

"But can they make an exact match?" John asked sceptically.

"No, that won't be possible because the welding node melts the metal. But let's see what they can do. Whatever happens, it will help convince a jury that Mitchell is your Abonar armourer, as the TIG is the critical common denominator for all the guns recovered."

"What else?" I asked as I looked into the remaining bags and crates. "How about these cloths, Myles? Where did you find them?"

"In Mitchell's workshop, under the bench, I think."

I looked at them through the clear plastic before passing them around. "What do you think, John? I'd say they're an exact match to the wrappings for the Tollgate Hotel guns."

John reached for the Abonar album and opened it at the relevant pages.

Myles looked on and asked, "what are those markings?"

"Cyrillic code," Hamish said helpfully. "But it's a smokescreen to deceive you into thinking the guns had been smuggled from the former Soviet-bloc."

"Interesting that," Marco interjected, "as our scientist identified the cloths with those Cyrillic letters on had been produced in Albania. It's called '*mutton cloth*' and is widely available here. It's used as cleaning rags in engineering workshops, just like the blue towelling wrapped around the MAC-10s and BAR. That's why Mitchell had them. He'd also have known from the packaging labels that the cloth comes from the former Soviet-bloc, which added nicely to his smokescreen."

I nodded as Myles continued, "okay, so Clive briefed us that the Abonar guns had been wrapped in cloths, so that's why I seized these. He also said they had handwriting on, but I didn't know it was Cyrillic letters."

"Well," I commented, "that's one of the critical bits of evidence we would have been searching for had John and I been invited along."

"Yeah, Guv, you've made that point before. It wasn't my choice. Don't blame me, please. I saw those same letters scribbled on some paper on Mitchell's workbench."

"Fantastic, Myles. Let's have a look at them."

"Um, I'm really sorry, but I left them there. I didn't know they were relevant."

"Bloody hell, Skip," John said, showing his own frustration. "As the Guvnor just said, that's another reason why we should have been with you."

"I know, I know. Now you've both made the point. Look, all may not be lost," Myles said, now reaching for another bag. "I did know about the handwriting, just not the Cyrillic code, so I grabbed every pen Mitchell had. They're all in here. Marco, what can you do with these?"

Marco smiled, "the scientists in the Chemicals lab can certainly make a comparison with the ink on the cloths, yes. But Michael, that will further dent your budget. I think you're going to have to re-mortgage your office."

"Happy to do so, Marco, so let's get it done. Good job Myles; your quick thinking may just have saved the day."

"Let's hope so, Guv."

"Yes, otherwise the Guvnor will be saying his usual '*Sugar, bloody, damn*'," John added mischievously.

I smiled as the others laughed at my expense.

We gathered all the items to take back to the Lab and I signed the SERCS' exhibits' register to show I now had custody of them. Once back on the surface, we put the lot in the boot of my police car. Having said our farewells and thank yous to Myles, I drove the others back to London. Having deposited everything in the Gun Room, Marco bid us farewell saying, "guys, now begins the long wait while we get the work done for you. You'll hear from me again in a couple of months."

CHAPTER 56

The Long Wait

Monday and Thursday, 15ᵗʰ and 17ᵗʰ September

Marco was kind enough to drip feed me with updates throughout August and into September. By the middle of the second month, he had built a convincing forensics case that linked the materials we had collected from the SERCS' exhibits' store to Abonar. Consequently, I made an appointment for he and I to brief Brian and Derek. John and Roger also came along to catch up on what we could now prove.

As we reached the end of our presentation, I invited our bosses to comment. Out of deference to his senior rank, we all waited for Brian to speak first.

"Right chaps, great work. Marco, my thanks to everyone at the Lab. Well, Michael, I'm convinced. You've got a very strong case now for getting SERCS to reinvestigate Mitchell. Derek, any observations from you?"

"Yes, I agree. Very strong case. Shows you were right to persevere with Abonar despite the Home Office. How do you want to proceed with SERCS?"

"I'll speak to DCI Bagshaw," Brian replied. "I want him and his ACC to come and hear this presentation too. Marco, are you happy to do it all over again in a day or two?"

"Of course. I'd be delighted now you've agreed to pay my bills."

"Ah, yes, that was a shocker, but clearly worth it. I may be lucky and SERCS will contribute something too."

On Thursday morning, we were back in the Gun Room; this time with a small contingent of senior people from SERCS. They included Arthur and Marcus plus their boss, ACC Basil Walker and his staff officer from the Pimlico HQ. Roger and John sat at the back, again, observing proceedings. I was grateful to them for their inputs when needed. John had been through the Abonar database and found Mitchell had called '*Horley Plating*'. He and Roger visited the company and obtained a statement from its managing director. He told them that, since 1995, Mitchell had been a regular customer. He had given them more than fifty semi-automatic pistols and revolvers in sandblasted bare metal to re-plate in a matt nickel finish. The manager instantly recognised the MABs, Colts and Smith & Wesson revolvers from the Abonar photographs. Marco and his colleagues had now matched the cloths, pens and plastic food bags found in Mitchell's workshop to the three recoveries in Whitechapel, Plaistow, and Gravesend. The evidence now amassed unequivocally connected him to Abonar. When we finished our presentation, it was Brian's turn to ask our SERCS colleagues what they wanted to do about Mitchell. As we had done, they waited for their boss to speak.

"Very good. Thank you, Marco, and Michael. I'm convinced," ACC Walker said to my huge relief. "I agree, without doubt, the evidence supports your case that Mitchell is responsible for Abonar. But what about the MAC-10s? I note you haven't found anything to say he's reactivating them."

"Nothing directly, no," Marco countered quickly, "but the fact I can match the spanner to every one of the silencers, and they also fit the screw threads perfectly on the MAC-10s, I'd say there's every likelihood he made them too."

I nodded in gratitude before adding, "and, Sir, there's the nine MAC-10 receiver locking pins. They confirm he was working on at least that number of guns in his workshop."

Brian chipped in too to say, "and, as Michael briefed you, Mitchell bought the ninety-five deactivated MAC-10s from Perkins that are turning up now reactivated. The Proof House confirmed the one found at Bown's address was one of those ninety-five. I think that's enough to go after them both Bown and Mitchell again."

"Thank you, yes, but as we didn't find where Mitchell was doing the work, could there be a second gunsmith reactivating the MAC-10s somewhere else? What do you think Brian?" The ACC asked.

Turning to me, Brian replied, "Michael, can you answer that."

"Yes, there's no chance of a second gunsmith. Having listened to his taped interview, Mitchell's so conceited he wouldn't want anyone else involved. He's craving attention for his gunsmithing skills, so no, this is all his own work. It means we must put him under surveillance again. This time, let's hope he leads us to wherever he's storing the remaining MAC-10s."

"That could take weeks," Marcus protested.

Brian countered, "then may I also recommend you go after Bown and Phillips, as we had originally planned when we were leading this."

Derek surprised me by helpfully adding, "we know from Michael's friendly that Bown cleared out at least one box from Stone Lodge. He may well have helped Mitchell clear out his workshop too. It's possible everything we're looking for is currently stashed at his sister's Chatham address."

"Thank you," I said, looking at Derek to acknowledge his support. Turning next to ACC Walker, I said, "if I may, Sir, I'd like to propose we go after the two couriers, Bown and Phillips, first. Bown's the weakest link in the conspiracy. Maybe Phillips is vulnerable too, given he's not been arrested before. If we can crack them both in interview, we should have the whole story ready for Mitchell's arrest."

"Hmm, okay, what real leverage do we have over Bown?"

Holding up Alice's i2 chart, I replied, "it's all here, Sir, and if he's as fearful of Mitchell as we think, once we explain how he exposed his co-conspirators, he'll want to talk."

"Okay, that works for Bown, yes," the ACC said, "but what about Phillips?"

With unwavering confidence I replied, "our analysis of the call data shows Mitchell used him to deliver the firearms and ammunition to Whitechapel, Plaistow and the Tollgate Hotel. That's why he must be arrested too."

"Alright, then he must be. Remind me Marcus, why didn't you go after Phillips in July?"

"We didn't know everything then that SO11 have on him now," Marcus said, trying not to sound like he was making excuses. "We housed him and that was it. Based on what Ackerman told us, the prize was always Mitchell and then Bown. He never mentioned Phillips, so we dropped him to focus on the others."

"Okay, Michael, if neither Bown nor Phillips talk in interview, can you rely on the call data alone to help convict Mitchell?

"Yes Sir, I can. Our i2 chart maps everything starting with Donovan, his family and solicitor in Manchester, and then all the way along the supply chain to Mitchell and Phillips and back again. It does the same to link Ackerman, Bown and Mitchell together too with both Ferris and McAuley."

"It's all impressively indisputable," Brian happily added.

"Yes, I can see that. Quite remarkable and mostly achieved, I understand, from sitting at your desks crunching data," the ACC nodded. "Right Marcus, how do you want to play this?"

"Okay, I'll make some time in the diary. It'll take us about a month to be ready for the arrest phase. We'll make a start on the surveillance next week."

Then turning to Brian he said, "Sir, it would help me enormously if you can lend us Michael from Monday."

Brian smiled, obviously amused by the irony of his about-face since our 'shocker-of-a-meeting' at the Home Office. "Yes, of course. That would be sensible. And, this time, might I suggest you take him along for the searches too?"

"Yes, Sir. I'd be very happy to," Marcus said, but chose to look down to avoid Brian's reproachful stare.

"Thank you," I said, extremely happy with this unexpected outcome, "I'll clear my desk."

CHAPTER 57

Another Kidnap

Friday, 19ᵗʰ September

I had my Friday mapped out to allow me the whole day to complete a proper handover for Roger to take on Corporate Services once more before I headed to Crawley on Monday. I thought for once I could get the whole weekend at home with the family too. However, I was interrupted when my pager sounded with its all too familiar shrill alarm. The message was to call the '*OCG Duty SIO*'. I dialled his number hoping it was something simple. It wasn't. We had another kidnap and Roy Richards was SIO again. Within minutes of activating the call-out procedure, I had a full team at their desks with me in Central 500 ready for when Roy arrived to brief us with Martin as his deputy.

"Okay," Roy began, "our hostage was abducted at gunpoint from his Islington home this morning, witnessed by his wife. She is now our victim. Red Centre is the family home. Green, proof of life calls are coming into the victim's Vodafone mobile. There's also a BT landline at the address but, so far, the kidnappers haven't called it. I want you to work your usual whizzy tricks once more, please."

"On to it now, Boss," I reassured him.

Roy continued, "the story is our hostage received £7,500 worth of cocaine on credit from his dealer and promptly lost it all when uniform stopped his associate and found it. The dealer wants the debt settled regardless. Of course, the hostage can't pay, as he didn't get the chance to sell any drugs. So the dealer's kidnapped him and is now demanding his wife raise the £7,500 by 9pm or they'll shoot him. That gives us just five hours."

"What's the intel on the kidnappers?" Harry asked, once more sitting in the 'Blue' chair. "Can you give me somewhere to position my surveillance teams?"

"Tottenham nick would be a good place for now," Roy told him. "I'll get Martin to put the details on CLIO. What we know about our kidnappers from the victim is that they're part of a Yardie gang from the Broadwater Farm Estate in Tottenham. Red suggests from all the background noises during the calls that they're on the move. They've blocked their number, so Green, I need it as soon as you can."

"Yup, I'll get that done too, Boss."

Within an hour, Ray at Vodafone had identified the kidnappers were using an Orange mobile to allow their captive to call home. Once again, he had been able to defeat their use of 1-4-1 to unblock the number. Keith at Orange had agreed to set up live monitoring, so we could begin tracing and tacking the mobile. I had updated CLIO with the registered subscriber's details.

Coming over to my desk, Roy asked, "so this subscriber, can we be sure he's our main kidnapper?"

"DC Ferguson is checking our systems now for what we know about the man," I told him. "Whoever has the mobile, though, is our principal kidnapper who's phoning the Red Centre for every proof of life call. Cellsite puts them in Tottenham and it's showing they're constantly changing location. I'm about to call out Toscas to get a fix on the mobile's position."

"Good, let me know how that develops."

"Guv," Chris called out, "the intel on the subscriber says he's known for firearms and drugs."

"Blue, get your team to plot up the street where the subscriber lives."

"Okay, Boss."

Minutes later, my console light started flashing. It was Keith calling again from the Orange Network Operations Centre.

"Sorry, but someone's just switched off your kidnapper's mobile."

"What?" I asked, annoyed that this meant I'd have to start all over again with tracing whatever the new number might be. "Are you sure and it's not dropped out of coverage or the battery's flat?"

"Yes, it's definitely been switched off."

"Sugar, bloody, damn. Okay, if it comes back to life, call me immediately!"

I had only just added this news to CLIO when my mobile pinged with a text, '*POL now*'.

I phoned Ray at Vodafone again, "What's the number calling our Red phone?"

"It's a BT landline," he advised, giving me the number.

Adding it to CLIO, I phoned Dara at BT Special Services, who gave me the subscriber. It was a phone box in Tottenham High Road, N17. I typed its details on to CLIO and that BT now had it on live monitoring.

Minutes later, Dave, who was once more in the 'Red Centre', phoned to update me on the latest call. "They're getting desperate for the money," he warned. "The hostage sounds terrified. The victim's stalling them, saying she's trying to raise the £7,500 from her friends. You better let the boss know there's no way she can get that much. Maybe a grand at the most in a couple of hours." He paused, knowing I was typing furiously to keep up. "So the kidnappers will call back every fifteen minutes." he added. "They've said if the victim doesn't raise the money by 9pm, it's all over for the hostage and they'll come for her next."

Roy stood behind me reading the computer screen as I updated CLIO.

"You better come up with a solution on the phones, Whizzy," he said quietly, "or I might be the first SIO to lose a hostage. We've got three hours before the 9pm deadline."

15 minutes later, Red sent his usual text, '*POL now*'.

While I waited for Dave's update following the call, Ray phoned to say it was a different BT number from before. I quickly set up a conference call with him and Dara at BT. The latter confirmed it was another phone box in Tottenham.

"Gents, I need a solution," I told them. "Ray, by the time you give me the incoming caller ID and I then phone Dara for the subscriber and location, we've missed any chance of getting to the phone box before they hang up. I need something instantaneous. What can you offer?"

"Nothing that's as fast as that from here," Ray said apologetically.

"What if we set up the victim's Vodafone to divert to the BT home number?" I suggested. "That way Dara you can grab the incoming caller ID and location at the same time in seconds?"

"That won't work," Ray interrupted. "Unlike BT, when you set up a divert from the handset, the caller will hear our automated message, '*Your call is being diverted, please wait*'. I suspect that'll spook them."

"Yes, it would," I said, quickly thinking it through. "Okay, but what if you set up the divert at the network end in Vodafone rather than on the handset?"

"That would work," Ray said more enthusiastically. "It would be seamless. No automated announcement."

"Dara, what can you do to speed this up too?" I asked.

"I can make anyone calling the home number think there's a delay while the line connects. That'll give us four extra seconds before they hear the ringing tone. If you also tell your Red to wait a few more seconds before they answer, we'll have time to get you the number and the phone box's location. How's that?"

"Perfect. Let's set that up and see how we get on. I'll leave this conference call running so we can update each other instantly too."

Exactly as Dara had proposed for the next incoming call, in seconds, BT had the location of another Tottenham phone box. Quickly checking the map, I could see the kidnappers were keeping to a small area. Its boundary to the north was Lordship Lane; the A10 to the west and south, and the High Road making up the third side of a triangle.

"Mr Richards," I called out as I typed to CLIO what was going on. "Heads-up everyone. Incoming call now from another Tottenham TK, this time Lordship Lane. I've got BT on my other line giving me the address." I paused before adding, "and it's now on your screens."

Blue shouted out, "I've got a team on their way there now."

"Michael," Dara's voiced sounded in my headset, "line's just gone dead. Call's finished. Any luck?"

I turned to Blue as I typed this to CLIO. He read the screen and looked across at me shaking his head, "Sorry, they couldn't get there in time."

Roy came over and I explained the setup.

"Blue, Vic, Martin, could you join us please?" Roy called out as he led the way to the SIO's corner office. Once we had all crammed into the small room, Roy briefed us. "I want your SFOs, Vic, strategically placed in this triangle of Tottenham ready to respond to whichever phone box the kidnappers use next."

"Sure Boss."

"Martin and Blue, split your teams up so you can cover the three phone boxes they've used previously, and any others you spot in the area. Okay, you all know what to do?"

The chorus of "Boss," signalled they did.

"Oh, and Whizzy, make this work," Roy told me with more than a hint of anxiety in his voice.

"Of course Boss. I won't let you down."

As soon as Dara gave me the location of the phone box used the next time, I called it out as I added it to CLIO. The room fell silent as Harry radioed the details to the teams around Tottenham.

"What's happening Dara?" I asked.

"They're still on the line," he replied earnestly.

"Blue, sitrep, please? Kidnappers are still on the line," I called out.

Clearly worried, he replied, "We don't have that one covered. I've got a team heading there now. Standby everyone."

"Line's dead, Michael. They've hung up," Dara abruptly announced.

"Blue?"

"Still running."

"The call's finished," I said at the same time as my mobile pinged with Red's '*POL now*' text.

"Sorry, we missed them, again," Harry announced.

"Sugar, effing bloody, damn," I exclaimed mutedly, just managing to contain my exasperation.

"Okay, okay, everyone, we've got fifteen minutes before we do that again," Roy said calmly. "Maybe we'll get lucky next time. Stick to the plan everyone. Stick to the plan."

As soon as Dara gave me the number for the next call, I knew it had featured before. "TK Lordship Lane now!" I called out, and Harry went through the same procedure as before.

The hostage was screaming down the phone to his wife as one of his abductors pushed a lit cigarette into the skin below his right eye causing it to sizzle as the flesh burned. He screamed and blinked rapidly as his tears diluted the stinging, acrid smoke. The other two men had a tight hold on him, so he could not turn away. So absorbed by the horror they were inflicting, they did not notice the armed police officers now moving rapidly towards them from their unmarked Range Rover parked only yards away.

"Armed police, get on the ground! Show us your hands!" each of the SFOs shouted; their weapons trained on the men now picked out in the torch beams of the MP5 carbines.

Another unmarked police car skidded to a halt alongside, and three OCG detectives ran forwards but stopped to avoid coming between the SFOs' weapons and their targets.

The arrests were swift and brutally efficient. Because the call was still ongoing, the victim heard for herself the events as they unfolded on the Tottenham street. She burst into tears with relief when her husband told her while crying, "I'm safe, love. The police got them. I'm so sorry. I'm so sorry." In Central 500, we were ecstatic. Once again, we had used a very clever CSP-developed technique to resolve another kidnap without losing our hostage.

Roy was so relieved he came over to shake my hand, saying, "thank you, again, *Whizzy.*"

Vic briefed me as I tidied up, "My team tell me the suspect doing all the torturing had a Tokarev-type pistol in his waistband. It's got weld marks all over it to obliterate the serial number." I nodded at this news of what was almost certainly another Abonar gun. It only reinforced why we needed to stop Mitchell from passing on anymore to violent criminals.

Returning to my office, it had gone 9pm. I would now have to come in over the weekend to finish clearing my desk. Sadly, doing so seemed a better option than home. The continuing juxtaposition between the excitement of Abonar and the coldness of my wife meant my office had become a welcome sanctuary. I told myself I just needed to get Abonar finished and then, for Rebecca's sake, I would put everything right at home.

CHAPTER 58

SERCS Crawley

Next four weeks, beginning Monday, 22nd September

Part way through reading Rebecca her bedtime story on Saturday night she announced, "Daddy, Mummy took me swimming with a man today."

From the way she said it, I could tell she knew her mother had done something wrong. Having tucked her in, I went downstairs to begin one of the worst conversations of my life.

Olivia explained she had begun an affair with a soldier almost half her age who was 'home on leave'. My marriage was over, and I was crushed. What made it worse was that she showed no remorse; no apology for what she had done to destroy our dreams. The irony was not lost on me that despite her relentless comments about where I was sleeping, it was she who had betrayed us.

It did not matter to her that I was building a new career as a respected Scotland Yard detective. While Abonar and our kidnap operations were proving to be the vehicle to do just that and secure a better future for us as a family, the exigencies of duty had finally taken their toll.

In some ways, committing to seeing Abonar through to its conclusion with SERCS was now a welcome distraction. The daily car journey to Crawley and back would provide valuable thinking time about how to recalibrate my life with a daughter I would now only get to see every other weekend. Fortunately, I held on to the house, which would provide Rebecca and I with a rock of stability and continuity. That was despite it representing a painful connection to a past life filled with objects now tainted by a hoped-for future that would never be. Olivia moved out on Sunday taking Rebecca with her. That first night I spent alone in the house felt so unreal. The empty cupboards where Olivia had removed her things with most of Rebecca's and, of course, the lifeless beds only added to my huge sense of loss. I had to dismiss thoughts about the day we had moved in only two years before and of all the promises we had made each other. Those included having more children, but then we'd suffered two pregnancy losses, which made Olivia's infidelity now even more devastating.

I am a stoic man, but this weekend left me completely heartbroken. Nothing can prepare you for a relationship destroyed by betrayal. It was especially hard for me when I hold so dear the values of honesty and trust, and Olivia had broken both. Some years later, Rebecca told me that night when she told me about her mother's affair was the first time she had seen her Daddy cry.

The SERCS Crawley Branch Office was a discreet building on an industrial estate outside the town. It looked like almost every other business unit in the complex. Nothing would seem out of the ordinary to the uninitiated observer. The only clues might be the unusual hours kept by its workers and visitors, and that there was no business name on the frontage. I drove down there that first Monday morning and parked my car on the forecourt alongside the array of assorted covert police cars, vans and motorcycles used by the squad. It felt very different to working at the Yard, and a lot more exciting for once being close to the action on the ground.

I spent the next three days in meetings getting to know the culture and personalities of the team. I was pleased at last on Thursday to be invited by Marcus to brief them. I kept the presentation short and focused on what more evidence we now needed to convict Mitchell, Bown and Phillips of the Abonar conspiracy. On finishing, I looked around the faces hoping for some constructive discussion.

"Okay Guvnor," one DS asked mischievously, "seeing as you say we missed a few things previously, how would *you* run this investigation?"

I looked at Arthur and Marcus for guidance, but they just folded their arms, stared at me, and waited with interest for my answer.

"First, we need to put Mitchell under surveillance again. We need him to lead us to wherever he hid the MAC-10s. Our friendly overheard him tell Bown he'd moved it all after being tipped off about Ackerman's arrest. He must have another premises under his control, and we've got to find it."

"I can't yet spare those resources," Marcus advised, "another team needs them for a week."

"Can we at least go technical and put the lump back under Mitchell's car?" I asked. "That way he might lead us to the property, and we wouldn't need a conventional team up behind him."

"Yes, we can do another feasibility study," he said, looking at Arthur, who nodded. "What else?"

"We must look at Bown's address in Chatham," I told him, holding up one of the three pagers John had given me back. "We know when he's there from the phone he uses to reply to his messages. We should put him under surveillance too when he is to see where he goes."

"Why?" asked one of the audience.

"I thought I'd been clear in my presentation," I answered, not wanting to sound annoyed. "It's because our friendly saw him remove a box from the gun club, and we need to find where he took it. It won't be at his Grove Park address, as he knows that's not safe. Bown's cellsite data shows he'd been back to the club on two other occasions beforehand, leaving late at night. It may be that Mitchell's got him to store everything at Chatham, including all the missing MAC-10s."

"Fair enough," Marcus said, "I'm happy to build that into the surveillance plan."

"Thank you, and as I've got the clone for Phillips's pager too, we should do more than house him as you did before. We need to get a full profile on him too."

"Yup, once I can spare the team, we can do that too," Marcus said. "Anything else?"

"That should keep us busy enough for the next week or so. I've also got Mitchell's clone pager, so I can let everyone know if he receives any messages to indicate he's gone back to supplying firearms."

After Marcus closed the meeting, I followed him and Arthur into his office for a more private conversation.

"Something else Michael?"

"Yes, if I may, I wanted to ask whether you'd consider applying for a 'Property Interference Warrant'?"

"For what purpose?"

"So we can get inside Mitchell's workshop and install a covert camera. I'd like to see what he's doing in there."

"I'll need some convincing. What are your grounds?" Marcus's tone warned me of his scepticism.

"Every tool he needs for his illicit gunsmithing is in that workshop," I explained. "Almost certainly, he's not expecting us back anytime soon. He hasn't seen hide nor hair of you since July, so he must feel pretty safe by now that he can get back to his illicit gunsmithing."

"Look, we were all shocked not to find your Abonar guns there after all his counter-surveillance," Marcus responded gruffly. "What makes you think he's now moved them back to the workshop?"

"Because everything he needs to reactivate the MAC-10s is in there. I doubt he's had time to do more than half of the ninety-five he got from Perkins. Each one is a lot of work. We need a camera installed to see exactly what he's doing inside his workshop."

Arthur seemed equally sceptical when he asked, "how can you be so sure he's got the MAC-10s either there or at Chatham?"

"Well, from the nine receiver locking pins DS Hurst recovered from Mitchell's workbench, we know there's at least that number still to be finished."

"Yes, but in the time since his arrest and us deciding to pick this job up again," Arthur protested, "he could have already finished them and all the others."

"If that was the case, Arthur," I countered, "we would have seen from the call data him trying to sell them, and we haven't. I'm convinced he's sitting tight until he gets them all finished. Then he'll offload the lot. The call data says he's not ready, and that's because he's working on them right now."

"That's all supposition, Michael," Marcus replied, wanting to play devil's advocate as he knew his bosses would do the same with him. "For property interference the lawyers will want hard facts," he pointed out forcefully, "and you're not giving me enough."

"Alright, so from what you learned the first time," I persevered, "Mitchell doesn't have a legitimate engineering business. And he's invested in some very expensive equipment that's really only any good to him for working on guns. Since leaving Longley's, that's all he's done. It's the only way he makes any money," I said, wanting to sound convincing. "Ackerman told you that too. Isn't that right, Arthur?"

"Yes, he did," Arthur confirmed in a tone that suggested he was beginning to accept my argument.

"That makes Mitchell a creature of habit," I pressed on. "Why else would he hang on to the workshop and all the equipment if he isn't using them for his illegal gunrunning enterprise?"

"But again, that's not enough to justify property interference," Marcus pushed back.

"Okay, how about we take it in stages, Guv," I offered, keen to find a compromise. "First, we get the lump back under his car. If that shows he's visiting the Knoll Business Centre again and long enough to be working on guns, then we move on to stage two, and install the camera."

"Okay, I'll go for that," Marcus replied positively at last. "Arthur, get that feasibility study done quickly on Mitchell's car, and put the TSU on standby to reinstall the lump."

"Sure, I'll have it done by this afternoon."

"Good, and I'll warm up the bosses to the idea of a covert camera," he said, finally smiling at me.

Arthur's feasibility study proved positive. In the early hours of the following Wednesday, October 1st, the SERCS TSU discreetly installed the tracker back under Mitchell's red Ford Mondeo. The device confirmed not only was he back to his counter-surveillance measures, but he was also visiting the Knoll Business Centre for hours each day. Disappointingly, it did not identify a third premises.

CHAPTER 59

Property Interference

Sunday night, 5ᵗʰ October

Satisfied we had now met his test for going ahead with the Property Interference Warrant, Marcus obtained authority for us to covertly enter Mitchell's workshop. Our mission was to install a surveillance camera over his workbench that would beam imagery via a microwave link to a video recorder discreetly placed in a vehicle parked nearby. Arthur had run the feasibility study into when and how to secure entry unobserved. It identified that the early hours of Monday morning offered our greatest opportunity.

My role was to arrange for Gary, the SO11 '*Locks Man*', to get us through Mitchell's workshop doors. He was one of only a handful of expert locksmiths shared by the police, military and intelligence services, and he worked for us in the SO11 TSU at Lambeth. With his skills and specialist equipment, Gary could make a key to fit any lock we needed to open. SO11 had invested in a mobile workshop, so he could park up close to the target premises. The SO11 TSU had built an enviable reputation for its expertise in covert entry. They had never been compromised. At the time of Abonar, knowledge of our capability to lawfully trespass in serious crime investigations was limited to a very small number of senior detectives. In addition, the intelligence gathered was rarely used in evidence. Hence, our covert visits inside their properties left many dangerous criminals guessing as to how we had exposed their enterprises. Regrettably today, due to multiple counter terrorism investigations revealing our capabilities in high-profile court cases, these techniques have become more widely known.

After the briefing at Crawley on Sunday night, Gary positioned his nondescript grey Leyland DAF van in the shadows opposite Mitchell's workshop and waited. Thankfully, neither the landlord nor any of the tenants had installed security cameras on-site. Nevertheless, the approach to Mitchell's unit was overlooked by a neighbouring house. The upstairs lights were still on. The detectives knew from previous reconnaissance that once these went out, they had a three-and-a-half-hour window to covertly enter Mitchell's unit before 4am. That was when the bakery staff next-door began work. A mobile security guard also visited shortly before 2am. He simply shone a torch at each door and gave it a rattle before returning to his van and leaving; all of which took no more than ten minutes.

Other members of the SERCS TSU positioned their nondescript vehicles in the streets approaching the business centre. Their purpose was to give Gary and the camera engineers advance warning of any potential risk of compromise. Years of experience meant they had an array of practiced contingencies to avoid someone surprising them. The camera engineers had parked their grey Mercedes van next to Gary's. At 12:45am, the lights went out in the neighbouring house.

Gary checked his watch. He had a maximum of one hour to make the keys and be back in his van before the security guard arrived.

"O-P from 6-5, permission?" Gary called on his covert radio.

"6-5, go."

"Heading out now."

With purpose in his stride, Gary walked with his ruggedised black toolbox over to Mitchell's unit. Like the others in the 'Covert Entry Team', he was dressed all in black, including a balaclava. He inserted the probe into the first lock and then removed it. Quickly, he checked the device had recorded the internal mechanism before doing the same with the second. Turning around, he headed swiftly back to the van, got in via the side door and slid it shut. He switched on the internal lights and, looking at the images of the two locks, thought, "*Easy. Not been defeated yet*".

His van was equipped with blackouts and soundproofing to prevent his work betraying what he was doing inside. Using the cutting machine, Gary crafted the two keys and checked them against the images. He nodded in satisfaction. Looking at his watch, Gary noted he had ten minutes in which to unlock the doors and be back in the van. From experience, he knew he needed only five.

"O-P from 6-5, permission?" Gary called on the radio.

"6-5, go."

"Is it safe to go again?"

"Yes, all good."

Instinctively, Gary held his breath as he tried the top lock. Turning the key slowly to avoid any sudden noise, he felt the teeth engage each lever as it opened. He breathed again.

Taking the second key from his top pocket, he pushed it smoothly into the lower lock. Again, he held his breath. Suddenly, a voice in his radio earpiece interrupted him, "all units from 6-7, we've got company. Security van, Egmont Road towards the T-P[53]."

"*Shit*," Gary thought as he extracted the key. He relocked the top one and, grabbing his toolbox, walked quickly back to the van.

The security guard was surprised to find his normal route blocked by a car whose female driver was making a complete mess of reversing into a parking space. "C'mon love, that's more than big enough for your Volvo, you could get a bus in there!" he shouted at her in frustration.

"All units from 6-5, I'm now clear."

The Volvo driver heard Gary's message over the radio earpiece, and quickly corrected her deliberately poor performance. Pulling into the space now with ease, she waved and mouthed "*Thank you*" to the van driver as he passed. Pressing the microphone button, she reported, "All units from 6-9, security guard now on his way in."

Shining his torch and rattling each unit door in his customary manner, the guard completed his checks. Returning to his van, he drove out paying no attention to the other two parked in the shadows.

"6-5 from the O-P, you're good to go again."

Gary returned to the door of Mitchell's unit. This time, he tried the second key in the lower lock first. Again, he felt the levers engage but then one prevented it turning further. Removing the key and dropping down on one knee, he took out a metal file and ground away some excess burring. Standing up, he tried it again. Relieved as it effortlessly opened the lower lock, Gary breathed again. He unlocked the top one too and announced, "from 6-5, we're in."

The side door of the other van opened, and the two camera engineers stepped out to cross the car park. As Gary passed them returning to his van, he handed over the keys. The first engineer carried in each hand a large black ruggedised briefcase. The second had a black rucksack on his back

---

53 T-P: Target Premises.

whilst carrying a black extendable ladder. The engineer in front dropped the briefcases at Mitchell's workshop door while he opened it and went inside. Moving swiftly to the alarm keypad, he silenced the now audible warning beep using the cancellation code Clive had noted. He then collected the briefcases, before going back inside followed by his colleague who closed the door behind them.

The two engineers worked quickly to get the job done. Within an hour, they had successfully installed a covert camera inside a light fitting in the ceiling, taking power from the existing electrical circuit. Next, one of them ran a cable up into the suspended ceiling and, climbing into the void above, pushed it through the insulation and out between a gap in the roof tiles. The second engineer was waiting on the ladder outside to grab the cable as it appeared. Quickly, he attached a small microwave box to give line of sight broadcasting to a receiver connected to a time-lapse video recorder. These were hidden in the boot of a Vauxhall Astra hatchback parked 50 yards away in Bellingham Crescent. Another member of the team was standing with it looking at a small TV screen checking the picture quality. It showed the headtorch of the remaining engineer inside moving around during his final tidy up.

"O-P from 6-8, pictures coming through. We're all good." He then locked up the car, leaving the eight-hour time-lapse recorder to start at 9am.

"All units from the O-P, let's pack up and withdraw."

At 7pm that Monday night, Myles stopped off at Bellingham Crescent to collect and replace the first video tape.

CHAPTER 60

Planning

Thursday, 9ᵗʰ October

Marcus invited Arthur, Myles and I to meet him in his office for our third confidential viewing of the tapes. Joining us for the first time was DI Russ Derby. He ran the surveillance teams, and Marcus wanted him and his detectives to now mix and match with the others for the final stages of the operation. We gathered around the television screen as Myles loaded the VHS tape into the player. We had previously viewed the ones for Monday and Tuesday. These quickly identified we had to accept some compromises; not least due to the camera's fisheye lens that gave a panoramic rather than finite view of Mitchell working. The time-lapse also caused us all to groan loudly with annoyance. In one frame Mitchell was in-view working at the milling machine and in the next he was elsewhere.

When the tape finished, the five of us kept staring at the now black screen with no one talking. I decided to break the silence, "okay, we can see that Mitchell is machining a lot of parts. That's very clear. Frustratingly, we can't see what they are and where he then puts them."

Looking at Marcus's face, I tried to guess how this might affect our plan to arrest Mitchell. From their expressions too, his long silence concerned the others. Again, I decided to go first, "okay Guv, what do you think? Should we go and get the warrants?"

"Yes, yes, go and get them," he announced to everyone's huge relief, "but not yet for Mitchell. Monday morning, I want three teams on this job. Arthur, I want you to take Bown's address in Grove Park. Michael, you take his sister's place in Chatham. Russ, you've got Phillips and his Rochester home. Myles, you'll be with me here as Controller. I want all your teams ready tomorrow for a briefing."

"As I've got the information on all three addresses," I said, "I'm happy to type up the warrants, if someone can then drive me over to Crawley Magistrates' Court to get them sworn and signed."

"I'll get DC Philpott to help you," Arthur offered.

"As for Mitchell," Marcus instructed, "we'll leave him until next Friday. That'll give us four days to arrest and interview Bown and Phillips; work through whatever they reveal, and then decide how best to tackle Mitchell."

We all nodded in agreement and stood up to leave. As I followed the others out, Marcus said, "oh, and Michael, remember, you're to stay in the shadows as much as possible."

"Yes Guv."

"Good, so on Monday you'll be with DC Philpott. Depending on where your pager tells us Bown is hiding, the main arrest team will go there. I want you at his Chatham address regardless. Okay? If the MAC-10s are there, I want you to be the one who finds them."

"Thank you, that's most kind," I replied, unable to hide an enormous smile.

"And one more thing, I want you to know you were right to persevere with Abonar. I wasn't happy when the Home Office told us to walk away, so let's hope after next week, we can both raise two fingers to Smedley. I'll be delighted to see Mitchell arrested and charged with everything you suspect he's done."

"Likewise, and thanks, again, for inviting me to be here."

As I walked into the main office, Clive was navigating his way between the desks towards me.

"I'm not sure whether I'm with you, Guv, or you're with me on Monday. But, since you're the DI, I suspect it's the former. Either way, how do you want to play this?"

"One moment, Clive, let me just grab DI Derby. Russ, do you have a moment, please?" I called after him.

"Sure, what do you need?" he replied turning round.

"I'm planning in my head what we can do ahead of Monday to secure Bown's Chatham address. Do you have the people to put it under twenty-four-hour surveillance ahead of us searching it?"

"What's your thinking?"

"Well, I'd hate for him to choose the very weekend before we raid the place to have another clear-out."

"But he could have done that weeks ago."

"Possibly, but I know he hasn't. His lack of activity on the phones means he's still got it all. Humour me please, Russ, can we get it done?"

"I'll check if we can spare someone over the weekend. Leave it with me."

A couple of hours later, Clive and I had the search warrants and were back at Crawley by mid-afternoon. Marcus then called the same group of four back to his office for a final catch-up.

"I need to give you some not so good news ahead of tomorrow's briefing with the whole team," he announced.

I looked anxiously at the others to see if they knew what was coming.

"The job is still on, don't worry, Michael," he assured me having noted my concerned expression. "The problem is I couldn't convince the ACC to let us carry firearms."

"What?" Arthur said, obviously alarmed.

"I know. I'm shocked too. It's body armour for everyone, but no authority to carry. The best they'll agree to is for Kent and the Met to have A-R-Vs on standby just in case."

"What reason did they give?" I asked.

"They want Bown and Phillips to leave their homes before we take them out on the street. That way, SFOs don't need to go busting through doors and we risk ending up in a siege situation."

My compatriots muttered audibly.

"Okay," I commented, "that works as there's also less risk of anything getting in the news and Mitchell finding out we're coming for him again."

"Agreed," Marcus confirmed, "and it'll be easier to control if we make the first two arrests without any fuss. Okay?"

I joined the others in nodding our agreement.

"Good, so let your teams know too, as I don't want any dissent at tomorrow's briefing."

CHAPTER 61

Grove Park and Rochester

Monday, 13ᵗʰ October

After a final 4:30am briefing on Monday for the whole team at Rochester Police Station, we headed out to the car park. As I got into Clive's car, I felt a mix of nervous anticipation and excitement at the start of this critical week for Abonar. The eight unmarked police vehicles, followed by two marked Kent Police A-R-Vs looked hugely impressive as we all left in convoy. Gradually we peeled off to go our separate ways to the three standby locations. Half-an-hour later, Clive pulled on to the pavement 200 yards to the north of our target address in Clandon Road. A hint of sunrise was just beginning to cut through the woodland opposite. The second vehicle in our search team had turned off beforehand to park up with an A-R-V in Yew Tree Close.

Clive spoke on the radio, "O-P from 4-6-7 permission."

"4-6-7 go."

"Sitrep?"

"No change. No sign of Subject Two. No lights on. T-P is currently occupied by one adult male and one adult female. They've been here all weekend. There's a blue Mazda four-door on the drive."

"Thanks O-P, we're now on the plot with Central 2-4-0."

Turning to me, Clive explained, "Right Guv, you asked, so we've had a Crops[54] officer buried in the hedgerow opposite the T-P since Friday. No sign of Bown."

"Well, that confirms the pager and call data that he spent the weekend at Grove Park. Let's hope DI Wilton and his team have better luck than last time."

---

54   Crops: term used for a surveillance officer who completely immerses themselves into the environment, sometimes wearing a total camouflage outfit, a 'ghillie suit'. They can stay put for days surviving on a ration pack and performing all bodily functions in situ. They clear up and take away with them all signs of their presence before leaving.

Arthur had his team parked in the streets around Bown's home. The MPS A-R-V had now joined them. Shortly after 9:15am, a voice on the surveillance radio interrupted the silence.

"All units from the O-P, Subject Two is out, out. Left in Balder Rise towards the TK on the corner. Standby."

While some detectives stepped from their vehicles to follow on foot, the remainder drove slowly to cover the junctions and wait.

Arthur called the MPS A-R-V to alert them to be ready, "Trojan 4-5-5 from Regional 4-1, Subject Two on the move south towards Marvels Lane, standby."

"All received Guv, we're rolling towards you."

Bown had now reached the junction with Marvels Lane. Turning right at the phone box, he looked back and immediately spotted the lone male surveillance officer following him on foot some 50 yards behind. The man stood out in the otherwise empty residential street. Bown knew his neighbours, and this was not one of them. He quickened his pace and crossed the road into Sydenham Place. It led into Alice Thompson Close, a dead-end for vehicles. Bown looked back again and saw the surveillance officer still following him now with a second man. About halfway down the cul-de-sac, Bown started to run. He moved swiftly between the industrial sized waste bins and along the cut-through that led on to the open meadow towards the Quaggy River.

"Trojan 4-5-5 from Regional 4-1, active message. Subject Two is running. Eltham College playing fields, Marvels Lane, go, go, go," Arthur shouted into the radio microphone.

With a squeal of tyres and gravel flying, the A-R-V driver turned sharply left from Marvels Lane and, at speed, headed along the driveway leading on to the playing fields and the College Meadow Pavilion. Arthur in his unmarked car along with two more police vehicles followed across the grass to block Bown's other escape routes. The two surveillance officers behind Bown were now running to catch him up. Bown looked ahead and saw the A-R-V crew deploying from their vehicle twenty yards in front with their guns drawn. He stopped. Looking all around for somewhere to run, he froze momentarily, unable to decide what to do. All his escape options were blocked.

"Robert," shouted DC Reece, the closest pursuing surveillance officer. "Give it up, mate. Give it up. You've got nowhere to go.

As everyone now closed in, Bown dropped to his knees. Anticipating an instruction to do so, he put his hands on the back of his head. His shoulders heaved, and he burst into tears. DC Reece and his colleague searched him while two of the

A-R-V crew provided cover with their semi-automatic pistols and carbines pointed directly at Bown's torso. DC Reece unclipped a black leather bag from around Bown's waist. Lifting it, the weight told him something significant was inside.

"Be careful," warned Bown, "it's loaded."

The Sergeant in charge of the A-R-V crew holstered his Glock pistol and stepped forward. He took off his baseball cap and dropped it upside down on the grass. Next, he pulled on a pair of latex gloves before taking the bag from DC Reece. He unzipped it and tipped the contents into the cap. Out fell a nickel-plated Smith & Wesson Model 36 snub-nosed revolver. "Standby guys, it's loaded," he warned.

Having cleared the gun, the Sergeant explained, "we've got five 38 calibre buckshot rounds. Not as deadly as 38 bullets, but still nasty at close range. And there's something else in the bag."

He put the revolver and ammunition back in his cap to look in the bag again. "Okay, we've got a CS gas canister too. By the weight of it, it's full. That's also a prohibited weapon. Nice one."

"Robert Bown," DC Reece said, now putting handcuffs on the kneeling man, "I'm arresting you for unlawful possession of a loaded firearm, CS gas, and conspiracy to supply illegal firearms and ammunition," and then cautioned him.

Within a few minutes, the detectives and A-R-V crew had cleared the area. No members of the public had seen the events unfold. Arthur took over and drove Bown back to Balder Rise to search the house. Thereafter, he took him to Gatwick Police Station for questioning.

Over in Rochester, Russ and his team were having a slightly later start while they waited for Phillips to leave home.

A voice on the surveillance radio channel got everyone's attention, "O-P to all units, Subject Three is out, out, standby."

It was almost 10am. Immediately, Russ had a problem. The Kent A-R-V crew had decided to take a comfort-break without telling him. They were no longer nearby. Consequently, Russ and his team were on their own. They could only follow Phillips while they waited for the armed officers to catch up.

Initially, Phillips was not aware of being followed. However, the sound of the siren from the approaching A-R-V made him nervous. He could see the blue lights heading his way. Stopping to look around, he immediately spotted the first surveillance officer. He was directly behind him, only a few feet away. As he looked to his left, another man on the opposite side of the road appeared to change course unexpectedly. Phillips panicked. He walked a little faster. Looking behind him only confirmed his fears that he was now being followed by at least two men. From their *clothing and appearance, he could not determine whether they were the gangland hitmen Mitchell had always warned would come after him, or plain clothes police.*

Not knowing quite where he might go, Phillips broke into a run and then a sprint. The A-R-V driver brought his car to a sudden stop to avoid colliding with the two unmarked SERCS cars approaching from the opposite direction. Phillips now realised it must be the police and they were after him. The SERCS cars quickly reversed to allow the A-R-V to go first.

Phillips sprinted as fast as he could, weaving and then slowing between the pedestrians in the hope his pursuers would lose sight of him. He headed towards The Esplanade where he knew there would be bigger crowds. Looking behind once more, he realised there was now no cover to hide him. The police officers were shouting at everyone to get out of the way. People in front moved to the side to avoid the man running at them. Phillips knew he was now totally exposed. The three police cars had also entered The Esplanade with their sirens wailing and were now gaining on him.

Phillips broke right towards the seafront where the vehicles could not follow due to the bollards. Running now to the end of the pier, he thrust his right hand into the hip pocket of his black leather blouson jacket. He felt the cold metal of the revolver as he fumbled for the handle. He knew he had to get rid of it before the police caught up with him. He heard their shouts as they closed in, "stop, armed police". He ran faster, his only option now was to ditch the gun and surrender.

Reaching the end of the boardwalk, Phillips stopped, keeping his back to the officers to hide his actions he held the revolver tightly against his tummy. Fearing his pursuers would see it and shoot him, he leaned slightly forward over the railings and let it fall into the murky brown seawater below. He had hoped he was far enough ahead for no one to see. But, on turning round with his empty hands now outstretched, he realised the detectives were much closer, and one had. Catching up with him, the first kept an eye on the tell-tale ripples and bubbles that marked the spot. Another grabbed Phillips roughly by his right arm and, with a sudden sideways kick, deftly took out his legs causing him to fall forwards on to the ground.

"Andrew Phillips?"

"Yes."

"I'm arresting you for conspiracy to supply illegal firearms and ammunition," the detective announced before cautioning him. "And what, my friend, did you just chuck in the sea?" he asked.

"Nothing," was Phillips's unconvincing reply.

Three hours later, the Kent Police Underwater Search Team recovered the gun. It was the same type as Bown's. However, Phillips had loaded his with five of the more lethal .38 calibre lead bullets.

The subsequent search of Phillips's home revealed various items of shooting memorabilia connecting him as a fellow Black Shod to Bown and Mitchell, but he did not have any other firearms or ammunition. The detectives then took him to Gatwick Police Station for questioning. Fortunately, none of the bystanders who had witnessed Phillips's dramatic arrest considered it worth telling the local media. Thus, Mitchell remained oblivious to the arrests of his two fellow conspirators.

CHAPTER 62

Chatham

At just after 8:45am, the Crops officer reported, "Central 2-4-0 from 4-6-7, occupiers of 122 now out and away in the Mazda. T-P is empty."

When Arthur called an hour later to let us know of Bown's arrest, I decided it was time to get our job done too.

"All units from Central 2-4-0, let's go," I called over the radio. The other units acknowledged.

"Central 2-4-0 from 4-6-7, you're clear. Street's empty."

I saw the Kent Police A-R-V pull up 50 yards south of us as we parked on the drive in front of the garage at the semi-detached house. Four detectives in the second car pulled up behind us. I was careful that nothing about our manner would attract the neighbours' attention. We had all come to a gentle halt before getting out and calmly walking up to the property.

Clive had collected the red battering ram from our car boot and joined me at the front door. DC Myers from the second vehicle stood behind us. DC Bannister moved a wheely bin alongside the garage and neighbouring fence. This allowed him and then DCs Connelly and Hughes to climb up and cross the low roof to the rear before dropping into the back garden.

Clive stood ready to slam the heavy metal ram into the door lock. Nodding to him, I announced over the radio, "from Central 2-4-0, door going in now".

Clive heaved the battering ram, shattering the upper glass panel and splitting the door frame around the lock. With his second blow, the door swung open.

"From Central 2-4-0, we're in."

With that, Clive and DC Myers quickly checked the ground floor rooms while I went upstairs. As we moved from room to room, we each shouted, "Police". The house was empty as we had expected.

"From Central 2-4-0, stand down everyone. The house is clear. Let's regroup in the lounge."

As Clive let the other three detectives in through the back door, I went to the front and saw the Kent Police A-R-V drive past. One of the crew gave me a nod and a wave. Looking across the road at the hedgerow opposite, I was surprised by the unexpected movement at its base. What I had taken to be a pile of leaves began rising, with an eruption of detritus. It was the Crops officer breaking cover to let me know where he was. He remained there watching, ready to warn if the occupants returned or anyone else took an interest while we searched the house.

"Right folks," I told the team. "DC Myers if you bring your camera and come with me, and DC Hughes joins us as Exhibits' Officer, we'll do the upstairs and loft. Clive, would you and DCs Connelly and Bannister search downstairs. Oh, and other than the garage, what's out the back?"

"There's a shed attached to the garage," DC Hughes advised.

"Okay, we'll work our way round to that too. Right, let's get this search done."

It was clear from the clothes and personal items which of the three upstairs bedrooms Bown was using. DC Myers stood ready with the camera while DC Hughes put the plastic crate containing all our exhibits' packaging on the bed. He and I then worked around the room. I focused on the wardrobe. Beneath his shoes, Bown had hidden a two-foot-long cardboard box.

"Mr Myers, would you please photograph this in situ before I move it?"

He took several pictures before I lifted it out. I could feel whatever was inside had considerable weight. I then placed the box on the bed. There was no external label to describe the contents. Opening it cautiously, I was surprised to see a complete but disassembled World War Two era Thompson M1A1 .45 calibre submachine gun. Bown had slid an empty 20-round magazine in between the three major components of the upper and lower receivers and the wooden stock. I checked the weapon was clear. The serial number had been obliterated with a TIG welder, no doubt to stop us connecting it to the Ralston Arms' inventory.

"Okay, that's our first relevant find. Mr Hughes, would you record this, please, as my exhibit MH/1, and package it."

"Er, Guv, are you sure you want me to exhibit it as yours? I thought the bosses wanted you to keep a low profile," his tone respectfully suggesting I change my mind.

"Yes, but one small trophy shouldn't hurt, and we can't go changing the facts. I did find it."

"Okay Guv, you know best."

We did not find anything else of relevance upstairs or in the loft. As we joined the others downstairs, Clive asked, "What do you make of this, Guv?"

handing me a percussion pistol dating from the mid-19th century that he had found on the mantlepiece.

"Sorry Clive, but unless Bown plans on being a highwayman, this is nothing more than an antique curio and quite legal to own."

"Oh, what a shame," he said, taking it back. "Then that's all we've found." DC Hughes showed him the packaged Thompson.

"Impressive. That's earned Bown a minimum five-year sentence. Good job, Guv," Clive said before noticing the exhibit number. "Um, Guv, should it be your exhibit? I thought..."

"Don't go there, Clive," DC Hughes interrupted him. "Guvnor's prerogative. He wants a trophy."

"Well, it's a good one, I'll give you that."

"Right DC Myers, if you and your camera come with me into the garage, the rest of you can work your way round the garden and shed, please."

Helpfully, the key was in the lock for the connecting door from the kitchen. Walking into the garage, it was clear from the clutter that the owners were not using it for their car. As I surveyed the scene to decide where to start, Clive appeared at the doorway.

"Guv, can you come and see these, please?" His tone forewarned of danger.

"What've you found?"

"Grown up fireworks, I think. They're in the shed. Follow me."

DC Bannister was searching under the hedgerow that bordered the rear garden, while DCs Hughes and Connelly were carefully removing items from the shed and putting them on the paved patio. I looked at the five six-inch tall cardboard canisters. Reassuringly, the wrappers described them as 'fireworks'. Next, DC Hughes brought out a box of flares of the type yachtsmen use, and two military-style 'Thunder Flashes'.

"These are perfectly safe to package as they are," I directed.

"Okay Guv," Clive said, sounding relieved. "Given we've found these," he continued with caution in his voice, "would you like me to check whether the Kent Police PolSA[55] team can join us?"

"I'd prefer not to," I told him. "I really want to keep this all very low key to avoid attracting the neighbours. We don't want them calling the newspapers. Just be methodical and thorough, please."

"Yes Guv," and Clive's tone revealed he wasn't entirely happy as he went back to searching.

---

55 PolSA: Police Search Advisor – an officer who specialises in planning and controlling complex searches involving high-risk crimes, such as counter-terrorism, looking for arms and explosives.

Returning to the garage, I found DC Myers still surveying the scene not having made a start. I told him what the others had found, and he immediately lost interest.

I looked around hoping to spot something out of place amongst the usual household items. Sadly, and very obviously, there were no boxes that could contain our missing MAC-10s. However, by the garage door was a large black plastic case standing upright. It was of the type sport-shooters use to carry rifles. Alongside it was a black motorcycle top-box. Both seemed incongruous amongst the otherwise household items.

"Mr Myers, would you photograph these two suspicious items before I move them."

Once he had taken pictures. I picked up the gun case and was immediately alerted to its potential contents due to the heavy weight. Carrying it back into the house I placed the case on the kitchen table with a thud. DC Myers took more photographs as I released the catches. Lifting the lid, I saw component parts for dissembled long- and short-barrelled firearms, plus assorted ammunition of different calibres, and a stun gun. After a few minutes of trial and error, I put together two sawn-off shotguns and two hunting rifles.

"Excellent," I announced cheerily, "they'll earn Bown another five years on each of these."

DC Hughes came through to the kitchen to log the exhibits as mine, again, and then packaged them. While he did so, DC Myers and I returned to the garage and the top-box. It was not locked so I lifted the lid carefully. Inside was a black plastic bin liner. Gently pulling it open, I looked inside. The bag contained three individually wrapped packages; each in an outer blue and white plastic shopping bag. Cautiously tearing this away on one, I stared in disbelief at the two smaller packs inside. They contained a white waxy substance separately wrapped in clingfilm.

"Holy, shit." I said, before realising I needed to moderate my reaction so as not to alarm DC Myers.

"What Guv?"

"I think we've just found C4 plastic explosive."

"Shit."

"No, no it's okay. It's perfectly safe just as it is. Take the photos, please, as I lift out the black bag and look underneath."

I could tell from the speed at which he was now photographing, DC Myers was keen to get the job done and leave. There was nothing else in the top-box. In total, we had found six separate packs of C4 plastic explosive.

"Right, change of plan," I told him. "We can't deal with this on our own. The rules say we need the Army. Let's withdraw to the kitchen, and I'll go and tell the others."

Clive's reaction was less controlled than mine, "What the fuck does Bown want with that?!"

"Don't know, but it means I need everyone to stop. Clive, would you now get in touch with Kent Police HQ and ask them to send over a couple of uniform while I call out the Army? Oh, and, please, no blue lights and sirens?"

"Sure Guv," he said, walking out into the back garden to make the call.

Standing in the kitchen, I telephoned the SO13 Senior Explosives Officer to get his advice. He arranged for the Royal Logistics Corps 11 EOD[56] Duty Officer from Deal Barracks to call me.

"I'll need you to set up a 250-yard cordon around the property, Sir," he said in very military, matter-of-fact manner, "and evacuate all the residents within that radius."

"Do I have to?" I asked, hoping to change his mind. "I'm trying to run a covert operation here. I don't need cordons and evacuations compromising everything. What can we do that's less conspicuous?"

"Well, we can turn off the blue lights and sirens before we get to you. Would that help?"

I would have laughed if it were not for the seriousness of the situation. We could not risk Mitchell seeing Bown's safehouse on the news.

"How about you get here and then decide whether we need cordons and evacuations?"

"Okay, I can agree to that, provided you all leave the premises and wait till we get there."

Grabbing everything else we had found and putting it in the boot of Clive's car; I withdrew the team to our two vehicles and repositioned them 100 yards away. While we waited, Clive organised for a local boarding up company to come and repair the front door.

The Army arrived in their standard white truck emblazoned with a yellow stripe down both sides along with the name of their unit, 'Royal Logistics Corps – Bomb Disposal'. Almost immediately and quite understandably, neighbours came out to watch. Thankfully, the uniform Constables who had joined us mingled with the anxious residents briefing them, as instructed, that we had

56 EOD: Explosives Ordnance Disposal.

found some fireworks which needed to be checked. Despite trying to keep the situation low-key, it did not take long for a journalist from the local newspaper to arrive. At that point, I had to agree to the cordon to keep him away.

"Right, you better show me where you found these explosives," the Ammunition Technical Officer asked me. The insignia on his khaki pullover indicated he was a Sergeant. Holding a large rucksack that he had taken from the truck, he followed DC Myers and I through to the garage. He placed his bag on the floor before taking from it the kit he needed. The first was an electronic portable field detector, which he switched on and then pointed its probe into the black plastic bag holding the explosives.

The detector's light went immediately to red, and the screen displayed some numbers.

"Yes Sir, as you thought, C4."

Next, he removed the packs from the bin liner and put them all on a set of electronic scales.

"Two point seven kilogrammes, Sir. That could certainly do some damage."

"But can we move it as it is?" I asked, noticing DC Myers hurriedly retreating to the kitchen.

"Oh yes, it's quite stable like this."

"Good, so what happens next?"

"I take it away, Sir, and send you a statement in a couple of days. In the meantime, you'll need to notify the Health and Safety Executive. They'll want the ins and outs of a duck's bottom about how you came to find it." His voice warned that completing the report would be a chore. "I'm happy all I need do is tell you it'll go bang if 'energised', detonated in your language, Sir," he concluded with a smile.

As the Sergeant then took out the forensic packaging needed to wrap the C4 he asked, "so, why were you searching this house anyway?"

"We came looking for illegal firearms, which we've found plus some ammunition. The C4 is an unexpected bonus. There's a couple of Thunder Flashes too."

"Okay, would you like me to check them over too?" he offered helpfully.

"Yes please, just to confirm we've packaged them safely."

Once he had finished with the C4, the Sergeant followed me through to the kitchen where Clive showed him the other items.

"Yeah, they're all fine Sir. Usual rules apply for storing them in a cool dry place," and smiling as he saw DC Bannister smoking in the back garden added, "away from a naked flame."

Fifteen minutes later, both the Army and the two Constables had gone taking with them the cordon tape. Very quickly, the street returned to its quiet suburban normality and the journalist left too. The two Kent officers did a great job playing down the situation. They made the whole episode seem so uninteresting to the journalist that he chose not to write about it. Thus, Mitchell remained oblivious to our closing in on him.

CHAPTER 63

Bown

Sussex Police had given us an upstairs office at Gatwick Police Station as our temporary 'Incident Room' for the week. By the time Clive and I got there with our modest collection of exhibits, the detectives who had arrested Bown and Phillips had theirs spread on a desk. Myles was sorting through them in readiness for the interviews. Only two appeared relevant.

"I'd like to open these, please, Myles," I asked him.

"Which ones, Guv?" he replied seeming a little distracted

"The ones with the revolvers Bown and Phillips were carrying. Everything alright?"

"Just tired, Guv, and I suppose a little disappointed. I had hoped this time we'd find a lot more at their addresses like the missing MAC-10s."

"Well, I don't think we did badly. Just look at what we got from Chatham. That's a bloody good result. It's also great leverage to get Bown talking. And we've got both him and Phillips carrying loaded firearms."

"Yeah, but is it enough to convince them to tell us everything about Mitchell?" he said, still sounding despondent.

"I bloody well hope so," I told him encouragingly. "Right, I want to look at the frames of these two revolvers."

Taking my 'Leatherman' multi-tool from my canvas briefcase, I selected the screwdriver. DC Myers stood ready with his camera while I removed the two-piece grips from both guns.

"Bingo! Mr Myers, I'd like you to photograph these marks, please. There you go Myles; these Cyrillic codes clearly connect Bown and Phillips to Mitchell and Abonar."

"Very good," he commented sounding happier. "I'll go and find Mr Wilton to ask who's doing the interviews. While I do that, I think you'll find these other two bags interesting too."

Myles slid them across the table. Each contained a pager. Having dialled the number for Pager C, the test message confirmed Alice's analysis, it belonged to Phillips. Running the same test for Pager D confirmed it was Bown's.

"Fantastic, we were right!" I exclaimed just as Myles returned to the room with Clive and DS Graham Murphy. "You see Clive, desktop investigations do have value," I said pointedly.

"Yes, Guv, I get that now," he commented respectfully. He then advised me, "DS Murphy and I will be interviewing the prisoners."

DS Murphy was a tall, powerfully built man in his late thirties. He looked like he would be very much at home in the three-quarters line-up on the rugby field. His unkempt, long curly ginger hair and scruffy facial stubble only added to the look of a 'bruiser'. I sensed Arthur had picked him in the hope his imposing, physical presence might be just what was needed to encourage Bown and Phillips to talk in interview.

In preparation, I reminded Clive and Graham of the key points to include in their questioning. I also handed them copies of the photograph albums and Alice's i2 chart; with an explanation of the relevant points they must put to Bown. I was about to follow them downstairs when Marcus walked into the room. "What's this about you having exhibits in your name?" he said almost angrily.

"I couldn't avoid it," I countered defensively. "I found them. We couldn't fudge it by saying someone else had."

"Yeah, yeah, I suppose so," he conceded, now sounding calmer. "Look, I don't really have a problem, but on your own head be it when you tell Brian."

Marcus then walked with me downstairs to join Arthur in the viewing room. We sat there watching through the one-way glass screen as Clive and Graham brought Bown into the interview room next door. I was struck by his appearance. Thinning dark brown hair; in his mid-forties; shorter than the two detectives; slightly overweight but, more strikingly, he looked exhausted and terrified. He sat alongside his solicitor facing us and opposite his interviewers. Clive had already put on the floor next to him all the exhibits they needed to refer to. On the desk he had the photograph albums and Alice's i2 chart. Having gone through the usual protocols of loading the tapes and cautioning him, Graham launched into the first question.

"So how long have you been a gunrunner delivering illegal firearms and ammunition?"

Bown lowered his head into his hands, took a deep breath, and then looked up directly at his accuser.

"I'll tell you everything I've done, but I'm not giving you names," his voice revealing a strong south London accent.

"Well, we know about your association with Anthony Mitchell, John Ackerman, and Andrew Phillips, so you'll not be telling us anything we don't know already. When and where did you all meet?"

He conferred briefly with his solicitor before saying in a resigned manner, "The Tudor and Stone Lodge Gun Club back in '91 or '92."

"So you'll know Kieran Walshe as well, then?"

"No comment."

"What about '*Mr Fixit*' in Eltham? Who's he?"

"No comment. Look, there are some serious London gangland criminals who go to that club," Bown protested. "There's no way I'm giving you their names."

"Who approached you first, Mitchell or Ackerman?" Graham demanded.

"Tony, er, Mitchell," he corrected himself. "He asked if I'd help him deliver guns to John. He said the two of 'em had been in business for a while. Tony had been supplying John with mostly handguns and ammunition. He said it had earned him about a quarter of a million."

"Was that why you also got involved, for the money?"

"Yes mostly, but then he and John had a falling out. John paid him once in phoney banknotes. That was his game too you see; shifting counterfeit currency and supplying guns to his mates in the biker-gangs."

"Who are they?"

"I told you; I'm not naming these people."

"What did Mitchell do about being paid in phoney money?"

"He wouldn't do business anymore with John directly. So John asked me if I'd act as his go-between. He had customers wanting guns, and Tony could supply everything they wanted. I was happy to do so, provided I got paid."

"Did Mitchell know you were acting for Ackerman?"

"Oh yes. It was good business for him. He just warned me to make sure whatever I brought back wasn't phoney money again."

"That confirms what Ackerman told us," Marcus whispered despite our room being soundproofed.

Graham continued, "so what was the first job you did for them?"

"John wanted four Smith & Wessons, which I collected from Tony. He'd wrapped 'em in cream-coloured cloths packed in an '*Emerald Margarine*' box. He prefers to package his guns that way. Tony gave 'em to me when we met in the car park at Crawley train station."

Clive thumbed through the photo album until he came to the relevant images of the Tollgate Hotel guns and asked Bown, "like these then?"

"Yeah, just like those, and with the same lettering scribbled on 'em."

"For the purposes of the tape," Clive said, "I've just shown Bown photographs on pages 17 to 25 in the album, exhibit BPH/4."

"What did you do with the four revolvers in the box?"

"Took 'em to Islington and handed 'em over to John in his local pub."

Turning to Marcus I commented, "maybe they were the ones destined for Moss Side. GMP got three back from a loft in January."

"Quite possibly," Marcus said, nodding back.

"How much did Mitchell want for them?" Graham asked, taking over again.

"Six hundred each, so two thousand, four hundred for the lot. I kept four hundred for my troubles and paid Tony the rest."

"So, Mitchell let you have guns on credit until Ackerman paid you?"

"Yeah, that's how it worked every time."

"And then what?"

"When John didn't have any business for us, Tony and I would still meet at the gun club. He'd get me to take guns he'd deactivated up to the London Proof House and then bring 'em back."

"What else was Mitchell doing for business?"

"He was selling guns to people who came to the club."

Graham thought he would try his luck, "Who?"

Bown smiled as he replied, "No comment."

"Okay, if not who, then what?" he persevered, trying not to sound irritated.

"Tony said he'd sold 'undreds of guns to a particular customer from Liverpool."

"What types?" Graham asked, realising the importance of this revelation.

"From what I saw 'im leave at the club for the man to collect, they were mostly rifles; a couple of AK47s; some other machine guns, shotguns, and a load of handguns, all with ammunition to match." Looking down he added, "and those guns on the floor you found in my sister's garage. They're from the same lot, only Tony hadn't been able to get rid of 'em as well."

"Why not?"

"The customer didn't need anymore."

"Why did you have them then?"

"Because when John got nicked in May, Tony asked me to clear everything he still had hidden at the club and keep 'em safe. I agreed to store 'em at me sister's."

"Where had Mitchell hidden them?"

"At the back of the bin shed."

"Is anything still there?"

"No, I went there three times for him and cleared it all."

"How did he convince you to do that, and not go himself?"

"I'd looked at 'em once, so Tony said my fingerprints would be on 'em. He bullied me into going, as I lived closer than 'im."

"Well, that confirms the cellsite data for Bown's mobile. It showed he made two late night trips to the gun club after Ackerman's arrest, plus the one our friendly observed," I told Marcus and Arthur, who nodded back.

"So what else did you collect?"

"That Thompson on the floor there."

"For the purposes of the tape, the Thompson referred to is exhibit MH/1. The other guns and case are exhibits MH/2 to 7," Clive interrupted.

"What about the black motorcycle top box also found in your sister's garage?" Clive asked, now pointing to it on the floor, "Exhibit MH/8."

"The top box is mine. What's inside is Tony's."

"The Army have it now, but what was it?"

"Plastic explosive. Tony only told me that only once I let 'im know I'd hidden it at me sister's. Originally, he'd said it was just '*bits and bobs*', so I didn't mind. When he said it was high explosive, I was furious. I mean' he'd made me drive round with a fucking bomb in the boot of me car!"

"Did he tell you why he needed it?"

"No. All he told me was it came from one of his customers."

"And the fireworks and Thunder Flashes. Where'd they come from?"

"We had them for our training."

"Training for what?"

"We did re-enactments of police raids."

"What, as the Black Shods?"

"Yes."

Clive paused, shaking his head at the thought of Bown running around dressed as a Ninja.

"So, these guns for the Liverpool customer," Graham cut back in, "when was this?"

"Late '95 into early last year."

"So the end-customers would be John Haase and Paul Bennett in Full Sutton Prison?" Clive then asked, confident in the knowledge he was right.

I watched Bown's face. He seemed thankful as he quickly answered, "no, I don't know those names."

"Sugar, bloody, damn," I said, turning once more to Marcus and Arthur. "That would have been the icing on the cake."

Graham carried on, "so how many guns did you deliver to Ackerman on Mitchell's behalf?"

"Around two hundred and fifty with ammunition for each one. Tony often bragged about selling John 'undreds more before I got involved."

"*Shit*," Marcus exclaimed looking at me, "and there was me agreeing with the Home Office to let Mitchell off with just a few licensing irregularities."

I decided it would be prudent to nod without commenting.

Clive then asked, "When did business between you, Ackerman and Mitchell re-start?"

"July last year. At first, it was revolvers and semi-automatic pistols of various types plus ammunition. Latterly, it was Tony's new MAC-10s."

"Tell us about them?"

"Well I knew from Tony he'd bought a load of 'em deactivated. I bought one off 'im too, which you found at my home the first time. He said he was working on reactivating 'em."

"When was that?"

"Last July."

"That would work with what Perkins told us," I commented. "He thought it would take a few months of trial and error before Mitchell could perfect his new design. July would be about right."

"Hmm," Marcus commented, "I'm very glad we're about to have another talk with Mitchell."

"What did Tony tell you about his new MAC-10s?" Clive continued.

"One time when he and I met in the Tesco's cafeteria in Horley, he told me what he was doing to improve the internals. He could tell I didn't quite get what he meant, so he drew a picture on a till receipt of his new breech bolt."

"Do you remember enough to draw it for us now?" Clive asked, sliding a sheet of paper across with a biro.

Bown took a few minutes to recreate a 3D drawing and slid it back saying, "there, like that."

"For the purposes of the tape," Clive explained, "Bown has drawn a rectangular block. What's this line here?"

"That's for the extractor. He said he'd machined it at forty-five degrees to stop the gun jamming."

Clive raised the paper so we could also see Bown's drawing.

"That's it," I commented, "and a pretty good likeness."

"How can you be so sure this is his design?" Clive asked.

"Because I've seen that many to know what they look like."

"How many?"

"Fifty."

"*Fifty!*" Marcus shouted. "Fucking hell. Michael, how many does that mean Mitchell's still got?"

"As many as another forty-five plus parts for maybe ten to fifteen more," I reminded him.

Marcus quietly repeated, "Shit, shit."

"When we interviewed Ackerman," Graham then pointed out, "he told us Mitchell had supplied him with only twenty in total."

"John's 'aving a laugh," Bown said, smiling. "No way it was just twenty. He's trying to make it sound better than it was. I took fifty up to him."

"How can you be so sure?"

"Because I counted 'em," he answered convincingly. "Over nine months until May this year, I took mostly MAC-10s up to John twelve times. I also took him ammunition and some other pistols. Often there were three or four in a box, and more than one box each time."

Clive quickly asked, "how were they packaged?"

"Same as before in either blue or cream cloths inside the Emerald Margarine boxes. Some he'd sealed with brown packing tape. Out of curiosity, I opened 'em, as they were really heavy. I did strip one down once to see if there was anything I could borrow for my own deactivated gun." He paused before saying disappointedly, "but there wasn't. Well not without a load more parts."

"How did you and Mitchell carry out these transactions?"

"Sometimes we'd agree to meet in car parks either at Crawley train station or Tesco's in Horley. Oh, and sometimes he just left the boxes for me behind the bins at the gun club."

"What else did Ackerman ask you to get from Mitchell?"

"I think I've told you everything already."

Clive persevered, "what about a CZ pistol with silencer and ammunition on January 17th this year?"

Bown looked uneasy and consulted his solicitor who shook his head.

"No comment."

Clive pushed Pager D across the table along with Alice's i2 chart, saying, "for the purposes of the tape, I'm now showing Bown the pager he was carrying when arrested today and SO11's analytical chart. Please explain why Ackerman messaged you three times on January 17th?"

Bown shrugged.

"You see on this chart here, it shows you called him back from the phone box near your house. Why was that?"

Again he shrugged.

"Then you messaged Mitchell to call you back at the same one. So what were you arranging between them?"

Bown looked down briefly before looking up at Clive, "Okay, yes, so John was giving me a hard time," he conceded. "John's customer was coming down from Scotland the next day to collect the pistol. Tony was late in getting it to me. That's why I messaged him. John had said he was one dangerous villain you couldn't let down. Tony finally met me at the gun club with everything in a box. I opened it and saw the CZ plus silencer and ammo."

"Excellent," Marcus said, "that ties in perfectly with your call data, plus what Ackerman told us, and MI5 observed."

"Yes it does," I said, rather pleased this also confirmed my bold theory about the call data. "The problem is," I added, "Ackerman won't now give evidence. We're going to have to trust the jury understands data analytics."

Graham then took the lead again, asking, "so, what was the next transaction you did for them?"

"The one John got nicked for."

"Tell us about that?"

"It was a different box this time, '*Opal Fruits*' I recall." He paused as if retrieving the image from his memory. "Yes, Tony sealed it with brown packing tape, but told me what was inside. Three of his new MAC-10s, three silencers, magazines, and a load of ammunition. He wanted three grand for the lot. I ran 'em up to John, and we met at his local pub."

"What was the detonator for in the box?"

"Don't know. I never opened it."

"Do you know who Ackerman's customer was?"

"Yes, John said it was the same big Glasgow villain who had the CZ pistol, but I don't know his name."

"How did you know Ackerman had been arrested."

"Because he didn't reply to the messages I left on his answerphone. I wanted to arrange to collect the payment for me and Tony. Eventually, I phoned his mate next door. He told me John had been raided and hadn't been home since. That was also why it was the last job I did for Tony."

"Why?"

"When I called him about John getting nicked, he was furious, cos it meant I couldn't pay 'im. He told me, *'Don't contact me again and don't come down to Brighton'.*"

"And when did you next speak to him?"

"After you raided my place and his."

"What happened?"

"He insisted that Andy and me meet him at the club for a pow wow. He got us to promise we'd never talk to the police like John had." Bown then slumped back in his chair as the irony struck him that he was now doing exactly that.

"What's the problem?" Graham asked him. "Broken your Black Shods honour code? There's no place for that now. We've arrested you in possession of a loaded firearm, more illegal guns and ammunition, CS gas and two point seven kilos of high explosive. You need to carry on telling us your side of the story."

Bown looked down at the desk and the tape machine recording everything as Graham continued, "When we searched your house in July, where were you?"

"Lying low at me sister's."

"In that search, we found three silencers of the same design as those you delivered to Ackerman. Where did you get them?"

Clive added, "we're now showing Bown photos of exhibits CP/5 to CP/7."

"Tony gave 'em to me as samples to show customers in the hope they might want one."

"And the three Uzi magazines?"

"Just spares he gave me. You can own magazines. They're legal."

Graham pretended to show interest by nodding before moving on, "I'm now going to ask you about three large deliveries of guns, ammunition and drugs made to Whitechapel last November, Plaistow in January, and the Tollgate Hotel in March. What was your involvement in these?"

"That wasn't me!" Bown immediately protested. "I only know of the last one, and that's because I read about it in the *'Kent Messenger'*, me sister's local rag."

"Who was involved then?"

"Look, this mustn't come from me, right."

Graham fired back, "we're not doing deals, Mr Bown, we just want you to tell us the truth."

Bown conferred with his solicitor for an agonising amount of time. I was desperately keen to hear what he would say. "Come on, come on, man, tell us the story," I uttered in frustration.

Turning back to Clive and Graham, Bown announced, "No comment."

"No, you've got to tell us!" I shouted, and Marcus and Arthur looked sideways at me in surprise.

"What if I said you're the weakest link in this whole sorry conspiracy?" Graham said almost menacingly.

"How so?"

"Because you used your sister's phone to contact both Mitchell and Phillips. You broke the Black Shod rule never to use an attributable phone. That's how we knew about Chatham. It's also how we got Andy Phillips's address in Rochester. I think they'd like to know that too."

Bown's expression made clear he was now panicking inside.

"So, you can see it really is in your best interests to cooperate and tell us about those three deliveries," Clive added.

Bown turned away briefly to consult with his solicitor again before facing Clive once more. "Okay, I'll tell you what I know." He then paused, thinking how to begin.

"And?" I shouted impatiently at him through the glass screen, despite knowing he couldn't hear me.

"Okay, so those three had nothing to do with me, right," he declared. "I recognised the handguns as the same as those Tony was getting me to deliver to John and the Proof House. You know, the ones in the cloths with those funny letters scribbled on 'em. I kept a copy of the newspaper to show Tony the next time we were at the club."

"What did he say when you did?" Clive continued.

"I asked him, 'is this your stuff?' and he said, 'it looks like it'. Now, a couple of weeks later Andy Phillips was there too. He and Tony got talking about the guns found at the Tollgate Hotel too. Andy bragged, '*I took those guns for Tony to give to another customer. They're for a reduction in someone's prison sentence*'." Bown said this in a voice I took to mean was his impersonation of Phillips's. Reverting to his own he carried on the story, "yeah, Andy said he wasn't that bothered about doing it for Tony, as he'd promised they'd all get found by the police and wouldn't be used."

"What did Mitchell say about that?"

"Well, he had the chance to deny it, but didn't. I took that to mean Andy was telling the truth."

Graham decided to take over, "so, when we searched Mitchell's home and workshop, we didn't find any MAC-10s. Where are they?"

"In a garage in Hove," Bown replied without needing to think.

"Yes!" Marcus and I both yelled in delight.

"Whereabouts?"

"Hmm, I don't know the address. He drove me there once in his Mondeo."

"Damn," I said in annoyance.

"How do you know the MAC-10s are there?" Graham asked.

"Sometime back, when he was first bragging about 'em, he took me to a garage block at the back of Longley's where he was then working. He wanted me to see these big metal tool chests. Inside were dozens of MAC-10s, some assembled and others in their component parts."

"But Longley's isn't in Hove," Clive corrected him.

"No, he's moved it all since to a new garage in Hove. The point I was making was I had seen those MAC-10s before he started work on 'em. That's when I bought mine off him."

Clive asked cautiously, "If we take you out later in a car, will you be able to find this place?"

"Yeah, I think so. If not the garage, then the block it's in, yes, for sure."

"I need to check again how you know the MAC-10s are in this garage?" Clive continued.

"Tony took me there. He made me stay in the car, though. That's why I can't tell you which one is his. But he came back with some MAC-10 barrels to show me saying he'd made 'em. He showed me how he'd added a screw thread for the silencers that he was also making. He also got a CZ pistol to show me, like the one I delivered to John. In fact, it may 'ave been the same one."

"So this would have been when?" Clive asked, wanting to extract everything from him.

"It must have been January, because it got dark early."

"Have you been back more recently?"

"No."

"Are you happy for your client to come out with us later to find that garage?" Graham asked the solicitor.

"Yes, provided I'm present for any follow-up interview."

"Agreed," Clive replied, before adding, "I've got one last question Mr Bown. Where did you get the loaded Smith & Wesson revolver you were carrying today?"

"Tony gave it me. Given all the big villains I knew he and John were mixing with, I wanted something for my protection. I would never 'ave used it other than to defend myself. That's why I loaded it with buckshot and not bullets."

Shortly after that, Graham terminated the interview and returned Bown to his cell. Minutes later, both he and Clive joined the three of us in the viewing room.

"Good job, guys," Marcus said. "Good job. Right, I want you to do the same now with Phillips. I don't want to run out of custody time, so I'll ask the superintendent for a 12-hour extension for him and Bown."

"Thanks, Guv," Graham said, "that will take the pressure off us."

Clive added, "and if Bown can't point out the garage, we'll need to do house-to-house."

"No," Marcus said forcefully. "No, I don't want that. Arthur, I want you and Myles to take Bown out now and find that garage. If he can't point out the actual one, just bring him back. We can't risk doing house-to-house until after we've nicked Mitchell. I don't want some unhelpful neighbour tipping him off."

"Sure, I'll go and find Myles now," Arthur said, and left the room.

Turning to Clive and Graham, Marcus said, "You better get Phillips out for interview."

They left the room looking happy at the prospect.

"Right, once I've got the custody extension done, I'm going back to Crawley. What will you do?" Marcus asked me.

"I'll stay and watch the interview with Phillips."

CHAPTER 64

Phillips

While I waited for the interview to start, I decided to call Derek with an update. I finished by asking where his enquiries had got to with Donovan.

"It's deeply frustrating. Gudgeon's backed the Prison Service into a corner demanding a letter from the Home Secretary. He wants it to say unequivocally that he's granting him early release."

"And that's the only way Donovan will now tell us where to find a sample?" I asked.

"I think it's still negotiable. Gudgeon's told Murray that Donovan's losing patience. He's accused the Home Office of over-promising and under-delivering. He's given them till Friday, or the deal's off. After that, he'll no longer pass on what he hears on the wing about the RPGs."

"That means he'll be stuck with them. No one else will want an RPG. So that's a hollow threat."

"Almost certainly, but we can't risk him then dumping these weapons and someone else making use of them."

"Agreed."

"So, on Friday, Murray will go back to Gudgeon telling him that once we've safely got the sample, Donovan will get a letter. That irritating lawyer, Smedley, is carefully crafting it ready to go. He's also drafting the script Murray needs to use when he speaks to Gudgeon on Friday. Both that and the letter will make clear the Home Secretary will only grant early parole if he's satisfied Donovan had nothing to do with either obtaining or holding the weapons."

"Sounds good. I'll call you again when there's more to tell from here."

I watched again through the one-way screen as Graham and Clive returned, this time with Phillips and his solicitor. They took up the same positions as before, with Phillips facing me. He too was older than I had expected; late forties, tall and thin, with fair hair that hadn't been brushed. His expression betrayed a deep nervousness about being in custody for the first time.

Clive and Graham went through the same protocols. This time, the only exhibits on the floor were Phillips's revolver, ammunition, and the pager. As before, Clive had the photo albums and Alice's chart on the desk. I listened as Phillips confirmed what we had also learned from Bown about their association through the gun club. Occasionally, he broke into cockney slang which sounded odd because he spoke mostly with a Kent accent.

"Moving on now to the three deliveries you made on behalf of Mitchell to Whitechapel, Plaistow and the Tollgate Hotel," Graham asked, "what can you tell us about them?"

"I didn't deliver them to those places," he reacted almost angrily. "I just left them behind the bins at the gun club for someone else to collect."

"What, you didn't take them to where the police found them?" Clive said disbelievingly.

"No, someone else did that. Tony only wanted me to drop them off at the club."

"Did you know what you were delivering?" Graham asked as he took over again.

"Tony said it was guns and ammo. I looked in the holdalls for the first two, and that's what I saw. Oh and there were some sealed up blocks of cannabis too in the first one. The third was all cardboard margarine boxes plus a heavy long gun wrapped in blue towelling and packing tape."

"Did Tony tell you who was collecting them?"

"No."

"Did you see who picked them up?"

"No. Didn't want to either, and I didn't want them to see me."

"So how could you be sure the right person collected them?"

"Not my problem."

"How did you get paid?"

"Cash. Tony paid me when we next met at the club."

"How much?"

"It worked out a monkey in total. Five hundred nicker for all three. One hundred and fifty each for the first two, and two hundred for the last one."

"Did Tony tell you who his customer was?"

"No name, but he did say it was for someone who needed help in getting his prison sentence reduced."

"Did he tell you who that was?"

"No and I didn't ask." Quickly, he then tried to excuse his actions by saying, "look, to be honest, I know it wasn't the right thing to do, but I didn't think it was that bad. You know; especially as you'd be recovering them. It wasn't like they'd be falling into the hands of villains. You'd be getting them."

"Why did you get involved then?"

"Money. I needed the money."

"Why didn't Tony deliver them himself?"

"He said he wanted to do me a favour by giving me the chance to earn some easy cash instead."

"Where did you meet Tony to collect each one?"

"His garage in Hove. He made me follow him in my motor and park round the corner, so I couldn't see which it was. Each time, he came back with what he wanted me to drop off and put it straight into the boot of mine."

"What's the address of his garage?"

"Don't know. It's somewhere in Hove. As I said, he made me follow him there."

"If we take you out later, would you be able to show us?"

Phillips conferred briefly with his solicitor before saying, "If you put in a good word with the judge that I helped you, then yes. I've never been in trouble before. I did this as a favour for Tony. As I said, it didn't seem too bad. He told me everything would get found by the police. They wouldn't be used in crime. And that's what happened, yeah?"

"That is what happened, but at the same time Tony was supplying these same types of guns to criminal gangs. They've been used in shootings and at least five murders."

"Whoa, that wasn't anything to do with me," Phillips protested, his voice now raised in alarm. "I only dropped off those three lots at the club. That's all I did. I never had nothing to do with whatever else Tony's been up to. He'll tell you that too."

"But you were arrested today carrying a loaded gun yourself?" Clive now asked pointedly.

"Yeah, I know, but that was for my own protection. Tony scared the be-Jesus out of me, saying not to talk to anyone, or his clients would top me. That's when I asked him for something I could carry, and he gave me the revolver with some ammo. I wasn't carrying it to do no armed robbery or anything, just personal protection."

I walked out of the room realising that was as much as Phillips would tell us. I consoled myself with the hope both he and Bown would show us Mitchell's garage. Going back upstairs to our makeshift Incident

Room, I waited for the others to return. Graham and Clive joined me five minutes later.

"Another good job, guys. Well done," I said smiling.

Clive responded with, "Yeah, but they're both so shit-scared it's easy getting them to talk. Mitchell will be a much harder nut to crack. He's an arrogant tosser and was totally uncooperative the first time."

"Hmm, let's hope when he hears of his fellow Black Shods' betrayal," I replied, "he'll want to set the record straight with his own version of events."

"Fingers crossed, yes," Graham answered. "The good news is that with Phillips's arrest we've given you at least one body for your original Abonar conspiracy. We're happy to add Bown to ours."

I let his comment go, as I considered both were part of the same big Abonar conspiracy.

Just then, Myles and Arthur walked in. Arthur spoke for them both, "We're going to need house-to-house once Mitchell's been arrested. He took us to The Martlet off Upper Drive in Hove, and to a block of garages there, but he couldn't pick out Mitchell's."

"Phillips is downstairs ready for the same treatment," Clive commented. "He's been to the garages three times. You may have more luck with him."

"Okay, we'll do him next," Myles accepted.

"Then we'll call it a day," Arthur added. "Mr Bagshaw got the extension, so we're good until midnight tomorrow."

Arthur and Myles took Phillips out to locate the garage. Like Bown, he was able to point out the block at The Martlet, but not the actual one. It was midnight when they returned him to Gatwick, and time for us all to go home. Clive dropped me back at Crawley to collect my car for the hour's drive to mine. I had left the bedroom lights on before leaving to give some sense of welcome on my return.

CHAPTER 65

Final Preparations

Wednesday and Thursday, 15th and 16th October

Late on Tuesday, Graham and Clive charged Bown and Phillips with conspiracy to supply illegal firearms and ammunition; unlawful possession of their Smith & Wesson revolvers and, separately, Bown with unlawful possession of explosives and his prohibited CS gas canister. The Custody Sergeant refused them bail. Both appeared at Crawley Magistrates' Court the next morning, where they were remanded in custody. To keep matters out of the public eye, we denied reporters access to the court.

Later that Wednesday afternoon, Marcus brought everyone together at Crawley to review the evidence. After a briefing from Clive and Graham on what they could put to Mitchell in interview, Marcus asked if there were any questions.

"If I may, Guv," I decided to go first, "will Bown and Phillips give evidence against Mitchell?"

"Bown yes, Phillips no," Graham answered.

"And Ackerman? I heard from the Home Office he won't, but is that really the case?"

"Yes. Someone got to him early on in prison. He's since told us he doesn't want to spend the rest of his life living in fear. So, he'll plead guilty; do his time, and move on."

"Any more questions?" Marcus asked… "No?… Good. I want everyone here for 8am tomorrow for a final day of planning. Russ, I want twenty-four-hour surveillance on Mitchell until his arrest on Friday morning. Make it happen."

"Sure, I'll get that organised," Russ confirmed.

"For everyone else," Marcus continued, "just to mark your dance cards now, there'll be a briefing on Friday morning at Brighton Police Station at 04:30."

He waited until the groans finished. "DI Wilton will lead the arrest and search of Mitchell's home. DI Hallowes will be there as our advisor. Graham and Clive, you did such a great job with Bown and Phillips, I want you to interview Mitchell. We'll sort out what the rest of you are doing tomorrow. That includes house-to-house enquiries at The Martlet to find Mitchell's garage."

As we dispersed back to our desks, Marcus signalled I follow him into his office.

"Quick heads-up for you and your team back at SO11."

"Guv?"

"I'm going to put the wind up Mitchell in the morning and I want to know how he reacts. I need you and your team monitoring his phones and pager for whatever it triggers."

I reached the Crawley Branch Office by 7:30am on Thursday. I called Roger to confirm he and the team were on standby in Central 500. Marcus came over to me as soon as he walked in the building.

"Your team all set?"

"Yes, Guv."

"Good, then come with me and Andrea outside, please." I then followed him and the office manager into the car park.

"Andrea, when you're ready, I want you to call Mitchell's mobile," Marcus instructed. "Here's the number," he said, handing her a piece of paper. "If anyone else answers, just ask for Tony. Okay?"

"Sure, what do you want me to say?"

"I've written a script on the back. Turn it over." Andrea did so and checked the wording.

"That's all I want you to say," Marcus continued. "Wait a moment for a reaction to confirm he's heard you and then put the phone down. Okay?"

"Yes, fine. What phone do you want me to use?"

"Follow me," he said, leading the way to a phone box close by. Marcus gave the handset to Andrea. Prefixing it with 1-4-1 to block the caller ID, he then dialled the number on the reverse of the paper. As Andrea heard a male voice answer, in a monotone she simply stated, "the police have arrested Bown and Phillips. Good luck."

As Mitchell asked, "who is this?" she put the handset down.

"That should stir the pot," Marcus said happily. "Let's see what he does about it."

As we walked back to the office, Pete phoned me to confirm he had the details of our trigger call. Once businesses opened around 8:30, Mitchell started using his phones. Within a couple of hours the pattern made sense. Roger and John had followed up on each one. Chris was helping them by researching the names and businesses on the Internet.

At lunchtime, Marcus came over to ask what had happened since Andrea's call.

"It certainly had an effect," I told him. "Mitchell's planning to travel. Looks like he's taking the train to catch the ferry in the morning to Cherbourg. He's also contacted a couple of firms that buy and sell engineering equipment. He's clearing out his workshop."

"Good, so he's planning to make a run for it." Smiling, he added, "I better warn Russ to be ready to '*widdle on Mitchell's strawberries*'."

An hour later, Marcus called the other two DIs, Myles and I into his office for one final catch-up.

"Russ, what's happening at the H-A?"

"Both Mitchell and his girlfriend are indoors. Haven't been out all day."

"Let your team know they may do a runner. If they come out with suitcases, arrest them. If he comes out alone and empty handed, follow and see where he goes." Marcus paused as he thought through his next instruction. "If he takes you either to the workshop or this elusive garage, arrest him once he's at the door, but not before. Okay."

"Sure."

Marcus finished, saying, "get that done and then join us in the main office. I'm going to give everyone a final health and safety briefing."

Fifteen minutes later, Marcus stood in the centre of the room with everyone forming a crescent around him. "Right, listen up," he began authoritatively. "First, it won't have escaped your attention that we found explosives at Bown's Chatham address, which he was storing for Mitchell. You'll also recall we found a detonator in the box he sent up to Ackerman." He paused for the acknowledging comments to subside before carrying on, "so, tomorrow, I need all of you involved in the searches to be extra, extra vigilant."

Again, he paused to wait for the groans to stop. "Thank you. So, DI Hallowes is coming along as our advisor on all things firearms, ammunition and explosives. If you find something you're not sure of, stop. For God's sake don't touch it. Get his advice. Understood?" and he looked around the squad members one-by-one checking for a nod.

He then turned to me. "Michael, would you like to comment?"

"Thank you, yes, I would. There's no evidence of Mitchell using or making improvised explosive devices," I reassured them.

"Can we have that in writing?" someone commented, which caused many to laugh.

I kept going once it stopped. "We will search systematically, room by room with Mitchell present. It may take longer but there's a reason for this. We need to find where he's hidden up to fifty or more MAC-10s." I checked their faces to confirm they had registered the significance. "Hence, I'm hoping his behaviour will give something away while we're searching. For that reason, DC Hughes here will be watching Mitchell the whole time for a reaction. With luck, he'll give away when we're getting warm to something he doesn't want us to find."

"I'm happy to do that, Guv," DC Hughes said helpfully, "but what's my signal?"

"Just say 'Guv, stop'. You and I will then confer. Everyone happy with that?"

"I am Guv," DC Hughes responded positively.

"Thank you, Mr Bagshaw, that's all I wanted to say."

"Okay, one last thing, and it won't surprise you, so I'm not interested in your moans about it. Once again, HQ won't authorise us to carry. Same as before, we'll take an A-R-V instead."

I left for home to get an early night ahead of finally meeting Mitchell.

CHAPTER 66

Day of Reckoning

Friday, 17th October

Clive collected me from Crawley, where again I had left my car, and drove us to Brighton Police Station for the briefing. Walking into the Parade Room, I noticed from the wall clock it was 4:25am.

Russ joined us followed by Marcus. "What news from the H-A, Russ?" Marcus asked him, looking at his watch.

"Sound asleep, Guv. Didn't go out at all yesterday."

"Good, almost time for us to wake him up then."

Marcus then ran through a few last-minute reminders on safety and objectives with the entire team. As he did so, Russ took a call on his mobile. Marcus glanced across at him, noting his anxious look.

"Lights just came on at the home address, Guv," Russ announced.

Marcus's reaction was instantaneous, "okay, no time to lose. Saddle up folks."

Russ kept on talking on his mobile, and then turned to warn Marcus, "Mitchell is out and heading for his car. He's alone and not carrying anything."

"Tell your team to follow him, Russ, and you better join them to find out where he's going. I saw the A-R-V in the car park; jump in with the crew and get after Mitchell. Everyone else, go to your ground-assigned."

Clive tugged my arm, "come on, Guv, we need to move."

He and I rushed back to our car. We were in pole position to leave. Clive attached the magnetic blue light to the roof as we headed out followed by a convoy of cars all making for different places across Brighton. Clive accelerated hard to catch up with the A-R-V. Our circulating blue light illuminated everything around us and made an impressive sight.

Mitchell had seen the car headlights following him. Given the hour, he had not expected another vehicle on the road. He changed course, but the headlights stayed with him. Then another vehicle joined behind it. Mitchell repeatedly checked his mirrors as he took several turns off his planned route. The two vehicles stayed with him.

Listening to the surveillance radio commentary, Clive said, "he's heading for Hove. It's either the workshop or his garage. I hope it's the latter."

"Maybe some last-minute tidying up to do," I commented.

Suddenly, Mitchell accelerated as he approached a set of crossroads. Looking back once more, he failed to notice the 'give way lines' ahead and raced through without slowing.

Coming in the opposite direction were two uniform Constables in their marked Sussex Police Vauxhall Astra. The driver braked sharply to avoid a collision. Mitchell did not register the accident he'd narrowly avoided. Instead, he focused on the two cars following him that were now held at the junction. They were letting another car go first, which he did not yet realise was the police car he had just forced to stop.

"Why's he in such a hurry?" the Constable driving said to his colleague.

"Best we stop and ask him."

Accelerating to get up behind Mitchell, the Constables were unaware of the now three unmarked SERCS surveillance cars following and the A-R-V racing to catch up. The driver switched on the blue lights.

"We've got a compromise," Russ called over the radio, "all units go, go, go. Rolling roadblock."

The three SERCS vehicles overtook the two Constables at speed followed by the A-R-V, all now with their blue lights on. The road ahead was straight. The leading surveillance car overtook Mitchell's Mondeo and cut sharply in front. The second pulled alongside keeping pace with Mitchell's decreasing speed as the one in front forced him to slow. The third now overtook the marked Sussex Police car and nudged in between it and the Mondeo to take up the rear of the formation.

When the lead surveillance car braked sharply, Mitchell had to do the same and stop. The A-R-V drew alongside. The crew were out in an instant and rushed over to Mitchell's door. With one hand firmly on the grips of their Glock 9mm pistols, the three SFOs were ready to draw if he posed a threat.

"Keep both hands on the wheel!" the first armed officer yelled. "Hands on the wheel, on the wheel! Stay in the car until I tell you to get out!" Then more calmly he instructed, "now turn off the engine."

Mitchell was totally compliant. He was also in shock.

The first armed officer carefully opened Mitchell's door.

"Get out nice and slow and keep your hands where I can see them on top of the door."

Mitchell complied. One of the surveillance officers stepped forward, "I'll take it from here guys, thanks." With that, he handcuffed Mitchell pulling both wrists firmly behind his back.

"Anthony Mitchell, I'm arresting you for conspiracy to supply illegal firearms, ammunition, and explosives," and cautioned him. "Are you carrying a gun?" he then asked.

"No, no I'm not," Mitchell replied falteringly. The arresting officer then patted him down to make sure. He found only a wallet, pager, mobile phone, and keys, which he placed on the car roof.

The driver of the marked patrol car kept his blue lights on as he pulled up behind the roadblock ahead. Getting out, he and his colleague walked over to find out what was going on. Eight men and women in casual clothes were now gathered around the red Mondeo, and the A-R-V crew were returning to their car.

Russ stepped forward noticing the Constables approaching and produced his warrant card.

"Regional Crime Squad. We've just arrested this man."

"What for, failing to give way?"

Russ ignored the attempt at humour and, instead, walked over to confer with the A-R-V crew.

At the same time, Clive and I came upon the scene. The arresting officer now held Mitchell as he watched the other detectives search his car. Clive and I walked across to observe. Passing the two Constables, I showed them my warrant card too, saying, "good morning gents. Would you do me a kindness, please, and divert any traffic away while we check out the suspect's vehicle?"

"Yes, Sir, of course. What's he nicked for?"

"Firearms offences. We shouldn't be long. I need a fifty-yard cordon front and back."

The two Constables eagerly carried out my instruction.

I was curious finally to be meeting Anthony Mitchell, the man my Abonar team had been so diligently investigating for almost six months. For a moment, I stood in the road a few feet away observing him as he waited at the open boot of his Mondeo. He looked his forty-five years. At around 5' 9" and puffy faced he was not an imposing man. However, his stocky build and thick neck gave him the appearance of being a bully. I now understood why Bown and Phillips had submitted to his demands they meet him at the gun club after his first arrest. His short fair hair explained why he had the nickname '*Blondie*', but it was receding, and the resulting high forehead only added to his thuggish look. He didn't have the appearance of the major gunrunner I had expected. He was certainly not what I imagined for someone who called himself a '*Black Shod*'. Instead, now standing in front of me, handcuffed with his head bowed, I saw all his vulnerabilities and human inadequacies exposed. My first impression was to think of him as almost not worthy of the huge efforts my incredible team had put into his arrest.

I stepped forward to see how he would react to me. The arresting officer acknowledged my arrival with a courteous, "Guv". Mitchell turned to look at me. His expression betraying his immediate interest in who the detective had deferred to. We exchanged glances. I held his stare and left him to blink first.

"Are you the man in charge?"

"Something like that, Tony, something like that," I told him.

"Can I know your name?"

"Right now, you don't need it. This is the arresting officer. He's the one you must pay attention to."

Mitchell looked at the badge on my warrant card now tucked into my jacket top pocket.

"Scotland Yard then?"

I chose not to give him the satisfaction of being right. Instead, I asked the detective searching the boot, "anything?"

"It's as good as empty, Guv. The one thing I've found and left in situ to get photographed is that lump of machined metal just there."

Taking my '*Maglite*' torch from my belt, I shone its beam where he pointed. It picked out a breech bolt for a MAC-10. As soon as the detective had taken a photograph, I reached in with my gloved hand and excitedly picked it up.

Watching me, Mitchell calmly stated, "it's deactivated".

I examined the machining. It was, and with the extractor set at ninety degrees, not the forty-five I wanted. '*Sugar, bloody, damn,*' I thought to myself. "Please log it and bag it anyway," I said to the Exhibits' Officer, "thanks."

Arthur had finally caught up and joined us. Summing up the scene, he said, "right, let's get Mitchell back to Baden Road. I want his car taken to Gatwick and thoroughly searched. Door panels off, floor linings out, the works. If you'd separate his car keys now from the rest, please, I'll take the others with me."

The arresting officer placed Mitchell in the rear left passenger seat of Arthur's unmarked car, and then got in the back alongside. Another detective got into Mitchell's and drove it away. Minutes later, we had cleared the road, leaving the two Constables to return to their patrol and a story to tell in the canteen.

Pulling up outside 30 Baden Road, Clive parked behind the car carrying Mitchell. As they saw us arrive, Marcus along with the detectives assigned to search the address started getting out of theirs. I walked over to where Mitchell was standing with Arthur.

"Can you get them to take these handcuffs off," he asked on seeing me.

"No, but maybe my colleague will bring your hands to the front while we're searching your home." The arresting officer followed my suggestion.

Naomi was understandably distraught at our presence as we came into the hallway. I was not surprised to see two packed suitcases just inside the front door ready for their departure.

DC Hughes and the arresting officer watched Mitchell for a reaction as we moved from room to room, starting upstairs. Having not found anything, and Mitchell not giving away any hint that we had missed something, we went downstairs to the lounge. I had only just invited Mitchell to sit and watch from an armchair when DC Hughes called out, "Guv, stop".

I went over to confer.

In a hushed voice, he said, "it's those papers DS Hurst is looking through."

I nodded to Myles. Taking a large plastic exhibits' bag, he then enthusiastically tipped a tall stack of mixed correspondence into it. He also scooped up another bunch of keys and dropped them into a separate bag. Looking back at Mitchell, I could see whatever Myles had found made him uneasy. We all then moved into the gun room.

"What's different since last time, Myles?" I asked.

"Well, for a start these three crates weren't here."

"So, let's begin with them."

Mitchell did not react as I opened the lids on each to reveal the contents. Instead, he calmly stated once again, "all legal and deactivated."

I inspected each gun and found they were and quite expertly done. Of relevance, though, to Abonar was that they were also of the exact same types recovered at Whitechapel, Plaistow and the Tollgate Hotel, in particular the M20s. DC Myers worked around us with his camera taking photographs. When Mitchell asked why we were bagging them up to take away, I chose to leave him guessing and not answer. I caught him studying my face. His expression suggested he'd now registered I was there as a specialist, and he nodded at me respectfully.

"Where did these come from?" Arthur asked Mitchell. "They weren't here before and they weren't in your workshop either. So where did you get them?"

"No comment."

"Did you deactivate them?"

"No comment."

"Your RFD authority was revoked in July," Arthur pointed out, "so where did you get these?"

"As I said the first time you arrested me; if you're going to interview me here and not at the police station, I want my solicitor present. Otherwise, no comment."

Myles bagged up a dispenser of brown packing tape as the only other item of relevance.

"Right, Mr Mitchell, we're going back to your workshop," Arthur announced.

"Arthur, Michael, I've seen enough," Marcus said as we left. "I'll be at Crawley if you need me. Good luck."

Once we arrived at the Knoll Business Centre, I watched Mitchell for a reaction as Myles unlocked his workshop door. Nothing. Clive keyed in the code he'd noted from before to silence the alarm. Mitchell shook his head, registering his own stupidity at not having changed it.

Inadvertently, I looked up at the light fitting to see if I could spot the covert camera. I was pleased not to. The arresting officer sat Mitchell on a stool in the only clear space available.

The other detectives waited while I surveyed the room checking the layout the covert camera had revealed as places of interest. Behind me was the lathe and sophisticated vertical milling machine Mitchell had been using. To my right against the wall were floor-to-ceiling shelves stacked with assorted lengths and thicknesses of bare metal. In front of me was the workbench. Beyond that against the far wall was the sandblasting machine. To my left was another shelving unit the same height as the other but stacked with a huge assortment of tools, pots, jars, and boxes. Summing it all up in my mind, it was clear Mitchell had everything he needed to both engineer component parts and prepare his firearms for nickel-plating. On the workbench, I spotted a new electric TIG welder. That alone told me he had not stopped working on firearms. Next to the bench were oxyacetylene tanks and a blowtorch for more industrial cutting and welding. I looked around at the sheer scale of the task ahead of us. It was daunting; particularly when we were looking for small as well as large component parts. I immediately understood why the first search in July might have missed essential evidence in this myriad of hiding places. That was not because it was an untidy mess, not at all. Mitchell had kept everything neatly stacked. There was just so much to examine.

I turned to my right and walked over to check a stack of assorted metals on the shelves.

"Guv, stop," DC Hughes alerted me.

I looked hard again at what Mitchell had seen me heading towards. Yes, here were the lengths of steel he would need to machine into his MAC-10 breech bolts but, in their raw state, they were of only limited evidential value. I had hoped what Mitchell had signalled was the hiding place for his finished ones but, sadly, not.

"DC Myers, photograph these in situ, please, with a ruler alongside for size comparison," I instructed.

I carried on checking for the tubing he needed for the MAC-10 barrels, but it was not there either. Whatever made Mitchell uncomfortable about me looking here, nothing I saw justified his alarm. I got DC Myers to photograph each shelf, so we could record of what Mitchell had in stock. Even if we did not recognise its relevance right now, we could always come back once we did.

Walking forwards, I looked to my left at the lower shelves. "Guv, stop," DC Hughes again alerted me.

Crouching down, I saw tucked away two large plastic crates on the bottom, one red the other yellow. I dragged them both out on to the floor. Each was extremely heavy, causing me to use more force to get them out, which told me immediately they contained guns. I looked at Mitchell for a reaction. He was staring, almost glaring back at me.

"Do you want to tell us what we're about to find?" Arthur asked him.

Mitchell's attitude changed to a shrug of resignation that we had found something important.

Lifting off a makeshift cover of blue towelling, I saw both contained rows of individually wrapped objects in white plastic carrier bags branded, '*SAMSON ARMS AND AMMUNITION*' in blue and red.

"DC Myers, please," I directed him to start photographing as I worked.

I lifted out the first bag randomly from the batch. It was heavy. I felt my heart pounding with excitement. I carried it over to the workbench to have a better look. Pulling the bag open revealed a MAC-10 submachine gun.

"They're deactivated," Mitchell said arrogantly, wanting me to think I was wasting my time. I chose to ignore him and carried on.

Carefully, I disassembled the weapon. Yes, it was deactivated, but it showed evidence of work being done to reactivate it. Mitchell had already welded in the new feed ramp and modified the grips to accept an Uzi magazine. He had also removed the sear to enable full-auto only. Lastly, he had removed the weld that would now allow the barrel assembly to slide out and the replacement to slot in. Disappointingly, the breech bolt was missing. All the springs he needed were attached to the deactivated one still in its place.

Returning to the crates, and now with Myles helping, I took out each bag and lined them up along the floor. One-by-one we unwrapped the MAC-10s and placed them on top of their plastic bags. I stripped and reassembled them in turn. Each had the SF Firearms markings that matched the Abonar finds. All still had their original serial numbers and deactivation stamps in exactly the places we had found the TIG welder marks on the Abonar MAC-10s. Some, but not all, still had the deactivated breech bolt in place, which were easy to lift out. As with the first one, Mitchell had obviously started work on many of them in readiness for his new breech bolt and barrel.

When Myles and I finished, we stood back to count the contents. In the first crate, Mitchell had forty complete MAC-10s ready to reactivate. In the second, were fifteen receivers with barrel assembly, and twenty frames incorporating the trigger mechanism and feed ramp. Next to the crates, I found a cardboard box branded '*Emerald Margarine*' into which Mitchell had put loose components. These combined with the contents of the second crate would enable him to assemble another fifteen complete MAC-10s. The assorted spare parts might make another five. In total, he was only days away from reactivating up to sixty live-firing MAC-10s. We had got to Mitchell just in time ahead of him flooding the criminal market with these fully functioning and easily concealable submachine guns.

"We'll take all of these, please. Myles, make them all your exhibits," I said as I turned to look at Mitchell again. "Where are your replacement breech bolts and barrels, Tony?"

He tried to maintain his disinterested expression, but I could tell he was rattled. Like a poker player, he was determined to keep a straight face from now on so as not to betray any weakness in his hand. I smiled and nodded hoping he'd sense I knew something he should be afraid of. It worked. His composure changed to unease. After nearly six months investigating Abonar, I was only too happy to see him looking so uncomfortable.

Turning to my right, I walked to the workbench. Again, I started on the bottom shelf. As I bent down, I froze for a moment to take in what was in front of me and smiled. It was a roll of cream-coloured mutton cloth just like the material the Abonar guns had been wrapped in. Next to it was a roll of blue industrial hand towel just like that used to wrap the BAR recovered at the Tollgate Hotel and the MAC-10s. I looked up at Mitchell, but he was now resolute in not giving anything away.

"We'll have these too, please," I said. "Photograph them in situ and then get them bagged and tagged."

Turning around, I walked to the sandblasting machine and looked in through its glass window. Mitchell didn't flinch. No alert. I was surprised. Surely, he would register something. After all, it was in this machine that he had prepared so many of his handguns for nickel-plating. I turned to look at him and, again, his face gave nothing away. "Sugar, bloody, damn," I said quietly to myself.

"Okay, photograph the sandblaster," I advised, trying not to show my disappointment. "Similarly, all the other heavy engineering kit we can't take with us. We'll take the portable TIG welder, though."

That concluded the search. While the others led Mitchell back to the car, I looked around the site. I was particularly interested in Unit 8, 'Lizzie's Wholesale Bakery'. Piled up ready to go in the recycle bins, someone had placed a stack of cardboard boxes branded 'Emerald Margarine'. As I picked one up, a woman's voice asked, "can I help you?"

I turned around to see who it was and, producing my warrant card, explained my interest.

"That's reassuring. I don't usually have people rummaging in my rubbish. I own the bakery. Yes, that margarine is only available wholesale for bakers like me."

Looking at Mitchell being placed back in the car, she added, "Tony often comes in asking if he can have the empty boxes. Says he finds them useful for sending things to his customers."

"Thank you," I said smiling at her helpful revelation. "If you don't mind, I'll ask one of the detectives to come over and get a statement from you."

"What's Tony done? You lot were here before, weren't you?"

"I'm sorry, but I'm not able to say very much right now other than we suspect him of firearms' offences."

I got back in the car with Clive to follow the others to Gatwick. As we pulled out of the car park, the TSU van drove past heading in to remove their covert equipment.

CHAPTER 67

Mitchell: Day 1

It had gone 1pm by the time we booked Michell into the Custody Suite at Gatwick Police Station and had then carried all the items seized up to our Incident Room. Seeing Arthur out in the corridor, I guided him into an adjoining empty office for a private chat.

"I'm not convinced from Graham's performance with Bown and Phillips that he's the right choice for interviewing Mitchell." I told him.

"Why's that?"

"Because Mitchell won't respond well to being challenged to confess his crimes to a man he'll consider a lesser adversary. We need to play to this man's ego. Graham won't do that. He'll just charge in with his usual, '*So how long have you been a gunrunner?*' routine"

"Mr Bagshaw wants him and Clive to do it, and that's how it's going to be."

"Okay, but I warn you, it won't go well."

Walking back into the Incident Room, Arthur announced, "right, Graham and Clive, I want you to take this interview in phases, okay?"

"Sure," Graham answered for them both.

"First, go back through everything Ackerman told us that Bown's now confirmed. Then go on to what Phillips told us about the three deliveries."

"Yup, that makes sense."

"Then take a break for a re-group up here before you move on to phase two."

"Okay, what do you have in mind for that?"

"Use the presentation material SO11 put together on the forensics and call data. If you haven't cracked him in phase one, I'm certain you will when he sees the weight of all that evidence."

"Is there a phase three?" Clive asked.

"Not sure yet. If the first two don't get him talking, we'll have a re-think up here. I suggest that's when you should put to him everything recovered from today's searches."

"Okay, DS Murphy and I will gather everything and head downstairs," Clive responded.

"I'll stay up here working through this pile of papers from his home," Myles commented, holding up the very full bag from Mitchell's lounge.

Arthur and I followed Graham and Clive downstairs to observe. They brought Mitchell through with his solicitor and took up the same positions as with Bown and Phillips. Exasperated, I watched as Graham performed his customary opening assault, followed by Mitchell's repeated, "no comment". I left Arthur to watch while I went back upstairs. To console my disappointment, I checked the exhibit bags for Mitchell's pager. I was delighted when the test confirmed it was Pager B.

Two hours later, Arthur, Graham and Clive returned. I knew from their expressions the interview had not got any better.

Graham spoke first, "bastard made no comment. We went through everything as planned, but nothing."

"Yeah," Clive added, "we gave him every chance to say what he'll be relying on as his defence, but zippo."

"We didn't get anywhere asking him about his garage at The Martlet either," Graham said glumly. "The team are just going to have to find it through good old fashioned detective work."

"Myles," Arthur interjected, "how are those house-to-house enquiries going?"

"I'm pissed off with the team," he replied, clearly annoyed. "They decided to have a long breakfast. So, by the time they started, most people had gone to work."

"What the…" Arthur began, but then realised it was pointless.

"Exactly," Myles commented. "I've told them they'll have to wait there until the neighbours come home. I don't care if they work late. I want the garage found."

"Myles," I asked, "anything amongst those papers to explain Mitchell's anxiety?"

"No, nothing yet. There are hundreds if not thousands of pages. I'm not about to make the same mistake, so I'm studying every one."

"How did he react to hearing Bown and Phillips had betrayed him?" I asked Graham.

"It shook him but, sadly, not enough to make him talk."

"In the next interview, exploit that betrayal," I advised. "Chip away at his vanity. Remember, he's a conceited sod. Keep firing at him what Ackerman,

Bown and Phillips have told you. Hopefully, it'll make him so angry, he'll say something in retaliation."

"We can try, Guv," Graham said dismissively while looking at Clive for a reaction.

"Stroke his ego too," I told them. "Don't forget, Mitchell's very proud of his expertise as a gunsmith. Talk about his obvious skills. Exploit his arrogance. Try and get inside his head that way."

Graham muttered, "psychobabble," and I could tell he was dismissing my more empathetic approach as not worth trying.

Myles chucked Clive the bag containing the keys he'd scooped up with the papers, saying, "Would you ask him about these too?"

Clive snatched them from the air and confirmed, "from the lounge today, yes?"

Arthur and I followed them downstairs again to the viewing room. As before, they repeated their old-style, adversarial interviewing technique. Unlike Scotland Yard detectives, they had not yet benefited from the new investigative skills training that the Canadian Mounties had pioneered.

"Arthur, this isn't working. They must play to his ego."

"Not their style, Michael. They know all they have to do is give Mitchell one chance to say what happened. The judge will do the rest if he doesn't. He'll direct the jury that Mitchell failed to mention when interviewed whatever he later relies on in court as his defence."

"That may be so, but we have a duty to find out who his customers are and stop them killing more people with the guns he's sold them."

"Noble idea, but I sense that's not going to happen."

Frustrated again, I left the room to go upstairs and help Myles.

He was surrounded by the papers he'd now separated into piles on the desk.

"Anything?" I asked optimistically.

"A few things, yes. Nothing earth shattering just yet. I'll let you know once I'm done."

An hour later, Graham, Clive and Arthur returned looking exasperated.

"I saw your opening launch," I told Graham. "So I know what happened. Another 'no comment' interview," I told him in a deliberately chastising manner.

"If you think you can do any better, Guv, perhaps you should have a go yourself," he retaliated.

"I wish I could, but your bosses and mine won't allow it."

Knowing it was late and I didn't have the appetite for a confrontation, I said, "let's stop for tonight. We'll chat tomorrow over a posh brew before you try again. It might seem 'psychobabble', Graham but when you talk to him again, I insist you stroke Mitchell's ego. You're not getting his cooperation with your old-style adversarial approach."

"To be honest, Guv, I don't really care," he told me forthrightly. "He can't fight the facts. He's had his chance to set the record straight. I say we just charge him now."

I noted Arthur had decided not to intervene, so I carried on. "Well, Sergeant, we're not doing that. Instead, we're calling it a day now. We still haven't found the barrels and breech bolts for the MAC-10s, and I'm not giving up until we do." Looking at him directly to reinforce I was pulling rank, "I want you and Clive to put Mitchell into his '*eight-hour rest period*' until the morning. I'll ask DCI Bagshaw to get the Superintendent to authorise extending detention for at least thirty-six hours. Now would you go and tell the Custody Officer that's our plan!"

With that, the two left the room, obviously unhappy but knowing I was right.

"I can't be here tomorrow," Arthur then announced as they left. "Long-standing family commitment. I'll leave it to you to run the show. Cheers." With that he walked out the room to follow the others downstairs, while I stared dumfounded at his departing back.

Regaining my composure, I turned to Myles, "it's gone 8pm, can you call the house-to-house team and find out how they're getting on, please?"

"I'll do that in a moment. Right now, I want to show you everything I've found."

He set out the papers he had selected, elatedly laying them down like a card player revealing his winning hand.

"I'll start with this one, Guv. A photograph of Mitchell's motorbike outside an open garage at The Martlet. Next, a load of deactivation certificates for what the Proof House called Tokarevs, plus MABs, and some MAC-10s."

I looked through them as he added, "here's the renewal for his renting Unit W11 at the Knoll Business Centre too. And what you're really going to like are these invoices. They're from *Samson* for thousands of rounds of 9mm ammunition, including the blue-tipped ones."

"Well done, Myles. Well done. Look, why don't you take that photo of the motorbike and compare it on-site with the block of garages Bown and Phillips pointed out. Hopefully, it will be obvious from it which one is Mitchell's."

"I'm on my way," he said excitedly.

"Call me when you've got a result. I have to wait here for Clive, as he's dropping me back to my car at Crawley."

CHAPTER 68

The Martlet Garage

It was 10pm before I set off for the final leg home to Hampton Wick. As I pulled out of the Crawley car park, my mobile rang. I answered it to hear an excited Myles tell me, "we've found the garage, Guv, and it's a real Aladdin's cave. The keys were on that bunch Mitchell was so concerned about that I found in his lounge. I could do with your help here, please, to identify exactly what we've got."

"Okay, I'm just leaving Crawley, so you're going to have to give me directions."

Forty minutes later, I drove through the entrance to The Martlet housing estate and round the back to a block of garages. The flashes from the camera being used by DC Myers guided me the final few yards. Myles was on his knees surrounded by forensic packaging materials and some very significant exhibits.

"Ah, Guv, glad you found the place. First, here's another roll of the mutton cloth already cut into strips."

My quick examination confirmed they were identical to the Abonar wrappings.

"Next, another '*Emerald*' brand margarine box with two more Smith & Wesson revolvers."

I checked them both. They had been refinished in matt nickel-plate, with their serial numbers obliterated using the TIG welder. I removed the grips and, once again, Mitchell had scratched into the frames his hallmark three-letter Cyrillic code.

"Now, you were looking for these, I believe," the excitement in his voice was very evident. "We've got sixty short lengths of smooth bore steel tubing in what I assume is 9mm. I think these are your missing MAC-10 barrels."

"Oh my goodness. Myles, they are," I said examining a couple. "Just as we suspected, he was very close to completing the reactivations."

"Not sure when he did all this," Myles added, "as the tracker didn't pick him up coming here."

"Maybe he made them all at the very start and has been adding them incrementally as and when he'd finished the other work."

"Maybe, maybe. Oh, and I found more silencers, albeit like Bown's, not yet painted black," and he passed me another exhibits' box.

"Yup, they're the ones. What else?"

"Have a look at what's in this '*Emerald*' box. It's gun barrels but rifled this time. Fourteen of them."

Picking them out to check, I confirmed, "so we've got seven here for MABs; four for the M20s or Tokarevs, and these last three are replacements for Smith & Wessons."

Walking to the rear of the garage, Myles pulled back a cover to expose a metal toolchest just like the one Bown had described. Lifting the lid he showed me another thousand rounds of the blue-tipped 9mm ammunition in their blue and white '*Samson*' boxes.

I moved around the garage carefully looking in every container and corner for where Mitchell could have hidden more evidence of his gun-making.

"Lost something?" Myles asked amused by my fussing.

"Not lost, Myles, can't find. Where are Mitchell's MAC-10 breech bolts?"

"Sorry Guv, I looked but they're not here."

"That means we've run out of options. Sugar, bloody, damn!" I said loudly to help vent my frustration.

"Yes, it's a bugger, isn't it?"

"Yes, it bloody well is Myles. Their continuing absence makes it even more important Graham and Clive change their approach with Mitchell. If not, we're never going to find them."

"Good luck with that. Those two old leopards will never change their spots."

"Well, they've got to, Myles. They've bloody well got to."

When we finished photographing, logging, and packaging everything, my watch told me it had gone 2am. I looked over at Myles and, like me, he was exhausted.

CHAPTER 69

Mitchell: Day 2

Saturday, 18th October

I managed around three hours sleep before I was back in the car heading to Gatwick for our agreed 8:30am start. It seemed so stark leaving and coming home to an empty house each day. Trying to disguise it by leaving lights on only added to the upsetting experience of coming home. As it was also the weekend, I missed the sounds of my daughter in the house. Again, I promised myself I would take a few days' leave as soon as Abonar was over and spend some meaningful time with her.

There were now only four of us working actively on Abonar. As promised, I took Graham, Myles and Clive for a briefing over a posh brew. Having found a table at the airport staff cafeteria, I began gently by asking, "so, Graham and Clive, given what Myles found last night, it's critical you work on Mitchell to tease out of him the whole story. I want you to be conciliatory and empathetic. More inquisitorial than adversarial. Yes?"

"Look Guv," Graham reacted gruffly, "that may work for you, but I've found confronting suspects with the facts saves an awful lot of time." Looking at Clive for agreement, he continued, "no jury wants to listen to a load of nonsense questions about the defendant's outlook on life and career in crime. They just want to know, did he do it, yes or no." Turning now to Myles for support, he added, "from what you found last night, it really doesn't matter whether Mitchell talks or not. Any jury will convict him. I recommend we charge him now, and then we can at least have Sunday off."

I saw Myles shrug supportively, so I firmly told them, "No. Absolutely not. I want you to ease out of Mitchell where he's hidden the missing breech bolts."

"Why's that so important to you, Guv?" Graham asked, as if finding them wasn't necessary.

"It's not just the icing on the cake for my Abonar investigation, if that's what you think. It's because they're interchangeable parts with other MAC-10s. Guy Savage deactivated loads of his, and they're the same pattern as Perkins's. That means Mitchell's breech bolts will fit those ones too. If we don't find them, and Mitchell tells someone where they are, that person will carry on reactivating MAC-10s."

"Well that certainly is a risk," Graham said, now in a conciliatory tone. "But Mitchell doesn't want to talk. I say we put to him what Myles found in the garage, and that'll be the end of it."

I could have pulled rank again, but turned to Myles hoping, as an aspiring DI, he'd say something to support me. "Myles, what do you think we should do?"

"I get why you want Mitchell to talk, Guv, but I sense Graham's right. I interviewed him the first time in July. He's arrogant, which means he won't give us the satisfaction of confessing to any of his criminality. I think Graham and Clive should question him about what we found in the garage, and then we charge him regardless."

"Okay, I also sense you want that because you're exhausted and need a day off too."

"Yes, Guv, that would be nice, wouldn't it?"

"Yes, I'd like one too."

Now turning to Clive, I asked, "so, what do you think?"

"One last interview and then we charge him," he told me without hesitation.

I sat back realising for the first time how uncomfortable the hard plastic canteen chair was to sit in. I was outnumbered three-to-one, with no authority to interview Mitchell myself, so I conceded, "okay, gents, have it your way. Give it your best shot."

Graham and Clive smiled, obviously looking forward to the sport of confronting Mitchell again.

The Gatwick Superintendent had extended Mitchell's custody to the full 36 hours, so we had until 1am on Sunday to finish. I took my seat in the viewing room with Myles and waited for the performance to begin. Clive had placed all the exhibits from the garage on the floor.

"So, Mitchell," Graham began, "last night we found the garage your mates Bown and Phillips told us was yours at The Martlet. As you can see, right little treasure trove you left for us."

"Oh not again, Graham!" I shouted, angered by his opening attack. Nevertheless, I decided to stay and watch.

"What have you got to say about all these new bits of evidence, then?" Clive asked, taking over. "I'd say they confirm you've been making and supplying illegal firearms along with ammunition. The sixty barrels show you've been reactivating MAC-10s too. But, saying that, I'm interested to hear your side of the story. So what have you got to say?"

"No comment"

And so it continued, with Graham and Clive going through the items individually and getting the same reply. I was actually grateful when Graham announced he was about to terminate the interview. "Okay, Mr. Mitchell. We've asked all the questions, so now it's your turn. Is there anything you'd like to ask us before we close?"

Defiantly he replied, "you know you told me Phillips said he'd been to the garage. Have you considered that everything you found is actually his and not mine? I don't suppose you'd thought of that have you? So, before you try and stitch me up with all his gear, I suggest you talk to him again."

Graham and Clive ignored the challenge and ended the interview.

"Okay, I watched it all, so I know how it went. No surprises with the result," I told them, trying hard not to do so in an '*I told you so manner*'. "That just leaves us to review all the evidence and work out what to charge him with."

I cleaned the whiteboards in our Incident Room and began to number and list the evidence. Thankfully, everyone contributed to the exercise and Myles copied it all into a document on his laptop. After an hour, I stepped back to review what we had amassed against Mitchell.

With some satisfaction I said to the others, "bloody good work guys. We've got him bang to rights on all these. There's enough to convince any jury he's the Abonar source. Let's go and charge him."

The team pushed back their chairs and stood up, eager to get downstairs and finish the job.

Myles let me know, "I got all that distilled ready to go into the CPS case file. Whoever prosecutes will need it. They'll want an idea of the picture on the lid of the Abonar jigsaw puzzle box."

I turned to have one last look at the whiteboards before leading the others out of the room. "Shame we didn't recover the breech bolts," I commented.

"You've done the best you could, Guv," Myles said sympathetically. "With what we've got here, Mitchell is going away for a very, very long time. As an accessory to murder, he should get life."

I stood behind the Custody Officer as Mitchell entered the Charge Room. His solicitor whispered that he was about to be charged. I looked directly at him as the Sergeant read out each of the nine offences.

Mitchell stood looking defiant as the Sergeant finished and cautioned him. "Right Mr Mitchell," he told him. "The DI here has convinced me to deny you bail. You'll remain in custody for court on Monday."

Mitchell looked straight at me. His expression betraying anger but also a hint of vulnerability at the prospect of being locked up in prison.

I seized the moment. "Tony," I began gently, holding his gaze, "while you're sitting in your cell waiting for whatever happens to you on Monday, think on this. I'm here to see we get justice for the many victims of your gunrunning and stop there being anymore."

The tension from when he was being charged seemed to lift from his face, so I continued. "The law allows you an opportunity now to talk to us when three rules apply. One, when it's absolutely necessary to prevent or minimise harm to others. Two, to clarify an ambiguity in one of your interviews. And three, give you one final chance to comment on information that comes to light when it's in the interests of justice that you do so. Do you understand?"

He nodded back.

"With all the weaponry you've supplied over the years that we know is still out there, all three of these apply to you."

Again, he nodded with an expression that told me he was thinking about what I had just told him.

I finished by playing to his ego, saying, "Tony, I've seen the quality of your workmanship as a high-class gunsmith, and I think you want someone other than a jury to appreciate your skills. I'd be happy to listen to you."

Turning to leave and so that Mitchell would hear, I said to the Custody Officer, "Skip, I'll be upstairs for another couple of hours finalising the case papers. My colleagues will top and tail matters down here with fingerprints and photograph. Do let me know if Tony wants anything."

CHAPTER 70

Mitchell's Epiphany

Myles was the first to join me upstairs. "You must be happy enough with those nine charges, Guv."

"I am but I'd be a whole lot happier if Mitchell takes the bait and now talks to me."

"I don't think he will."

"Well, I hope what I said plays on his conscience. He is an ex-Special after all."

Graham and Clive joined us a few minutes later.

"How is he?" I asked.

"Quiet," Clive replied.

Together, we worked on putting together the case file. It was nearly 9pm. I was beginning to look forward to having Sunday at home and then being back in my own office on Monday. My thoughts were interrupted by the phone ringing over in the corner. Myles answered it.

"Guv, Mitchell wants to talk to the officer in charge."

"Did he ask for me by name?"

"No, only '*the officer in charge*', and by my reckoning that's you."

Graham glared at me suspiciously. As I left the room, I heard his voice but not the words he spoke. He sounded angry and surprised. I went downstairs alone and cleared it with the Custody Officer to speak with Mitchell through the open hatch in the cell door.

"Yes, Tony, how can I help you?"

He got up from the bed and walked over, bending down slightly to look at me through the hatch.

"You know, you're the only person who's called me by my first name. Thank you for the courtesy. Will you tell me yours?"

"Yes, it's Michael."

"Thank you, Michael. And you're a DI from Scotland Yard, aren't you?"

"Yes."

"Um, which branch?"

"Let's just say Specialist Operations."

"And you're the officer in charge?"

"Right now, yes. You asked to see me. How can I help?"

"I want to talk to you but without my solicitor, and on your own."

"That's a little unorthodox Tony. I'll need you to confirm it in writing on the custody record."

"Of course. Can you get me out and we can talk in the interview room?"

The Sergeant wrote out the necessary certificate on the custody record and Mitchell signed it. I asked the Gaoler to bring us two teas and some sachets of sugar, which he then did. On leaving us, he told me, "I'll be just outside, Sir."

I broke open the plastic seals around the first of two cassette tapes ready to load them into the '*Neal*' recorder.

"Michael, please, no tapes," Mitchell said firmly.

"Tony, as you well know, the convention is I record our conversation."

"No tapes. I want to tell you everything, but no tapes."

"Okay, I'm here to listen to whatever you want to say." I was now torn between wanting him to talk and knowing I had to follow procedure. "Yes, Tony," I continued, "but you'll remember from your days as a Special, I must caution you first. And, if we're not taping it, I'll need to make contemporaneous notes. For both our sakes, we need some form of reliable record. Agreed?"

"Yes," he conceded, "you can take notes."

I opened my daybook and put my pen down on the table before adding, "and you do realise whatever you tell me now may need to be repeated later on tape?"

"Yes, and if that happens, I can decide whether to make no comment; say you got it all wrong, or something else."

I stopped myself from smiling at his extraordinary arrogance and quickly read out the caution from the laminated card stuck to the desktop. Looking at Mitchell's face, I could see he was in turmoil about where to begin.

"Okay, Tony, let me start. I've been to the Royal Armouries' Pattern Room where they've got one of your MAC-10s along with every other subsequent variant of the Ingram. That's quite an achievement getting yours in there. Your design is unique. Arguably, it's the best there is."

"Yes, and that's all due to my breech bolt with the extractor cut at forty-five degrees. And did you see how I welded in a new feed ramp and modified the grips to accept the much better Uzi magazine?"

"Yes, we did." I replied, now realising I was right about his ego, and he was keen to let me stroke it. So I continued, "and that combination means your MAC-10, unlike the others, never jams."

"Absolutely right, Michael. It's bloody perfect."

"Well, it certainly proves your worth as one of the best gunsmiths I've met," I commented, deliberately enticing him to say more.

"Thank you. I take great pride in my craftsmanship. It's nice to have it recognised."

"What are you most proud of, Tony?"

"Well, the MAC-10 of course, but I've done a great job bringing new life to those Smith & Wessons, MABs, Colts, and other tired old guns. What did you make of my silencers?"

"Very efficient."

"Thank you, yes. I've found my design is almost completely silent."

"Terrifying, though, for the person on the wrong end."

"That's why you need an expertly designed silencer. It gives the shooter the ultimate level of surprise."

"True, but lethal," I said now feeling uncomfortable about releasing his demons, but knowing I had to keep drawing the story out of him. "Where did you test them?"

"Oh, at the gun club using one of my MABs."

"And the rangemaster didn't challenge you?"

"Why should he? He knows I'm a gunsmith and RFD. I'm quite entitled to test my workmanship there."

"And that perfect MAC-10 breech bolt, Tony, I'm disappointed we didn't find any."

He smiled mischievously and shrugged his shoulders.

"Does that mean you didn't make them?"

"No, Michael, no," he replied instantly. "I made them alright on my milling machine. I've got the dimensions programmed in, so producing them is virtually automated."

"One flaw in your design was you chose not to rifle the barrels. Why was that?"

"It's not a flaw," he answered petulantly. "Why would I waste time doing that? The MAC-10 is for close quarters combat, which is fifteen yards max. It'll hit anything within that range regardless of whether the barrel is rifled or smooth?"

He stopped as he noticed my expression change to shock as I recalled Brockwell Park and what that meant for the victims. I decided to change the subject, "I'm surprised, Tony, why you chose to supply the criminal market."

"I only agreed to sell off-ticket guns because the client said they were part of a scam to con the Home Secretary into releasing prisoners early." Like Phillips, he said this as if it was a perfectly justifiable reason. "Since none of my guns nor the ammo would ever be used in crime, I thought it was all very acceptable to have them recovered by the police and get paid."

"Do you know who these prisoners were? Were they John Haase and Paul Bennett?"

"No, I never knew their names. All he told me was they were two big-time Liverpool drug dealers, and they needed a favour to get their sentences reduced when they came to trial. He also told me they were on remand at Full Sutton Prison."

"Who told you?"

"The guy who arranged it all."

"Who?"

"Someone I knew at the gun club made the introduction. I never actually met the guy who took them to Liverpool. He paged me and I called him back from a phone box so he couldn't trace me." Leaning back in his chair and putting both hands behind his head, he went on, "I left whatever he wanted behind the bins at the gun club to collect, which was where he also left me the cash. Neat really, as he never knew who I was, and I didn't need to know him. Both totally anonymous to each other."

"Who made the introduction?"

"Sorry, Michael, but I'm not ready to give you that just yet." He took his hands down to rest them on the table as he leaned forward saying, almost menacingly, "like the guys in Full Sutton, I may want to trade names for a favour. You'll have to wait until I work out what it'll be."

I felt uncomfortable allowing him to get any nearer, so I leaned back gently to create some distance and asked, "why did you go to the trouble of adding so much ammunition?"

"He asked me to. He said it would look convincing to the police that way. That the guns really were for some criminal end-user, and not just deliberately left to be discovered."

"That was quite a scam you were part of, and it even fooled the Home Secretary."

Laughing he said, "yes, but then it all went quiet after that Liverpool job. I was suddenly holding a load of stock with no customers." He paused and smiled, adding, "so, I was very happy to renew the arrangement a few months later when the guy came back asking me to do it all over again. Easy money, and no risks, or so I thought."

"So, those three most recent finds at Whitechapel, Plaistow and the Tollgate Hotel. Who were they for?"

"Well, I didn't know where the first two ended up. Nothing was in the papers or on the news. I only found out what happened to the third when Bob showed me an article in his local paper."

"Who were they all for, Tony?"

"Another inmate at the same prison as before."

"And his name?"

Mitchell hesitated.

"So you do know his name, Tony? Your face tells me you do."

"Yes, but like the others, I'm going to hold on to it for now. Sorry, Michael, but his name is worth something as collateral. When the moment's right, I'll want to trade it in. This isn't the right time."

"We know it's Fred Donovan from Manchester. We know he's got a family friend in Eltham, along with Kieran Walshe at the gun club who you were paging and calling to arrange everything."

Mitchell smiled as he contemplated how to respond.

"Tony, I can see it in your face," I told him, knowing I needed to keep pushing him. "Once again, it's telling me your customer was Fred Donovan and Kieran Walshe was one of his arrangers. Those are the names, aren't they?"

"I'm not ready to confirm either way," he said, leaning back and placing his hands behind his head once more. "As I told you, I don't yet know what they're worth to me." And then moving forward slightly, he added, "but I can tell they're worth a lot to you."

"Tony, they'll have no value whatsoever if someone else talks before you do. I suggest you get in first and maximise the benefits for yourself right now. And you can give me the name of the middleman in Eltham as well."

He leaned a little further forward and quietly replied, "I get your frustration, Michael, but no, I'll take my chance. When I'm ready, I'll ask to speak to you personally."

"Make sure you do, Tony; I'll be waiting."

"You know Michael, I was playing a game with you all," he then announced arrogantly, as he reclined once more. "I wanted you to know about my craftsmanship as a gunsmith. There was nothing in the papers or on the news, and it disappointed me. That's why I added the MAC-10s and silencers to the third package. I knew they'd do the trick to get people talking about my workmanship and, clearly, they did."

Trying not to sound irritated by his conceit, I said, "yes, Tony, they certainly got our attention."

"I also needed to up the money they were paying me, you see. I couldn't envisage the scam going on forever. I mean how many more government officials and Ministers could these prison inmates continue to fool?"

"But Tony, you were selling off-ticket guns well before the Liverpool scam."

"You don't want to believe everything that fucking snake John Ackerman said about me."

"But you told your Black Shod mate, Bob Bown, that you'd supplied hundreds of guns well before that first scam and since. You must have known they were going to dangerous gangland criminals. What was that all about?"

"Money. That's all. Nothing more than money." Lowering his hands back down to the table, he went on, "sitting here now, yes, I regret it. I blame John for persuading me to get involved. He cheated on me with his phoney money, and that's when I sent Bob instead."

"How much did you charge?"

"Oh, between £400 and £600 per handgun, and up to £1,200 for each MAC-10. The ammunition and silencers would command additional prices. Similarly, I could charge more for adding a barrel extension with a screw thread and silencer."

"Bob said you told him you'd made a quarter of a million from all this. Is that right?"

He laughed and with a deceitful smile replied, "no, no. I was bragging. I've made less than ten percent of that."

"Your smile suggests Bob got it about right, Tony."

Defensively he reacted sharply, "look, I had lost my job at Longley's and was running short of cash. If that hadn't happened, perhaps I wouldn't have got into this. That's how it was, and I regret it."

I let him continue thinking on that point. I chose not to ask anything in the hope he would fill the silence with more admissions of regret, and he did.

"I also know my stupid pride probably led you to me?"

"How so?"

"You said it yourself, I'm a skilled engineer and gunsmith. I couldn't help myself with wanting to prove that. I needed everyone to see the quality of my work. I couldn't let some tatty old guns turn up." Leaning towards me again, he continued, "I had a reputation to protect. I knew I had to convince you the guns recovered were for a real end-user and not just scrap. That's why I had so many refinished in nickel-plate." Then sounding pleased with himself, he added leaning back again, "I also got a lot more money for them in that condition."

"Of course," I said to indicate interest despite having my head down writing my notes.

"Yeah, I thought I'd disguised my enterprise by building up a legitimate deactivation business alongside. I was very good at it. That's why Ralston Arms sent me so much work. I bet you haven't worked out how I did it, though?"

"I'm listening Tony," I replied, still hiding my irritation as it was paying dividends.

"Well, it meant tricking the Proof House into believing each gun I deactivated was a new submission, but most were clones. *And they never noticed.*"

"Clones? I've not heard that term before. What's a clone?"

"It's simple, effective, but time consuming for me. It works like this." He suddenly became animated with his hands as if working on a gun to illustrate each point. "I'd take a few guns from a box of live-firing ones sent over by Ralston Arms and deactivate them to the legal standard. I'd then give them to Bob to deliver to the Proof House for stamping and certification. When they came back, I'd mill out their serial numbers and deactivation marks; weld new metal into those areas and refinish the surface." Smiling he went on, "I then stamped them with the serial numbers from others I hadn't deactivated and resubmitted them."

"That's a lot of work."

"Yep, and that's how I created dozens of clones. The best ones to work on were the Tokarevs."

"So, let me just check my understanding. Bob then took them back to the Proof House, each now stamped with a serial number borrowed from a still live-firing gun in your possession as if they were first-time submissions."

"Yes, that's it exactly, Michael, and the staff never realised. They stamped them again and issued another deactivation certificate." He laughed at the effectiveness of his deception. "My workmanship was so good they never spotted it. I could submit the same gun up to three times. That's when it became too difficult to hide what I was doing to clone them."

"Wow, that's ingenious," I said, genuinely shocked by his revelation. "So what happened to all the ones you hadn't deactivated?" I then asked.

"I'd use the TIG welder to obliterate their serial numbers. I'd add a few more touches to make it look like the Proof House's deactivation stamp had been removed too. That way," he continued smugly, "if anyone was to recover the number forensically, I could claim it left my hands properly deactivated. Someone else must have reactivated it afterwards. I kept the Proof House certificates to prove it just in case."

"But you left the pistols you call Tokarevs with their original rifled barrel, which meant they couldn't have been reactivated."

"Yes, but I assumed from the Cyrillic markings I put on the frames and cloths you'd think they'd been smuggled in with replacement barrels. I thought you'd think the same about all the others I didn't have time to work on beyond removing their serial numbers and armourer's marks."

"We realised very quickly your Cyrillic markings were an elaborate smokescreen."

"Oh, you did," his voice betraying obvious disappointment. "Oh. I spent hours doing that, and you worked it out quickly. How?"

"I'm not going to tell you now Tony," I said, letting my pleasure show.

"Well, anyway," he continued, "when the Liverpool job finished, I was happy to let John take as much of the surplus as he could find customers for. It was him who put the guns on the street, not me. I only hope you've charged him and Bob with all that."

"You're all charged as co-conspirators, Tony."

"Oh really," he replied, clearly surprised and indignant at the prospect.

"We recovered one of your so-called Tokarevs in Tottenham a few weeks back used in a kidnap. You see, Tony, for all your pride, ingenuity and craftsmanship, there are real-life consequences for the victims of your trade."

"That is as maybe, Michael, but I'm just the craftsman," he replied dismissively. "I'm not the guy who sells them on. I'm not the one who puts the gun in the hands of the criminal who uses it. That's someone else, not me. Not guilty."

"And then there's the murder of Devon Dawson, killed with one of your MAC-10s."

"Is that what the last charge is all about?"

"Yes, and it makes you an accessory to his murder. Once we find the one used in a quadruple murder in Brockwell Park, you'll be charged with those too."

"Oh. Oh well, we'll have to see," and his expression showed that bothered him.

"So how many off-ticket guns have you sold?"

"Around six hundred. Most of them, though, went towards the scam to get the Home Secretary to reduce those prison sentences."

"The total recovered in Liverpool was one hundred and fifty, Tony, and we got sixty-five back in the latest one. What happened to the other four hundred or so?"

"Gone elsewhere."

"Where?"

"More collateral for another day, Michael, not now."

"What did you tell Ralston Arms you'd done with the ones you hadn't returned?"

"We had an informal arrangement whereby they allowed me to sell them as part-payment for my deactivation work."

"And the Thompsons and BAR?"

"The same. I got those originally for the Liverpool scam, but the guy didn't want them. He told me he needed more modern guns." Smiling again, he went on, "he wasn't happy when I slipped in one or two Thompsons along with some other surplus wartime guns, Brens and the like. Hence, I was stuck with the BAR and another Thompson." He paused to think before continuing. "Yeah, unfortunately, I trusted Bob with the latter. He loved all that Second World War stuff. I finally managed to offload the BAR and get some money for it when I put it in with the ones found at the Tollgate Hotel. I was glad to be rid of it quite frankly."

"Have you got any more, Tony?"

"No, you've successfully cleared me out now." And leaning back again with his hands behind his head, he added, "I thought I had time to finish the MAC-10s, and then that would have been it for good."

"Tony, for it really to be the end of it, you need to tell me about your customers. A complete list of names, contact details, and dates. If not, like the murder of Devon Dawson, every time one of your guns turns up with your unique hallmarks, you're going to be charged with supplying it."

"I do understand why you want me to give you names. I know it's because you want my help in getting the guns back. But I'm not ready to do that today. You'll understand, I too will want to do a deal to get my own sentence reduced."

He paused before saying excitedly, "tomorrow, Michael, as a sign of my goodwill, I want to show you something really big."

"Like what?"

"Something really, really big I know you want to find."

"How big? Big guns, big weapons? What?"

"Big, that's all you need to know. If you take me out in the morning, I'll show you."

"Tony, you're now a high-risk prisoner. You have customers who will no doubt want you silenced. They might even use one of your guns. I can't just take you out without knowing exactly where we're going and what it is you want to show me."

"Okay, okay. It's AK47s and somewhere you've been before."

"Where?"

"Hove." He then feigned a yawn. "Look, I'm tired and entitled to my rest period. Thank you for recognising my craftsmanship. It means a lot to me. Now if you don't mind, I'm done for the night."

I finished by getting him to read through my pages of notes and signing them as an accurate record of our conversation. Having explained to the night-duty Custody Officer the rather unconventional approach to the interview, she countersigned the notes too. I watched as Mitchell was led back to his cell.

As I left the Custody Suite, Graham, Myles and Clive were waiting in the corridor.

"We were in the viewing room, Guv. Saw and heard it all," Graham said, before pausing a moment. "Well done," and he smiled as he went on to say, "shame he wants to play games over the names."

"And he's as good as given you Donovan, which kiboshes his chances of early release," Clive commented looking happy too. "And he's admitted to being involved in the Liverpool scam."

"I expect you'd like us back in the morning to help you retrieve whatever it is that's 'something really big' he wants to give you," Myles added nodding with respect.

"Yes, and I better phone Mr Bagshaw too and let him know. Back here tomorrow at 8:30 please," I told them.

CHAPTER 71

Mitchell: Day 3 – "Something Really Big"

Sunday, 19ᵗʰ October

Once again, I had only a few hours to get home and sleep before returning to Gatwick. Whilst I had become accustomed to the empty house, I missed the humdrum of Rebecca being there and my checking whether she was asleep. I loved it when she rolled over and smiled. It told me she knew I was watching over her. Losing those precious moments as I came home late and went out early only added to my anger at Olivia's betrayal.

On the way back to Gatwick, I phoned Marcus to update him, and he agreed to meet me later at the police station. Having parked the car, I walked into the building and upstairs to our temporary office. Finding none of the others in yet, I went down to the Custody Suite and chatted with the Gaoler while he made me a cup of coffee. The Custody Officer joined us to advise that Mitchell wanted to phone his girlfriend. Before I left the previous night, I had warned the Sergeant to blank anyone who telephoned asking about Mitchell's welfare and not to let him call home, and they had done just that. I waited until Marcus joined us before going with him to see Mitchell in his cell.

"I hear you'd like to call Naomi?" Marcus asked after I made the introductions.

"Yes, I do."

"Well you can, but I'm conscious we need to protect you. As Michael has told you, you're now a high-risk prisoner. We need to make sure no one gets to you." Holding Mitchell's stare, he went on, "we think once your former gangland customers hear of your arrest, they'll want to make sure you don't talk. That means you need to warn Naomi not to speak to anyone too. Is that clear?"

"Yes. Can she come and see me?"

"Yes, and that would help me, as I want to speak to you both about going into 'Witness Protection'. Do you understand what that means?"

"Yes, something like you're going to change our identities and we'll have to live a whole new life elsewhere."

"That's about it, Tony, but only once you've served whatever sentence your barrister can negotiate. You'll also have to cooperate with us fully and plead guilty at court."

"I need to talk to Naomi before I can agree to anything like that," he said hesitatingly. "This is going to affect her too. As I said to Michael last night, I'm not yet ready to cut a deal. That doesn't mean I'm not interested in hearing what you can offer."

"Yeah, but first, we're going to get you out of your cell and interview you on tape," Marcus told him firmly. "I want to go over everything again you told Michael last night."

"That's okay with me as long as you don't expect me to do it with those two clowns again."

"Mr Mitchell, I'll decide who interviews you," he said sternly.

The Gaoler closed the cell door and I walked with Marcus into the Custody Office. As we passed an empty room, he said, "Michael, a private word," and pushed the door open for us to go inside.

"Guv?"

"I had a call last night from DS Murphy. As you can imagine, he's just a bit pissed off with you speaking to Mitchell without him and Clive. I understand why you went ahead without them, though. I even told him you were right to do so. It's also evident from what happened, you did a great job getting Mitchell to talk. Well done."

"Thank you, and thanks for letting me know about Graham and Clive. What will you do now about the follow-up interview with Mitchell?"

"You know he's right. I can't risk putting him back in the room with them. Chances are, he'll clam up, and that'll destroy any hope of further cooperation."

"Yup, I agree, and we do need him to confirm on tape everything he told me."

"Yes, but you can't do it either. You've already put me in a difficult position with Brian. I told him I'd keep you out of the evidence trail, so you wouldn't appear in court. Now you're pivotal to getting Mitchell to confess, your day in court is guaranteed."

"Ah, yes, but I'm hoping you can tell Brian it was unavoidable."

"I can, but you can't do the interview either. DS Hurst and I will do it instead."

"Fine, that's a good compromise. I imagine Mitchell will be happy with that too."

"Don't you worry about him," he said curtly. "What I want from you, though, is to keep him thinking you're now his new best friend. I'm as keen as you are to find out what he wants to show us, so for now, I'm prepared to make some exceptions."

"While you do the interview, Guv, I'll arrange for an A-R-V to escort us to wherever Mitchell wants to take us."

"Do, but before you go anywhere, you better let me have a photocopy of your notes from last night. Myles and I will need them."

Marcus and Myles were in good spirits when they joined Clive, Graham and I an hour later.

"How did it go?" I asked.

"He's an arrogant tosser," Marcus said, letting his frustration show. "But he confirmed what you had in your notes. He's still not giving us the names of his contacts and customers. He maintains he'll only do that once he's worked out what deal he can get. Absolute tosser."

"So did he say what it is that's 'big' and where he's taking us to?" I asked.

"Something about AK47s and we've got to go back to his unit at the Knoll Business Centre."

Mitchell squinted at the bright October sunshine as we left the Custody Suite and walked out into the station yard. Clive had handcuffed his left wrist to Mitchell's right, and the two of them walked uncomfortably together towards the unmarked Volvo that Myles was driving. I sat in the front seat while Clive sat Mitchell in the back. Marcus and Graham were in another car and the Sussex Police A-R-V was waiting for us on the other side of the station gates.

We travelled in convoy with the A-R-V following. As we pulled up right outside Mitchell's workshop, the A-R-V driver took up a controlling position in the centre of the car park. His two crew members then walked over to the door and stood guard. Myles grabbed the camera bag and Mitchell's keys from the car boot. Clive made Mitchell get out on his side, deliberately dragging him by the handcuffs across the rear seats. I glared at him, and he stopped to let Mitchell get out on his own. Myles unlocked the workshop door and cancelled the alarm. Once more, those of us who could, put on a pair of forensic latex gloves.

Mitchell could not wait to show us what we had missed the first time. "Michael, climb up to the top shelf there and push to one side the pile of steel," he said excitedly. "Then tell me what you've found."

As I climbed the stepladder, I cursed myself for not finding whatever was up there before.

"Do you see them now?"

"Yes, I've got them." On the shelf were five breech bolts with integral gas recoil piston rods. They were in raw polished steel, indicating Mitchell had machined them recently.

"Do you know what they are?" he asked almost mockingly.

"Congratulations, Tony, on getting round the problem that you don't have the equipment to cast these in one piece. You've machined the piston rod and bolt separately and then screwed them together. "

"Yes, but what are they?" he asked.

Marcus looked at me with an expression that said I better be right.

"They're the principal component parts for a Kalashnikov AK47 or its Chinese equivalent Type 56 assault rifle."

"Very good," Mitchell responded in both a patronising and genuinely congratulatory tone. Marcus looked relieved. I passed the items down to Myles and he placed them on the workbench before photographing them.

"You better log them as my exhibits MH/19 A to D," to which Marcus visibly winced in acknowledgement of another potential problem with Brian.

"Who's your customer for these, Tony?" I asked.

"It was to be someone in the Loyalist paramilitaries, but he never came back," he replied, sounding disappointed. "I chucked them up there in case anyone else wanted me to reactivate an AK."

"They look very recent, when exactly was that?" I asked.

Smiling, he quickly replied, "look Michael, I've seen your chart. I know what you can do with dates and telephone calls, so I'm not giving you anything that'll help work out who my customer was."

"We'll be taking you back to Gatwick and interviewing you again Mr Mitchell, so you can tell us then," Marcus said irritably. "Now, let's get on with whatever else it is you want to show us."

"I think components for AK47s intended for the Loyalists is big in its own right, don't you?" And now smiling broadly, Mitchell added, "especially when you didn't find them the first time."

"Right, Tony, what's next?" I said, annoyed both by the truth in what he'd said and at his games.

"What, you want a prize for getting my test right?"

"Really, Tony. You either tell us, or we'll rip this place apart until we find whatever it is ourselves."

Conceding to my point, he answered, "you'll need a screwdriver."

I took out my Leatherman multi-tool and asked, "Standard or Phillips?"

"Phillips."

"Where?"

"The sandblaster. Pull it away from the wall. Unscrew the back panel and look inside."

I switched off the machine and unplugged it. Then I did as instructed, and removed the back, which I then handed to Myles.

Inside, neatly stacked within a compartment not visible through the glass at the front were five neatly stacked, heat-sealed clear plastic bags.

"Myles, some photos of these in situ, please, and another exhibits' bag."

Once he had finished, I reached in and gently lifted one of the bags. Its contents seemed unusually heavy at around two kilos. Taking it out, I saw it contained four shiny rectangular blocks of recently machined steel.

"More photos please, Myles."

I used the blade of my Leatherman to slice open the bag before tipping the contents on the workbench.

"Well, Michael, what do you think?" Mitchell asked eagerly. "Do you like your prize?"

"What are they?" Marcus asked me.

"To use one of Marco's expressions, Guv, these are Tony's 'kryptonite'. They're four of your unique MAC-10 breech bolts, aren't they?"

"Yes, they are, and I imagine you're much happier now."

I ignored his remark and asked, "how long did it take you to make each one?"

"A few hours."

Returning to the sandblaster, I reached back inside and removed the other heat-sealed bags. Each contained four more fully functioning Abonar MAC-10 breech bolts. Mitchell had just surrendered twenty in total. There was another packet in the machine, but much smaller and I lifted it out too. The contents were the extractor claws, and I counted them through the plastic: twenty again to match the number of breech bolts.

"Thank you, Tony. You know us finding these means it's now undeniable you manufactured all the MAC-10s recovered with your unique breech bolt."

"Yes, and I thought from our conversation last night you'd appreciate having them. It completes your investigation. I also want people to know that the one in the Royal Armouries that's mine isn't just any MAC-10, it's a '*Mitchell MAC-10*'."

"Fucking tosser," Marcus said very loudly, summing up what we all thought at that very moment.

"The name's already taken, Tony," I told him, taking great pleasure from my next words. "They're known by the investigation name. They're called the 'Abonar MAC-10'." I was pleased to see the growing look of disappointment on his face.

"Myles, log, bag and tag these please. The twenty breech bolts will be my exhibits MH/20A to MH/20T. The bag of extractor claws is MH/21. Right, Tony, what else?"

"That's it, Michael. That's the lot. You've now got everything."

I wanted to say, "*What about the RPGs?*" but realised he was serious. This really was the lot.

Back at Gatwick, Marcus and Myles interviewed Mitchell about the latest finds to confirm what happened in the search. They also spoke to him and his girlfriend about going into Witness Protection. Naomi refused and Mitchell wouldn't go in on his own. Thereafter, he withdrew his cooperation.

The following morning, Mitchell appeared at Crawley Magistrates' Court and was remanded in custody to await trial at the Old Bailey.

CHAPTER 72

Sample

Sunday, 27th October

After my month's absence, I spent Monday back in the office catching up with my team. Brian and Derek organised a meeting with everyone involved in Abonar for me to brief them on the outcomes. That included not only my team, but also Marco and Hamish, along with our principal contacts in the CSPs. The event achieved its objectives of not only providing a great opportunity to update them on our success, but also demonstrate how each person's contribution made it possible.

As I headed back to my office, Derek caught up with me. "Thought you'd be interested to know the Home Secretary gave us the green light for negotiations on the RPGs to begin again. Gudgeon is seeing Donovan tomorrow."

"Well, I hope you have as much luck with that strand of Abonar as we did with ours."

John and I spent most of the week drafting briefing documents about what we had learned from the firearms investigation. In particular, guidance for Firearms Licensing Officers, the London and Birmingham Proof Houses and the Home Office to warn them of Mitchell's many deceptions.

That weekend was the first I had been able to spend at home in a while, albeit on my own. My estranged wife had refused, however, to let me see Rebecca. In an unexpected way it was just as well, because at 4pm on Sunday, my pager sounded. I called back and spoke to Ray at Vodafone.

"What have you got for me my friend?"

"Your target mobile, Michael, the one for Gudgeon has just called the mobile for Colin Murray. That was straight after a call Gudgeon received from a London number. Oh, and Murray has just called your boss, Commander Jackson, on his mobile. Thought you'd like to know."

"Thanks, Ray. Has Gudgeon made or received any other calls today?"

"Yes, just one incoming from a BT number."

"Okay, give me the number and I'll call Special Services."

As soon as I ended that call, I phoned Karen at BT and gave her the number.

"Michael, it's a phone box in Eltham. You've had the number before."

"Okay, Karen, please remind me of the address."

"High Street at the junction with Archery Road."

"Damn, of course."

"Problem?"

"I don't know yet. But, as you said, we've seen that number multiple times. Thanks."

I sat back in the armchair and made a note in my daybook that I had now pulled from my briefcase. As I finished writing, my mobile rang again.

The number displayed told me it was Commander Jackson.

"Sir, how can I help?"

"I've just had a call from Colin Murray. He's had one from Donovan's solicitor, Gudgeon. He's told us where we can find what he describes as an RPG. I've tried calling Derek Hamilton, but it keeps going to voicemail. Are you able to get to a lockup garage in Eltham if I give you the address?"

"Sure. I'm ready with pen and paper."

I phoned the on-call SO11 Duty Officer, DI Steve Wiley, and briefed him. He agreed to go to the garage with his DS and keep it under observation until I got there. Since I didn't have access to a police vehicle, I had to telephone the Chief Inspector Information Room once more and ask for a fast car run. While I waited for the traffic car to arrive, I called the SO13 Senior Explosives Officer. He agreed to come in an unmarked vehicle and meet me. As the traffic officers navigated the route, I telephoned Brian. Thankfully, he answered.

"Sir, sorry to bother you on a Sunday, but I thought you'd want to know. Gudgeon's given us an address, an empty lock-up in Eltham, where we'll find a sample." I then explained what I had arranged to secure its recovery.

"I'll alert the DAC and keep trying to raise Derek for you," Brian said, helpfully. "I'll also speak to the CID at Eltham to arrange for their SOCO to get the phone box fingerprinted quickly."

The traffic officers dropped me off a few streets away from where I had agreed to meet Steve. It was now dark and easy to move about relatively unnoticed. I walked the short distance to where he was waiting in his unmarked car.

"Thanks ever so much for turning out like this."

"No problem. Frank, my DS, is hiding over in the garage block keeping watch. He says the right-hand door of yours is half-open. I told him not to go inside. I've been looking out for anyone who might be observing us, but there's no one around. Whoever picked this place did so for its remoteness."

"Hmm, yes. I just need Expo[57] to get here and then we can go and see what we've got."

As I spoke, the Chief Expo, Graham Eastwood, arrived in his unmarked Range Rover driven by one of his team. As Steve and I walked over to join him, Graham removed a large kitbag from the boot.

"Have you had a look at it yet, Michael?"

"Not bloody likely, Graham, that's your job. We've been keeping the garage under observation until you got here."

"Okay, well let's go and have a butcher's[58]. I'll get Charlie to follow us in the car."

As we walked up the unlit, leaf strewn drive, Graham asked, "so, you've been told there should be an RPG in here?"

"Yes, that's the message passed to us."

"Well, that should be okay to handle, provided the safety's in place."

Steve kept watch from the entrance to the drive twenty yards behind us. Frank flashed his torch from the shadows to signal it was clear to approach. Charlie slowly reversed the Range Rover and stopped behind us as Graham and I reached the garage. It was in a remote block on the far side of a council housing estate. All were in a very poor condition. Judging by the height and number of weeds growing in the old tarmac driveway, they were not in regular use. Checking our surroundings, I noted we could not be overlooked. "*The ideal place for someone to choose for the drop-off*", I thought. Graham checked the double garage doors for a booby trap, and quickly convinced himself it was safe to go in. He then pulled back the right-hand door and I shone my torch inside. The beam picked out a short roll of beige carpet on the floor right at the back. Nothing else was inside except rubbish and fallen leaves that had blown in over time.

"If you stand guard, Michael, I'll go in. Just keep shining your torch on that carpet."

I did as Graham asked and watched intently as he pulled on a pair of latex gloves. Next, he knelt on the concrete floor and carefully began to unroll the carpet.

"It certainly feels heavy enough to have an RPG in here," he announced as he did so.

---

57 Expo: police term for SO13 Explosives Officers – former military bomb disposal technician.
58 Butcher's: abbreviated cockney rhyming slang for 'look', as in 'butcher's hook'.

Very quickly he revealed a dark green cylindrical object just under a metre long wrapped in a clear plastic sleeve. Holding it up for me to see, he removed the wrapper and checked the Cyrillic markings printed in white on the black label alongside the trigger mechanism. It had a large white arrow pointing forwards to indicate the correct direction in which to aim at a target.

"Okay, it's a live anti-tank rocket, what we call an '*RPG 18*'. It's got a viable warhead. Safety is still on. Almost certainly Bulgarian-made. We saw a lot of these in the Balkans," Graham explained authoritatively.

"Please tell me you don't need to cordon off the place!" I asked, recalling my unwanted experience at Chatham.

"Heavens no. I'm going to wrap it up again, shove it on the back seat and take it down to DSTL at Fort Halstead. They'll give you a report in due course. I suggest you and I drive away and leave the place as we found it. I'll get the weapon photographed and send you the pictures."

I made a note of what Graham told me was the serial number before he rolled-up the carpet. He then put it with its deadly contents into the back of the Range Rover and strapped them in. He also wedged his kitbag alongside to stop it from rolling around.

"Right, I'll call you tomorrow with an update," he said as he got into the Range Rover. Moments later, he had gone.

My mobile rang as I re-joined Steve. I could see from the screen it was Derek.

"Michael, Brian called me. What have we got?"

"According to Expo, a viable Bulgarian anti-tank rocket. Apparently, it's an RPG 18."

"Oh, fucking hell. I'm so sorry I wasn't available earlier. I seem to have been out of signal range. What's Expo done with it?"

"He's taking it now to Fort Halstead. We should have photos tomorrow. In the morning, I'll get Hamish to run a search on the serial number. What have you got from the surveillance?"

"Nothing. This came out of the blue. I wasn't expecting the sample for another week. Shit. Something must have spooked Donovan into moving this forward. Any likely witnesses or CCTV?"

"No. The garages aren't overlooked; there's nobody about, and there's no CCTV, which is certainly why whoever made the drop picked this place. There are no forensic opportunities either."

"Shit. Okay, I'll come and find you tomorrow for a catch-up."

CHAPTER 73

Uncomfortable truth.

Monday, 21st October

Monday morning was a period of frenetic activity. Derek called an urgent meeting in the Fordham Suite to review how he and his OCG team had been caught unawares. His cologne added a sweetness to the aroma of stale pipe smoke emanating from John. Also around the table were Roger and three of his DCs from the RPG strand of Abonar, together with his analysts, Emily and Natasha. Along with John, I had brought in Chris, Pete, and Alice. DC Des Overton had also dialled in on the teleconference line to add his support from Full Sutton Prison. Alice gave me one of her looks that showed she was delighted to be involved again.

"Right everyone," Derek began, "I'm sure we all know each other, so no need to waste time on introductions. Thanks, Des for dialling in. I want to review in an open and blame-free manner what we know about yesterday's delivery." Trying to sound calm and confident, he continued, "we need to reconstruct the events building up to Murray receiving that call from Gudgeon."

Just then, Anton walked into the room without knocking, interrupting Derek's flow, and causing him to look uncomfortably surprised. I was amazed to see Anton too, and with neatly cut short hair.

"Good morning. I understand a bit of a screw-up yesterday, Derek," he said scathingly. "The DAC called to tell me the Commissioner's keen to rectify the situation, so I've been summoned back."

"Oh, I was just explaining how this would be an open and blame-free review," Derek said feebly.

"Well, good luck with that," Anton said sarcastically. "As you will no doubt appreciate, the Commissioner is all over this like a rash. Hence, he and the DAC want me here."

"Anton, I can handle this. Anyway, I thought you were starting at Kennington today as the new Chief Superintendent."

"I was, but then I got a message from on high telling me to be here instead. So, I'm not happy about this either Derek. Now, let's get on with reconstructing what happened and learning what we need to do to make damned sure it doesn't happen again."

"Sure, Anton, it'll be good to have your input," Derek said, clearly annoyed at being usurped. Like many in the room, I felt uneasy at seeing two senior officers trying very hard not to have a spat in front of us.

"Right, what do we know?" Anton asked, looking around for someone to give him an answer.

"I'll speak for my team, Boss," Roger announced. "From what I've quickly ascertained this morning, it's clear we took our eye off the ball at a crucial moment. I'm sorry."

I was immediately impressed by his candour at taking the hit on behalf of his team. That could not have been easy; especially when he was hoping for promotion.

"Okay, Roger, so what have you learned?" Anton now softened his manner towards him. It was also clear to Derek that Anton was asserting his recent promotion to now lead the review.

"Des, would you like to brief us on what you've got from the prison?" Roger asked.

"Certainly. So, Donovan made a call to his home number last week. That followed a visit from his wife the weekend before. Gudgeon last saw him on Thursday."

"What do we know about the call?" Derek asked, deciding to try and recapture his lead.

"Well, I sent the tape down to your team on Thursday, Guv."

"Roger, who did you task with listening to it?" Anton asked.

"DC Roberts but, to be fair, he had other priorities."

"What?"

Falteringly, Roger responded, "yes, I know with hindsight…"

"Des, have you listened to the tape?" Anton asked, without waiting for Roger to finish.

"Yes, I have. In essence, Donovan discussed a project to redecorate the family home. The man he spoke to said he would send over a sample of wallpaper and, if they liked it, he'd order some more and send them over express delivery."

"Holy shit!" Anton exclaimed. "And you didn't think to escalate that to us immediately?"

"Guv, Mr Baxter, if that's you, no," Des replied apologetically. "I hadn't really been taken into the confidence of Mr Hamilton's team, so I wasn't exactly sure what you wanted me to listen out for." Des's tone let us all know he was deeply embarrassed. "As I do every time, I put the tape in the despatch immediately, so you'd get it on Friday and could listen to it yourselves."

"Okay, okay," Anton said, dismissing Des's excuse. "So what do we know about their communications? Michael? Pete"

"Sir, we've reviewed them this morning," I began to explain. "BT confirmed the Donovan home number had once again been diverted. This time to the second anonymous Orange mobile. It seems realising this had suddenly come back to life had been missed."

"What a screw-up!" Anton exclaimed. "Okay, so do we know where it was at the time?"

"Yes," I answered calmly, "as with the previous calls, it was in Eltham."

"Derek, since you'd stood down Michael's team from this strand of Abonar, what were you doing to monitor the phones?" Anton asked, clearly annoyed.

Derek kept quiet, looking across at Roger, who glared back, now realising he was being '*thrown under the bus*'. Roger hesitated for a few seconds, which only amplified his growing embarrassment before speaking. "I'm sorry Mr Baxter, that seems to have fallen through the gaps too."

Anton threw his arms up in obvious despair and looked directly at Derek to say something.

"Look, I don't operate a blame culture," Derek said hurriedly, "so let's see what we can recover from the situation."

"Derek, let me be very clear," Anton said, instinctively brushing back his hair only to find he didn't need to anymore. "Whilst you might not operate a blame culture, the Commissioner wants someone at this table to carry the can. *Capisce?*"

"Yes," he replied uncomfortably. "Okay, Michael, I want you and your team back on this job. I want you to reconstruct the call data to see how this happened. I also want you monitoring every number we've got." Almost not pausing for breath, Derek went on, "next time there's the slightest hint on the phones of something happening I want to know immediately."

Maintaining my respectful calm, I nodded saying, "Sir, consider it done."

"Roger, I need you to find the resources to put Walshe under 24-hour surveillance," Derek almost barked.

"Sir." Roger's one-word reaction indicated his deep frustration. I looked at him quizzically. I knew there had been no indication from our early analysis of the Abonar data that Walshe was involved with the RPGs. Roger just shrugged back at me, indicating he was more comfortable complying with Derek's instruction than challenging it.

"Good, good. DC Overton, are you still on the line?" Derek then asked.

"Yes, Mr Hamilton, Sir," Des's tone sounded like those of my staff when they sensed I was about to ask them 'to do me a kindness'.

"What can you do for me?"

"I'll do everything I can to give you advance notice of visits and phone calls. From now on, I'll make sure we've got someone listening in real-time. Donovan has to pre-book calls, so that should be easy. Mr Hallowes and his team can then look out for any diverts again to other numbers."

"Yes," I added, "with advance warning we can certainly do that and monitor the TK near the Donovans' home."

"Great," Derek said, sounding more confident. "I want maximum effort, everyone. No taking your eyes off the ball this time. Are we clear?"

Just then, Anton took a call on his mobile. He chose not to leave the room, so everyone waited quietly until he finished.

"That was the Commissioner's staff officer," he explained. "Michael, you, Derek and I have been summoned to the Home Office for a meeting at 2pm with that irritating man Smedley. We better get ready with some extra copies of the weekend's papers down our trousers. I sense we're going to get a thrashing. From what I've just heard, we bloody well deserve one. I'll meet you both downstairs at 1:45."

CHAPTER 74

The Thrashing

As the three of us walked across to the Home Office, the conversation between Derek and Anton was undeniably tetchy. Respectfully, I kept a few paces behind them so as not to intrude. I could tell Derek was still deeply embarrassed. Anton was making clear his annoyance in anticipation of Smedley playing our apparent failures to his advantage. Minutes later, we were ushered into the same meeting room at the Home Office as before. This time, Smedley was already sitting at the table along with four others. Commander Jackson was one of them, along with the man, Wheeler, from before. I did not know the other two men.

Anton waited for Derek to pick his seat before manoeuvring me a little further away, saying quietly, "I want you next to me, slightly apart from Derek. Take your lead from me. Don't say anything unless I invite you to. It's Derek's operation, so let him take the heat. Okay?"

"Understood, Sir."

"Right, some introductions might be in order," Smedley announced once we were all seated. Helpfully, the two men I did not know introduced themselves as Nick Duckworth, the Director General of the Prison Service, and his deputy, Colin Murray. I nodded to them in acknowledgement that I knew their names.

Smedley then got straight to the point. "Right, I understand Scotland Yard unexpectedly took delivery of an anti-tank rocket yesterday courtesy of Donovan and his associates. As you can imagine, the Home Secretary wants to know the details?"

"We were taken by surprise," Derek answered with unexpected candour. "We didn't have our assets in place, and we were not able to intercept the delivery before it happened. Currently, we're reconstructing events to see what we can learn for next time."

"Well, I'm not about to cast blame, Mr Hamilton; only to recommend this doesn't happen next time." His voice was surprisingly calm as he carried on, "Mr Duckworth, would you like to comment?"

"Thank you, yes, I would. Yesterday's events mean we must now give Donovan a benefit. My recommendation is that Colin now sends Gudgeon the letter we promised after we received a sample. I've prepared the following to come from me as Director General."

He cleared his throat before reading from the file in front of him. "*Further to previous conversations on this matter, the Home Secretary confirms he is prepared to review the terms and length of sentence currently being served by Fred Donovan. This will begin with a reduction in his security categorisation. In addition, he will be referred to the Parole Board at the first opportunity. Both benefits are on the strict understanding that Fred Donovan continues to supply information necessary to enable the police swiftly to recover the remaining weapons. In addition, he does so without any risk of them falling into criminal hands, and there being no evidence of collusion on his part in the supply of the said weapons.*"

As Nick finished, Smedley's mood had changed to anger. He did not wait for our reaction. Instead, he looked directly at Derek and said, "let me be crystal clear, this Home Secretary has no intention of letting Donovan have early parole." Annoyed, he continued, "your job is to make sure he doesn't have to. It's not my job to interfere in operational police matters, so I expect you to carry out your duties to the best of your abilities." He paused for effect before ending with, "and I will then have great pleasure in advising the Home Secretary when that is done. Good day gentlemen."

He then gathered up his papers and walked out the room.

"Useless little drama queen!" Anton muttered in contempt as the door closed.

Nick Duckworth was the next to speak. "Gentlemen, can that be done? Can we stop Donovan getting any benefit?"

Anton replied, confidently saying, "yes, we can Nick. Whatever happens, we'll make sure Donovan doesn't benefit from this. That's even if he drops the weapons on us again without warning."

"Thank you, that's very reassuring, Anton. And what about the firearms job? I see SERCS arrested Mitchell again. Has he implicated Donovan?"

"Michael," Anton answered, "perhaps you could update us, as you interviewed him?"

I briefed them that Mitchell had as good as implicated Donovan and knew it was a similar scam to the one involving Haase and Bennett, which he had also contributed to. I finished by saying, "and, no doubt, we can expect Mitchell to want to trade a reduction in his sentence too."

"Oh dear," Nick said, mopping his brow. "Well at least he'll be dealing with the Met this time and not Customs. He won't be able to fool you in the same way."

"No, he won't," Anton said smiling.

"Very good to know Donovan was in on it up to his neck, though," Nick continued. "That's most helpful, Michael, thank you. Once you've resolved this job with the RPGs, Anton, I'll write to Gudgeon. I'll advise him that we know of his client's manipulation of the firearms in a wilful attempt to deceive the former Home Secretary, and so Donovan can't expect early parole."

"Thank you, that seems entirely right," Derek added. "And at some point, Michael and I will also need to visit Donovan in prison and question him about the scam."

"Well, I'll leave that for you to organise once this job is completely finished. Anton, are you happy for me to fax my letter to Gudgeon by close of play today? I think it's important we advise him quickly of the Home Secretary's decision."

"Certainly, Nick. If Gudgeon gets it tomorrow, that then gives Derek enough time to put all his assets in place for whatever happens next."

CHAPTER 75

The Drop

Wednesday, 23rd October

For the next forty-eight hours, we waited for Donovan's reaction to the Prison Service letter. It came by way of Gudgeon scheduling a visit for Wednesday morning. Almost as soon as he left Full Sutton, DC Overton called to advise that Donovan had booked a call home for 3pm. Derek had opened Central 500 in anticipation. Des waited, ready to listen to the call. I put BT on standby in case someone diverted the home phone again.

At 3pm, Donovan dialled the home number, but it did not divert. His wife answered. "I've got a letter to say we've got what we wanted. I'll leave the rest to you," he told her before hanging up.

The surveillance team from GMP followed Mrs Donovan out of the family home to the phone box at the end of the street. She made a brief call before returning. Karen from BT called me almost immediately to advise that the number dialled was the phone box we knew about in Eltham High Street. I added its details to the CLIO log.

Reading my screen, Derek shouted out, "Blue, what's surveillance got on the Eltham phone box?"

From his regular seat, Harry calmly said, "I'm checking."

"What do you mean 'checking'?! What did they see?"

"I'm checking, Boss," he answered testily this time, "the O-P's not answering the phone or radio."

"Shit. Michael, where's Clever Trevor and his Toscas kit?"

"The Orange mobile is still switched off, Boss," I told him, "so Trevor can't make a start. He's still on standby at Eltham Police Station."

"Shit, shit. Blue, have you got through to the O-P yet?"

"Yup, bad news I'm afraid Boss. He was on a comfort break and missed it."

"Oh, fucking hell," Derek exclaimed. "What about the team plotted up around it?"

"Without the off from the O-P, they didn't have a target," Harry told him.

"Okay, how about the team over at the block of garages where they dumped the previous sample?" Derek asked, his voice now full of desperation.

"No change there, Boss, still no one about," Harry reported.

The tension in the room was palpable and not helped by Derek's own high levels of anxiety that, like his cologne, he found hard to contain.

An hour later, we were all hoping for a development when my mobile rang. It was Ray from Vodafone.

"What news?" I asked him, "please make it good."

"Just like last Sunday, about eight minutes ago, your subject Gudgeon received a call from a BT London number. I've passed it over directly to Karen to check. No doubt she'll call you in a minute with the subscriber. I thought I'd get in first. So, immediately after it, Gudgeon phoned the Prison Service chap, Murray, on his mobile, and he's then called your boss, Commander Jackson. It's so helpful they're all using Vodafone mobiles. I better get off the line now to free up yours for Karen's call."

Before I could alert Derek to the development, Anton walked into the room. Without displaying any emotion he simply instructed, "Derek, Michael, my old office, please. Now would be good."

I followed Derek out and turned right into Anton's former office. Apart from the furniture, it was almost bare, as he had already moved his belongings over to Kennington.

"I'm waiting for a call from BT," I told them as we stood in the room. "I expect you know already, Mr Baxter, Gudgeon just phoned Colin Murray."

"Yes, I do, and Commander Jackson has just phoned me."

"Sorry, I seem to be out of the loop here," Derek complained.

My mobile rang. "May I take this, Sir? It's likely to be BT."

Anton nodded and waited for me to finish.

"Michael, it's Karen. The number you're looking for is a phone box in Hither Green."

I wrote down the address and thanked her before ending the call. Showing Anton my note I suggested, "I should pop back into 500 and give Harry the details?"

"There's no need," Anton said calmly. "Close the door, and both of you sit down. I'll explain."

I did so, choosing the only spare chair next to Derek.

Again rather dispassionately in the circumstances Anton advised, "okay, as I think you've now realised, a few minutes ago Gudgeon called Colin Murray. He told him there's a white Ford Escort van parked in Hither Green near the station. It's got fourteen RPGs in the back."

"Shit," announced Derek, "we don't have any intelligence about how they did that."

"I know, Derek. I know," Anton told him, still sounding calm. "I considered that might happen, so I put in place a contingency. I've got it covered and will let you know how it develops." Then with a hint of mischief in his voice, he said, "you better get your OCG team down there to keep watch and wait for Expo." Passing Derek a scrap of paper, he added, "here's the address the van's parked outside and its registration."

Derek hurriedly left the room leaving me alone with Anton.

"What do you need me to do, Sir?"

"Let Harry know to stand down his teams," he said coolly. "It's no longer a proactive surveillance operation. I need the OCG to make it look like we're genuinely searching for the van, though."

"I don't understand. Wouldn't it help to have Harry's teams deployed around it until the OCG get there?" I asked, unsure of his rationale.

"No, there's really no need," and he smiled, which I found disconcerting. "We can leave it all to the OCG now. It's their job. Keep your team on in 500 until I tell you to stand them down too. Okay?"

"Um, yes, but I don't get it Sir. What's just happened?"

"Don't worry, Michael, it's all been sorted," and not only did he continue to smile but he winked at me too.

Now realising what Anton's contingency might have been, I commented, "damned shame about the O-P taking a comfort break right at the most critical moment."

"Yes, quite an unfortunate coincidence," he said, now grinning more broadly. "I suppose one good thing to come from this is there'll be no prosecution." Nodding at me with one eyebrow raised, he went on, "that would have created a very public stink for the Home Office when it got to court; especially if Donovan demanded the credit. Right, you better get back to 500."

I returned to the room mulling over the obvious disruption to Derek's operation that Anton had discreetly engineered. I also passed on his instruction to Harry to stand down the surveillance teams.

By now, Derek had deployed four of his detectives on standby at Eltham over to Springbank Road near Hither Green Railway Station. He tasked them to keep watch on the van until Expo arrived.

"Boss!" a detective suddenly shouted from the far side of the room.

"What?" Derek asked, sounding flustered and picking nervously at his right thumb.

"The guys are saying they've checked the length of Springbank Road, but the van's gone."

"Shit, what do you mean?" Derek asked, completely unable to fathom what was happening. "It must be there!" he shouted. "Okay, tell them to start house-to-house. Knock on every bloody door if need be! Get more people down there to help. Tell them to check for CCTV. I've got to know what's happened to that van. Don't let me down!"

Twenty minutes later, the same detective as before shouted out, "Boss, I've got an update."

"What is it? I only want good news," Derek replied, but his voice revealed he was already resigned to it not being so.

"Not really Boss," the detective confirmed Derek's fears. "The team did the house-to-house as you asked. According to neighbours, they only noticed the van when a white tow truck pulled up and took it away."

"What do you mean, took it away?" Derek sounded desperate for facts.

The detective relayed, "The tow-truck driver hitched it up by the front axle and drove off with it. He was so purposeful and professional; the neighbours didn't think it suspicious." He paused before adding what he hoped might be helpful, "one remembered the driver wore blue overalls, but didn't notice a name on them or on his truck. Sorry, Boss, that's all they've got."

I watched Derek for a reaction, but he was clearly in a state of shock and stood there frozen.

One of my team had checked the van's registration number on the PNC. As with all the other vehicles used in the previous Abonar drops, predictably, there was no current owner.

Anton walked back into the room and asked, "any news on the van, Derek. I've got Expo standing by."

"It's been towed, Anton. A frigging tow truck beat us to it," he said with obvious despair.

"What, has someone nicked your van?" Anton said, and I detected with a wry smile.

"It certainly looks that way."

Anton turned to walk out but stopped to say, "I better let Colin Murray know it's been stolen so he can tell Gudgeon. Michael, watch the phone lines, please, to see how he and the Donovans react."

About thirty minutes later, Ray at Vodafone alerted me to the call from Colin Murray to Gudgeon. As soon as that one ended, Gudgeon telephoned the Donovans' home. The GMP surveillance team then reported the same woman as before left the house and went to the phone box. We were ready when Karen at BT passed on to me the mobile number the woman had dialled. It was not one we knew already. Beverly took the details from me to check for a subscriber. The call lasted only three minutes. According to the surveillance officer, the woman returned home looking distraught.

My console light flashed, and I could see from the screen Pete was calling me from the TIU.

"Yes, what can you tell me about it?"

"Predictably, Sir, it's an Orange mobile. We're on to them for the subscriber and live monitoring."

"Thanks, Pete. I'll get the paperwork signed off and down to you as soon as I can.

Stepping out into the corridor to get a break from the tension in Central 500 and Derek's cologne, I noticed Anton still in his old office on the phone. He ushered me in and indicated I sit down while I waited for him to finish the call.

"Was that Colin Murray, Sir?" I asked, having made some sense of the overheard conversation.

"Yes, it was, and I think it's time you took off the live monitoring on his number. In fact, I want you to stand down all your Abonar monitoring activities."

"May I know why?"

"You and your team have done enough now. Cancel everything, and I mean everything, even that latest Orange mobile."

"Shouldn't we at least do something to identify the subscriber?" I suggested. Then with a smile I proposed, "It might add to the rest of the smokescreen you're deliberately creating."

Smiling back he said, "no, there really is no need. Instead, I'll tell you about Colin Murray's call just now with Gudgeon. I know you'll like it."

With that he recounted what Murray had just explained to him…

"Mr Gudgeon," Colin began, "I need to tell you the police couldn't find the van in Springbank Road. By the time they got there, it had gone. They believe it's been stolen."

"Stolen?"

"Yes, that appears to be what's happened, as it wasn't where you said they'd find it."
Then, disdainfully he asked, "was it left unlocked like the other three from before?"

"I don't know. How would I know that?"

"It's a common factor according to my information from the police."

"Look, my client is still entitled to early parole. It's not his fault the police took
too long, and some car thief stole the van."

"That's not quite how we see it, Mr Gudgeon," he said, now enjoying hearing the
man's discomfort. "You see, without the police confirming the weapons were safely
delivered to them, I can't see how your client can realistically expect any benefit."

"He kept to his end of the deal; you must honour yours!"

"Hmm, but my Director General made it very clear in his letter to you the
conditions that had to be met. It appears very much that some other criminals now
have the weapons." He then paused to relish his next comment as he slowly said,
"perhaps you should read again the last sentence of his letter."

"But you already had the sample," Gudgeon protested.

"That may be so Mr Gudgeon," Colin was now really loving this long-awaited
opportunity to crush him. "But I also understand from the police that the call you
made to me on Sunday and again today was preceded by ones to you from London
phone boxes. Therefore, the information did not come from your client as you led
me to believe."

Once more he paused before delivering the coup de grâce, "therefore, your client
can hardly claim he got the information from an overheard conversation from
inside the prison. I'm sensing some collusion in this matter."

Gudgeon reacted angrily, "I'll need to take instructions before I can comment further."

"Yes, that seems eminently sensible. Good afternoon, Mr Gudgeon."

Colin ended the call feeling delighted. After months of dealing with a man for
whom he only felt contempt, he clenched both fists and let out a triumphant, "yes,
take that you lying bastard".

"You see, Michael, Abonar is over. Your job is done," Anton told me and
still smiling added, "shame the RPGs went astray, but I wouldn't worry about
them turning up again."

Anton could see I was about to ask for confirmation of what he meant but
raised his hand to stop me. Leaning forward he said, "the Commissioner is
delighted we got the result he wanted. Donovan isn't getting any benefit, and
he'll serve out his sentence. Between us, SO11 just saved the Home Secretary
from a very messy political situation."

He paused before adding, "what do you think, should I put Derek out of his misery now, or leave it a little longer?"

I grinned back as he quickly answered his own question, "nah, he can wait. I need him to carry on making it look convincing the weapons have vanished. Stand down your team in 500. You've got five minutes, then I'm giving you a lift home. We can get a pint on the way. Go on, get it done."

CHAPTER 76

Justice

I sent Donald Manross at INTERPOL all the information about how Mitchell reactivated the Abonar MAC-10s, including photographs of the distinguishing hallmarks. As he had promised, Donald turned these into an INTERPOL *'Orange Notice'* that he circulated worldwide. We had several dozen responses from various European agencies to advise they had one of our Abonar MAC-10s. John and I sifted through the photographs they sent to confirm some were indeed made by Mitchell. We delivered this new evidence to the CPS, asking they add each one as an additional count to Mitchell's indictment. One involved the MAC-10 recovered after the Dublin shooting. The CPS responded that our case was already complex enough without these additional matters. As a compromise, and after much persuasion, they did agree to add one more from the UK.

It was a tense time in south Manchester in early 1998. Two rival factions in Moss Side and Longsight were engaged in a gangland feud that had already left four dead. It was a partly cloudy day when, at approximately 12:50pm on Monday, 23rd March, two uniform Constables were on foot patrol in Moss Side. They spotted a couple of known Longsight gang members riding bicycles who had deliberately come on to their rival's turf.

"What are those two up to?" PC Hunt said to his colleague. "Shit, they're making a run for it." He shouted into his radio, "Charlie Kilo from 18-42, chasing suspects, Fairman Street, Moss Side."

"18-42 from Charlie Kilo, direction and descriptions?"

Breathing heavily he kept up the commentary, "two males... IC1s[59]... Late teens... Wearing dark hoodies and bandanas... Both on mountain bikes... I'm chasing one towards Brentwood Street. He's carrying a red Nike sports bag. 16-36 has gone after the other one."

"Tango 3 on-way."

---

59   IC1: race code at that time for 'white'.

"Tango 6 as well."

"18-42 from Charlie Kilo, where are you now?"

"He's fallen off. He's fallen off. Corner of Fairman and Brentwood Street… Assistance! Urgent assistance! He's got a gun!"

On hearing the shout for assistance, his colleague turned around and ran back to help. He found PC Hunt slowly walking backwards with his hands raised saying, "easy mate, easy, you don't want to shoot an unarmed police officer."

The teenager he was pursuing had pulled a MAC-10 from his sports bag and now had it pointed directly at the Constable's chest. Gently, PC Hunt continued retreating while praying the man wouldn't kill him.

Seeing the second Constable now trying to outflank him, the gunman hurriedly stuffed the MAC-10 back in the bag, successfully remounted his bike and fled up the street.

"Are you okay?" his colleague asked PC Hunt on joining him, still breathless himself from the foot-chase.

"Yeah, just a little shaken. I don't think he realised it, but his bandana had slipped. That was Malachi Rowlands."

Four days later, police recovered the Nike sports bag from where Rowlands had thrown it over a fence. Still inside was the MAC-10 cocked and ready to fire the sixteen blue-tipped 9mm bullets in its magazine. It was an Abonar MAC-10. PC Hunt had been very lucky Rowlands had not squeezed the trigger.

Malachi Rowlands was nineteen years old when he was arrested by GMP detectives. The judge later sentenced him to ten years imprisonment.

Understandably, we wanted this MAC-10 included in the case against Mitchell. Just like the one used to murder Devon Dawson, and the others found in Moss Side, we needed the jury to understand the real-life consequences of his manufacturing and supplying his reactivated MAC-10s. It was not as he thought, a mark of his craftsmanship as a gunsmith. Instead, his actions caused very real harm to communities and the police officers who strived to protect them. As I had said to Mitchell, I wanted justice for his many victims, and this episode became '*Count 10*' on the indictment against him.

***

Prior to his trial, Mitchell was moved to Belmarsh Prison where I hoped he would allow me to visit and debrief him. As it was one of the London prisons within my remit, we monitored all his communications, correspondence and visitors. Within a few weeks of him arriving, he received in the post a sequence of three photographs without an accompanying letter. The first was of a ladder against a wall. The second of a light aircraft. The last of a dead rabbit.

When I asked his solicitor about visiting to continue our conversation about his customers, he told me Mitchell was reluctant to cooperate. That was because he had interpreted the photographs as a threat. To him they meant he would be sprung from prison; escape in a private plane and be taken somewhere to be murdered. Consequently, we lost a major opportunity to recover some of the guns he had supplied before they could cause more harm.

***

On Tuesday, 30th March 1999, the case against Mitchell, Bown and Phillips was listed for trial at the Central Criminal Court. I arrived well before the 10am start to meet our Prosecution Counsel, Terence Powell, QC. We met in the echoey public area, so moved to a quiet corner to hold a private conversation. Standing in his gown and taking off his wig, he invited me to sit.

"Michael, I've found this a most interesting case," he began, "but, I'm sorry, I have to tell you about an unwelcome change."

"What, may I ask?"

"I received an instruction last week about Mitchell from the Director of Public Prosecutions on the advice of the Treasury Solicitor."

"Really, what does it say?"

"To entirely redact from the prosecution case all the evidence that implicates the former Home Secretary and his officials in Abonar. They don't want any mention of them being hoodwinked by prisoners into allowing a trade to secure their release in return for information about where other criminals had hidden firearms."

"Why? What possible reason could they give?"

"They consider it's not in the public interest to expose in court the naivety of a government department and a former Cabinet Minister." Terence's tone indicated his own contempt at this decision. "Their failures cannot be made public. I'm truly sorry. I know from the brief just how much work you and your team put into the Abonar investigation."

"Sugar, bloody, damn, so officialdom gets its way in the end!"

"If by that you mean some government officials get to suppress the full facts about Abonar, then yes, I'm sorry, that is exactly what's happening."

"What does it mean for the rest of our case today?"

"For Mitchell, well, we can expect some further plea-bargaining once the CPS tell his barrister."

"That's scandalous!"

"Having read the papers and now had to re-write my '*Opening Note*' describing the case to the judge and jury, I'd say, yes, it is."

"Is there anything we can do to reverse it?"

"No. The D of P-P has directed every aspect of the case involving the scam cannot now be mentioned."

"That's outrageous," I said angrily, suddenly conscious from the echo that my raised voice could be overheard.

"Yes, it means even if Mitchell pleads guilty, I'm prevented from alluding to the scam. Consequently, the former Home Secretary, his officials, and several Customs officers can all now relax. I won't be exposing in open court for the media to report on how they were so easily fooled by career criminals."

"Well, at least we've got solid evidence against Mitchell for everything else."

"Yes, I'd say from what you've amassed the judge will know the full extent of his gunrunning and its consequences for his victims."

Just then, Myles walked over to join us. The look of anger on his face warned he too had just learned of how our case had been undermined.

"Have you heard what those idiots in the CPS have agreed to?" he asked angrily.

"Yes, it's a disgrace. Mr Powell just told me we're prohibited from mentioning in our evidence anything to do with Donovan and Mitchell attempting to deceive the former Home Secretary."

"Not just that, Guv, they've agreed with Mitchell's barrister to drop '*Count One*' and then '*Seven*' to '*Ten*'!"

"What?!" I said in shock.

"Yes, it's a fucking disgrace. Look…" Myles said, now showing me his copy of the indictment.

Stabbing his finger at the page, he angrily explained, "the CPS have completely withdrawn 'Count One' against Mitchell. That concerns him supplying the guns GMP recovered from the loft in West Gorton."

Then with increased anger he added, "and they're leaving on file, not to be proceeded with, 'Counts Six' to 'Ten'. 'Six' relates to Mitchell supplying Bown with all those items you found at Chatham."

"Damn them, what are they thinking of?" I said, now even more furious. "And what about the others?" I asked him.

Pointing again at the indictment Myles replied, "'Seven' to 'Ten' concern Mitchell supplying his MAC-10s: the one used to shoot at PCs Kennedy and Thompson in Moss Side; the one GMP recovered after the foot-chase in Ardwick and, you're not going to like this; the one used to murder Devon Dawson."

"No!" I shouted in disbelief.

"And the one he supplied that Malachi Rowlands used to threaten PC Hunt in Moss Side. All not to be proceeded with." Myles finished, looking totally exasperated.

"That makes it virtually impossible for us to charge Mitchell with anymore of his MAC-10s that turn up in future. There goes my leverage," I commented, now dumbfounded by the CPS's decision.

Turning to Terence I then asked, "did you know about this?"

"No, not at all. They must have agreed that while you and I have been talking."

Moments later, I barged open the door to the CPS office with Myles and Terence following. Myles helpfully pointed out the CPS lawyer he had spoken to. The man looked up from the case files on his desk, and immediately appeared uneasy at our rapid approach. He was in his mid-20s, which meant he had only recently qualified as a solicitor and been appointed to the CPS. His small round-framed glasses only reinforced my impression that he had no experience of real life beyond what he had read from law books. He would not comprehend the horrors of Brockwell Park and the murder of Devon Dawson. Also, he would have no perception of the violence still being inflicted by the gangs Mitchell had armed.

I looked at the name plate on his desk before addressing him, "Mr Topping?"

"Yes."

"I'm DI Hallowes, the SIO in the case of Mitchell and others. DS Hurst and Mr Powell here just briefed me on your decision to withdraw six of the ten counts against Mitchell. Why?"

"We've agreed to a plea-bargain," he answered, somewhat flustered by my challenge. Then with wholly misplaced piety continued, "it's in the public interest we avoid a costly trial. Mitchell will plead guilty to the remaining four and Bown and Phillips will plead to all theirs."

"Well, that's not a deal I've agreed to," I told him firmly.

"Maybe, but *I* represent the prosecuting authority, not you," he countered haughtily. "I've determined it's in the public's best interest we proceed today as I've just described."

"I want to speak to the Senior Crown Prosecutor," I demanded. "I've got victims and families who want justice. They expect this case to expose the full facts, not some watered-down CPS version. They want Mitchell to get what he deserves and that means going to prison for a very long time."

"I have already spoken to the Senior Crown Prosecutor," Topping said defiantly, "and he agrees with me. Furthermore, he's spoken to other government officials, and they also consider this is the right outcome."

"You can't do that!" I shouted. "What we're now left with in respect of Mitchell are just the counts involving illegally transferring firearms." Exasperated, I told him, "you've decided not to proceed with the four on his indictment where his MAC-10s were used in shootings and threatening police officers. You've also withdrawn the one involving the murder of Devon Dawson, damn it! Mitchell armed all of these gunmen with both his MAC-10s and ammunition. How can that be justice?"

Topping replied dismissively, saying, "there is enough evidence in the remaining four counts for the judge to sentence him appropriately."

Myles was equally angry and asked, "why have you also decided not to proceed against Mitchell with 'Count Six'? That's the one involving Bown clearing out the gun club for Mitchell and hiding his guns, ammunition and explosives. What the hell is that about?"

"Bown will plead guilty to that," Topping countered, again, "and that's sufficient. Mitchell won't, so we'd have to go for an expensive trial when he's unlikely to get any greater penalty if found guilty."

Terence intervened at this point to check with Topping what he was now left with to prosecute. "So, can I confirm that Mitchell will plead guilty to illegally transferring an undisclosed number of MAC-10s through Bown to Ackerman? That's 'Count Two'."

"Yes, Mr Powell."

"'Count Three', to illegally transferring the CZ pistol through Bown and Ackerman to Joseph McAuley?"

"Yes."

"'Four', to illegally transferring three MAC10s, silencers, magazines and ammunition through Bown and Ackerman to Paul Ferris?"

"Correct."

"And 'Five', to supplying all three consignments of guns and ammunition that police then recovered in Whitechapel, Plaistow and at the Tollgate Hotel?"

"Indeed, but you're not to make any mention of how the former Home Secretary and his officials along with Customs got caught up in that."

Myles and I looked at each in shared fury.

"Why aren't you proceeding with '*Count One*'," I asked curiously. "That's where Mitchell got Bown to supply Ackerman with four Smith & Wesson revolvers; three of which were later recovered by GMP in a loft along with two MAC-10s. Bown was ready to be called by us today as a witness for the Crown against Mitchell. He would have given convincing evidence about this and all the other offences in their conspiracy. Your decision to a plea-bargain makes no sense."

"Mitchell won't plead guilty to that, but Bown will, and that's good enough for the CPS," Topping replied in his annoyingly indifferent manner as if justice was only about economics. He then glared at Myles and I as if we were nothing more than an irksome, petulant children.

Myles passed his own judgement on this setback, "what he's telling you, Guv, is they don't want you talking to the media afterwards about the involvement and interference of government officials in Abonar."

"Worse than that Myles, I sense they've also decided it's too risky to prosecute Mitchell for being an accessory to whatever crimes his MAC-10s get used in. That's because, as he hinted at when I spoke to him, he'll do a deal. I sense that might be to go public and tell the media about the scam that hoodwinked Customs, a former Minister and his officials."

"Maybe so, Guv, maybe so."

Frustrated, I sought solace from Terence, "Mr Powell, am I right that the maximum sentence for the remaining four counts against Mitchell is fifteen years' imprisonment on each?"

"Yes," his tone suggested some hesitation as he tried to guess where my thoughts were heading. "The sentencing guidelines recommend a shorter one if he pleads guilty, though."

"Can you have a word with the judge as part of this plea-bargain?"

"On certain points I can, yes."

"Can you persuade him to sentence Mitchell based on the cumulative effect of his crimes, so he gives him at least fifteen years?"

"I can make the point, but the judge alone determines the sentence."

"Well, I'm expecting him to give Mitchell that," I said sternly.

Myles added, "Mitchell's an accessory to multiple murders. The judge will know that from reading the file. Whilst he didn't pull the trigger, he supplied the guns and ammunition for the person who did. If Mitchell had pulled that trigger, he'd be getting 'life', so fifteen is a reasonable compromise."

"Gentlemen," Terence said, his voice raised to quell our own, "I sympathise but with what the CPS have left me to prosecute, there's no longer any evidence that connects Mitchell to violent crime. It's now just a series of unlawful transactions to which, sadly, we cannot attribute an actual victim."

I felt crushed. he was right. We could not now secure justice for any of Mitchell's victims.

When the usher called out the defendants' names, Myles and I followed Terence into '*Court 4*'. The judge looked on in surprise as Terence then explained how the CPS had withdrawn certain evidence from the case and left five of the counts against Mitchell '*on file not to be proceeded with*'.

Once the three defendants' barristers had made their '*Pleas in Mitigation*', the judge retired to consider the sentences. On his return, he summed up the case against each defendant. In respect of Mitchell, he said, "*I find it regrettable that I am unable to deal with you for your part in the disgraceful deception practiced on officers of HM Customs and the former Home Secretary.*"

I stared at Mitchell as he sat in the dock slightly apart from Bown and Phillips. I wanted the satisfaction of seeing his face fall as he heard the judge sentence him to fifteen years. To my dismay, though, the judge gave him eight in total: six on "*Count Two*'; four on '*Count Three* and two on '*Count Four*' both concurrent, and two consecutively on '*Count Five*'. He also made a confiscation order of £27,750, as the apparent proceeds of Mitchell's crimes, and directed the destruction of all the exhibits in the case.

Mitchell caught my stare and smiled. It told me he knew he'd succeeded in doing a very cheap deal to reduce his sentence. He had conceded nothing whereas the CPS had given away any chance of us ever achieving real justice for his victims now and in the future.

The judge sentenced both Bown and Phillips to four years' imprisonment.

In his closing remarks, the judge generously commended the Abonar investigation team.

***

On 8th June 2000, Assistant Chief Constable Trevor Pearce of the newly formed National Crime Squad awarded members of my team and those from SERCS with commendations for our roles in Operation Abonar. My citation reads, "*For outstanding detective ability in the prosecution of eight criminals involved in the illegal supply of firearms. Also commended by the Judge at the Central Criminal Court.*"

***

Mitchell's dreadful legacy has cast a long shadow of terror. Abonar MAC-10s have continued to be used in murders, woundings, gang violence and robberies; the most recent to my knowledge in 2009. In some, even though the weapon was not recovered, forensic examination of the spent cases found at the crime scene showed the tell-tale crescent-shaped hallmark caused by his breech bolt.

One of the most murderous uses of an Abonar MAC-10 was a gang-related drive-by shooting on Churchill Parade in Aston, Birmingham, at 4:08am on 2nd January 2003. It was a revenge attack resulting from escalating gangland violence. A burst of fully automatic gunfire came, coincidentally, from a red Ford Mondeo as it passed a small crowd of partygoers standing on the street. The intended target escaped unharmed. However, Charlene Ellis and her twin sister Sophia, aged 18, their friends Letisha Shakespeare, aged 17, and Cheryl Shaw, plus another bystander, Leon Harris, were all gunned down. Charlene and Letisha died of their wounds. The others were left with horrific injuries. Four men, each in their twenties, were subsequently convicted of this merciless attack. Three were jailed for thirty-five years, and one for twenty-seven. Mitchell, however, has not been held to account for his part in arming them.

Today, the Royal Armouries hold at the National Firearms Centre in Leeds three Abonar MAC-10s along with many other examples of the actual guns from Operation Abonar.

CHAPTER 77

Co-conspirators

Derek Hamilton and I did visit Fred Donovan in Full Sutton Prison. I wanted to meet the man who had instigated Abonar. Nothing about him was remarkable. He was in his mid-40s, flabby and unfit, and not very tall. He was surprisingly inarticulate too when he spoke, which left me wondering how he had been able to convince so many people to back his scam. I reconciled myself by assuming it was only his offers of money accompanied by some threat or menace that made things happen for him.

To our disappointment, we had been instructed by the CPS, on the advice of the D of P-P, that it would not be in the public interest to prosecute Donovan for his part in the conspiracies alongside Mitchell and the others. That foreshadowed what then happened at Mitchell's trial. Thus, it was with some pleasure we were allowed to tell Donovan that he would not receive any credit. Instead, he would get a downgrading of his prison security status from High-Risk to standard Category A. Donovan knew he was entitled to that anyway for his good behaviour. He was clearly angry we would not give him more, because as we left, he warned me, "*You'll be hearing from my solicitor*".

The Prison Service did not reduce his security category again for the remainder of his sentence. Consequently, Donovan did not receive parole when he first became eligible. He left prison in October 2000, just six months before his automatic release date. However, we remained determined to see justice done in any way we could.

With the help of the information Chris discovered, GMP reinvestigated Donovan's finances. It took them several years of painstaking detective work to uncover all the evidence to confirm he had concealed the proceeds of his drug trafficking. It was these that had enabled him to purchase the firearms recovered. In October 2006, GMP charged Donovan with deceiving the court at his original 1995 trial about the true value of his assets.

In April 2008, at Knutsford Crown Court, Donovan pleaded guilty to concealing those assets and two other matters under the Drug Trafficking Act, 1994, and the Proceeds of Crime Act, 2002. Some weeks later when he returned for sentencing, the judge gave him two years' imprisonment and ordered the confiscation of all his remaining realisable assets.

Concurrent to this, Donovan engaged new solicitors to push for a judicial review. He wanted to claim redress for his perceived breach of the Home Secretary's agreement to release him early. He also contested the seizure of his assets. He named both the Director General of the Prison Service and me in his action. Bizarrely, he also continued to claim recognition for Mitchell's arrest and the recovery of all the Abonar firearms and ammunition.

In response, I outlined in my affidavit how we had very clear evidence of both his deception and active part in the conspiracy to acquire the firearms and ammunition. I warned that I would disclose these in court if he continued to pursue the action. I advised that if the judge decided against him, as he most certainly would, we would push for Donovan to be tried for those offences too.

Donovan's legal case was undermined by his wife, who in return for a lighter sentence, admitted her part in laundering the proceeds of her husband's drug dealing between 1995 and 1997. In 2009, Donovan finally abandoned his legal action against me.

***

Paul Ferris, John Ackerman, Joseph McAuley, Constance Howarth and Arthur Suttie were each jailed for their individual and collective parts in the various conspiracies involving the possession and transfer of illegal firearms and ammunition. Ackerman was sentenced to six years, and McAuley to four.

At his trial, Ferris admitted to involvement in criminal activity when he visited Ackerman, but not to collecting the MAC-10s. Instead, he claimed Ackerman was meant to supply him with a box of counterfeit currency. He accused Ackerman of tricking him by then swapping it for one containing the MAC-10s. The jury agreed with the prosecution that police and MI5 had caught Ferris red-handed, and his claims of innocence had a '*hollow ring*'. The trial judge, Henry Backsell, also said he was convinced Ferris had "*Arranged, paid for and taken delivery of a lethal parcel of weapons*". He went on to say, "*He could hardly dare to speculate on the potential for death and destruction they might have caused had they reached their intended destination*".

Ferris was on record for his many complaints about being a victim of 'police fit-ups'. Hence, the detectives from Strathclyde Police, who had so diligently gathered the intelligence and evidence against him were delighted to see him finally convicted. To Don McGregor's personal delight, the evidence was so overwhelming, Ferris was unable to repeat his earlier performances imitating 'Houdini'.

In July 1998, Ferris was sentenced to ten years' imprisonment. However, he appealed. At the subsequent hearing in May 1999, his barrister made the case for reducing the sentence. Ironically, it was because the man who supplied the MAC-10s, Anthony Mitchell, had received only eight years. Lord Justice Belden sitting with Mr Justice Harrison and Mr Justice Lyas agreed. Lord Justice Belden said, "*Bearing in mind the eight-year sentence given to this man* [Mitchell], *it is clear to us that the sentence imposed on Paul Ferris was too high*". They reduced it to seven years.

***

Derek Hamilton was unable to gather sufficient evidence to arrest Kieran Walshe for his roles in organising the illegal transfer of firearms and ammunition. Nonetheless, I passed the file to Kent Police for their Force Intelligence Unit to record the information. In 2005, along with three other gang members, Walshe was sentenced at Woolwich Crown Court to twenty-one years' imprisonment for his part in an armed robbery in north London.

***

I sent the file detailing Patrick Gudgeon's involvement to GMP to review. The CPS determined there was insufficient evidence to mount a prosecution with the likelihood of a successful conviction. In addition, they felt he had been so discredited by the Donovan family, few amongst the criminal fraternity in Manchester would ever use him again as their solicitor. Hence, he was neither arrested nor interviewed in connection with the Abonar conspiracy. In 2015, though, the *Solicitors' Regulation Authority* successfully prosecuted Patrick Gudgeon for misconduct in a totally separate matter at a Solicitors' Disciplinary Tribunal. In September 2016, he was struck off the Solicitors' Roll.

***

The Labour MP for Liverpool, Peter Kilfoyle, campaigned for twelve years to have Michael Howard investigated over the early release of Paul Haase and John Bennett. In 2005, the Home Secretary tasked Scotland Yard with running a new and independent investigation. It was titled, '*Operation Ainstable*', and led for the most part by Detective Superintendent Graham McNulty. By coincidence, he and I had been on the same Detective Inspectors' Course in 1997. The objective of Ainstable was to identify whether Haase and Bennett had conspired to pervert the course of justice by deceiving HM Customs; their trial judge and then, in turn, the former Home Secretary, Michael Howard.

After a very thorough investigation, Graham's team arrested Haase and Bennett along with two women, Debbie Haase and Sharon Knowles. A search of their Knowsley Village and Walton homes in the suburbs of Liverpool found clear evidence of their involvement in the scam. Of particular relevance was a set of Polaroid pictures taken by these women of the guns in 1995 and 1996 while Haase and Bennett were in prison. Graham's team had also arranged for the forensic re-examination of every item recovered twelve years before. Scientists found unequivocal evidence in the form of fingerprints from both women on some of the packaging used to wrap the firearms and ammunition. Graham charged all four with a conspiracy to pervert the course of justice. His investigation was a triumph after what had gone before. Merseyside Police had previously been unable to find evidence to connect anyone to the thirty-five caches of weapons recovered.

In the subsequent trial at Southwark Crown Court, the prosecution counsel, Maltby Grenfell QC, made various observations about the case that had strong parallels with Abonar. He explained to the jury that some of the cars in which the guns were found had been bought or stolen shortly before the defendants told their Customs' handler where to look. In others, the garages where the guns were stashed had been rented by people who had either given false details or were otherwise untraceable. "*These various features*," he added, "*indicate that the series of seizures was a set-up. In other words, Haase and Bennett were not genuinely informing on real criminal activities or telling authorities about the guns in fact used by criminals, but, with their undoubted contacts and resources, set up a scheme, the purpose of which was to reduce their sentence*".

I gave a statement covering what Operation Abonar had revealed about the deception. I was surprised to learn that Mitchell gave evidence too. He explained his involvement in supplying many of the firearms and ammunition, knowing they were an essential part of the scam to hoodwink Customs, the judge, and the Home Secretary.

On Wednesday, 19th November 2008, the jury found all four defendants guilty. Haase was jailed for twenty-two years and Bennett for twenty. Haase's wife, Debbie, was sentenced to four years, and her friend, Sharon Knowles, to five.

David Lynch, the original trial Judge in 1995, who recommended to the Home Secretary that Haase and Bennett be released, also gave evidence at their 2008 trial. He said he was "*influenced by the report from their handler, Customs Officer Paul Cook,*" who had told him, "*It is highly unlikely that they would revert to a life of crime upon their release*".

From how journalists have reported on the trial, it appears that Michael Howard could not accept he had ultimate responsibility as Home Secretary when he had allowed the scam to happen by agreeing to trade at Ministerial level with career criminals. Extraordinarily, he seemed to blame it entirely on the judiciary. He told reporters, "*People try to deceive judges all the time and it's quite difficult to devise a system which would be fool proof when it comes to deceiving judges*". He brushed aside that he too had been deceived. As the former Minister entrusted with upholding the law, he should have taken full responsibility; especially for his own failure to investigate the facts and so prevent the scam. The same can be said for the government officials who advised him. The whole sorry debacle contradicts Michael Howard's very personal assertion that "*Prison works.*"

EPILOGUE

The Abonar Legacy

Using our evidence from Abonar to push for a global policy shake-up, I started the lengthy process of recommending improvements to domestic and international firearms regulations, including more robust deactivation standards. For two years, starting in June 1999, the MPS loaned me to the Home Office to work with Peter Storr, Director of the Policing Organised Crime Unit. My role was to develop the UK's position for our Ambassador to the United Nations in Vienna to negotiate on an international treaty to counter illicit firearms trafficking. Our efforts contributed to what is today the '*UN Firearms Protocol Against the Illicit Manufacturing of and Trafficking in Firearms, Their Parts, Components and Ammunition*'. This international treaty supplements the '*UN Convention Against Transnational Organized Crime*'. It provides a broad set of standardised controls on legal firearms and ammunition to prevent their diversion to the illicit market.

Article 5 of the Protocol established one common international standard for deactivating firearms to prevent any possibility of reactivation. I wrote this jointly with a Canadian colleague, Doug Dalziel, and used the lessons learned from Abonar to convince others to support it. Article 5 was the only provision that passed without amendment. On 31ˢᵗ May 2001, I had the privilege of addressing the United Nations General Assembly in New York, giving the speech on behalf of the UK Government to confirm our commitment to ratifying the Protocol. Today, Article 5 is the basis for the 'EU Deactivation Standard' that finally came into force in the UK on 28ᵗʰ June 2018. This makes the possibility of reactivation impossible.

***

Abonar was ground-breaking. We were confronted by a gunrunning network that relied on anonymous communications to frustrate our attempts to identify them. It was the first time Scotland Yard employed such wide-ranging and pioneering techniques in the lawful exploitation of telecoms data to solve a case. Today, thanks to our work, they are commonplace in serious crime investigations.

Subsequently, I led a team who then wrote the 'ACPO Manual of Standards for Accessing Communications Data for Serious Crime Investigations'. At times, it felt like we were flying the aeroplane while building it; while writing the manual on how to do so, hoping someone was creating the airstrip for us to land. The latter being the regulatory framework allowing us to do it all. Ultimately, our initiative grew into a national training course hosted by West Mercia Constabulary at their Hindlip Hall HQ. It was run by the hugely energetic DC Graham Blomfield along with industry leaders from the CSPs. I had the pleasure of being its 'Course Director'. Over the years, we trained hundreds of staff both from TIUs in every UK law enforcement agency and their equivalents in the CSPs. Together we succeeded in bringing a high degree of professionalism to these critical roles in supporting serious crime investigations.

***

All the police officers who worked on Operation Abonar went on to have illustrious careers, with at least two achieving very senior rank and others being honoured by Her Majesty the Queen for their services to policing.

***

On 31st July 2011, I retired as a Detective Chief Superintendent after more than thirty years policing in London. I had accepted the appointment as Emergency Services Commissioner for the state of Victoria in Australia. Before I left, colleagues in MI5 invited me to Thames House for a farewell gathering. I had expected, perhaps, a small gift as a memento of our long-standing friendship, such as the customary MI5 'Regnum Defende[60]' wall plaque or cufflinks. I was both delighted and humbled when instead Hamish handed me a package that felt far more substantial. Inside, he and his team had created a very personal gift. On an oak plinth, they had mounted one of my original 1997 exhibits from Operation Abonar, an Abonar MAC-10 breech bolt. The accompanying brass plaque simply reads, 'ABONAR MH 20A'.

---

60   Regnum Defende: MI5 motto, which means, "Defend the Realm".

Abonar MAC-10 RHS (Safe-Fire switch inside the trigger guard)

Abonar MAC-10 LHS (Semi- and Full-auto select-lever on the frame)

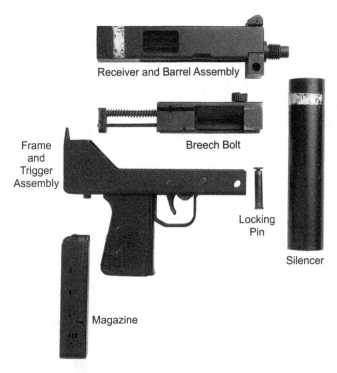

Receiver and Barrel Assembly

Breech Bolt

Frame
and
Trigger
Assembly

Locking
Pin

Silencer

Magazine

*Ingram MAC-10 breech bolt with 90-degree
extractor claw*

*Abonar MAC-10 breech bolt with 45-degree
extractor claw*

SF Firearms markings and the obliterated serial
number and deactivation mark

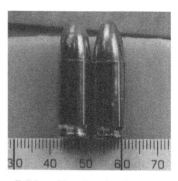

IMI 9mm blue-tipped and copper-
jacketed bullets

Whitechapel

Plaistow

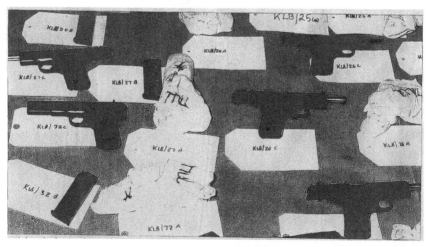

Newspaper photograph of the 'Tokarevs' (Chinese M20s) from the Tollgate Hotel

Cloths with the three-letter Cyrillic codes

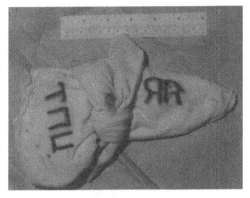

'Tokarev' (Chinese M20)

Colt

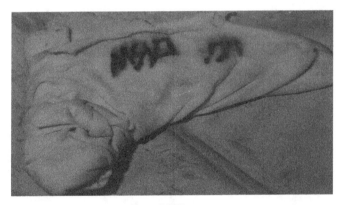

MAB

BAR wrapped in blue towel and packing tape from the Tollgate Hotel

Chinese Model M20 copy of the Russian Tokarev with obliterated serial number

Other obliterated markings on the slide-top

French MAB Model D refinished in matt nickel plating with barrel extension for a silencer (under the screw-on cap).

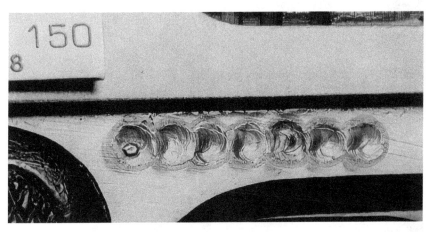

Close-up of the serial number obliterated by the TIG welder.

Cyrillic codes scratched into the Abonar handguns

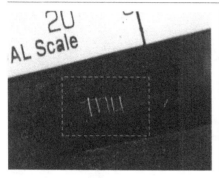

'T' - Tokarev (Chinese M20)

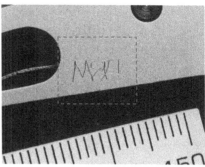

'M' - MAB

'C' - Colt

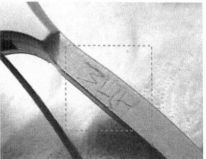

'W' - Smith & Wesson

Abonar Colt with area of refinishing

Untouched Colt with Iraqi arsenal mark

Abonar MAC-10 with silencer recovered from a shooting in Dublin in May 1997

Joseph McAuley's CZ Model 27 with barrel extension and silencer

John Ackerman's MAB Model D

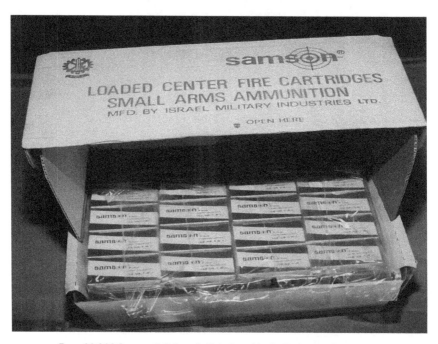

Box of 3,000 Samson IMI 9mm bullets found in the Baden Road gun room

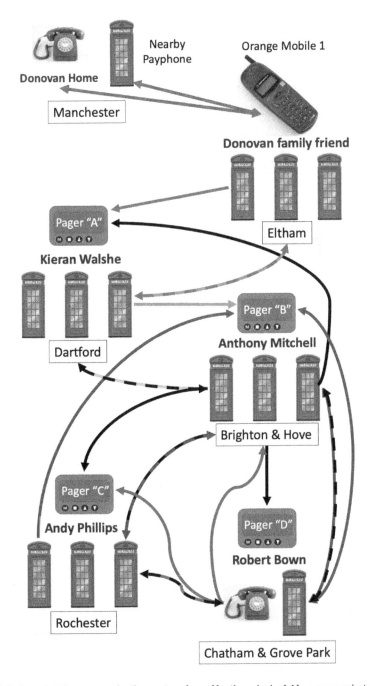

'Mind map' of the communications network used by the principal Abonar conspirators

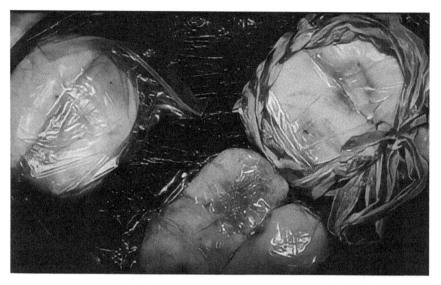

C4 plastic explosive found in the garage at Chatham

One view of the workshop at Unit W11, Knoll Business Centre

Twenty of the Abonar MAC-10s being readied for reactivation

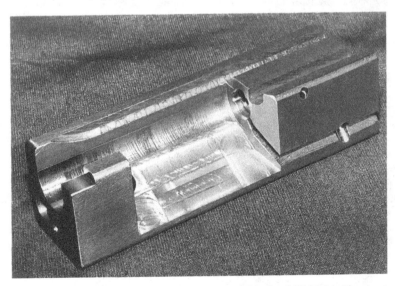

One of the Abonar MAC-10 breech bolts exhibited as 'MH/20A to T'

INTERPOL Orange Notice for Operation Abonar

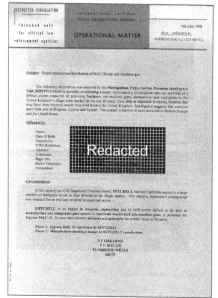

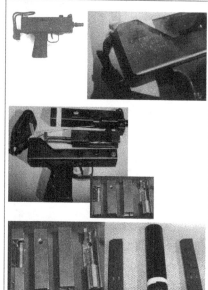

(front)   *(back)*

Author's MI5 retirement gift

About the Author

2009

Michael Hallowes is a thirty-year veteran of policing London, reaching the rank of Detective Chief Superintendent before being appointed in 2011 as the Emergency Services Commissioner for the state of Victoria, Australia. He served with the Metropolitan Police Service in both Specialist Operations and Specialist Crime and worked on some of the most high-profile investigations of the time, including the arrests of the '*Mardi Gra Bomber*' and the '*London Nail Bomber*'. He is the only serving British police officer to have addressed the UN General Assembly in New York (on countering the illicit arms trade). He also led the vanguard of detectives and industry colleagues who pioneered the use of telecoms data in serious crime investigations. For thirteen years he was also a Hostage Negotiator. He holds eighteen policing awards and commendations. Today, Michael lives in London and works in the voluntary sector.